April 3, 2017

Dear Dr Shaun

Thanks so very much for always supporting me

Sincerely
[illegible]

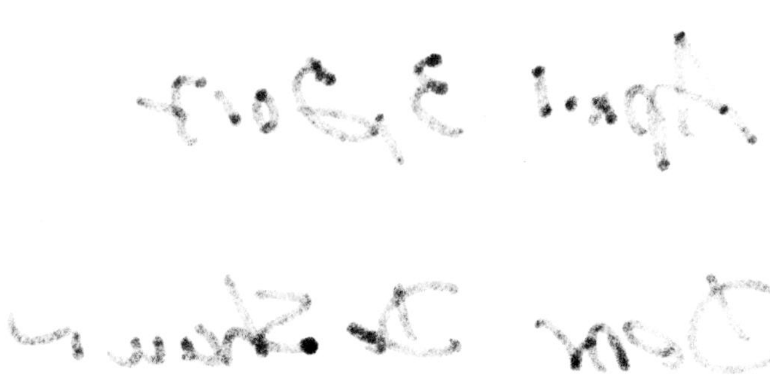

Part of the FEEDS® Series

And

Memoirs and Occasional Papers

Association for Diplomatic Studies and Training (ADST)

Xlibris, Bloomington, Indiana

FEEEDS® Series and ADST MOPS Book 

The Rise of Africa's Small & Medium Size Enterprises:

Spurring Development & Growing the Middle Class

By Ambassador (Dr.) Robin Renee Sanders

View from a former U.S. Diplomat & CEO-FEEEDS®

Introduction

Ambassador Andrew Young

Foreword

Mr. Aliko Dangote, President & CEO Dangote Group

Library of Congress Control Number: 2016920538

ISBN:	Hardcover	978-1-5245-6854-2
	Softcover	978-1-5245-6853-5
	eBook	978-1-5245-6852-8

Print information available on the last page.

Rev. date: 02/08/2017

To order additional copies of this book, contact:
Xlibris, Bloomington: Indiana
1-888-795-4274
www.Xlibris.com
Orders@Xlibris.com
751710

For my family and friends who in 2014-2015 crossed over and now walk among the ancestors. . .

Devon, Anne, Miriam, and Ade

To my loving parents who always have supported me and continue to do so in every endeavor I undertake. . .

Geneva Sanders and Robert M. Sanders, Jr.

And

To the incredible "Africa SMEs," entrepreneurs, business cooperatives, and social enterprises that I have had the pleasure to work with over the years – I salute your evolution and commitment. *

You are the true "Soft Power" of the Continent!

---

*Phrase "Africa SMEs" is intentional and meant to include African nationals, African immigrants and the greater Africa Diaspora

Contents

List of Figures

Introduction

I have been saying for more than three decades two key things about the future of Sub-Saharan Africa's development: its economic growth lies with its youth and the region's progress will be driven by job creation, particularly by small and medium size enterprises (SMEs). Here we are nearly 30 years later with the focus on these two key things being addressed in earnest by African governments, and donors such as China, the United States, the European Union; philanthropists, and foundations.

But the real driving force in this direction – especially making SMEs one of the answers to Africa's economic growth and growing its middle class – has been Africa's young people. Africa's burgeoning youth are creative, innovative, and bullish on finding their own path to employment and improving their quality of life by starting their own SMEs in response to unemployment (and under-employment); they are hopeful about their future and the future of the Continent. It is all happening in real time right before our eyes. It is inspiring, encouraging, and empowering to see Africa SMEs create solutions for economic development sectors from agriculture to financial services.

When I was Mayor of Atlanta and co-chair of the Atlanta Olympic Committee, I stressed the importance of the role of business in planning for the games to ensure that the city was not left in debt and that urban areas were developed, modernized, and revitalized. Many of the businesses involved in building and providing support services for the Atlanta Games were small and medium size enterprises. African SMEs can and are doing the same thing for Africa – as Ambassador Sanders notes – "they are spurring economic growth and helping to grow Africa's middle class."

I have known Ambassador Sanders since she worked for me on loan from the Department of State as part of its program to share career diplomatic experiences in cities around the United States. Ambassador Sanders picked Atlanta as her city to work and my office in which to be assigned. I told her then that I expected her to move up through the career ranks of the U.S. Diplomatic Corps and become an Ambassador.

Not only did both of those things happen, but I swore her into her first U.S. Ambassadorship to the Republic of Congo, along with Secretary Colin Powell, and again when she became the United States Ambassador to the Federal Republic of Nigeria and Permanent Representative to the regional West African organization called ECOWAS. *

Robin was the first woman to serve in all three posts, as well as the first African American to head the U.S. Embassy in Congo-Brazzaville.

Her book outlining the role and contributions that Africa SMEs are making today is groundbreaking because she underscores that their efforts are not just about job creation, but about transformation, the transformation of a Continent which will host the largest population in the world over the next decades. The Ambassador is right.

She is not arguing that SMEs are the silver bullet, but she is saying that they are a key part of the way forward for economic growth, transformational development, and contributing to the success of the Sustainable Development Goals for Sub-Saharan Africa Region.

Ambassador Andrew Young

Founder, The Andrew Young Foundation
Former UN ambassador and mayor of Atlanta
Civil Rights Leader

---

*See Photographs 1-2, Secretary Colin Powell, Ambassador Young, and Sanders in ante-room before the swearing-in ceremony at the State Department's Benjamin Franklin Room.

Foreword

When I started as an entrepreneur nearly four decades ago, it was way before most governments, and international donors saw and understood how such initiatives could be totally transformative – not only to develop the economy of a nation, but more importantly to change the quality of life of the average person, particularly the life of the ordinary African citizen.

From my early experience in having a small and medium size business, I learned to be both innovative and creative – the pillars of entrepreneurship – in order to move my trading company forward. This is why support for small and medium size enterprises (SMEs) and entrepreneurs is so important to me today. SMEs and entrepreneurs not only help address the challenge of unemployment, but also find new solutions to some age-old challenges. For Africa, this is especially true. When one looks at the emerging markets and growth around the globe in the twenty-first century, nowhere is the potential more progress evident than on the African Continent. It is home to 1.5 billion people, with roughly 60 percent of that figure representing talented young Africans under the age of 35 years.

As Ambassador Sanders points out in her very timely book, the contribution that Africa's SMEs are now making, and will continue to make, will spur the Continent's economic development and grow its middle class. I believe so strongly in these two value-added elements of SMEs to Africa's future that I spend a great deal of time highlighting these linkages, contributing to training, and making entrepreneurship a key component of what the Dangote

Foundation does. * In addition, the Dangote Group employs some 24,000 people around Africa, as part of its effort to help reduce unemployment on top of its support for SMEs and entrepreneurship.

What I like the most about Ambassador Sanders' book is the bold declaration that now is the time for SMEs and entrepreneurs to be seen more as synergetic contributors to development – maybe even the primary one. She also stays focused on the messages coming from today's young Africans – what they are saying and what they want – as illustrated in the book's chapter on *@The FEEEDS Index*, based on polling data from Gallup Analytics®. Young Africans are saying that they want to start their own businesses, that they see entrepreneurship as the path to improving their quality of life, and that they want to make a contribution to their country's national growth and welfare.

As I travel around Nigeria, Africa, and the rest of the world, I have a lot of opportunity to meet young Africans who discuss their hopes and dreams and talk to me about starting and growing their businesses. Hence, it is extremely important to assist the SME sector by doing such things as linking large and small enterprises through industry clusters, improving access to finance, and creating capacity building initiatives. Added to this is an emphasis on *partnerships*, something that I have advocated strongly for, over the years. Partnerships must be part of the support to help Africa SMEs grow. Investors, financiers, philanthropists, policy makers, innovators, advocates, and even African stock markets – all have a role to play, but in line, and in tune with the SME community's desires, needs, and focus.

Ambassador Sanders has long been an SME advocate way before it became in vogue to be so. She has continued this work under her *FEEEDS Advocacy Initiative*, and her book reminds us that we all need to step up our game on SME development and entrepreneurship, particularly by operating outside our traditional comfort zones. If we really want to see Africa transform in the next decades, this is the path we must all follow. Africa's future rests with Africa's youth; we all must ensure that they succeed. Entrepreneurship is the way forward for us to help them get there and permanently set the Continent on the path to success.

Aliko Dangote

President & CEO Dangote Group and Chairman Dangote Foundation

* Founded in 1994, the Dangote Foundation is one of the oldest Africa-owned and primarily Africa-focused foundations based on the Continent.

Author's Preface

I have always been inspired by Africa way before I ever set foot on the Continent – believing in *Africa Rising* and the opportunities that the outcomes from this phrase can mean to change the life of the everyday person. I have also always thought of Sub- Saharan Africa collectively and inclusively, encompassing all of us – African nationals, immigrants, and the greater Africa Diaspora. So, in this light I use the terms Africa and Africa SMEs and entrepreneurs as opposed to African to be all-inclusive as I talk about my perspective of the changes that have taken place over the last decade or so as small and medium size enterprises (SMEs) in the region and are a combination of all of the above – African nationals, African immigrants, and the greater Africa Diaspora – who are doing great things as SMEs to spur development and grow economies and the middle class.

This book is about Sub-Saharan Africa. It is about Africa SMEs and entrepreneurs. And, it also is a slice of life of some of my time on the Continent. I have personally experienced a lot of change, growth, and resilience – including being on the front lines of some of the challenges, transitions, successes, and remarkable historical events that have brought Sub-Saharan Africa to where it is today.

I have also lost some colleagues and friends along the way during my journey in the region both African and American. But through it all, I was always inspired by the culture, creativity, commitment, and perseverance of those I have interacted with, particularly in the hundreds of villages and rural communities I have had the honor to visit and work throughout both my diplomatic career and now as CEO-FEEEDS. Getting to know the heartbeat of a nation was something I always tried to do no matter what the obstacles were. I have traveled from as far flung as Sudan's *Nuba Mountains*, camped at the foot of the country's 3,000-year-old *Nubian Meroë Pyramids* and the 5-million-year-old desert orange dunes of Namibia's *Sossusvlei*, visited slave trade departure points in Congo, Angola, and West Africa and pygmy and bushmen villages, and crossed the region from corner to corner as far out as Mozambique's *Bazaruto* Archipelago to the Mauritanian markets in the Sahel, have seen gorillas, including silver backs, *in the mist* and been literally everywhere else in between.*

Thus, I have experienced the transitions and changes that have come about in the region, but the spark, innovation and potential that I see, hear, and experience from Africa SMEs and entrepreneurs demonstrate that they are today one of the region's greatest S*oft Powers and game changers for forward progress.* I am convinced that Africa SMEs will do more than any other collective group to change, lead, and serve as a "community of innovators" to advance development. It was Africa SMEs that pushed the envelope and got donors, foundations, and investors to sit up and take notice – throwing out the old *income-generation* model and creating a path to do the reverse – *generate-income* – through entrepreneurship and small businesses in order to determine their own destiny, play an enterprising development role in their countries, while also contributing to the global good of the region. I have been talking about Africa small businesses for nearly 15 years, and what I thought their impact and role would be going as far back as 2003 in Congo, and as a result worked to do more hands-on, practical things since then to put policy into practice. I started working with young African national adults as early as 2003 on their initiatives to be small business owners and then in 2011 began writing about the potential and impact that Africa SMEs were going to have on the region's economic growth, nation-building, and growth of the middle class in my Huffington Post (HuffPost) and blog articles during that period, and more recently through my work today as CEO-FEEEDS.

The goal of this book is to applaud the Africa SME and entrepreneur. You are innovative, inspiring, and inimitable. And...you have led the way for others to follow.

---

*Phrase comes from the movie "Gorillas in the Mist."

The Scene Setters

"Small and medium enterprises (SME) are playing an important driving function in the economic growth; they occupy a determining role in employment and wealth creation and are an important vector in the process of diversification of the economy. It is in consideration of these characteristics that the Government of the Republic of Congo is implementing its policy of promoting SMEs, which is the 'missing link' in its economy between large companies and a myriad of micro enterprises. I, therefore, welcome Ambassador Sanders' book which is a very significant contribution in her support of Congo SMEs (and also those entrepreneurs who she helped when she lived here), and certainly she continues today to help elsewhere in Africa and internationally. My best wishes for the success of this book and its author whose commitment I warmly appreciate, as well as her support during the difficulties experienced in the 2002-2005 period in Congo, and most importantly for our friendship over many years."

—Yvonne Adelaide Mougany, Minister of Small and Medium Size Enterprises, Republic of Congo

"Ambassador Sanders and I work together over several years, when I was then-Managing Director of Nigeria's Bank of Industry (BOI), on a number of key projects, but none so important to both of us than the development, training and assistance to SMEs and entrepreneurs from all over Africa, especially as regards to access to financing. In addition, we wanted Africa's Banks to see Africa SMEs differently so a great deal of the joint BOI-Western Union-FEEEDS-ADM efforts were to ensure that Pan-Africa SMEs had a chance to meet directly with local Bank executives to pitch their business concepts, and discuss funds for expansion and growth. Ambassador Sanders' book is incisive and puts into perspective the game-changing role that Africa SMEs and entrepreneurs are playing in developing the Continent."

—Evelyn Oputu, Former Managing Director, Bank of Industry, Nigeria, and Founder of the Ovie Brume Foundation

"The role of information, communications, and technology (ICT) in the last 20 years cannot be overstated. ICT, and as a result knowledge management, have played a critical role in transforming societies, and the lives of millions of people in emerging region's around the world such as Africa, and particularly for its ever-growing small and medium size enterprises. Africa's young people today are not only able to manage information that heretofore they would not have had access to, but more importantly, they have taken these tools much further in creating economic development solutions through enterprising businesses. In this, her second book, Dr. Sanders continues to be insightful as to how ICT is redefined from its traditional framework to its role in culture, economic development, and wellbeing."

—Dr. Frederick G. Kohun, University Professor of Computer & Information Systems, School of Communications & Information Systems, Founding Director, Doctoral Program Information Systems & Communications, Robert Morris University, Pittsburgh

Part One: The Backstories

"Africa SMEs are the lifeblood of economic growth, employment, and innovation. African entrepreneurs are remaking the Africa Growth story. From a reliance on development aid to a surge in creative business ventures that are solving deep seated problems, the entrepreneurial spirit is taking over the Continent.

It is the new development model. The essence of this entrepreneurial spirit is sweeping across Africa. Its origins, its key dynamics, and its implications for the future are all undeniable."

—Eric Guichard, Founder & CEO Homestrings

Chapter One: Context and Conditions: The Rise of SMEs

Framing Analysis – Touch of History

As Erving Goffman, a prominent Canadian social scientist and writer, emphasized, it is important to have a "framing analysis" when discussing or studying any element of human society, from its political, economic, business, and organizational issues to cultural trends, social relationships, and unexpected, unplanned changes within a community or group.[1] [2]

Hence, a short backstory "frames" and puts into perspective the developmental challenges of Sub-Saharan Africa (SSAfrica) over the last 40 years. This framing sets the stage and explains why and how Africa small and medium size enterprises (SMEs) and entrepreneurs became so important to the Continent, and moreover, the contributions they are making in a

---

[1] Lermet, C., & Branaman, A. (Eds.). (n.d.). *The Goffman Reader.* Retrieved July 22, 2016 from http://people.brandeis.edu/~teuber/goffmanbio

[2] Goffman, E. (1973). *The Framing Analysis: An Essay on the Organization of Experience.* Boston: Northeastern University Press.

range of areas from job creation to economic growth to spurring the region's middle class.[3]

The story on Africa SMEs and entrepreneurs begins with a quick look back at how donor aid was focused, used, and in many cases, misused – and as a result, how and when from my practitioner's point of view, Africa SMEs stepped into the void and became a key development tool for the region.[4]

[3] SSAfrica, when used, will mean Sub-Saharan Africa. This book focuses on the 47 countries that make up that region, and not North Africa, although on occasion 1 or 2 North African countries might be used as an example. The word "Continent" also will be used to mean Sub-Saharan Africa, and as a matter of the author's style and point of emphasis will always be capitalized.

[4] As noted in my Preface at the beginning of the book I will use the terms "Africa SMEs," "Africa entrepreneurs," and "Africa SMEs and entrepreneurs" to be inclusive of African nationals, African immigrants, and the Africa Diaspora small businesses as to me they are the best and broadest terms to capture the spirit of the variety of small business activity that we see today in Sub-Saharan Africa (SSAfrica) because of the ties, links, and connections among and between these groups as a result of birth, as result of self-definition and the slave trade, and as a result of the global movement today of people and goods and services. In addition, I capitalize the terms "Diaspora" and "Continent" because of the importance and emphasis I place on both. If there is a point I need to make to distinguish between these groups, I will do so by using the specific term, but otherwise "Africa SMEs," "Africa entrepreneurs," etc., will be used interchangeably throughout this book and is intended to be all inclusive – African nationals, African immigrants (including those who have returned home after many years of living abroad), and the greater Africa Diaspora.

SSAfrican nations from the post-independence era to early 2000s presented a series of ensample issues politically, socially, developmentally, and economically, which at times included challenges in national governance, leadership, and as pawns in Cold War and other politics.

For many of the region's nations, these challenges lasted throughout the four decades following their independence, which for most countries began around 1956 and ran through the 1960s.[5] [6] (NB: A select few countries received their independence earlier – Liberia in 1847 and South Africa in 1910. Ethiopia was occupied briefly by Italy from 1935 to 1941 but is not considered to having been colonized).[7] Exceptions after the 1960s were Angola (1975), Seychelles and Djibouti

[5] *Mapping History.* Africa History. (n.d.). University of Oregon. Retrieved July 30, 2016 from http://mappinghistory.uoregon.edu/english/AF/AF01-04.html

[6] *A Chronological List of Independence Dates for Africa.* (n.d.). Education. Africa. About.Com African History. Retrieved July 30, 2016 from http://africanhistory.about.com/library/timelines/blIndependenceTime.htm

[7] Ibid.

(1976), Namibia (1990, I was there), and Eritrea (1993).[8] [9]

Certainly there is recognition that many of the challenges of the region were a result of the long-lasting impact of a number of events: from European trading control, missionary work, and political influence as early as1870; to the 1884-1885 Berlin Conference, when European nations formally divided up the Continent based on political and economic interests; and, then to the colonial period and term mandate or protectorate systems, which for many African nations ran from the 1900s to the 1960s (most

---

[8] Ibid.

[9] I served in Namibia during this period as a junior diplomatic political officer as part of the embassy team to open the U.S. embassy and assist in the U.S. Government's efforts to support Namibia's transition to independence.

countries became independent during the 1960s except where noted above). [10] [11] [12] [13]

The results of all of these decisions, events, and actions continued to impact modern-day Africa with the region being used in Cold War politics (West and non-Western), followed by what I would call the post-Cold War period of disengagement – manifesting itself in

---

[10] Craven, M. (2015). Between Law and History: The Berlin Conference 1884-1885 and the Logic of Free Trade. *London Review of International Law*. 3(1). pp. 31-59. Retrieved April 16, 2016 from http://lril.oxfordjournals.org/content/3/1/31.full

[11] *Berlin West Africa Conference*. (n.d.). *Encyclopædia Britannica Online*, s. v. Retrieved April 26, 2016 from http://www.britannica.com/event/Berlin-West-Africa-Conference

Scramble for Africa. (2015, May 11). New World Encyclopedia. Retrieved May 11, 2016 from http://www.newworldencyclopedia.org/p/index.php?title=Scramble_for_Africa&printable=yes

Additional background: Proposed by Portugal, the Berlin West Africa Conference (Nov. 15, 1884-Feb. 26, 1885) took place in Germany to negotiate which of the European imperialists including Britain, France, and the host country would secure colonial rule. Portugal pursued control of the Congo estuary known as the Congo River basin but was overruled, resulting in a neutral territory, free for trade and shipping. The resulting scramble for Africa, with a new resolve to forbid slave trading, saw the map of the area redrawn as the Congo Free State. No territory could be formally claimed prior to being effectively occupied, except on the occasion when colonial powers countermanded the agreement for personal gain.

[12] Oliver, R. & Atmore, A. *Africa Since 1800*. (2005, February). (5th Ed). Cambridge, United Kingdom: Cambridge University Press. [First published 1967].

[13] Mapping History. (n.d.). Africa History. University of Oregon. Retrieved July 30, 2016 from http://mappinghistory.uoregon.edu/english/AF/AF01-04.html

disinterest (the West) and a combination of disinterest and lack of capacity (the former Soviet Union) for nearly a decade.

All of these stages had a profound impact on Africa's development. Yes, SSAfrican governance and leadership (or lack thereof) over the 40-year span from colonial independence (1960s-2000) also played a big part in the political, economic, and development challenges the Continent faced during this period, and into the millennium. But donors – both non-Western and Western – are equally at fault during this period because they:

- Primarily viewed the region as a source for commodities and extractive resources, without a focus on strategic engagement;
- Did not see the importance of national development strategies being connected to the use of donor resources – or if national strategies existed, they were ignored;
- Had little to no interested in demanding good governance and transparency;

- Dismissed SSAfrica as unimportant as a political and economic partner during most of the four-decade post-independence period.

In the mid-to-late 1990s some Western and non-Western countries slowly began to see the value of engaging differently with the region. China was the first that I would put in this category, beginning in the mid-1990s. Other donors began to change their views toward the end of the 1990s; 1997 is where I would put the turning point in U.S. policy, when former President Clinton's national security team encouraged him to make his first trip to the region, which he did in 1998; EU countries, Japan, as well as other nations were all beginning to view the region very differently around this same time.[14]

So, let's fast forward to today. We clearly see a shift-change, not only by African nations demanding a more engaged and strategic partnership, but also by the range

[14] I was a member of then President Clinton's National Security Council's (NSC) Africa Office at that time.

Wilson, J. (2004). *The Politics of Truth: Inside the Lies That Led to War and Betrayed My Wife's CIA Identity.* New York: Carroll & Graf.

of countries that now view SSAfrica as an important political, economic, and emerging market region, particularly China (currently the region's largest trading partner). The list today is pretty expansive as European countries, the United States, India, Japan, the United Arab Emirates, Brazil, Turkey, and others – are all extensively engaged now in the region. However, recent domestic turmoil has impacted the external focus of both Brazil and Turkey and their pro-active involvement in the region has slightly diminished. Others like Indonesia and Malaysia began to get involved much later in the region particularly in areas such as timber. It is important to note, regarding past European colonial ties, that these ties kept many African countries close politically and economically over the years. But, as older African leaders pass on, Africa's young adults and youth are less connected to that past sense of historical obligation to a previous colonial power. Thus, one certainly sees outreach to a vast number of other global players by Africa's younger generation, and leaders.

The different country relationships we see today on the Continent are because Sub-Saharan Africa is fundamentally a different region from what it was a decade and a half ago. Today's political and economic picture looks very different from that of the early 2000s. There are more evolving and maturing democracies on the Continent since then – even though much still needs to be done to address poverty, and improve social sector issues like food security, health, and education, with some countries continuing autocratic rule, non-transparent political processes, and restrictions on human rights, and press/social media freedoms (e.g., Zimbabwe, Democratic Republic of Congo, Angola, Cameroon, both Sudans, Equatorial Guinea, and Gabon to name a few). In addition, there was also a robust economic upturn in the region beginning around 2011 with many SSAfrican economies having the fastest growing gross domestic product (GDP) levels in the world.[15] [16]

---

[15] Organization of Economic Cooperation and Development. (2011, June 6). *Africa Should Embrace New Economic Giants and Boost Social Inclusion.* Retrieved May 2016 from http://www.oecd.org/newsroom/africashouldembraceneweconomicgiantsandboostsocialinclusionsaysafricaneconomicoutlook2011.htm

[16] Seria, N. *Africa's Growth May Not Meet Poverty Targets, UN Says.* (2011, January 18). Bloomberg. Retrieved July 22, 2016 from http://www.bloomberg.com/news/articles/2011-01-18/africa-s-growth-not-enough-to-meet-poverty-targets-united-nations-says

We all had heard it: Of the ten fastest growing economies in the world during 2011-early 2015, seven of those were in Sub-Saharan Africa.[17] [18] This was during the time when the GDP norm for the rest of the world was quite low as a result of the 2008 economic crisis and subsequent recession.[19]

Botswana during this period maintained a double-digit growth rate for 10 years up to that point, and growth for 2016-2017 has only dropped to just above 5 percent.[20] Other nations such as Angola, Cape Verde,

---

[17] *Lions on the Move: The Progress and Potential of African Economies.* (2010, June). McKinsey Global Institute. McKinsey & Company. Retrieved July 24, 2016 from http://www.mckinsey.com/global-themes/middle-east-and-africa/lions-on-the-move *MGI Lions on the Move: African Economies Full Report*.pdf (2010, June). Found at Africa Pop Up Store. Retrieved August 9, 2016 from http://www.africapopupstore.com/documents/MGI_Lions_on_the_move_african_economies_full_report.pdf

[18] *Bulging in the Middle: A Boom in Sub-Saharan Africa Is Attracting Business Talent from the Rich World.* (2012, October 20). *The Economist.* Retrieved May 2016 from http://www.economist.com/news/middle-east-and-africa/21564856-boom-sub-saharan-africa-attracting-business-talent-rich-world?zid=304&ah=e5690753dc78ce91909083042ad12e30.

[19] *The Origins of the Financial Crisis: Crash Course.* (2013, September 7). *The Economist.* Retrieved July 25, 2016 from http://www.economist.com/news/schoolsbrief/21584534-effects-financial-crisis-are-still-being-felt-five-years-article Shah, A. *Global Financial Crisis.* (2013, March 24, Last Updated). Issues. *Global Finance.* Retrieved July 25, 2016 from http://www.globalissues.org/article/768/global-financial-crisis

[20] United Nations Development Program. (2015). *Botswana.* Retrieved May 2016 from http://www.bw.undp.org/content/dam/botswana/docs/Publications/Botswana%60s%20GDP%202015.pdf

Ethiopia, Ghana, Mozambique, Nigeria, Republic of Congo, Rwanda, Sierra Leone, and Zambia enjoyed high single or double-digit growth during the 2011-early 2015 period, with GDPs in the 7-15 percent range.[21] These previously high GDPs will likely run the range from 1-4.5 percent in 2016-2018 as institutions like the International Monetary Fund (IMF) adjusts its estimates over this period. In fact, the IMF SSAfrica Chief Mohammed Salsi noted in a November 11, 2016 interview that overall for the region growth estimates were 1 percent for 2017-2018, with slight more optimistic country specific rates for countries like Rwanda and Senegal (3%), and Kenya (6%, although if it does not get it rising fiscal deficit in check this positive rate will not be sustainable.)[22] Furthermore, global commodity prices are projected to remain low for petroleum exports,

[21] Organization of Economic Cooperation and Development. (2011, June 6). *Africa Should Embrace New Economic Giants and Boost Social Inclusion: African Economic Outlook 2011.* Retrieved May 2016 from http://www.oecd.org/newsroom/africashouldembraceneweconomicgiantsandboostsocialinclusionsaysafricaneconomicoutlook2011.htm Seria, N. *Africa's Growth May Not Meet Poverty Targets, UN Says.* (2011, January 18). *Bloomberg.* Retrieved July 22, 2016 from http://www.bloomberg.com/news/articles/2011-01-18/africa-s-growth-not-enough-to-meet-poverty-targets-united-nations-says

[22] (2016, November 1). Global Business [Television broadcast] China Global Television Network.

metals, coffee, copper, and cacao, presenting challenges for many African nation which rely on these single export commodities for revenue or foreign exchange.[23] (NB: This growth projection could change, however, if some African economies begin to truly diversify from being a single commodity-based economy.)

Although there is a decline in the fast pace growth of the region's GDP, Sub-Saharan Africa is still seen as an important emerging market in which to be involved.[24] Data indicates that these smaller GDPs, which began in early 2015, were driven not only by lower commodities prices, but also by currency and foreign exchange issues, and, in many cases, the need for better macro-economic policies.[25] [26] But

---

[23] World Bank. (2016, January). *Sub-Saharan Africa Analysis. Global Economic Prospects 2016.* Retrieved August 9, 2016 from https://www.worldbank.org/content/dam/Worldbank/GEP/GEP2016a/Global-Economic-Prospects-January-2016-Sub-Saharan-Africa-analysis.pdf

[24] World Bank. (2016, April 11). *Africa: Low Commodity Prices Continue to Impede Growth* [Press Release]. Retrieved May 2016 from http://www.worldbank.org/en/news/press-release/2016/04/11/africa-low-commodity-prices-continue-to-impede-growth

[25] Ibid.

[26] *Sub-Saharan Africa-Navigating Headwinds. Regional Economic Outlook.* (2015, April). *International Monetary Fund.* p. 36. Retrieved July 24, 2016 from https://www.imf.org/external/pubs/ft/reo/2015/afr/eng/pdf/sreo0415.pdf

keep in mind, the downshift from global high GDPs to these smaller GDPs doesn't diminish Africa as an investment and growth destination, especially, in my view, if more resources are directed to Africa SMEs and entrepreneurs.[27] Africa was the place to be during the extraordinary economic boom and investment highs of 2011-early 2015, and it is still the place to be for business even with the new normal of lower GDPs.

According to an April 2016 World Bank brief, a few countries are projected to weather the current downturn better than others, like Cape Verde, Cote d'Ivoire, Mauritius, Senegal, and Zambia with the remainder in East Africa such as Ethiopia, Rwanda, and Tanzania (NB: Zambia's difficult 2016 election could change its positive projection.)[28] [29] Moreover, This Is Africa in late 2016 noted four SSAfrican countries

---

[27] *Bulging in the Middle: A Boom in Sub-Saharan Africa is Attracting Business Talent from the Rich World.* (2012, October 20). *The Economist.* Retrieved May 2016 from http://www.economist.com/news/middle-east-and-africa/21564856-boom-sub-saharan-africa-attracting-business-talent-rich-world?zid=304&ah=e5690753dc78ce91909083042ad12e30

[28] Ibid.

[29] World Bank. (2016, January). *Sub-Saharan Africa Analysis. Global Economic Prospects 2016.* (Retrieved August 9, 2016 from https://www.worldbank.org/content/dam/Worldbank/GEP/GEP2016a/Global-Economic-Prospects-January-2016-Sub-Saharan-Africa-analysis.pdf

which further improved their business environments – Mauritius (49), Rwanda (56), Botswana (71), and South Africa (74) – all being in the top 100 on its ranking list of 190 countries.[30]

The main point is that the positive economic indicators during 2011-early 2015 further added to Western and non-Western countries, more foreign investors, businessmen, and companies thinking about SSAfrica differently – as a multi-dimensional region with positive stories, challenges, but most importantly, economic and investment potential. This shift coincided with many more African nations (not all) driving their own growth, demanding more respect and a different type of relationship and partnership from foreign countries. In addition, during this same period, there was tremendous growth of African businesses, financial institutions, and local investors which also contributed to the region's attractiveness and development.

---

[30] Across Africa, 3 in 4 Countries Improve Business Environment. (2016, November 7). News. This Is Africa Online. Retrieved November 7, 2017 from http://www.thisisafricaonline.com/News/Across-Africa-3-in-4-countries-improve-business-environment?ct=true

SSAfrica's demand for a different type of relationship, becoming a sought-after emerging market, along with the pivot by many new foreign donors and investors to the region seemed to coincide with several African nations beginning to make positive changes to improve both their leadership and governance. At nearly the same time, there was also a realization that how and where development aid had been used needed to be re-examined and changed, particularly as to why – despite more than an estimated $US3.5 trillion spent during the 40-year post-colonial period, with many of the same critical poverty, economic, and development challenges remaining.[31]

It was clear with the look-back on 40 years of post-independence policies that the impact of various foreign politics, plus past internal African domestic policies, had not contributed to improving the lives of the majority of the people in the region.[32] Furthermore,

---

[31] Shah, A. *Foreign Aid for Development Assistance.* (2014, September 28). *Global Issues.* Retrieved April 13, 2016 from http://www.globalissues.org/article/35/foreign-aid-development-assistance

[32] Hirvonen, P. *Stingy Samaritans: Why Recent Increases in Development Aid Fail to Help the Poor.* (2005, August). Global Policy Forum. Retrieved April 2016 from https://www.globalpolicy.org/component/content/article/240/45056.html

a 2014 Organization for Economic Cooperation and Development's (OECD) report which reviewed how development financing had been deployed from 2000 to 2014 stated that there was a *lack of commitment* to Africa's true growth.[33] This 2014 OECD report also projected that there would be an early downturn in aid to SSAfrica in 2017, a trend already begun in 2016.[34] The United Nations (UN) was similarly concerned about this same lack of commitment and development progress in the region, which it had called for also almost 40 years earlier in its "Resolution 2626."[35]

Indeed, there was what I think of as a *convergence* of all of these elements and events that helped start the transformation and improvements in the development

---

[33] Organization of Economic Cooperation and Development. (2014). Development Aid Stable in 2014 But Flows to Poorest Countries Still Falling. Organization for Economic Cooperation and Development. Retrieved April 2016 from http://www.oecd.org/dac/stats/development-aid-stable-in-2014-but-flows-to-poorest-countries-still-falling.htm Organization for Economic Cooperation and Development. (2014). Global Outlook on Aid Results of the 2014 DAC Survey on Donors' Forward Spending Plans and Prospects for Improving Aid Predictability. Retrieved April 2016 from http://www.oecd.org/dac/aid-architecture/GlobalOutlookAid-web.pdf

[34] Ibid.

[35] United Nations. (n.d.). *Resolutions Adopted on The Reports of The Second Committee.* (1970-1971). Retrieved April 2016 from http://documents-dds-ny.un.org/doc/RESOLUTION/GEN/NR0/348/91/IMG/NR034891.pdf

approaches we see today by countries, donors, international and non-governmental organizations (NGOS), and the private sector.[36] This convergence, as well as the 40-year void before it, played a big part in how young Africans began to see themselves and what they wanted. It especially contributed in large measure to Africa's *Generation-Xers* and *Millennials* finding their own way to address the development challenges they faced, and allowed for Africa SMEs to later enter the mix and become so important.[37]

I saw this convergence and change in development approaches begin to take place on the ground in the early-to-mid 2000s by a number of countries. The

---

[36] *UN – NGO Relations*. (n.d.). United Nations. UN Non-Governmental Liaison Service. Retrieved April 2016 from http://www.un-ngls.org/orf/ngorelations.htm

Additional Information: The United Nations Non-Governmental Liaison Service defines non-governmental organizations (NGOs) as having been active with the United Nations since its founding in 1945. NGO work related to the UN comprises a number of activities including information dissemination, awareness raising, development education, policy advocacy, joint operational projects, and providing technical expertise and collaborating with UN agencies, programs, and funds. This work is undertaken in formal and informal ways at the national and country levels, and at the UN headquarters itself.

[37] Generation-Xers (1960-1970) and Millennials (1980-1990) are slang terms that moved into the mainstream that describe persons born between those years.

United States for example—still behind China at that time in doing so—began to expand its development outlook, raised its development aid levels to the region, and became more creative in its support of projects and various avenues for debt forgiveness. China in the mid-2000s was ahead of most other countries as it held its first annual comprehensive diplomatic conference with African leaders in November 2006, even though its business and development practices were not considered transparent at that time, nor was it providing sufficient skills transfer.[38] By far, during the mid-2000s, in my estimation, the Nordic nations (Norway and Sweden especially) were the most creative and flexible in their approach to development. The Dutch were not far behind.

MDGs and SDGs – The Challenges and The Positives

As these new approaches to development began to take shape on the ground in the early 2000s, they coincided with the coming together of the global community to

[38] *African Leaders, China to Meet on Investment.* (2006, November). *Washington Times.* Retrieved July 30, 2016 from http://www.washingtontimes.com/news/2006/nov/1/20061101-115934-5178r/

better: address worldwide poverty issues; implement and coordinate actions; and, improve the impact and results of development funding. As a consequence, we saw the creation and adoption of the UN Millennium Development Goals (MDGs), in 2000, the global development framework created to reduce worldwide poverty, gender inequality, and address key social and economic disparities, which ran until 2015.[39] Meanwhile, the entrepreneurial spirit of young African adults was already beginning to take hold in the region, even if the term "SME" was not yet in vogue in the early 2000s.

The MDGs had a slow start; neither African governments, donor nations, nor the private sector did much in the first years as many of them tried to figure out in practical terms how to translate these goals into reality. It seemed to me, in the field at that time, that it took large donors three to four years from the adoption of the MDGs to truly revamp and better target their

[39] United Nations Development Program. (2015, July 6). *The Millennium Development Goals Report*. Retrieved April 2016 from http://www.undp.org/content/undp/en/home/librarypage/mdg/the-millennium-development-goals-report-2015.html

approaches and policies. African governments took a little longer, into years 7-8, in my estimation, to begin to ramp up their planning and policies. However, for most African nations it was a struggle to meet their domestic contributions to the MDGs, with many falling short of the UN goal of 0.07 percent of Gross National Income (GNI) even by 2015.[40] From my perspective, it was during this lag period while countries were pivoting that Africa SMEs and entrepreneurs, in name and purpose, stepped into the gap.

As the 15-year clock on the MDGs began to run out, one could see in the last five years that many more nations, particularly in Africa and Southeast Asia, begin to improve their internal planning, coordination, resource commitment, and engagement on the global development goals and targets. During the September 2015 UN session, nations reviewed the progress and shortfalls of the MDGs, and adopted the next fifteen-year (2015-2030) plan, called the "Sustainable Development Goals" (SDGs).[41] The SDGs are now

---

[40] Ibid.

[41] *Sustainable Development Goals: 17 Goals to Transform Our World.*

the policy centerpiece for global development for governments, donors, NGOS, and the engaged and committed private sector.[42] Why is this important to the discussion on Africa SMEs and entrepreneurs? Because many of the SDG targets are the exact areas in which Africa small businesses had been working in during the void years, and are working in today – creating jobs, forming new responses to development challenges, and contributing to the greater good to address poverty in addition to making money for themselves and their families.

It is important to note that as a result of the global MDG effort, "extreme poverty" was cut by more than half, from 1.9 billion people worldwide to 836 million people – 236 million of that number live on the African Continent today.[43]

(2015). United Nations Retrieved April 2016 from http://www.un.org/sustainabledevelopment/sustainable-development-goals

[42] Ibid.

[43] United Nations. (2015, July 6). *The Millennium Development Goals Report 2015*. Retrieved April 2016 from http://www.un.org/millenniumgoals/2015_MDG_Report/pdf/MDG%202015%20rev%20(July%201).pdf

I remain bothered by the term "extreme poverty," because I have seen, firsthand, people living in poverty in many places in the world – from Angola to Burma, and Congo to Cambodia. Whatever people face, where they are, poverty is poverty to them, whether or not those of us who are safe, fed, educated, dry, and have lights on want to distinguish between "extreme poverty" and "poverty."

Turning to SSAfrica in particular in this development discussion about current poverty levels, many African citizens, despite living in resource-rich countries, did not benefit from the economic boom on the Continent from 2011 to early 2015.[44] As the region's economies slowed, which started for some countries in early 2015 and likely will run through 2016-2018, many countries still face high poverty and unemployment (particularly among the Continent's youth). In addition, many struggle with health, education, food/nutrition security, and climate change challenges, on top of

---

[44] *Bulging in the Middle: A Boom in Sub-Saharan Africa is Attracting Business Talent from The Rich World.* (2012, October 20). *The Economist.* Retrieved May 2016 from http://www.economist.com/news/middle-east-and-africa/21564856-boom-sub-saharan-africa-attracting-business-talent-rich-world?zid=304&ah=e5690753dc78ce91909083042ad12e30

some having the world's highest income inequality. Countries such as Angola, Central African Republic (CAR), South Africa, and Namibia over the last decade are cited as having some of the highest income disparities in the world, according to *Global Finance Magazine*, based on the GINI coefficient, used by many respected world institutions to measure wealth distribution.[45] [46] Furthermore, Liberia is cited as having the largest number of people in Sub-Saharan Africa who live on less than $US2.00 per day.[47] [48] South Africa also has two other distinctions worth mentioning, in this discussion on poverty levels. On

---

[45] Pasquali, V. *Income Inequality and Wealth Distribution by Country.* (2012, August 22). Project Coordinator Bedell, D. *Global Finance Magazine.* Retrieved July 23, 2016 from https://www.gfmag.com/global-data/economic-data/wealth-distribution-income-inequality

[46] Central Intelligence Agency. (n.d.). *Country Comparison: Distribution of Family Income - GINI Index.* World Fact Book Library. Retrieved July 24, 2016 from https://www.cia.gov/library/publications/the-world-factbook/rankorder/2172rank.html

World Bank/IBRD-IDA. (2012). *GINI Index (World Bank Estimate).* Retrieved by search for each country July 24, 2016 from http://data.worldbank.org/indicator/SI.POV.GINI?locations=ZA

[47] Ibid.

[48] Ibid. *Global Finance Magazine*, like World Bank and CIA World Fact Book, defines GINI coefficient. This book used the definition from Global Finance which stated: "GINI coefficient is 'a statistical measure of the extent of income distribution or consumption of expenditure among household deviates from a perfectly even distribution." An additional poverty measure which is used is the number of people living under $US2.00 per day.

top of its high income inequality, which mostly affects its black population, South Africa also is home to the largest number of millionaires in the region with 46,800, and the region's second largest per-capita income of $US11,040 –a figure mostly representing white income levels, although this is slowly changing.[49] (FYI: On millionaires in the region, Nigeria is third with 15,400; Kenya fourth at 8,500; and Angola fifth with 6,500.)[50] Mauritius has the highest per capita in the region at $US21,470; Namibia falls third at $US10,440, but this too doesn't reflect the income of most in the majority black population.[51]

Certainly, there is recognition that the MDGs helped reduce the stats on the world's poor, particularly

---

[49] Sedghi, A., & Anderson, M. (2015, July 31). *Africa Wealth Report 2015: Rich Get Richer Even as Poverty and Inequality Deepen.* Global Development Datablog. Africa. *The Guardian.* Retrieved July 24, 2016 from https://www.theguardian.com/global-development/datablog/2015/jul/31/africa-wealth-report-2015-rich-get-richer-poverty-grows-and-inequality-deepens-new-world-wealth

[50] Ibid.

[51] Ibid.

The country with the second largest number of millionaires on the overall Continent is in North Africa, Egypt at 20,200.

for regions like SSAfrica.[52] [53] But, this reduction in poverty levels needs to be viewed in balance with the region's population growth. In March 2016, the World Bank noted that although the share of Africa's poor fell "from 59 percent to 43 percent, many more [people] are poor," because the region's population had grown apace, increasing the likelihood that there are "330 million poor in SSAfrica up from 280 million in 1990."[54] [55] (NB: Nowadays, the poverty level is defined

---

[52] United Nations Development Program. (2015, September 28). *Assessing Progress in Africa Toward the Millennium Development Goals.* MDG Progress Reports – Africa. Retrieved July 24, 2016 from http://www.undp.org/content/undp/en/home/librarypage/mdg/mdg-reports/africa-collection.html

[53] *MDG Report 2015.* (2015, September). Joint Publication. United Nations Economic Commission, African Union, African Development Bank Group, United Nations Development Program. Retrieved July 24, 2016 from http://www.afdb.org/fileadmin/uploads/afdb/Documents/Publications/MDG_Report_2015.pdf

African Development Bank. (2016). *Africa's Recent MDG Performance.* Report. Retrieved July 24, 2016 from http://www.afdb.org/en/topics-and-sectors/topics/millennium-development-goals-mdgs/africa%e2%80%99s-recent-mdg-performance/

[54] World Bank/IBRD-IDA. (2016, March). *While Poverty in Africa Has Declined, Number of Poor Has Increased.* Region-Africa. Retrieved July 24, 2016 from http://www.worldbank.org/en/region/afr/publication/poverty-rising-africa-poverty-report

[55] World Bank. (2012). [data set]. Retrieved July 24, 2016 from http://databank.worldbank.org/data/views/reports/ReportWidgetCustom.aspx?Report_Name=POV_REG_1&Id=be849c9d&tb=y&dd=n&pr=n&export=y&xlbl=y&ylbl=y&legend=y&isportal=y&inf=n&exptypes=Excel&country=SSA&series=SI.POV.NOP1,SI.POV.DDAY&zm=n

as less than $US2.00 per day, whereas previously it was defined as less than $US1.25 per day, although many Africans remain below that level.) Just think of how many more people are struggling just to stay above or at those levels. Those in the region who struggle at the less than $US2.00 per day level, I worry often about, as they are the *fragile poor:* as one life change, could mean the difference between surviving or not. Thus, the region and the countries with the highest inequality income figures will have even more work to do as they begin to implement the new SDG framework.

This *backstory* – post-independence to the onset of the MDGs, through the ups and downs of donor approaches, and African governments then not making real progress to combat poverty and create jobs – all provide clarity and underscore both the how and why young adult African nationals and their Diaspora counterparts turned to entrepreneurship to help fill the nearly 43 percent gap in job creation

---

This 2012 report has a slightly higher estimate of 388.8 million poor, so there has been some improvement between 2012 and 2016 as the 2016 report has 330 million poor.

needs.[56] [57] In the post-MDG and inaugural SDG period, development areas needing the most attention can be best understood by taking a look at the following *facts and stats*, which highlight the degree of challenges in the region and why and where many Africa SMEs and entrepreneurs have emerged and stepped up in response, putting further into perspective the important role they are playing in Africa's landscape today.

Facts and Stats – What Today's Landscape Looks Like

- 75 million: the current number of young Africans looking for work now, out of 1.2 billion worldwide of working-age looking for jobs. This means that the lack of jobs is a worldwide

[56] *MDG Report 2015.* (2015, September 2015.) Joint Publication. United National Economic Commission, African Union, African Development Bank Group, UNDP. Retrieved July 24, 2016 from http://www.afdb.org/fileadmin/uploads/afdb/Documents/Publications/MDG_Report_2015.pdf

[57] World Bank/IBRD-IDA. (2016, March). *While Poverty in Africa Has Declined, Number of Poor Has Increased. Region-Africa.* Retrieved July 24, 2016 from http://www.worldbank.org/en/region/afr/publication/poverty-rising-africa-poverty-report

youth issue.[58] [59] (NB: I do not use the word "employment" in this book because it conjures up images of 8 hours a day, employed by someone else – versus entrepreneurship and starting one's own SME.) SSAfrica will, however, need all these tools: SMEs, entrepreneurship, formal employment, and vocational opportunities to address its huge job creation needs.

- 19 million: the number of young Africans of working-age who will be added yearly over the next 15 years to the 75 million already seeking jobs according to both the International Labor Organization (ILO) and the African Union (AU),

---

[58] *Global Youth Unemployment: A Ticking Time Bomb.* (2013, March 27). *The Guardian.* Retrieved May 2016 from http://www.theguardian.com/global-development-professionals-network/2013/mar/26/global-youth-unemployment-ticking-time-bomb

[59] International Labour Organization Document. (2015). *Global Employment Trends for Youth 2015: Scaling Up Investment for Descent Job for Youth.* Geneva. ILO.org. p.9. Retrieved July 5, 2016 from http://www.ilo.org/wcmsp5/groups/public/---dgreports/---dcomm/---publ/documents/publication/wcms_412015.pdf

the political body of African States, based in Addis Ababa, Ethiopia.[60] [61] [62]

- 18 million: the number of jobs that need to be created per year until 2035 to meet the minimal demand of the working-age population of the region; and, as noted by the IMF, SSAfrica in 2035 will have the largest working-age population in the world, greater than all other world regions combined.[63]

---

[60] Ibid.

[61] *Welcome to The Youth Division of African Union Commission.* (n.d.). Department of Human Resources, Science, and Technology. African Union Youth Division. Retrieved July 30, 2016 from http://www.africa-youth.org/

[62] The African Union, or AU, is the overarching membership-based political organization for most of the nations of the African Continent, except Morocco (by choice). In July 2016, it asked to re-enter the AU after 30 years.) The AU is governed by a rotating Assembly Chairperson among the various countries and is managed day-to-day by a secretariat called the African Union Commission (AUC), and a director called a chairperson. It has eight internal committees, such as the Peace and Security Committee, Political Affairs, Trade and Industry, etc. The AU transitioned to its current name and organizational structure in 2002 from the Organization of African States (or OAU). The older form, the OAU, was founded originally in 1963 after most African states received their independence from their former colonial power.

[63] International Monetary Fund. (2015, April). *Sub-Saharan Africa-Navigating Headwinds.* Regional Economic Outlook. p. 36. Retrieved July 24, 2016 from https://www.imf.org/external/pubs/ft/reo/2015/afr/eng/pdf/sreo0415.pdf

- 547 million: estimated number of Africans living without electricity and energy. The reality is that this number is probably closer to 600-640 million in 2016 (1.2-1.6 billion people worldwide are in the dark daily with no power/lights).[64] [65] [66]

- $US1.25: the average amount that 90 percent of Liberia's and Burundi's populations live on per day, and 54 percent of SSAfrica's overall population, with few opportunities to improve the quality of life of their families, have access

[64] Shah, A. Poverty Facts and Stats. (2016, January 7). Last modified May 2016. Global Issues. Retrieved May 2016 from http://www.globalissues.org/article/26/poverty-facts-and-stats

Mascarenhas, H. 45 Surprising Facts About Extreme Poverty Around the World You May Not Have Realized. (2014, May 22). World.Mic. Retrieved May 2016 from http://mic.com/articles/89717/45-surprising-facts-about-extreme-poverty-around-the-world-you-may-not-have-realized#.ZTbscq6sy

[65] African Development Bank. (2016). *Light Up and Power Africa – A New Deal on Energy for Africa.* The High Five. Retrieved July 30, 2016 from http://www.afdb.org/en/the-high-5/light-up-and-power-africa-%E2%80%93-a-new-deal-on-energy-for-africa/

[66] Parke, P. *Why Are 600 million Africans Still Without Power?* (2016, April 1). Africa View. World. Africa. *CNN.com* Retrieved July 30, 2016 from http://www.cnn.com/2016/04/01/africa/africa-state-of-electricity-feat/

to education, clean water, etc.[67] [68] As noted earlier, in 2015, the donor community such as the World Bank, OECD, UNDP and many other organizations began using less than $US2.00 per day as the poverty measure (this change also is reflected in the SDGs) to reflect the higher costs of basic needs for over 700 million people worldwide.[69]

- 842 million/1.2 billion: current number of people living in hunger/living in fear of hunger in the world today (this includes those in the U.S.).[70]

---

[67] World Bank/IBRD-IDA. (2015, September 30). *Why did the World Bank Decide to Update the International Poverty Line, and Why Now?* FAQ: Global Poverty Line Update. World Bank/IBRD-IDA. Retrieved July 30, 2016 from http://www.worldbank.org/en/topic/poverty/brief/global-poverty-line-faq

[68] Glenn, P., & Crabtree, S. *More Than One in Five Worldwide Living in Extreme Poverty.* (2013, December 23). Gallup. Retrieved May 2016 from http://www.gallup.com/poll/166565/one-five-worldwide-living-extreme-poverty.aspx

Mascarenhas, H. 45 Surprising Facts About Extreme Poverty Around the World You May Not Have Realized. (2014, May 22). World.Mic. Retrieved May 2016 from http://mic.com/articles/89717/45-surprising-facts-about-extreme-poverty-around-the-world-you-may-not-have-realized#.ZTbscq6sy

[69] World Bank/IBRD-IDA. (2015, September 30). *Why Did the World Bank Decide to Update the International Poverty Line, And Why Now?* FAQ: Global Poverty Line Update. Retrieved July 30, 2016 from http://www.worldbank.org/en/topic/poverty/brief/global-poverty-line-faq

[70] Martin, P. *Capitalism and Global Poverty: Two Billion Poor, One Billion Hungry.* (2014, July 25). Centre for Research in Globalization. Global

- 239 million: Portion of the 842 million noted above in Africa who face hunger daily. A bit of good news: stats on worldwide hunger show improvement as the worldwide figure of 842 million represents 209 million fewer hungry people than three years ago, (2013), when over a billion-people faced daily hunger.[71] Much credit must be given to the implementation of the MDGs in reducing worldwide hunger.[72] [73]

- 37 percent: Reflects percentage of the population in the region that do not have access to clean water.[74]

Research. Retrieved July 24, 2016 from http://www.globalresearch.ca/capitalism-and-global-poverty-two-billion-poor-one-billion-hungry/5393262

[71] Ibid.

[72] Ibid.

[73] Kalama, M. (2014, September 9). *Africa Live.* [Television broadcast, 1 p.m.] China Global Television Network.

[74] United Nations. (2000-2015). *Access to Water.* International Decade for Action "Water for Life." Retrieved August 25, 2014 from http://www.un.org/waterforlifedecade/africa.shtml

Facts about Water: Statistics of the Water Crisis (2014, August, 12). The Water Project. Retrieved August 25, 2016 from https://thewaterproject.org/water-scarcity/water_stats

In addition, many people in SSAfrica are without adequate shelter or affordable housing; worldwide the figure is 1.6 billion, 640 million of that figure being children.[75] [76] [77] Region-wide aggregate statistics about the affordable housing issue could not be found, but the following samplings provide the bleak picture of shortfalls in these countries:

Kenya: 250,000;

Nigeria: 24 million;

Namibia: 252,000;

Senegal: 120,000;

South Africa: 10 million;

Zimbabwe: 1 million; and

---

[75] Habitat. (2015). *World Habitat Day 2015 Key Housing Facts*. Retrieved May 2016 from http://www.habitat.org/getinv/events/world-habitat-day/housing-facts

[76] Ibid.

[77] Shah, A. *Poverty Facts and Stats*. (2013, January 7). (Last Modified May 8, 2016). *Global Issues*. Retrieved May 2016 from http://www.globalissues.org/article/26/poverty-facts-and-stats

Mali and Malawi: 80-90 percent of residents in these countries are without adequate housing.[78]

Furthermore, 14 million more people in 2016 were added to the region's adequate shelter issues as a result of displacement by conflicts in the region.[79] I need to say more about lack of shelter/affordable housing as I currently work in this sector in Nigeria: the crisis needs even more attention than the above numbers reflect. Specifically, I do not think the new 2015-2030 SDG framework really stresses sufficiently how much more effort is needed to address not simply shelter, but affordable housing. This is one thing I point out in all my lectures – if you fall in the $US1.25-to-$2.00 a day poverty level or just above the poverty threshold, it is likely you do not have adequate, affordable housing or permanent shelter.

[78] *Global Homelessness Statistics*. (2014). Homeless World Cup. Retrieved May 2016 from http://www.homelessworldcup.org/homelessness-statistics/#africa

[79] United Nations High Commission for Refugees. (2015). Global Appeal 2015 Update. Retrieved April 9, 2016 from http://www.unhcr.org/ga15/index.xml

From my perspective, African and donor governments and institutions must find creative partnerships, special memoranda, strategies for mortgages, and financing options to make a sizable dent in the affordable housing challenges on the Continent. I have either walked through, worked, or visited sites, villages, and camps for refugees and internally displaced, in a number of countries in Africa, and also in Southeast Asia (from Angola, CAR, both Congos, Kenya, Mali, Nigeria, Senegal, South Africa, Sudan, Burma, Cambodia, India, Indonesia, and Vietnam to name a few) where the daily living and shelter conditions for many of the world's poor are heartbreaking.[80] (NB: Shelter also is an issue in the U.S. where reportedly 2 to 3 million people are homeless or lack minimal shelter.)[81]

---

[80] *Global Homelessness Statistics.* (2014). Homeless World Cup. Retrieved May 2016 from http://www.homelessworldcup.org/homelessness-statistics/#africa

[81] Habitat. (2015). *World Habitat Day 2015 Key Housing Facts.* Retrieved April 16, 2016 from http://www.habitat.org/getinv/events/world-habitat-day/housing-facts

Kalama, M. (2014, September 19). *Africa Live.* [Television broadcast, 1 p.m.] China Global Television Network.

International Labor Organization. (2015). *World Employment Social Outlook Trends.* Retrieved April 16, 2016 from http://www.ilo.org/wcmsp5/groups/public/---dgreports/---dcomm/---publ/documents/publication/

The leadership role of Africa SMEs and entrepreneurs becomes even more important in light of the critical poverty and development facts and stats noted above. Yes, worldwide some progress was made under the MDGs in combating hunger and improving water, sanitation, and education, but unfortunately nearly a billion-people entered the 21st century unable to read or sign their names; two-thirds of these were women, and many of those live in the SSAfrican Region.[82]

However, the bright light is that in all these areas and challenges noted above are where I have found the *value-added* of Africa SMEs and entrepreneurs and also where they have shown their muster and leadership, as many of these poverty stats are linked to job creation, education, agriculture, health, and clean water issues. The innovative responses by Africa SMEs to these development issues have become

---

wcms_337069.pdf

Shah, A. *Poverty Facts and Stats.* (2013, January 7). (Last Modified May 8, 2016). *Global Issues. Retrieved May 2016 from* http://www.globalissues.org/article/26/poverty-facts-and-stats

[82] United Nations Children's Fund. (1999). *The State of the World's Children.* Retrieved April 17, 2016 from http://www.unicef.org/sowc99/sowc99f.pdf

catalysts for change in the region. In the end, one cannot *be hungry, thirsty, homeless, without good infrastructure, and in the dark AND progress.* Indeed, Africa cannot progress, transform and meet its industrialization agenda without a full-time focus by national government, donors, and business on these areas, and SMEs can help.

Enter – The Entrepreneurship of Small and Medium Size Enterprises

Africa SMEs and entrepreneurs have *entered* the development picture in a big way, pushing both African nations and donors to see their role dramatically differently as a way to combat current and future poverty challenges. Africa's tremendous job creation gap needs to match its large youth population. If not this will affect the success of the SDG framework in the region over the next 15 years, and impact African governments' planning, budgets, urban development, and ability to provide social services. Therefore, given the previous historical perspective and current development issues, the Africa

SME/entrepreneur role is critical and pivotal to the Continent's forward progress. But before we begin to look at what these small businesses are actually doing, it is important to add that *Africa's population growth is estimated to continue to grow at roughly 2.4 percent. If that variable increases at all, the expected population in 2050 will be much higher than 2.4 billion currently now predicted.*[83] [84]

Thus, Africa's job creation gaps now and in the future, will always be driven by its ever-increasing population growth – meaning jobs, and population estimates, will always be moving targets, requiring constant creativity and vigilance just to keep pace with the rising number of people in the region in in their wage-earning years. Social sector projections for people at the other end of the age spectrum (older Africans) will also have to be adjusted as life expectancy increases.

---

83 United Nations. (n.d.). World Population Prospects: Key findings and Advance Tables 2015. Revision. Retrieved April 17, 2016 from http://esa.un.org/unpd/wpp/publications/files/key_findings_wpp_2015.pdf

84 United Nations Development Program. (2015, September 28). *Assessing Progress in Africa Toward the Millennium Development Goals.* MDG Progress Reports – Africa. Retrieved July 24, 2016 from http://www.undp.org/content/undp/en/home/librarypage/mdg/mdg-reports/africa-collection.html

The ability of African governments, donors, investors, and the private sector to respond to these two synergistic and symbiotic issues – job needs and youth population growth – are fundamental to the region's ability to combat poverty and ensure a positive trajectory for economic development. Africa SMEs are a huge part of the solution to addressing these issues.

Part Two: #AfricaSMEs (Hashtag SMEs)

"African SMEs have led the way in making governments, donors, and others see the positive role they play not just in contributing to job creation, but more importantly contributing to creative ways to address economic development.

We see this in Kenya and East Africa extensively in the information technology sector – adopting mobile platforms and creating mobile money applications to help improve the quality of life of the average African. I doubt whether many of the innovations we see today would exist without the creativity of African SMEs, and supporting these entrepreneurial initiatives should be a top priority."

—Erastus Mong'are, Founder & CEO Startup Africa

Chapter Two:
#AfricaSMEs – Innovative and Their Instagram-like Impact!

Now let's talk more precisely about what Africa SMEs and entrepreneurs are doing that is making them so important! The first is their potential for Instagram®–like impact or insta-impact.[85] [86] In many cases, they are pioneering or creating work-around solutions to some age-old economic development issues, with most ideas reflective of the mobile, digital environment we live in today.

Keep in mind, I am using the terms "SMEs" and "entrepreneurs" interchangeably and symbiotically

---

[85] In 2010, Stanford graduates Kevin Systrom and Mike Krieger created a mobile application called Instagram, a social networking site which provides instant sharing of photos and videos. Facebook bought the site for $US1 billion in 2012. CNBC.com reported that the site as of December 2015, had 400 million users. See: www.instragram.com, http://www.dailymail.co.uk/news/article-2127343/Facebook-buys-Instagram-13-employees-share-100m-CEO-Kevin-Systrom-set-make-400m.html, http://www.businessnewsdaily.com/7662-instagram-business-guide.html, and http://www.cnbc.com/2015/09/23/instagram-hits-400-million-users-beating-twitter.html

[86] In my view, pictures tend to provide an instant reaction and can have an instant impact (insta-impact) depending on who is in the picture or of what the picture shows or reflects. My analogy of connecting Africa SMEs to the term is because in many cases they are disruptive and are having an immediate impact on the sector in which they operate, or the creative idea they project.

because from my perspective, in order to be either, one has to have certain traits as part of the small business makeup. I call them the three I's:

> Being *innovative*, *imaginative*, and have the potential for *"insta-impact"* on whatever sector or endeavor in which the small business is operating – either with a new twist on an old solution or fundamentally the rare new idea.

In some cases, these *solutions or new twists* can simply address an old problem via an Internet application: many of the trendsetting 30 billion applications downloaded worldwide in the last four years were created in the developing world, and a fair amount of that figure on the African Continent.[87] In fact, "apps" (downloadable applications) and other economic development or business solutions abound in SSAfrica.[88] These twists include addressing access

---

[87] World Bank. (2012). *Maximizing Mobile. 2012 Information and Communications for Development.* Retrieved May 2016 from http://siteresources.worldbank.org/EXTINFORMATIONANDCOMMUNICATIONANDTECHNOLOGIES/Resources/IC4D-2012-Report.pdf

[88] "Apps" is computing slang for software that is downloadable on a mobile device. Dictionary.com defines the term as follows: "an application, typically a small, specialized program downloaded onto mobile devices."

to the Internet in difficult environments such as the creative "brck" work-around solution in Kenya, providing Internet hotspots and power solutions in isolated rural areas on a unit that looks like a brick.[89] Or the Songhai Program's climate and nutrition smart food security and environment project (biofuels and renewables) in the Benin Republic, growing organic, non-GMO foods while training a cadre of young African farmer-entrepreneurs.[90] [91] [92]

Source: *Apps.* (2016). Dictionary.com. Retrieved July 2, 2016 fromhttp://www.dictionary.com/browse/app

[89] A rugged powered mobile Wi-Fi device which provides Internet connectivity to people and devices in difficult environments, particularly rural areas. Multiple devices can be connected to it and it also has backup power. See: *BRCK.* About Us. (2016). BRCK Education. Retrieved May 17, 2016 from http://www.brck.com

Beal, V. *Wi-Fi Definition is Not Wireless Fidelity.* (2010, July 14). Did You Know. Webopedia. Retrieved July 8, 2016 from http://www.webopedia.com/DidYouKnow/Computer_Science/wifi_explained.asp

[90] The Songhai project is based in the Republic of Benin and trains and educates farmers to be farmer-entrepreneurs. It also develops climate-smart, non-GMO agricultural products and technology appropriate to the environment where it will be used. The Project is the brainchild of its director, Father Nzamujo, who has used his entrepreneurial talent to create a unique sustainable project for the last 25 years. Sanders first came into contact with Songhai in 2003 in Republic of Congo (located in the Central Africa Region). Songhai will be discussed in more detail later in the book.

[91] Non-GMO – food that has not been grown with a genetically-modified organism. GMO is the abbreviation for genetically-modified organism.

See: *GM Basics.* (2016, August 22). Home Page. Food and Safety Standards. Retrieved July 4, 2016 from https://www.food.gov.uk/science/novel/gm/basics

[92] *The Songhai Centre.* (n.d.). About Us. Retrieved May 27, 2016 from http://

This brings me to the second part of the Africa *SME-Entrepreneur* good news story – their role in spurring the region's still growing but small middle class, and helping to nation build.[93]

In my view, there are several important ways the current crop of SMEs play into the Continent's nascent middle class: creating things that make the lives of Africa's nationals easier (savings in time and resources); entering the middle class themselves as their income and spending power increase; and improving their own quality of life and sense of *wellbeing*—the latter an increasingly important measurement used by some institutions (including FEEEDS) as an indicator of how people are doing and feeling about their life, future, and where they live.[94] [95]

---

www.songhai.org/index.php/en/home-en

[93] Sanders, R. R. *SMEs Development Enterprise Role in National Building: Recognizing the Valuable Role of SMEs in National Development.* (2011, June 22). FEEEDS®. BlogSpot. Blogitrrs.blogspot.com. Retrieved August 3, 2016 from http://blogitrrs.blogspot.com/2011/06/smes-development-enterprise-role-in.html

[94] *National.* (n.d.). Definition. Oxford Dictionary. Retrieved July 30, 2016 from http://www.oxforddictionaries.com/us/definition/american_english/national

[95] Center for Disease Control. (2016, May 31). *Well-being Concepts. Health-related quality of life (HRQOL).* National Center for Chronic Disease Prevention and Health Promotion, Division of Population Health. Retrieved

Prominent institutions such as the World Bank have various wellbeing indices on a range of topics (e.g. poverty, health, water); the Paris-based OECD's *Better Ways Index*, Gallup's *Well Being and Life Evaluation Indices*, and government-funded ones like the United Kingdom's *Personal Well Being Index,* all include polling around *life-quality or happiness* as a measurement of how people are feeling about their lives or where they live.[96] [97] [98]

July 31, 2016 from http://www.cdc.gov/hrqol/wellbeing.htm

[96] The World Bank has various topical wellbeing indices, including specific country wellbeing indices. As an example, see the Tajikistan Index at: *Listening to Tajikistan.* (2015, November). World Bank. Retrieved July 4, 2016 from http://pubdocs.worldbank.org/en/472971449038116674/TJK-Wellbeing-v13.pdf

[97] OECD. (n.d.). *Better Life Index.* Retrieved July 4, 2016 from http://www.oecdbetterlifeindex.org/

[98] The Paris-based Organization of Economic Cooperation and Development (OECD), founded in 1961, and composed of 35 members. Its mission is to promote, improve, and measure the economic and social wellbeing of people around the world. It is also a forum in which governments can work together to share their experiences on economic, social, trade, and environmental issues. It was an outgrowth organization developed from the work and benefit done by The Organization for European Economic Cooperation (OEEC), which was created in 1948 after World War II to manage the Marshall Plan to rebuild Europe. The Marshall Plan was financed by the United States.

See: OECD. (n.d.). About Us. Retrieved June 15, 2016 from http://www.oecd.org/about/ and OECD. (n.d.). About History. Retrieved June 15, 2016 from http://www.oecd.org/about/history/

[99] [100] The United Nations also has commissioned several "happiness reports," and *Harvard Business Review* looked at the "Economics of Well Being" as far back as 2012.[101] [102] I would argue that for Africa SME owners that there is probably a strong sense of satisfaction, even if they face other challenges that affect their wellbeing and that of their families.

In essence, what I am arguing is the *ideal;* Africa SMEs/entrepreneurs have the potential to contribute to a wide range of factors which can help improve the

---

[99] Gallup. (2016). *Well Being.* Topics. Retrieved July 4, 2016 from http://www.gallup.com/topic/category_wellbeing.aspx

NB: Institutions spell wellbeing differently in their text or indices. How the term wellbeing appears in specific titles and names of indices represent how it is expressly written by that institution. Elsewhere in the manuscript, it will appear as wellbeing as I am referring to more than just "being well." See: http://edwardpinkney.com/?p=333

[100] Office of National Statistics, Government of the United Kingdom. (2016, May 5). *Personal Well Being.* Frequently Asked Questions. Retrieved July 4, 2016 from http://webarchive.nationalarchives.gov.uk/20160105160709/http://www.ons.gov.uk/ons/guide-method/method-quality/specific/social-and-welfare-methodology/subjective-wellbeing-survey-user-guide/subjective-well-being-frequently-asked-questions--faq-s-.html

[101] Helliwell, J., Layard, R. & Sachs, J. *World Happiness Report.* (2015). United Nations. Retrieved July 4, 2016 from http://worldhappiness.report/wp-content/uploads/sites/2/2015/04/WHR15.pdf

[102] Fox, J. *Economics of Well Being.* Harvard Business Review. (2012, January-February Issue) Retrieved July 4, 2016 from https://hbr.org/2012/01/the-economics-of-well-being

quality of life and eventually contribute to wellbeing even if that is not the case right now.[103]

SSAfrica SMEs – Impact on Job Creation and the Middle Class

Since I am emphasizing that SMEs and entrepreneurs can help spur the growth of the region's small middle class, it is important to look at the data on how large it is today, and discuss some of the factors which might affect its growth.

Currently the data on Africa's middle class is wide ranging, inconsistent, and pretty much all over the map. Somewhere from 18, 30, 120, to 300 million people make up Africa's middle class, depending on what US dollar figure is used to determine middle-class levels, whether net worth and/or income are the indicators, whether the same indicators are used to measure different countries, and which of these

[103] It is important to note that there are some who do not feel wellbeing indices tell the whole story or are a good measure of issues or how citizens feel, particularly because some can be subjective. I am not one of those. I do believe wellbeing indices, if anything, can help gauge a society's direction, or feelings about institutions even though they may not be an absolute or perfect measure.

measurements an organization uses. [104] [105] [106] [107] [108] [109] Starting at $US1.25-$US2.00 per day income (poverty levels or just above), the threshold measuring SSAfrica's middle class can be anywhere from $US4.00

[104] Mwiti, L. *Special Report: 18 million, not 300 million: That's the size of Africa's 'Real' Middle Class—And It Could Disappear.* (2015, October 29). Africa. *Mail & Guardian.* Retrieved July 4, 2016 from http://mgafrica.com/article/2015-10-27-18-million-thats-the-size-of-africas-middle-classand-with-chinas-woes-it-could-just-be-wiped-out

The African Development Bank. (2011, April 20). *The Middle of The Pyramid: Dynamics of The Middle Class in Africa.* Market Brief. Section 2.2, p. 2. Retrieved August 7, 2016 from http://www.afdb.org/fileadmin/uploads/afdb/Documents/Publications/The%20Middle%20of%20the%20Pyramid_The%20Middle%20of%20the%20Pyramid.pdf

[105] Rosen, A. *A Credit Suisse Report Just Debunked a Huge Claim About the Size of Africa's Middle Class.* (2015, November, 19). *Business Insider.* Retrieved May 2016 from http://publications.credit-suisse.com/tasks/render/file/index.cfm?fileid=C26E3824-E868-56E0-CCA04D4BB9B9ADD5

[106] Credit Suisse Research Institute. (2015, October). *Global Wealth Data Book 2015.* Retrieved July 4, 2016 from http://publications.credit-suisse.com/tasks/render/file/index.cfm?fileid=C26E3824-E868-56E0-CCA04D4BB9B9ADD5

[107] International Monetary Fund. (2015, December 26). *Africa's Middle Class Spearheads Economic Growth.* IMF Survey. Retrieved July 5, 2016 from http://www.imf.org/external/pubs/ft/survey/so/2013/INT122613A.htm

[108] Melber, H. *The Myth of Africa's Growing Middle Class. (2016, May 26).* Opinion. *Independent Online (IOL).* Retrieved July 5, 2016 from http://www.iol.co.za/news/the-myth-of-africas-growing-middle-class-2026750

[109] African Development Bank. (2011, April 20). *The Middle of The Pyramid: Dynamics of The Middle Class in Africa.* Market Brief. The African Development Bank. Section 2.2, p. 2. Retrieved August 7, 2016 from http://www.afdb.org/fileadmin/uploads/afdb/Documents/Publications/The%20Middle%20of%20the%20Pyramid_The%20Middle%20of%20the%20Pyramid.pdf

to $20.00 per day, with $US4.00 at the lower end of middle class in many of these reports.[110] [111]

Some data-focused organizations prefer to count net worth as the determinant rather than disposable income (or they require both) to measure who is in Africa's middle class. Regardless of how one measures, there is discernable evidence that Africa's middle class is growing, even if that growth is very slow and small.[112] [113] [114]

South Africa is considered to have the region's largest middle class at 4.3 million, but as noted above, it also

---

[110] *Africa's Middle Class - Few and Far Between. Africans Are Mainly Rich or Poor, But Not Middle Class. That Should Worry Democrats.* (2015, October 24). *The Economist.* Retrieved May 2016 from http://www.economist.com/news/middle-east-and-africa/21676774-africans-are-mainly-rich-or-poor-not-middle-class-should-worry

[111] Fletcher, P. *Africa's Emerging Middle Class Drives Growth and Democracy.* (2013, May 10). 2013. *Reuters.* Retrieved July 4, 2016 from http://www.reuters.com/article/us-africa-investment-idUSBRE9490DV20130510

[112] Ibid.

[113] Oxfam. (2016, January 18). *62 People Own the Same as Half the World, Reveals Oxfam Davos Report.* News. Retrieved July 16, 2016 from https://www.oxfam.org/en/pressroom/ pressreleases/2016-01-18/62-people-own-same-half-world-reveals-oxfam-davos-report

[114] Organization for Economic Cooperation and Development. (2016). *Divided We Stand: Why Inequality Keeps Rising.* Home Page. OECD.org. Retrieved July 5, 2016 from http://www.oecd.org/els/soc/dividedwestandwhyinequalitykeepsrising.htm

has one of the world's highest income inequalities.[115] [116] Nigeria follows with the next largest middle class, followed respectively by non-Sub-Saharan countries like Egypt, Tunis, and Morocco, but income inequality is high in these countries too.[117]

Whatever the country-specific figure is or how one is calculating, some on the Continent will expect and be expected to make the transition to the middle class over the next decade. Moreover, the continued growth and development of Africa SMEs and entrepreneurs over the next decade should help increase middle-class numbers. As I mentioned, when I talk about Africa SMEs spurring the middle-class, they do so in three ways: creating services and products for people already in the middle class;

---

115 Pasquali, V. *Income Inequality and Wealth Distribution by Country.* (2011, August 22). Project Coordinator Denise Bedell. *Global Finance.* Retrieved July 1, 2016 from http://www.gfmag.com/global-data/economic-data/wealth-distribution-income-inequality and, earlier retrieved from April 14, 2014 from http://www.gfmag.com/tools/global-database/economic-data/11944-wealth-distribution-income-inequality.html#axzz2x0eRLqkL

116 Mwiti, L. *Special Report: 18 million, not 300 million: That's the Size of Africa's 'Real' Middle Class—And It Could Disappear.* (2015, October 29). Africa. *Mail & Guardian.* Retrieved July 4, 2016 from http://mgafrica.com/article/2015-10-27-18-million-thats-the-size-of-africas-middle-classand-with-chinas-woes-it-could-just-be-wiped-out

117 Ibid.

entering the class level themselves; and providing jobs, which sets the stage for their employees to follow. If this doesn't happen, then something is terribly wrong.

The Important Critical Mass SMEs – Needing More of a Hand-up

What I see lacking in the plethora of data and commentary on Africa SMEs and entrepreneurs is a comprehensive global plan (possibly needing to be incorporated into the SDGs) that includes measures to ensure that middle-class growth is achieved, not fluctuating, floating, or vulnerable, but on a constant, upward trajectory. Factors include credit, access to finance, pension, insurance, sustained economic enabling environments, which can propel small businesses forward, helping them not only protect their company assets, but also move their owners and employees into the middle class.

It is clear to me, however, that within the Africa SME and entrepreneur sector, there is a group, I would target and that I call the *critical mass,* which I define as making $US10,000-$US250,000, with 1 to 20 employees, sole proprietors and those in the informal sector (unregistered businesses). This is the group I would argue we need to help the most over the hump so that they are solidly and securely (not minimally) into Africa's middle class or finally have registered businesses. The goal should be for donors, foundations, venture capitalists, and the private sector to ensure this critical mass group is not *vulnerable* to fall out of the middle class or lose their businesses at the first sign of financial difficulty or unexpected life changes. My definition of critical mass SMEs includes *registered and unregistered companies* and is based on my work in the sector with both types of SMEs, designing SME training programs, meetings with Africa SMEs from all over the Continent, and engaging in dialogue with those with whom I have directly worked with in the past and today. *VC4Africa* notes in its 2014 report that when it canvassed its SME online community (including startups) that most received between $US80,000 and $237,000 from private equity and venture capital firms looking to invest in small businesses in the region.[118] These levels, coupled with access to finance and credit, will need to be larger and donor, foundations, investments, and award grants consistently need to increase to help *this* SME critical mass group both enter, but more importantly remain in the middle class, or keep their business if they are in the informal sector. There is also another target group on which I want to expound.

The IMF 2015 report on Africa's middle class referred to earlier in Chapter 1 discusses a "floating middle class" (those just holding the line at $US4.00); this is the group, if you remember, I call "fragile" because any increase in food or fuel prices (including a natural disaster) could sink them back below the poverty level at a moment's notice.[119] Therefore, to truly increase the size of Africa's middle class,

[118] Heilbron, M. *Private Equity & Venture Capital Investments in Africa Growing Fast – Will We See a Quick Shift Towards SMEs?* (2014, March 3). Venture Capital for Africa. Retrieved June 25, 2016 from https://vc4a.com/blog/2014/03/03/private-equity-venture-capital-investments-in-africa-growing-fast-shift-towards-smes-expected/

[119] International Monetary Fund. (2015, December 26). Africa's Middle Class Spearheads Economic Growth. IMF Survey. International Monetary Fund. Retrieved July 5, 2016 from http://www.imf.org/external/pubs/ft/survey/so/2013/INT122613A.htm

African and donor governments need to include in any global strategic plan more help to *the fragile and critical mass groups* so that they first reach, and second, stay in the middle class; I do not see type of planning happening now.

When middle class numbers increase, there can also be a small dent in upper-class numbers as some will transition from middle to upper class. If there is more of a comprehensive plan, we should be seeing more of this kind of movement as well during the next decade. That being said, movement at all levels or from one to another (poverty to middle, middle to upper) is all good. Whether the current middle class comprises 18, 30, 120, or 300 million people in the region, the truth is probably somewhere in between these figures as it is difficult to both *assess* and *access* accurate data for many African countries. According to Reuters (2013), the 18 million as the size of Africa's middle class would represent about 3.3 percent of the population, while 120 million would represent a little over 10 percent of SSAfrica's 1.1

billion.[120] [121] [122] Indeed, assisting more of Africa SMEs to become part of the middle class will help stabilize the estimates and data.

In addition to the impact on the middle class, Africa SME growth can help change income inequality and disparity. The richest on the Continent represent 0.2 percent of the region's population but hold 30.6 percent of the wealth; we know that this disparity impacts GDP.[123] [124] Therefore, as SMEs and entrepreneurs

---

[120] Rosen, A. *A Credit Suisse Report Just Debunked a Huge Claim About the Size of Africa's Middle Class.* (2015, November, 19). *Business Insider.* Retrieved May 2016 from http://publications.credit-suisse.com/tasks/render/file/index.cfm?fileid=C26E3824-E868-56E0-CCA04D4BB9B9ADD5

[121] Fletcher, P. *Africa's Emerging Middle Class Drives Growth and Democracy.* (2013, May 10). *Reuters.* Retrieved July 4, 2016 from http://www.reuters.com/article/us-africa-investment-idUSBRE9490DV20130510

[122] World Bank/IBRD-IDA. (2015). *Sub-Saharan Africa Population.* [data set]. Retrieved August 15, 2016 from http://data.worldbank.org/region/sub-saharan-africa

United Nations. (2015). *World Population Prospects: Key findings and Advance Tables.* Revision. Retrieved April 17, 2016 from http://esa.un.org/unpd/wpp/publications/files/key_findings_wpp_2015.pdf

[123] Mwiti, L. *Special Report: 18 million, not 300 million: That's the Size of Africa's 'Real' Middle Class—And It Could Disappear.* (2015, October 29). Africa. *Mail & Guardian.* Retrieved July 4, 2016 from http://mgafrica.com/article/2015-10-27-18-million-thats-the-size-of-africas-middle-classand-with-chinas-woes-it-could-just-be-wiped-out

[124] Organization for Economic Cooperation and Development. (2015, May 21). *In It Together: Why Less Inequality Benefits All. OECD.org.* Retrieved July 5, 2016 from http://www.oecd.org/els/in-it-together-why-less-inequality-benefits-all-9789264235120-en.htm

increase their job creation numbers, manufacturing output, and value-added exports, these can help reduce income inequality, all of which in turn add to increased GDP.

A reminder though: SMEs are not a silver bullet to all the poverty and quality of life/wellbeing issues in the region, but they can be:

- A built-in sustainability vehicle.
- A counter-driver to security challenges.
- A wealth of talent to help bring new ideas to the fore, like no other group.

I have already talked about Africa's "youth bulge," a term referring to the large number of young people on the Continent from which most of Africa's entrepreneurs hail. Age data defining Africa's youth also varies widely per institution: AfDB, 15-24 years; African Union, 15-35 years; World Bank/ILO, 15-24 years; Gallup, 15-29 years; and OECD, under 15 years. It is important to keep these institutional age definitions in mind when examining the progress made and the progress that still needs to be made in job creation and middle- class growth in each country.[125]

[126] [127] [128]

We know Africa's youth bulge (no matter what age range one is using) will be pivotal in helping to break barriers on "poverty," by using their creative contributions as Africa SMEs or entrepreneurs to make a difference. We also know small businesses spur middle-class growth (the US, China, India, Indonesia, and up until 2014, Brazil, are all good examples of

---

[125] Williams, S. *Africa Youth. The African Development Bank and the Demographic Dividend.* (2012, March 30). African Development Bank. Retrieved July 5, 2016 from http://www.afdb.org/fileadmin/uploads/afdb/Documents/Generic-Documents/AFDB%20youth%20doc.pdf

[126] *African Youth Charter.* (2006, June). Banjul. African Union Commission. Retrieved July 5, 2016 from http://www.un.org/en/africa/osaa/pdf/au/african_youth_charter_2006.pdf

[127] World Bank Group/IBRD-IDA (2016). *World Bank and International Labor Organization Use 15-24 Years of Age to Define Africa's Youth or Youth Bulge.* [data set]. Retrieved July 5, 2016 from http://data.worldbank.org/indicator/SL.UEM.1524.ZS

International Labour Organization Document. (2015). Global Employment Trends for Youth 2015: Scaling Up Investment for Descent Job for Youth. p. 9. Geneva. ILO.org. Retrieved July 5, 2016 from http://www.ilo.org/wcmsp5/groups/public/---dgreports/---dcomm/---publ/documents/publication/wcms_412015.pdf

[128] *Generation 2030/Africa.* (2014, August 12). Retrieved July 5, 2016 from http://data.unicef.org/gen2030/index.html

this). For SSAfrica this would be no different as the *insta-impact* of helping both the fragile and critical mass groups cannot be underestimated to the overall economic direction of the region.

As for GDPs, it was a struggle to find sources detailing the exact contribution that Africa SMEs provide to countries or the region. The closest estimates for SMEs in emerging markets like Sub-Saharan Africa show that formal small businesses (meaning those registered with their governments) contribute about 33 percent to national GDPs, and 45 percent to job creation.[129] However, it remains hard to determine how much *informal* SMEs (those not registered with their governments) add to GDP.[130] On the issue of

---

[129] African Development Bank. (2013, July 22). *The AfDB SME Program Approval: Boosting Inclusive Growth in Africa.* News and Events. Retrieved July 5, 2016 from http://www.afdb.org/en/news-and-events/article/the-afdb-sme-program-approval-boosting-inclusive-growth-in-africa-12135/

[130] World Bank Group/IBRD-IDA. (2015, September 1). *Small and Medium Enterprises (SMEs) Finance.* Finance Brief. Worldbank.org. p. 8. Retrieved July 5, 2016 from http://www.worldbank.org/en/topic/financialsector/brief/smes-finance

Other key figures on SMEs in emerging markets like Asia, Africa, and Latin America, in this same study, include estimated global totals of: "365-445 million micro, small and medium enterprises (MSMEs) of which 25-30 million are formal SMEs; 55-70 million are formal micro enterprises; and 285-345 million are informal enterprises."

informal SMEs, *the World Bank Small and Medium Enterprises (SMEs) 2015 Finance Brief* stated that there are approximately 285-340 million informal SMEs in emerging areas such as Africa, Asia, and Latin America. (NB: the report also noted that there are more unregistered SMEs in emerging regions than those registered with their governments.)[131] Therefore, whatever the actual number of informal SMEs is, they de facto make some contribution to GDP. One 2015 news report on China Global Television Network's Africa Live claims that the informal SME and entrepreneur sectors, or "grey economy," contributes $US4 billion to the region's GDP.[132] I also would assume that the estimates on the total number of informal SMEs could be way under or over the reality, given the difficulty in obtaining accurate data on unregistered Africa SMEs.

---

[131] Ibid.

[132] (2015, December 9). Africa Live. [Television broadcast]. China Global Television Network.

Leaving data aside and taking a philosophical approach for the moment, one could look at summing up the contributions of Africa SMEs as:

One self-sustaining person, group, or communities of purpose that generate-income through a creative or business entrepreneurial effort and then shares that forward.[133]

It is as simple as that. So now let's look at how international institutions and African governments define SMEs as this impacts funding and resource availability, which slows down their growth and the realization of their full potential and contribution for Africa's tomorrow and its future.

---

[133] I am using the terms "generating-income" or "generate-income" to mean making your own money.

Chapter Three:
Current State of Play – The "Future-Morrow" for SMEs

When one scripts the current state of play for Africa SMEs, including the fragile and critical mass groups, in what I like to call their *Future-Morrow* role (a mashup of the words "future" and "tomorrow"), it is important to take into account a few things in addition to the void they filled left by gaps in development, such as how they are defined by funders, and what other funding obstacles are in their path?[134]

First, one of the key change-agents that made Africa SMEs and entrepreneurs the new face of development and job creation was. . .*Technology!* I have been an avid information systems and communication advocate over the years, and could see the transformation that technology and mobile phone use would provide for the Continent as early as 2000s when I was living in the region.[135] I began to focus on technology uses and

[134] Future-Morrow is a phrase used by the author to mean the future and tomorrow, or in today's lingo, a "mashup" of the words "future" and "tomorrow."

[135] I later received my doctorate in the field of information systems and

the importance of self-sufficiency for the region when I was working in the Republic of Congo in 2003, (even though I was not thinking about the terms "SMEs" and "entrepreneurship" at the time as neither words were part of my daily passion in 2003). All this is, however, is worth a short side-bar story on my experiential work and building partnerships in the Congo where technology, interest in small business, and *smart development* all came together for me.

The Congo Side-Bar Story (With a Bit of Atmospherics)

I had been in the Republic of Congo for a few months, arriving in-country as the first woman diplomat and first African American to hold the post as the United States Ambassador there.[136] The Republic of Congo

---

communications.

[136] There are two Congos divided by the mighty Congo River, the second longest river in Africa after the Nile. The Congo River has the world's second largest discharge and rainforest after the Amazon River, is the world's deepest river; and crosses the equator twice. I served as U.S. Ambassador to the Republic of Congo, a French-speaking nation in the Central African Region of the Continent, whose capital is Brazzaville. Republic of Congo is across the Congo River from the Democratic Republic of the Congo (also French-speaking), whose capital is Kinshasa and is known by the abbreviation DRC. Republic of the Congo is also sometimes called Congo-Brazzaville, or Congo-Brazza.

was still finding its footing after a devastating civil war (1991-1997), followed by a fragile post-conflict period, which ran at least 10 years from 1997 to 2007.[137]

During my time, there from 2003 to 2005, many Congolese still suffered from the trauma of the war and the fragility that comes in the post-conflict aftermath. The infrastructure was devastated, buildings were destroyed (including the U.S. Embassy), there was little to no commerce, and many other services remained non-functional or unreliable (such as using mobile phones for calls, electrical power, clean water, etc.). This is when I learned to text (2003), as I relied on texting for

---

See: *Congo River Facts.* (n.d.). Africa Facts. Retrieved July 30, 2016 from http://interesting-africa-facts.com/Africa-Landforms/Congo-River-Facts.html

Congo River. (2013, June 13). Research Begins Here. New World Encyclopedia. Retrieved July 30, 2016 from http://www.newworldencyclopedia.org/entry/Congo_River

[137] It took about 10 years for all of Republic of Congo's society – people, places (cities and villages), institutions, and infrastructure – to truly bounce back from the devastating civil war and also become home to a generation of young people who had not lived through the civil war. It was not until the mid-2000s that most countries re-opened their embassies and investments began to return. In 2016 it had an election which was questioned by the international community based on concerns that a constitutional referendum to allow a presidential third term was not transparent; the opposition leader was arrested after the elections and there also was some post-election violence and blocking of the press.

nearly all of my local communication. (NB: I have been texting my head off ever since; it remains my default communication tool to this day as I would rather text than call any day.) But texting in Congo was more a matter of survival because of the vast destruction of most of the infrastructure during the civil war.

Despite the devastation, what I also saw was resilience, with my own U.S. Embassy local staff (many who had protected Embassy property during the civil war) and with local Congolese. There were few streetlights, and those that worked were mostly on four main streets. Lights were out most of the time; food selection, fresh or otherwise, was scarce in Congo's capital Brazzaville while I was there (only two small grocery stores that I can remember, and the main market, which also didn't have much then.) Everything was expensive since most things were imported. I and the rest of the U.S. Embassy American staff most often had to cross the mighty Congo River on the Embassy-owned small Boston whaler boat, to DRC's capital Kinshasa to buy larger quantities of groceries.[138]

---

[138] U.S. Embassy Brazzaville is the Embassy of the United States in the

[139] Most schools and hospitals had been destroyed; downtown still had bullet-riddled buildings, or buildings with no roofs or other parts blown off by rocket-propelled grenades or tracer surface-to-air missiles from the civil war, including the old U.S. Embassy building. Our old U.S. Embassy Brazzaville structure was burnt, without a roof, but remained standing on the main road which ran parallel to the banks of the Congo River in downtown Brazzaville (more commonly called Brazza).[140]

I remember one evening a few months after arriving in Congo, seeing young people huddled or lying under the few streetlights that worked in Brazza, which were those near the two main hotels still open, the Chinese-built soccer stadium, and on one of the main cross town streets that ran near the United Nations

---

Republic of Congo whose capital is Brazzaville, and the U.S. Embassy Kinshasa is in the capital of the Democratic Republic of Congo, whose capital is Kinshasa. The Embassies are across the Congo River from each other. I had an office in both embassies, as I had to travel across the Congo River to Embassy Kinshasa to read classified materials.

[139] Ibid.

[140] The book will use the terms "Brazza" and "Brazzaville" interchangeably, and refer to the capital of the Republic of Congo and both are commonly used.

Development Program (UNDP) Office. The rest of the city was most often dark at night. I would pass by these groups of young people almost every night who were under these streetlights, while I was on my way to a work event in the U.S. Government-owned armored vehicle (required because of spurts of violence and gun fights that still erupted in Brazza; on several occasions I had to institute lockdowns of Embassy staff movements because of security).[141] I couldn't make out what these young people were doing lying in the street as I thought it unsafe because of the fragile security environment – so I asked my driver, Casimir, to stop one night, as curiosity had gotten the best of me.

I got out of the car and walked over to the very weak, broken streetlight and looked down to see what they were doing. They were reading! I spoke to them (in my still very weak French at that time), just to hear their stories – some tragic as many lost loved ones during the civil war, but all wanted to ensure they received an education, could read (particularly English), and make a living. They

[141] "Lockdown" is a term used by the U.S. State Department and its embassies, requiring embassy employee to remain where they are because the local environment is unsafe.

actually used the words "make money" (I noted that they didn't say "be employed"), since the term "make money" sounded so strange to me then as I wasn't sure exactly what they meant. But they explained they didn't want to depend on anyone else for their money or livelihood.

Although I had only been in-country for a few months, this encounter gave way to my singular focus and commitment to find a way to help, and for the U.S. Government to help. Although, the terms SME and entrepreneurship were not really as prevalent in the development sector nomenclature then as they are today, but what these young people described were exactly these two things.

In 2003, the main donor emphasis and model was still on "income-generating projects," but what I heard that night in Brazza was the reverse – *generating-income,* which we all know today is something completely different.[142] I took this as a personal charge for my

[142] I am using the term "donor" here in the broadest sense meaning foreign governments, NGOs, and development-focused foundations providing assistance. In early 20002, the numbers of donors we see today were not operating in the region in assisting in SSAfrica's development. Today, donors range from the private sector to eminent persons and their

time in Congo, and it is why I have been so committed to Africa SMEs and entrepreneurship ever since. Life is always about concentric circles for me (time, place, people, and events) and reflecting on where and how things overlap. The concentric circles which overlapped in my Brazza experience where I found a great (and the right) development partner to work with, and my development focused move from income-generating to generating-income. I continued to work with the older development models supporting projects identified by my team for monies from Embassy Brazzaville's Ambassador's Self-Help Fund. But my real passion had become to find a way to help young Congolese on this goal of generating-income, and identifying partners (what is called public private partnerships today) to help since I knew our Embassy budget was not going to be enough to make an impact.[143]

---

foundations, etc.

[143] Most of Embassy Brazza's income-generating projects fell under the U.S Ambassador's Special Self-Help funds, which were $US25,000 small grants used to assist community-based around the globe and are managed by U.S. Embassies. The goal of the Self-Help Program is to improve the basic economic and social conditions of a village or community, and should benefit the greatest number of people possible. Projects must be completed within one year, and grantees can apply again for an attendant or different project.

The like-minded development partner in this case was my UN colleague, Mr. Aurélien Agbénonci, who was both the UNDP Resident Representative and the United Nations Coordinator (he headed UNDP and also was responsible for overseeing the coordination of all other UN agency activity in Congo).[144] Agbénonci had a similar sense of the environment, as I did, and he too strongly believed it was important to do something "uniquely different," to help Congolese overcome the pervasive social and economic destruction and trauma left by the civil war. Both partner-institutions (U.S. Embassy Brazza and UNDP) shared a *commonality of purpose* – wanting to help address the various societal challenges, which developed as an outgrowth of the conflict.

See: *Special Self-Help Fund (SSH)*. (n.d.). Diplomacy in Action. Department of State. Retrieved July 3, 2016 from http://www.state.gov/p/af/pdpa/ssh/

[144] Mr. Aurélien Agbénonci, from the Republic of Benin, served as UNDP Resident Representative and UN Coordinator in the Republic of Congo, 2003-2008, and in Central African Republic (CAR) as the United Nations Resident Coordinator, UNDP Resident Representative in Central African Republic, and Deputy Special Representative for the United Nations Multidimensional Integrated Stabilization Mission in CAR (MINUSCA) from 2014 to 2016. As of April 2016, he is the Minister of Foreign Affairs and Cooperation for the Republic of Benin. Also, see: United Nations. (2014, April 25). *Secretary-General Appoints Aurélien Agbénonci of Benin Deputy Special Representative and Resident Coordinator for Central African Republic.* Meetings Coverage and Press Releases. Retrieved May 2016 from http://www.un.org/press/en/2014/sga1458.doc.htm

My time in the Republic of Congo also prompted a great appreciation and understanding of how effective public-private partnerships (PPPs) can be, if they are done right, particularly in sharing ideas, implementation, responsibility, and resources.[145] In this case, in Congo, everything came together: a sense to try something different, the opportunity to work with a great partner in UNDP under the leadership of Mr. Agbénonci and with both his and my committed, capable, and talented staff staffs. All these elements were needed to get something *unique* accomplished under difficult circumstances and a difficult security environment.

My sense is that this desire to generate-income was probably happening everywhere on the Continent around that same time, contributing to the other drivers and catalysts (unemployment, social sector needs) that sparked growth of today's Africa SMEs. The

[145] Public-private partnerships, or PPPs, are when two or more entities/organizations/institutions come together to advance a particular issue, project, or purpose. In this case, the PPP was created between the U.S. Embassy Brazzaville in the name of the U.S. Government, and the United Nations Development Program (UNDP) Brazzaville for the UN agency, UNDP. PPPs were not as prevalent or creative in 2003 as they are today. But during my time in Congo (2002-2005), a PPP was still a fairly new thing for a U.S. Government entity such as an embassy to do with a UN agency.

Congo experience certainly made me understand what these young people wanted, but I also understood that what they wanted was very different from donor project assistance or income-generating projects.

Both partner-institutions zeroed in on the lack of reliable Internet access in Congo as there were 1 or 2 very small cyber cafes in Brazzaville then (that I can remember), which faced constant electrical power outage; and, there were also no standing libraries left in the city after the war (this began to change, though, as I was departing in 2005).

In sum, the issues the UNDP-U.S. Embassy Brazza PPP set out to address were:

- Assisting with generating-income as opposed to income-generation;
- Ensuring better, reliable Internet access;
- Using all new technologies available, video conferencing, mobile platforms;
- Establishing a training center; and

- Providing a safe location in which to do all of the above.

After a lot of creative thinking, we created the UNDP-U.S. Embassy Multi-Educational Resource Center, or "UNDP-U.S. Embassy-MERC."[146]

Agbénonci and UNDP had an empty building on their compound which needed to be refurbished after the war, but it had power, a generator, and was safe and secure. Embassy Brazza had the ability to purchase computers, building materials, English books by the truckload, and other resource materials, equipment,

[146] The UNDP-U.S. Embassy-MERC infrastructure was finished in 2004 with both partners needing time to marshal approvals, resources, all supplies, equipment, and material, and get two buildings completely refurbished and supplied with electricity. The MERC became operational in 2005, with an opening ceremony attended by nearly everyone in town and Congolese officials from the Ministry of Foreign Affairs, Education, and so on. The MERC responded to everything on the to-do list noted above.

The MERC PPP remained in effect until 2009. Agbénonci and I determined we would sign an MOU which would remain in effect for 5 years. Our thinking was that within that 5-year time line, Congo would truly be out of post-conflict mode then and there would be a wide variety of other options available to provide additional new technology access for young Congolese. That of course did happen for Congo and the Congolese, including on the U.S. side, with a new Embassy facility opening in 2010, where I am honored that my name appears on the plaque on the entrance wall for my work in Brazzaville.

and supplies. Both partners had supportive staff to oversee and run the UNDP-U.S. Embassy-MERC.

The U.S. Government did not have much interest at that time in developing any on-ground big projects as part of U.S. Embassy Brazzaville's presence in Congo, since there was no U.S. Agency for International Development (USAID) office in the capital.[147] Therefore, all the support for the MERC had to come from my Embassy's small public diplomacy budget. Notwithstanding, I have to thank immensely then-USAID Assistant Administrator for Africa, Lloyd Pierson, who came to Brazzaville on a three-hour trip (I worked with Lloyd in Namibia when I was a junior diplomat and he was at the Peace Corps).[148] I showed

---

[147] USAID has the primary responsibility for managing projects in foreign countries under the U.S. Government's development assistance program. Therefore, it is more difficult and challenging to have large projects on the ground in foreign countries without a USAID mission in country. The term used for countries without a USAID mission is "non-presence post/embassy."

[148] Lloyd Pierson was appointed to senior Administration positions by three U.S. Presidents. Nominated by President George W. Bush as the Assistant Administrator for Africa at USAID, he also previously served as Chief of Staff/Chief of Operations at the Peace Corps. Pierson testified multiple times on Africa issues before the U.S. Congress. He serves on the Advisory Board for the Nigerian-American Leadership Council.

See: Lloyd Pierson. (n.d.). LinkedIn Profile. Retrieved May 19, 2016 from https://www.linkedin.com/in/lloyd-pierson-63276018

Lloyd the MERC space and discussed the concept; he immediately understood what I, Agbénonci, and our staffs were trying to do. Having seen enough of the city's devastated infrastructure, Pierson simply said, "What can I do to help, Ambassador?" I said, "I need more computers than I have money for in my small budget." He said, "I will see what I can do." Needless to say, I got the additional computers, help with the video conferencing equipment, and UNDP covered the refurbishing of its space, reconnected power to the building, provided security, and installed the ISDN line for teleconferencing so we could provide remote training.[149] The Embassy's carpenter, Patrick, built all the computer desks and tables. UNDP also refurbished another small room near the MERC for Embassy Brazzaville to use as a library or "American Corner," which also had computers, English books, and movies.[150] In the end, UNDP and Embassy Brazza

[149] ISDN is the abbreviation for integrated services digital network, which as defined by Webopedia as the "international standard for sending voice, video, and data over normal telephone lines." See: Beal, V. *ISDN - Integrated Services Digital Network*. (n.d.). Term. Webopedia. Retrieved July 31, 2016 from http://www.webopedia.com/TERM/I/ISDN.html

[150] There was a main MERC building, responding to all the elements on the to-do list noted above, and UNDP also allowed U.S. Embassy Brazzaville

opened one of the first post-civil-war cyber, educational training facilities centers in Brazzaville for young students and adults and those interested in starting small businesses. The UNDP-U.S. Embassy MERC achieved the goals set out in the PPP document:

> *Create a center for learning, training, and business workshops, co-located with library in a secure location that had reliable power for dependable Internet access, a trained staff, and was open to the public.*

We also allowed Congolese Ministries to use the facilities for their training programs. The MERC did not get any high-level attention from the U.S. Government, but within UNDP headquarters in New York, the Center, the PPP effort, and Agbénonci, I, and

---

to open a small library in a separate building with English-language materials and movies under a USG program called "The American Corner," to which Embassy Brazza provided personnel and additional computers. Without UNDP Brazzaville's help at that time, the U.S. Government would not have been able to establish an American Corner in Congo. I will forever be grateful to Mr. Agbénonci, UNDP Headquarters in New York, and the entire UNDP staff for allowing us to have an American Corner and more importantly for the great PPP that created the UNDP-U.S. Embassy MERC. Prior to coming to Brazza, I was the Director of the Africa Office of Public Diplomacy at the State Department, so knew where and how to get the resources we needed for the American Corner.

our staffs received high accolades. The venture was cited as a "best practice partnership on PPP's" and on how to turn policy on economic development and new technologies into something tangible and useful.[151]

The MERC partnership forever changed how I wanted to engage as a diplomat and underscored for me how important it is to turn *policy into practice*. It also sparked my early commitment in what we now call SMEs and entrepreneurial thinking. The MERC helped a lot of young Congolese start or develop their ideas for small businesses and we offered a range of programs that helped on entrepreneurship and other educational needs.

The impact of the MERC on the community, to me, was unmistakable. It provided many other positive intangibles in Brazzaville's post-conflict environment, most notably computer access and new uses on mobile platforms such as texting to send MERC info to others who could not come to the center – texting became a multiplier effect. We know based on Pew Research

---

[151] USG is an abbreviation meaning the United States Government.

that texting today is the most common use of mobile phones for 80 percent of those with cell phones, and we also know the importance that technology's mobility provides to the Africa SME story; this potential was evident in the MERC project back in 2003.[152] [153] [154]

One of the first young adults who came to use the new MERC was a good example of the impact it had in the community. I remember Agbénonci and I watched, initially bewildered, while a young man moved the computer mouse vertically up the side of the desktop monitor – since that is of course what mice do – they run vertically up the wall. (We finally got that after watching him for a while.) This young man had never sat in front of a computer, seen or used the accessory

---

[152] Pew Research Center. (2015, April). *Cell Phones in Africa: Communication Lifeline. Texting Most Common Activity, But Mobile Money Popular in Several Countries*. Global Attitudes and Trends. Retrieved July 3, 2016 from http://www.pewglobal.org/2015/04/15/cell-phones-in-africa-communication-lifeline/

[153] *Mobile Phone Users Worldwide*. (2013-2019). The Statistical Portal. 2016. Statista. Retrieved July 2, 2016 from http://www.statista.com/statistics/274774/forecast-of-mobile-phone-users-worldwide/

[154] World Bank. (2012, December 10). *ICTs Delivering Home-Grown Development Solutions in Africa*. Retrieved August 7, 2016 from http://www.worldbank.org/en/news/feature/2012/12/10/ict-home-grown-development-solutions-in-africa

we call a "mouse," or experienced the Internet.[155] The MERC gave him a chance to broaden his horizons, learn to use a computer, and have free Internet access; he could have spent several more years in the *technology wilderness* without this exposure. This was an *Ah-ha Moment* for me regarding the impact that technology was going to have overall on the Continent and its development. I never forgot the visual of that young man and the computer mouse as it underscored how one experience, exposure, or event can change a person's life and path. Both Agbenonci and I received awards from the Congolese President upon our departure from the country for our work on the MERC and other development contributions during our tenure there. My medal of merit (Medal of Honor) from the President of the Republic of Congo as well as the Congo parliamentary declaration giving me the title and status of "Ordre Du Mérite, Le grade de Commandeur," I recently donated to the State Department's new

[155] In 2004, computers were still mostly in two large parts: the large desktop monito with all its innards, and the separate floor hard drive. He was running the mouse up the side of the desktop monitor.

museum called the Diplomacy Center (See Photograph 3, Sanders receiving "Ordre Du Mérite").

Concurrent with the MERC project, my staff and I still had committed to find a way to address the desire of many young Congolese to learn English.[156] Thinking *entrepreneurially*, I got permission from the regional security officer to use a sister location of Embassy Brazza called *Villa Washington* permanently for *English Clubs* three evenings a week.[157] At these clubs, young Congolese could practice English and where the hard-working Embassy Brazzaville staff member Distel Kandza, could share additional English materials, hold English language workshops and show American movies.[158] During the summer, we brought in English

---

[156] The American Corner at the MERC provided access to English-language books, but we did not teach English there.

[157] Villa Washington was one of the locations in the city of Brazzaville, which the U.S. Government owned that was not being used that much since Republic of Congo's civil war. It was not in great shape at the time I was living in Congo, but both I and the previous U.S. Ambassador David Kaeuper tried to use it for various things when we were given permission by the regional security officer to do so. Bio on Kaeuper at: http://photos.state.gov/libraries/somalia/323250/pdfs/amb-kaeuper-bio.pdf

[158] The MERC creation and success would never have come to fruition without the buy-in from the U.S. Embassy and UNDP Brazzaville staffs. They were hard working and committed to helping Mr. Agbenonci and I turn our vision into reality. I know we both owe them a debt of gratitude, and I wholeheartedly thank them. In particular, I want to thank the

language professors from the University of Washington to help on grammar and syntax. When I visited Congo in late 2015 on a FEEEDS trip, the first time since I left 11 years ago, I was pleased to discover that these clubs, now much more expansive and comprehensive than I could have ever dreamed, were still active. I had the chance to go to Villa Washington at the invitation of the then-sitting U.S. Ambassador, Stephanie Sullivan.[159] Ambassador Sullivan was kind enough to ask me to address the current clubs. I was touched that the assembled group thanked me for my expanded efforts 11 years ago, noting how important the clubs were then and now. The visit to Villa Washington was one of those concentric moments I spoke of earlier. I never thought I would get back to Congo and certainly never expected to engage with members of the Embassy's English Clubs. Villa Washington in 2015

---

talented and committed Embassy Foreign Service National employees from Distel Kandza, my technology guys Bertrand Nsossolo and Dhercy Makaya, and Patrick Kissambou (one of the world's creative carpenters ever!). Distel was, for me, a triple talent that I had hired a few months before, and was incredible doing triple duty helping at the MERC, running the English programs at Villa Washington, and at the American Corner. I saw Distel and Dhercy when I visited Congo in 2015, and have been in touch with Bertrand via Skype and email over the years.

[159] U.S. Ambassador Stephanie Sullivan was appointed as Ambassador to the Republic of Congo in August 2013.

was like a Hilton Hotel compared to when I used it in 2003.[160] I laughed inside when I saw the roof on the multipurpose room, as before in 2005 it didn't have one. In the raining season, we just got soaked. Also, during the 2015 trip, I had the opportunity to send one more person to the English Clubs. I was eating lunch at the Olympic Hotel (still one of Brazza's main hotels), and a young waiter asked me if I had been the previous U.S. Ambassador in Congo, and if so, could he practice his English with me. He said he wanted to be an entrepreneur so he would not have to work at the hotel all his life. I chuckled again inside, saying to myself, "How fortuitous for me to meet a young Congolese entrepreneur." We chatted, and I told him about the Villa Washington English Clubs. He was so pleased (as was I) that there was somewhere he could go to practice his English. It was all a very nice life book-end for me, albeit with 11 years in between.[161]

---

[160] Hilton Hotels and Resorts® is a brand name of a well-known luxury hotel chain. See: http://www.hiltonworldwide.com/ and http://www3.hilton.com/en/index.html?WT.srch=1

My use of the term here is hyperbole to underscore just how much Villa Washington had changed and been refurbished and upgraded from when my staff and I used it for English clubs in 2002-2005.

[161] I also want to thank all the U.S. Ambassadors to Congo after I left for

My love of PPPs, entrepreneurial thinking, and creative solutions to economic development challenges was born in Congo. I spent the rest of my diplomatic career using my voice, energy, creative thinking, and resourcefulness to seek out like-minded entrepreneurial partners both within and outside the U.S. Government.[162]

E-Empowerment of Mobile Devices, Apps, & Knowledge Management

Fast forward to today. Not just in Congo but everywhere in SSAfrica and in the developing world, technology has been one of the big drivers of change, adaptation, evolution, and, in some cases, revolution (i.e., 2010-2011 Arab Spring Revolutions in North Africa, where mobile phones and social media played

---

supporting the MERC and also being kind enough to include my name on the new U.S. Embassy building in 2010. They did not have to do that, and I am touch by this. I saw the plaque for the first time, which includes my name in 2015 when I visited the Embassy.

[162] I had great PPP partners domestically and internationally after the Congo experience such as Ambassador Marcharia Kamau in Namibia (who as of 2016 is the Kenyan Permanent Representative to the United Nations), Africare (one of the oldest American NGOs working in SSAfrica), and Evelyn Oputu, Omowale Orungunde, former Katsina Governor Shema, former Diamond Bank Managing Director Alex Otti in Nigeria, Father Godfrey Nzamujo in Benin and Gallup World Poll in the US.

a big role in disseminating information to encourage political change).[163]

The ability to create apps and the availability of smart and better feature phones in the hands of 680 million Africans in 2016 underscore the pervasive role mobile technology has had in helping Africa SMEs and entrepreneurs expand the global reach of their products and services. [164] [165] Of the six billion worldwide devices, and 4.7 billion users predicted for 2017, the Continent's growth projections for the number of devices and users are staggering and

---

[163] O'Donnell, C. New Study Quantifies Use of Social Media in Arab Spring. (2011, September 12). Washington University Study. University of Washington. Retrieved July 31, 2016 from http://www.washington.edu/news/2011/09/12/new-study-quantifies-use-of-social-media-in-arab-spring/

The Arab Spring kicked off by social media in Tunisia started in December 2010, and ran through early January 2011 in Tunisia with the government's removal. It was also called the Jasmine Revolution there. Other countries in North Africa and the Middle East followed afterwards.

[164] *The Mobile Economy Sub-Saharan Africa 2015.* (2015). GSMA Intelligence. GSM Association. Retrieved August 8, 2016 from https://www.gsmaintelligence.com/research/?file=721eb3d4b80a36451202d0473b3c4a63&download

Mobile phone users worldwide 2013-2019. (2016). The Statistical Portal. Statista. Retrieved July 2, 2016 from http://www.statista.com/statistics/274774/forecast-of-mobile-phone-users-worldwide/

[165] Qureshi, R. Ericsson Mobility Report. Data and Forecast Page. (1996-2016). Ericsson. Retrieved July 2, 2016 from https://www.ericsson.com/mobility-report

continue to outpace all other global regions. Nigeria alone clocks in at 100+ million mobile devices, the most in the region.[166] [167] [168] [169]

Nigeria's mobile phone numbers will become even more staggering if its current estimated population of 182 million reaches reportedly 440 million by 2050.[170] (NB: There is a distinction between number of subscriptions and actual mobile phone devices; many people

---

166 World Bank-IBRD/IDA. (2012, December 10). ICTs Delivering Home-Grown Development Solutions in Africa. Retrieved August 7, 2016 from http://www.worldbank.org/en/news/feature/2012/12/10/ict-home-grown-development-solutions-in-africa.

167 Fick, M. *Smart Africa: Nigerian Group Target 100% Mobile-First Market.* (2016, January 28). Telecoms. Ft.com. *Financial Times*. Retrieved July 3, 2016 from http://www.ft.com/cms/s/0/0ad2bbe4-c044-11e5-846f-79b0e3d20eaf.html#axzz4DO2DXW00

168 The goal of GSMA is to represent the interest of the mobile phone industry. See: *Global Data.* (2016, July). GSMA Intelligence. Retrieved July 3, 2016 from https://www.gsmaintelligence.com/

GSMA Mobile Economy. (2016, July). Retrieved July 3, 2016 from http://www.gsmamobileeconomy.com/

169 The abbreviation GSM means Global System for Mobile Communication, more commonly referred to as GSM. It is the technology which has been adopted by most countries as the way to make a call on a mobile phone. Smith, M. GSM vs. CDMA: What Is the Difference and Which Is Better? April 21, 2014. Make Use Of. Retrieved July 3, 2016 from www.makeuseof.com/tag/gsm-vs-cdma-difference-better/

170 World Bank-IBRD/IDA. (2016). *Nigeria Population.* Retrieved August 8, 2016 from http://data.worldbank.org/country/nigeria

Emekalan, K. *Africa Live.* (2016, July 11) [Television broadcast, 1 p.m.]. *China Global Television Network.*

subscribe to more than one provider, may have more than one phone/device, or may have one subscription providing service to multiple devices. The figure that I am referring to is *actual number of discrete devices.*)[171]

It is not just technology but really mobile technology, which has propelled the growth and success of Africa SMEs. Even if their business is not a technology company, SMEs use technology in other ways to support the success of their businesses and engage customers. Technology allows Africa small businesses to have knowledge in the palm of their hands – and more importantly, knowledge management.

The knowledge management aspect cannot be underestimated as it is not only *Information,* and the ability to *Communicate* across economic, social, and political spectrums and the globe, regardless of location, but *Technology's* (ICT) by-products, which has removed all barriers to collaboration, creativity, and

---

171 *The Mobile Economy Sub-Saharan Africa 2015.* (2015). GSMA Intelligence. GSM Association. Retrieved August 8, 2016 from https://www.gsmaintelligence.com/research/?file=721eb3d4b80a36451202d0473b3c4a63&download

interaction among communities, be they communities of purpose, ideas, innovators, villages, neighborhoods, cities, or countries. *ICT* and its twin sister *knowledge management* have made the difference! ICT has contributed to the range and variety of Africa SMEs and entrepreneurs, making them not only possible and fascinating, but also cutting-edge, clever, and solution-oriented, while helping their owners generate-income (make money) and improve life-quality in some way for themselves or others.

Knowledge management is as important as the mobile device itself is in Africa today, fueling knowledge-based activities, and in some cases, more knowledge-based African communities. SMEs and entrepreneurs used ICT and knowledge management to their advantage much earlier than donors did. (I wrote an article in Huffington Post [HuffPost] in December 2012 on just how far ahead the developing world was, particularly SSAfrica, in using mobile and e-empowerment services over the West.)[172]

---

[172] Sanders, Ambassador R.R. *Mobile Services and E-Empowerment – The Developing World Has the Advantage.* (2012, December 12). World News. *The Huffington Post.* Retrieved August 3, 2016 from http://www.

I am making a big tent argument here about ICT and knowledge management for Africa SMEs and entrepreneurs: whether the sector is finance, creative arts, energy, manufacturing, agriculture, or infrastructure – technology has made the difference. ICT tools have allowed for each Africa entrepreneur, personality, community, or company, but more importantly, each idea and each discovery to have its own voice, vehicle to success and income possibilities, providing for a life-change. Technology is the great equalizer in the region – answering economic, social, and development challenges along the way. ICT provides Africa SMEs with what "reality TV" has provided for the individual – propelling them forward, side-stepping traditional processes, obstacles, resource limitations, and the sometimes unfair or unwilling gatekeepers along the way.

---

huffingtonpost.com/amb-robin-renee-sanders/post_4203_b_2253551.html (NB: More commonly called HuffPost nowadays.)

Sanders, Ambassador R.R. *Mobile Services and E-Empowerment – The Developing World Has the Advantage.* (2012, December 6). *FEEEDS* BlogSpot. Blogitrrs.blogspot.com. Retrieved August 3, 2016 from http://blogitrrs.blogspot.com/2012/12/mobile-services-e-empowerment.html

The Future-Morrow: Defining, Financing, and Counting SSAfrica SMEs

I talked before about the economic and middle class pluses, and I provided my simplest definition of an Africa SME: *one self-sustaining person, group, or community of purpose, generating-income through a creative or business entrepreneurial effort and sharing that forward.*

As part of this definition, let's add whatever skills set, business idea, social enterprise, and tools which create work and income for the innovator (or co-innovators) AND provide jobs for others.

But for funders, they define SMEs mostly by size, and at times by valuation. The most prevalent measurement that defines an SME is employee size. Why is employee size an important discussion on helping Africa SMEs do and grow more? Because size and valuation are connected to how many donors provide SME funding assistance and finance. Thus, it is worth being more descriptive as to what the definitions are as we look at my mashup concept called the *Future-Morrow.*[173] Since employee size impacts funding levels, we all want to ensure that Africa SMEs, particularly the fragile and critical mass groups I talked about earlier, are all adequately funded in order to have the best chance to secure their continued success and growth in the Future-Morrow of the region. The definitions for SME employee size varies widely around the world:

European Union,10-250;

China, 500 or fewer;

Brazil, 250 employees or fewer; and,

Egypt, 10-50 employees; while

[173] Future-Morrow is my phrase used to mean the future and tomorrow or in today's lingo a mashup of the words "future" and "tomorrow."

India measures its SMEs by valuation per priority sector, not by number of employees.[174] [175] [176] [177] [178] [179]

In the region, Kenya and South Africa have specific employee numbers which have to be met per SME category, while others have various ranges:

Kenya, micro (1-10), small (10-50), and medium 150-1000);

South Africa, very small (6-20) and small (6-21);

---

[174] *Small and Medium-sized Enterprises.* (2016, July 2). Retrieved July 3, 2016 from https://en.wikipedia.org/wiki/Small_and_medium-sized_enterprises

[175] Dudovskiy, J. *SMEs In China Overview.* (2016, August 8). Home Page. Research Methodology. Retrieved July 3, 2016 from http://research-methodology.net/small-and-medium-enterprises-in-china-overview/

[176] *Micro, Small, Medium Size Enterprises.* (2015, March 16). FAQ. Reserve Bank of India. Retrieved July 3, 2016 from https://www.rbi.org.in/commonman/English/scripts/FAQs.aspx?Id=966

[177] Inter-American Development Bank. (2016, October 28). *Assessing Results of Programs Supporting the SME Sector in Brazil. News and Views. Office of Evaluation and Oversight.* Retrieved July 3, 2016 from http://www.iadb.org/en/office-of-evaluation-and-oversight/assessing-results-of-programs-supporting-smes-in-brazil,18216.html

[178]*Inter-American Development Bank.* (2016). Retrieved July 6, 2016 from http://www.iadb.org/en/inter-american-development-bank,2837.html

[179] Katura, T.N. *The Role of SMEs in Employment Creation and Economic Growth in Several Countries.* (2014, December). Catholic University of Eastern Africa Lecturer. Vol 2:12. International Journal of Education and Research. Retrieved August 18, 2016 from http://www.ijern.com/journal/2014/December-2014/39.pdf

Ghana, small (1-50) and medium (50-250);

Cameroon, 21-100;

Congo-Brazzaville, small (1-5), medium (5-20) and large (20-100); and

Nigeria defines SMEs as having 1-100 employees.[180] [181] [182] [183]

[180] Ibid.

[181] *SME Ghana Award Definition.* (2016). SMEGA. Retrieved September 4, 2016 from http://www.smeghanaawards.com/introduction

[182] *Finance for All: Promoting Financial Inclusion in Central Africa.* (2016, March 23). ECCAS Regional Conference, Congo-Brazzaville. Afriland First Bank. Retrieved September 4, 2016 from https://www.imf.org/external/np/seminars/eng/2015/brazzaville/pdf/AfrilandENG.pdf

[183] Republic of Congo Documents & Reports. (2009). World Bank. Retrieved September 4, 2016 from_http://documents.worldbank.org/curated/en/316651468244180464/708380ESW0P1070000Final00030-06-09.docx

The US, with 28 million small businesses, defines SME employee size as 1-500; about 975 businesses in the US have 1,000 or more employees.[184] [185]

If sustaining the success of Africa SMEs (particularly for sole proprietors where many entrepreneurs fall) is important for the Future-Morrow of the Continent then African governments, the donor community and investors (particularly venture capitalists) need to pay more attention to the employee sizing issues. I believe that sizing definitions may continue to impact whether sufficient resources are available for Africa SMEs to steadily grow, and add to the world's creative ledgers of addressing some of the region's economic development issues. I mention the employee size figures because I have seen recently an ironic twist – not yet in great numbers, but something to watch (or something I am

---

184 *Ngozi Bell. Region III Advocate.* (n.d.). SBA. Professional Bio note. https://www.sba.gov/advocacy/region-iii-advocate-ngozi-bell

185 My FEEEDS Advocacy Initiative has partnered from 2014 to 2016 with Gallup® and its Managing Partner Jon Clifton to host a data-driven event on key Africa issues from elections to business. The 2016 event focused on the important role of SMEs in meeting the Continent's job creation needs, and former President Obama's 2016 US-Africa Business Forum. Allafrica.com has severed as the media partner, and others such as the Africa Society and GB Group Global have each served as additional partners respectively in 2014 and 2016.

watching, at least): where and how SME assistance money is being directed, and what companies are showcased as model examples of Africa SMEs; some certainly have more than 100 employees or either valuations greater than million dollars. This by no means diminishes those companies at these levels, since they are, in my opinion, equally important. But they have more financing avenues available to them than the smaller SMEs in the critical mass group.

If one uses the television show *Shark Tank* (which I absolutely love, showcasing American entrepreneurs seeking investment funds) as a measure of SME employee size, one would see that the average size is about 1-20.[186] In the context of the Future-Morrow for the region, job and economic needs are so great that there needs to be more *universality* on the employee size standards for Africa SMEs so that donor financial

[186] *Shark Tank* is a U.S.-based weekly television production that airs on the ABC Network. The format—described as a structured reality program—consists of self-made multi-millionaire and billionaire tycoons investing in America's inventors and entrepreneurs who pitch the panel in hopes of securing a deal that would make them millionaires. See: *Shark Tank*. (2009 – present). ABC.com. Retrieved August 8, 2016 from http://abc.go.com/shows/shark-tank. Note: Site doesn't keep hyperlink. To view site cut and paste into browser

assistance, venture capital funds, and training can be focused, targeted, flexible, and as creative as possible. In SSAfrica, the important Future-Morrow SME groups that really need help are:

- The fragile and critical mass groups I talked about above;
- The Startups; and
- The broader Africa SME businesses which have been operating for 3-5 years, having under 100 employees.

This is where I would put the energy to get SSAfrica over the hump on economic development, filling more of the job creation gap and adding to GDP and the middle class. There also must be a concerted effort to mentor and help those unregistered small businesses get registered and connect to the financial and credit system.

The other important aspect of the Future-Morrow is ensuring a better handle on the total number of

SSAfrica's register and unregistered SMEs. I have already talked about how varied the numbers are on the size of Africa's middle class, sometimes as varied as 18-300 million, with the figure of 300 million coming from an AfDB 2011 estimate.[187] [188] The same numbers game applies to how many formal and informal SMEs there really are in the region and overall in emerging markets. (NB: World Bank 2015 SME figures for all emerging markets stated that there were 365-445 million registered micro, small and medium enterprises (also called formal), and 285-345 million unregistered (also called informal).[189]

[187] Mwiti, L. Special Report: 18 million, not 300 Million: That's the Size of Africa's 'Real' Middle Class—And It Could Disappear. (2015, October 29). Africa. Mail & Guardian. Retrieved July 4, 2016 from http://mgafrica.com/article/2015-10-27-18-million-thats-the-size-of-africas-middle-classand-with-chinas-woes-it-could-just-be-wiped-out

African Development Bank. (2011, April 20). *The Middle of the Pyramid: Dynamics of The Middle Class in Africa*. Market Brief. Section 2.2. p. 2. Retrieved August 7, 2016 from http://www.afdb.org/fileadmin/uploads/afdb/Documents/Publications/The%20Middle%20of%20the%20Pyramid_The%20Middle%20of%20the%20Pyramid.pdf

[188] Rosen, A. *A Credit Suisse Report Just Debunked a Huge Claim About the Size of Africa's Middle Class*. (2015, November, 19). Retrieved May 2016 from http://publications.credit-suisse.com/tasks/render/file/index.cfm?fileid=C26E3824-E868-56E0-CCA04D4BB9B9ADD5

[189] World Bank/IBRD-IDA. (2015, September 1). *Small and Medium Enterprises (SMEs) Finance*. Brief. Retrieved September 4, 2016 from http://www.worldbank.org/en/topic/financialsector/brief/smes-finance

International financial institutions, think tanks, and African governments need to do more research to obtain more accurate SME numbers for the region; more specific numbers also will better assist donors, African governments, and investors in addressing financing and investment needs. If these figures do not become clearer, it will remain challenging to know whether projections of impact and contributions on GDP and other areas are on track.

Specifically, for the SSAfrican region, I have heard a range of figures at different international fora and in researching for this book, but no exact figure on the number of total SMEs. The best information, which provides a good idea on the number of SME and entrepreneur, is a 2016 IFC brief stating that they make up 90 percent of businesses in the region.[190] Anecdotally, my educated guess is 30-35 million is probably closest to the reality of registered and possibly another similar number of unregistered Africa

[190] International Finance Corporation. (2016). *SME Initiatives*. Sub-Saharan Africa. Retrieved September 4, 2016 from http://www.ifc.org/wps/wcm/connect/REGION__EXT_Content/Regions/Sub-Saharan+Africa/Advisory+Services/SustainableBusiness/SME_Initiatives/

SMEs and entrepreneurs. I take into account, in this estimation, on top of the anecdotally figures I have heard, latest reports on India and China (2014), which state they had the largest number of registered SMEs respectively at 48 and 50 million. We can assume that in 2016 many more millions exist in both those countries.[191] A better handle on the exact number of SSAfrica's SMEs is very important so that everything can be done to assist and support their success in order to have the best Future-Morrow as possible; without accurate numbers, the right amount of training and assistance for SMEs will not be planned for by governments or donors.

African million-dollar club companies also have an important role to play in the Future-Morrow of SMEs as they can help incubate, mentor, and become donors themselves. I see this happening–– the reaching back to bring others along by larger African companies

---

[191] Goyal, M. *SMEs Employ Close to 40% of India's Workforce, But Contribute Only 17% to GDP.* (2013, June 9). SME Biz. Economic Times. Retrieved July 3, 2016 from http://articles.economictimes.indiatimes.com/2013-06-09/news/39834857_1_smes-workforce-small-and-medium-enterprises

At the time of this writing, neither 2015 nor 2016 figures on China's number of registered SMEs were found in my research efforts.

and foundations––but not often enough. The African million-dollar companies also need to take into account these same issues on SME employee size and the number of SMEs needing help and be as creative and flexible as possible on financing as they seek to help their newer, and hopefully future, business colleagues move forward.

Whether a business falls into my critical mass group, or whether an African company has entered the quarter-million or million-dollar club, they are all change-agents and have a role to play in the region's growth. The goal is for all of these businesses to do their part in helping the Continent *leapfrog* over development stages and make dents in the tough *facts and stats* discussed in Chapters 1 and 2.

Chapter Four: SMEs' Leapfrogging Effect: Prime Development Sectors

Africa SME interventions in key sectors can help the region *leapfrog* over many of the development and poverty hurdles already discussed. The sectors I see with the most potential to do this are on what I call my *Top Eight List* (TEL). The TEL is where I see both the critical mass group and the more stable group of Africa SMEs playing bigger roles in development. The list is meant to be illustrative, not exhaustive, and contains my top eight because SME input in these sectors can help *leapfrog development* stages in these areas as well as provide that all-important *insta-impact* -- the two requirements to make my TEL.

Other Africa experts may emphasize different sectors. Two TEL areas – infrastructure and manufacturing – include a "where more help is needed" segment, recommending additional support needed by national governments or donors to help Africa SMEs become more competitive in the sector or options to help expand big business-SMEs partnerships. The sectors on my TEL are as follows: infrastructure/construction, power, services (I include agriculture and assistance to small farm holders in this TEL), manufacturing, housing, software development, tourism, and what I call the *Ah-ha-Moment* solutions.[192]

The Top Eight List (TEL) – Key Sectors for Africa SMEs

1. *Infrastructure and Construction* – No matter how small, or what sub-segment of infrastructure improvements are needed from roads, rail and bridges to sub-contracting on construction projects, brick-laying, or building support infrastructure in airports and ports – there is a role for Africa SMEs to play. Just think...if you have been through an African airport recently, particularly newer or renovated ones, those small food concessions, kiosks, and/or franchise operations from KFC, and Mickey D's to Nandos (American and South African companies) are

[192] The larger agriculture sector is not on my TEL list, but large agricultural production is an important sector for growth and development, and jobs. It is a longer-term development sector and is fundamental to Africa's economic diversification. SME-driven small farms like aquaculture, organic farms, small food and cosmetic processing, and assistance to existing small farm holders through apps and tools and seeds are on the TEL and examples appear under services or manufacturing.

mostly run by Africa SMEs.[193] There is nothing wrong with playing the supporting role in bigger business projects, and African SMEs are doing this. However, more need to be involved in the larger projects in this sector as well. I recognize that it is sometimes hard for SMEs to get in the door on big business and government projects or procurements. I see this with the African SMEs I advise, even with their good ideas and project skills – but it is happening a little more, albeit slowly, and their involvement in these bigger opportunities will help with the Continent's overall transformation. Ambassador Andrew Young talks about this in the *Introduction* of this book, noting his efforts to ensure that SMEs, particularly from minority groups, were included in the planning and construction opportunities, as well as participated as service provides for the 1996 Olympic Games in Atlanta, Georgia. As a result, SMEs were contractors or subcontractors in the building of, or in providing services to, the stadiums or Olympic Village. Ambassador Young was a strong early pioneer of the view that it was critical

---

[193] The term "KFC" and "Mickey D's" are American slang which refer to fast food chains Kentucky Fried Chicken and McDonald's headquartered, respectively, in Louisville, Kentucky and Oak Brook, IL, USA. Nandos is a South African company headquartered in Johannesburg, South Africa.

not only to ensure SME inclusiveness, but also to ensure that they had the opportunity to work directly with big businesses.[194] [195] [196] (See Photograph 4, Ambassador Young and Sanders at 2016 US-Africa Policy Forum.)

Where More Help Is Needed – Big Business Links & Government Frameworks

In the infrastructure and construction areas, Africa SMEs (particularly the critical mass group) rarely are given the opportunities to work with or be linked to big businesses that have large African government projects in a contracting or subcontracting role. It is important for African governments, within their country context, for these linkages to happen, or for

[194] *Ambassador Andrew Young.* (n.d.). Biography. Biography.com

Retrieved July 1, 2016 from http://www.biography.com/people/andrew-young-jr-9539326

See books by Ambassador Young: *The Making of Modern Atlanta,* (2012), and his books on his life *A Way Out of No Way* (1994), and *An Easy Burden: The Civil Rights Movement and the Transformation of America* (1996).

[195] Weisman, Steven R. *Atlanta Selected Over Athens for 1996 Olympics.* (1990, September 19). *New York Times.* (Retrieved May 2016 from http://www.nytimes.com/1990/09/19/sports/atlanta-selected-over-athens-for-1996-olympics.html

[196] The 1996 Olympic Village today is called Centennial Park – a thriving upscale business and cultural section of the city. Ambassador Young's book, the "*Making of Modern Atlanta,*" highlights the importance of SME inclusiveness and the key role SMEs in development.

governments to create more mechanisms or set asides which will secure some Africa SME participation. Big businesses, be they international or national, also need to see Africa SMEs as key partners to have in either government or other private sector business deals; new local content laws help with this, but a bigger percentage of procurement set asides will also be needed.[197] [198] [199] [200] More expansive SME set asides

[197] Hussain, M.N. *Linkages Between SMEs and Large Industries for Increased Markets for Trade: The African Perspective.* (2000). Strategic Planning and Research Department. Economic Research Paper No. 53. African Development Bank. Retrieved July 1, 2016 from http://www.afdb.org/fileadmin/uploads/afdb/Documents/Publications/00157640-EN-ERP-53.PDF

[198] Kennedy, K. *Key Barriers to Kenya's SMEs Growth – Study.* (2016, June 23). Retrieved from Capital Business July 1, 2016 from http://www.capitalfm.co.ke/business/2016/06/key-barriers-to-kenyas-smes-growth-study/

[199] Badal, S. B. *How Large Corporations Can Spur Small-Business Growth.* (2013, January). Retrieved July 1, 2016 from http://www.gallup.com/businessjournal/160109/large-corporations-spur-small-business-growth.aspx

[200] Local content is the term which refers to the legislative effort by more and more SSAfrica countries to ensure that local or national companies and workers are included in opportunities to participate in business opportunities, particularly in sectors which foreign companies have dominated, such as the oil and gas sectors as well as other extractive industries. The trend is called "resource nationalism," as quoted from March 2016 article by King Woods & Mallesons (KWM) – a global law firm with an Africa practice on the issue. African governments want both a greater control and financial benefit deriving from its country resources for its people. KWM lists the following SSAfrica countries such as Angola, Ghana, Kenya, Mozambique, Nigeria, South Africa, Sudan, Tanzania, and Uganda as either having already or are in the throes of initiating local content legislation.

See: Sonal, S., Wagacha, N., and Nyayieka, S. (Anjarwalla & Khanna,

are not prevalent at the moment on the Continent. Examples such as the U.S. SBA's 8(a) program for *disadvantaged small businesses* (minority, women, etc.) encourage the involvement of SMEs with these backgrounds in government contracting opportunities such as infrastructure projects, procurement, etc.[201]

I have seen the tough environment for Africa SMEs to get direct contracts from African governments, and for international and national big businesses to have the confidence to give them a chance in larger infrastructure and construction projects. Of course, it is about making money and knowing a company can deliver on a project, so partnering and/or subcontracting with an Africa SME might be scary for an established business. Big business-SME frameworks still remain hard to do even in developed countries, like the US or OECD countries,

---

Kenya, ALN). *A Review of Local Content Regulations in The Upstream Oil & Gas Sector in Africa.* (2015, March 16). Insights. King, Woods & Mallesons. Retrieved July 31, 2016 from http://www.kwm.com/en/uk/knowledge/insights/a-review-of-local-content-regulations-in-the-upstream-oil-and-gas-sector-in-africa-20150316

[201] United States Small Business Administration. (n.d.). *About the 8(a) Business Development Program.* Contracting. Retrieved August 27, 2016 from https://www.sba.gov/contracting/government-contracting-programs/8a-business-development-program/about-8a-business-development-program

where one might think these linkages are easier to create. However, there are ways to build that confidence and those relationships such as having more cluster industry centers or special economic zones where big and small businesses can work together. These are not yet that prevalent in the SSAfrica Region (there are a few), but these are solutions that can help overcome the big business-SME confidence hurdle. On the flip side, the service environment of a cluster can help SMEs gain additional export capabilities and know-how.

France's big business-SME framework called "competitiveness clusters" is another idea worth considering (or modifying so that it fits in the Africa context). These government-supported competitiveness clusters are located around France and are more of a hybrid – serving as a combined small business agency and industry cluster, connected to national policy planning where SMEs and large businesses can come together. In addition, France's new state-of the-art *Station F Startup Campus* is another smart idea to help SMEs, providing computer work space and support services for more than 3000 startup companies.

Having more African countries create (also within their cultural context) one-stop small business administrations, agencies or ministries would also better help Africa entrepreneurs address financing, mentoring, loan guarantees, and access to credit issues for larger projects. As more African governments create these SME-focused agencies/institutions/ministries, they also could keep databases of qualified or pre-approved Africa SMEs which could also help in addressing *confidence concerns* large companies might have and help further build the big business-SME partner relationship. The U.S. SBA has these same primary responsibilities for America's small businesses, but it was created only in 1953. I say "only in 1953" because the U.S. started its industrial revolution in the late 1800s and by the 20th century was considered the largest industrialized nation.[202] [203] Thus, SBA's

[202] *The Industrial Revolution in the United States.* (n.d.). Teacher's Guide Primary Source Set. Library of Congress. Retrieved July 1, 2016 from http://www.loc.gov/teachers/classroommaterials/primarysourcesets/industrial-revolution/pdf/teacher_guide.pdf

[203] Kelly, M. *Overview of the Industrial Revolution: The United States and the Industrial Revolution of the 19th Century.* (2015, October 16). American History. About Education. Retrieved July 31, 2016 from http://americanhistory.about.com/od/industrialrev/a/indrevoverview.htm

creation in 1953 was very late in the industrialization game, which also underscores just how challenging it is to create a single institution, backed by policy and financial resources to assist small businesses in which big business and commercial banks too have faith.[204] I am not suggesting an exact replica for SSAfrica of the U.S. SBA, but each African country should seek to come up with a model within its own national context that better responds to its SMEs, and their never-ending quest for access to financing, loan guarantees, insurance, and credit. Rwanda, Ghana, Kenya, and Liberia have some semblance of this, with South being the most advanced – all which will be discussed more in the chapter on sustainability.

2. *Power* – This would include all forms of electrical power: traditional, renewable and off-grid. The number of people without light in the region – 600 to 640 million as mentioned in Chapter 1 – is fundamentally

---

Industrial Revolution. History. (2016). A+E Networks Digital. History.Com. Retrieved July 31, 2016 from http://www.history.com/topics/industrial-revolution

[204] United States Small Business Administration (n.d.). About Us. Retrieved July 1, 2016 from https://www.sba.gov/about-sba/what-we-do/history

a show-stopper for the Region's growth on just about anything you can think of regarding development.[205] Lack of electrical power impacts food production, manufacturing, health, education – the list is simply endless. Africa SMEs can be subcontractors on national grid projects or provide services and equipment for power generation and distribution companies. But the centerpiece for SMEs in this sector, in my view, is providing real-time data on supply and demand, meter support and services; assisting in off-grid sector development and independent power plants or IPPs (small targeted self-contained power supply options for companies, villages, economic zones, or neighborhoods), or renewables from solar-powered buses (United Nations Environment Program offices in Nairobi demoed one during the May 23-27, 2016, Environment Conference); and supplying creative solar

---

[205] African Development Bank. (2016). *Light Up and Power Africa – A New Deal on Energy for Africa.* High Five. Retrieved July 30, 2016 from http://www.afdb.org/en/the-high-5/light-up-and-power-africa-%E2%80%93-a-new-deal-on-energy-for-africa/

Parke, P. *Why Are 600 million Africans Still Without Power?* (2016, April 1). Africa View. World. Africa. CNN.com Retrieved July 30, 2016 from http://www.cnn.com/2016/04/01/africa/africa-state-of-electricity-feat/

recharging options for mobile phones, lights, and other devices.[206] [207]

3. *Other Services (includes agriculture)* – Beauty and cosmetic businesses in Africa (such as shea butter and salons) tend to be success gold mines on the Continent. Even in post-conflict Republic of Congo when I was there using the old income-generating model, U.S. Embassy Brazzaville's most successful rates of return on our loans were from beauty salons and cosmetics shops. Today, this category – services – for me can includes anything for Africa entrepreneurs that provide or respond to whatever might be needed, such as: retail, the agricultural sector (apps, training for small

---

[206] *Sustainable Innovation Expo-UN Environmental Program.* (2016, May). Climate Action. United Nations Environmental Program. Retrieved July 2, 2016 from http://www.sustainableinnovationexpo.org FYI: Demoed is slang for demonstrated.

[207] The U.S. Government Power Africa Initiative has both grid and off-grid components to its assistance in this area. Its on-grid goal was to add 30,000 megawatts (mw) of power, and as of July 14, 2016, remarks by then President Obama's Special Assistant on Africa, the initiative had added 22,000mw to Africa's electrical power output. Also under the United States African Development Fund (USADF), smaller businesses in the off-grid sector can apply for grants up to $US100, 000. See: United States Agency for International Development. (2016, August 17). *Power Africa.* Retrieved August 1, 2016 from https://www.usaid.gov/powerafrica

United States African Development Foundation (USADF). (n.d.). Home Page. United States African Development Foundation. Retrieved August 1, 2016 from http://www.usadf.gov/apply-for-a-grant/

farm holders or farmer-entrepreneurs, developing seeds, new tools, organic farming, and small food production); technology services like African-developed data cloud storage; and, Uber®-like car/transport services such as *TaxiJet* in Cote d'Ivoire or the Egyptian "pink taxis" driven by women for women, addressing female safety issues in the country (I tweeted about these when they were first launched).[208] [209] [210] More SME technology examples are discussed in

---

[208] Uber®, a registered trademark, is a unique online transportation company that was the creative idea in 2008 of Travis Kalanick and Garrett Camp in response to not being able to get a taxi on bad weather day in Paris. This is a good example of one of the "Ah-ha Moments" I was talking about above in TEL #8, when an idea is a response either to address an old issue or to overcome an existing or new challenge. Uber's new approach is an alternative transport option for riders, and as well as an alternative income option. It is a disruptive force in the taxi and other traditional commercial and public transport services worldwide. See https://www.uber.com/our-story/

[209] Veselinovic, M. *Tired of Catcalls? Pink Taxi Promises to Drive Women Around Cairo Peacefully.* (Updated 2016, April 7). African Start-up. *CNN World.* CNN.com. Retrieved July 2, 2016 from http://www.cnn.com/2015/12/09/africa/pink-taxi-cairo/

[210] *Keep Up with TaxiJet Cote d'Ivoire.* LinkedIn. Retrieved August 6, 2016 from https://www.linkedin.com/company/taxijet-cote-d'ivoire

TaxiJet App Cote d'Ivoire. (2016, May 24). *Global Business.* [Television broadcast, 2p.m]. China Global Television Network.

TaxiJet in Cote d'Ivoire was created to address gaps in transport services there. Although Egypt is not an SSAfrican country, the "pink taxi" example is used to underscore the point of how SMEs are responding to almost any challenge or obstacle out there – in this case female safety in public transportation, which is a big issue in places like Egypt and India in recent years.

TEL #7 and in Chapters 9 and 10, but it was important to highlight that any general or unique service or operation that is responsive to a need (particularly food security or agriculture) or a challenge in the region is an opportunity for Africa entrepreneurs.

4. *Manufacturing* – Small-to-medium scale manufacturing of a wide range of products such as food and cosmetic processing, medicine, household goods, furniture, clothing, and leather goods (e.g., purses, shoes, etc.) – are all winning areas for Africa SMEs and entrepreneurs. SMEs in food processing are some of my favorites as CEO-FEEEDS because they are serving a double duty – providing an income for the SME and its employees, while also contributing to the reduction of hunger (remember those staggering stats – 842 million hungry people worldwide, of which 239 million are in Africa).[211] For SMEs to further grow the sector, they will need to be able to access trade and export opportunities, make more value-added

[211] Martin, P. *Capitalism and Global Poverty: Two Billion Poor, One Billion Hungry.* (2014, July 25). Centre for Research in Globalization. Global Research. Retrieved July 24, 2016 from http://www.globalresearch.ca/capitalism-and-global-poverty-two-billion-poor-one-billion-hungry/5393262

products (i.e., like China's plan to build car factories in South Africa and Republic of Congo), and produce more items in response to in-country demand by the growing consumer class for manufactured goods. The in-country manufacturing base for many African countries is low, about 11 percent of GDP, when it should be around 39 percent according to briefs during the 2016 US-Africa AGOA Ministerial on SME issues, as well as an April 2016 *CGTN* news report discussing the region's manufacturing challenges.[212] [213]

---

[212] Tafirenyika, M. *Intra-Africa Trade: Going Beyond Political Commitments.* (2014, April). Africa Renewal Online. United Nations. Africa Renewal. Retrieved August 8, 2016, and July 6, 2016 from http://www.un.org/africarenewal/magazine/august-2014/intra-africa-trade-going-beyond-political-commitments

Ancharaz, V., Mbekeani, K., & Brixiova, Z. *Impediments to Regional Trade Integration in Africa.* (2011, September). AfDB Economist Complex. Africa Economic Brief. Vol 2: Issue 11. Africa Development Bank. Retrieved August 8, 2016 from http://www.afdb.org/fileadmin/uploads/afdb/Documents/Publications/AEB%20VOL%202%20Issue%2011 AEB%20VOL%202%20Issue%2011.pdf

World Bank. (2016, January). *Sub-Saharan Africa Analysis. Global Economic Prospects 2016.* Retrieved August 9, 2016 from https://www.worldbank.org/content/dam/Worldbank/GEP/GEP2016a/Global-Economic-Prospects-January-2016-Sub-Saharan-Africa-analysis.pdf

(2016, May 11). *Global Business.* [Television broadcast, 2 p.m.] China Global Television Network. (NB: This was the most up-to-date stat that could be found at the time of this writing. Institutional stats were older.)

[213] I attended the September 2016 US-Africa AGOA Ministerial as a member of the U.S. Trade Representative Advisory Committee on Africa (TACA), and the special workshop on issues for SMEs.

(2016, April 30). *Africa Live.* [Television broadcast, 1 p.m.] China Global Television Network.

The manufacturing share of SSAfrica's GDP, although growing, was only around 10-14 percent in 2014, as per the *Economist,* and hovered around the same in 2016.[214] But digging in a bit deeper, McKinsey & Company's earlier 2010 analysis on "*What's Driving Africa*" underscored why improvements in manufacturing are so critical. They noted that "...each 15 percent increase in manufacturing and services, as a portion of GDP, is associated with a doubling of income per capita."[215] The point is that per capita increase is a reflection of a growing middle class. Here again is another way that Africa SMEs are spurring the growth of the middle class – as they increase manufacturing, they help increase per capita on top of entering the middle class themselves and setting the stage for their employees to do the same.

I believe new technologies are again going to be pivotal in how Africa SMEs and entrepreneurs begin

---

214 *Manufacturing in Africa: An Awakening Giant.* (2014, February). *Economist.* Retrieved May 12, 2016 from http://www.economist.com/news/middle-east-and-africa/21595949-if-africas-economies-are-take-africans-will-have-start-making-lot

215 McKinsey & Company (2010). *What's Driving Africa.* McKinsey & Company Report. Johannesburg, South Africa: McKinsey and Company.

to respond to the voids in the manufacturing sector. It may not necessarily be in heavy production, but the new kid on the block is 3-D printing, which opens a lot of new manufacturing opportunities for small businesses. As 3-D printing becomes more readily available and cheaper, Africa SMEs more and more will be manufacturing their own equipment, as well as, *finally*, having the unlimited ability to make their own spare parts. Songhai, which I mentioned I work with, started using 3-D printing for its spare parts as far back as 2011; as a Songhai Board member, I had the opportunity to see early on how this new technology, 3-D printing, was going to be another new tool and game-changer for the Continent, as drones also have now become.[216]

---

[216] Songhai Centre is a development project and natural laboratory providing sustainable socio-economic solutions. Songhai is headquartered in Porto-Novo (Benin Republic) under the incredible leadership of Director Father Godfrey Nzamujo, author of *Songhaï: When Africa lifts Up Its Head.* Sanders is on the board and worked with Songhai both during her diplomatic career and since creating FEEDS in 2013.

Where More Help Is Needed – Manufacturing Centers & African Regional Trade

Indeed, increasing Africa SMEs' role in all manufacturing opportunities could aid in doubling the per capita for the region and individual countries. These opportunities have become even more important in 2016 as the economies and manufacturing bases in places like China and Brazil tighten and because, at the same time, African countries are seeking, finally with a bit more vigor, to diversify their commodity-based economies. If African governments begin to establish more economic zones and industry clusters, these also could serve double duty as manufacturing centers. African national governments can assist their SMEs further in the manufacturing sector by helping on taxes, providing incentives, ensuring better transport systems to improve delivery of goods and services, and opening more avenues for 3-D printing opportunities.

Regional Economic Communities (RECs) like the South African Development Community (SADAC, with 277 million people), the Economic Community of West African States (ECOWAS, with 335 million people), the East African Community (EAC, 150 million), the Common Market for Eastern and Southern Africa (COMESA, whose population includes East and Southern Africa), and the AU must also continue to reduce barriers to African regional trade which will help expand markets for SME products with the goal of many more of them from the SME sector into bigger companies. The goal of course would be to set the stage for larger growth and for SMEs in this sector to become bigger businesses and move into more heavy manufacturing and help shore up the industrialization agenda for the region.[217] [218] Bottom line, if African

[217] *Regional Integration: Uniting to Compete.* (2014). Mo Ibrahim Foundation. Retrieved from http://static.moibrahimfoundation.org/downloads/publications/2014/2014-facts-&-figures-regional-integration-uniting-to-compete.pdf (NB: This side describes in detail the role of The RECs.)

Southern African Development Community. (n.d.). SADC Facts & Figures. Retrieved November 25, 2016 from http://www.sadc.int/about-sadc/overview/sadc-facts-figures/

ECOWAS 2015 Outlook. (2015, January 16). inAfrica24.com. Retrieved November 25, 2016 from http://inafrica24.com/modernity/ecowas-outlook-2015-gdp-growth-projected-7/#sthash.9wlbadQ2.dpbs

East African Community. (n.d.). Overview of EAC. East African Community. Retrieved November 25, 2016 from http://www.eac.int/about/overview

[218] Tafirenyika, M. *Intra-Africa Trade: Going Beyond Political Commitments.* (2014, August). Africa Renewal. United Nations. Africa Renewal Online.

governments help more SMEs enter the manufacturing sector by addressing some of the above issues and providing incentives, then small businesses can be an additional driver to help create the reportedly "6-14 million jobs the manufacturing sector has the potential to produce for the region over the next decade."[219]

5. *Housing* – There are huge deficits in the African housing market as was highlighted in the facts and stats section in Chapter 2. Affordable housing is a sector where SME entrepreneurial skills and services are helping, but an area that I would argue more Africa SME companies need to consider. Furthermore, African governments need to provide more creative financing support for sovereign-backed mortgages and off-taker guarantees. Affordable housing is also another one of those sectors in which FEEEDS works. There is insufficient housing to shelter the region's poor, or to provide for its growing middle class. I am working

---

Retrieved August 8, 2016 and July 6, 2016 from http://www.un.org/africarenewal/magazine/august-2014/intra-africa-trade-going-beyond-political-commitments

[219] Statement made by the then-United States Trade Representative, Michael Froman, during the September 2016 US-Africa AGOA Ministerial opening ceremony, which I attended.

with one SME group that is providing training in skill needed for the affordable housing sector: carpenters, brick layers, electricians, etc. Housing is also another one of those *double-benefit* sectors like food security – where an SME or social enterprise is providing vocational training, along with addressing a key development sector such as the region's huge housing deficit or food needs.

6. *Climate Smart Tourism* — In May 2016 I tweeted about comments from the representatives of both the United Nations World Tourism Organization (UNWTO) and the UN's Environment Agency (UNEP), in synergistic events in Johannesburg, South Africa, and Nairobi, Kenya, that noted that 1 in 4 future jobs in the region would be in the tourism sector.[220] Right now, North Africa is the big winner in the sector, but climate smart tourism offers a huge opportunity for countries

---

[220] *UN Environment Assembly Opens in Nairobi Aiming to Ensure Healthy Planet, with Healthy People.* (2016). News. The United Nations News Centre. Retrieved July 2, 2016 from http://www.un.org/apps/news/story.asp?NewsID=54014#.V3f7vod0xwE (NB: The conference was held in Nairobi from May 23-27, 2016)

(2016, May 14). *Global Business.* [Television broadcast, 2 p.m.] China Global Television Network.

below the Sahara. In North Africa, Morocco holds the top tourism spot since the 2011 Arab Spring security issues plagued Egypt, while South Africa holds sway as the only SSAfrican country on the world list of top 5 tourist destinations, according to UNWTO.[221] [222] [223]

UNWTO underscored, during its *First World Conference of Tourism and Development* held in Beijing in 2016, that Africa is on trend to attract 130 million tourists by 2030, and that "tourism [would be] one of the most dynamic economic sectors making a significant contribution to the SDGs."[224] [225] If this turns out to be true, then this is a prime sector for the Africa SMEs to

---

[221] Ibid.

[222] African Development Bank. (2015). *Africa Tourism Monitor 2015: Tourism in Africa Is On the Rise, But Has Not Yet Reached Its Full Potential.* News and Releases. Retrieved July 6, 2016 from http://www.afdb.org/en/news-and-events/article/africa-tourism-monitor-2015-tourism-in-africa-is-on-the-rise-but-has-not-yet-reached-its-full-potential-15284/

[223] *UNWTO Tourism Highlights.* (2015 Edition). United Nations World Tourism Organization. Retrieved July 6, 2016 from http://www.e-unwto.org/doi/pdf/10.18111/9789284416899

[224] *Opening Address by Tourism Minister Derek Hanekom.* (2016, May 7). Indaba Africa's Top Travel Show. Indaba Tourism Conference. Indaba. Retrieved August 1, 2016 from http://www.indaba-southafrica.co.za/news/INDABA-2016-opening-address.aspx

[225] *UN Conference Spotlights Role of Tourism in Fighting Poverty and Building Peace.* (2016, May 21). *Johannesburg Life.* Retrieved August 1, 2016 from http://www.johannesburglife.com/index.php/sid/244260705

tap into as service providers, suppliers of technology-based travel and location apps, small boutique hotels, guest houses, hospitality, food/catering, cultural event planners, and so on.

In addition, the *Day Three Schedule* at the later May 23-27, 2016, UNEP conference focused specifically on the tourism-SME link, with a session that stressed the need to "integrate SME development funding into climate change areas [like tourism]."[226]

Given Africa's unique, *only place in the world* environment for much of the nature's animal big game, along with incredible vistas, climate smart *cultural tourism* for the region is a big opportunity for Africa SMEs, especially since SSAfrica is one of the earth's areas most affected by climate change. Africa small businesses can contribute to reducing the carbon footprint by developing environmentally-friendly tours, apps, cultural events, facilities, renewables, or helping existing tourist facilities *go green.* African governments

---

[226] *Sustainable Innovation Expo-UN Environmental Program.* (2016, May). Climate Action. United Nations Environment Program. Retrieved July 2, 2016 from http://www.sustainableinnovationexpo.org

also should seek to include more of its SMEs in their climate change discussions and planning.

7. *Software Development* – I discussed extensively the importance of technology for Africa SMEs in Chapter 3, particularly apps, innovative software development, and new technology uses, which have been pivotal in addressing economic transformation. The apps and software developed by many Africa SMEs from the creative arts to services (including drone use), data protection and cloud services – are all things Africa small businesses and entrepreneurs are doing today and where additional innovation is limitless. Software development also will always be a go-to sector for Africa SMEs.[227] During two Pan-African SME training programs in 2012 and 2013, run by Nigeria's Bank of Industry, Western Union, FEEEDS, and USAID's Africa Diaspora Marketplace (henceforth referred to as BOI-WU-FEEEDS-ADM, which will be discussed further

---

[227] Slang expression, previously defined and cited in Chapter 2. Apps, considered a computing slang for software downloadable on a mobile device. Dictionary.com defines the term as follows: "an application, typically a small, specialized program downloaded onto mobile devices." Source: *Apps.* (2016). Dictionary.com. Retrieved July 2, 2016 from http://www.dictionary.com/browse/app

in Chapter 7), there were several SMEs developing software services to help their fellow Africa SMEers.[228] If you were an Africa SMEer too busy or without staff to manage your own bookkeeping, financial records, and inventory, all that could be outsourced via African-owned cloud services – which were like smaller versions of the American company *Intuit®*, which produces *QuickBooks®* and other great software tools for small businesses. These Africa-focused services were specifically designed for the African context and for Africa-based servers, and were designed and owned by Africa SMEs. [229] There were at least four SMEers from Kenya and Ethiopia which competed in our programs for additional resources to grow their companies and add more cloud support services for streaming, media and file storage. Last, but certainly not least, and my favorite sector (or non-sector, really) is...the *"Ah-ha Moment"* category.

---

[228] BOI-WU-FEEEDS-ADM – these four entities – Nigeria's Bank of Industry (BOI), Western Union (WU), FEEEDS Advocacy Initiative, and USAID Africa Diaspora Marketplace Initiative held two large Pan-African SME training, programming, and access to credit events in 2012 and 2013. Details of these training events will be discussed later in the book.

[229] *Intuit.* (2016). Featured Products & Services. Intuit. Retrieved July 1, 2016 from http://www.intuit.com/

8. *Ah-ha Moments* – This is a category that includes what I call the rare *not thought of before response* or *the new response to an age-old challenge.* Hence, if technology was the big game-changer, then any creative response to address the poverty statistics, encourage development, help Africa's females, or leapfrog some of the Continent's economic transformation challenges noted on the TEL list falls into the Ah-ha Moment category.[230] I see these all-important Ah-ha Moment solutions happening all over the region; I tweet about them as I am sure some of you do. Some are complex, and some are so simple that they are startling as they produce that *Ah-ha.* Developing solutions like a *WhatsApp*®-type application which works around high-cost mobile phone data plans is an example of an Ah-ha Moment solution. (I was introduced to *WhatsApp*® in 2013 in Burma by my cultural guide when I could not access

[230] Future-Morrow cited earlier: my term which I use as a mashup of the words "future" and "tomorrow" and means what you want both your future and your tomorrow to look like.

my T-Mobile® service because of the local government regulatory environment.)[231] [232]

In this category, *one can do well by also doing good* (as the saying goes), developing creative solutions for critical economic development sectors on the TEL list, or by addressing some of the poverty facts and challenging stats in education, health, food security, etc., mentioned in Chapter 2. There are several self-evident apps or tools (or the *no-one-ever-thought-of-before apps and tools,* or if they did, failed to act*)* that either have been developed or used differently by young African entrepreneurs or governments that are plentiful today in the region. Some entrepreneurial solutions which exemplify the Ah-ha Moment category to me include:

- Drones that deliver medicine in rural areas, survey water, and land resources; traveling

[231] "WhatsApp" was developed in 2009 by Ukrainian-born Jan Koum in California with the assistance of his former Yahoo colleague Brian Acton and a number of others to address the high cost of data texting in developing countries. Facebook bought "WhatsApp" in 2014. "WhatsApp" is a registered trademark.

[232] *The World's Billionaires – 2016 Ranking.* (2016, August 9). *Forbes.* Retrieved August 9, 2016 from http://www.forbes.com/profile/jan-koum/

cyber cafes on luxury buses providing Internet for rural and hard-to-reach areas or Internet to those who cannot afford a permanent subscription. (NB: Some of these traveling cyber cafes, usually with 20 laptops, are also cashless. In places like Rwanda, these ICT-buses provide Internet access for free.)[233]

- The app iCow, one of my favorites, functioning like a mercantile or commodity exchange for small farm holders, helping them have better knowledge management of their cows' gestation periods, best milk prices, etc.

- South Africa's kiosk banks (mini bank-like stalls) or shops where mobile devices can be used to pay bills, do money transfers, etc., and, of course, Kenya's well-known M-Pesa money

---

[233] Tafirenyika, M. *Information Technology Super-Charging Rwanda's Economy.* (2011, April). Africa Renewal. United Nations. Africa Renewal Online. Retrieved July 31, 2016 from http://www.un.org/africarenewal/magazine/april-2011/information-technology-super-charging-rwandas-economy

Buses in Rwanda used to teach IT skills. (2013, October 18). Business. *BBC.com.* Retrieved August 8, 2016 from http://www.bbc.com/news/business-24574998

transfer company, which helps its customers receive credit, pay bills, or transfer funds to their relatives, friends, or other SME businesses or customers.[234] [235] [236]

- InVenture, one of the cloud-type Africa services focused on SMEers mentioned in TEL#3, helps small businesses track their daily accounting via their mobile phones and also helps Africa SMEs improve their credit scores. [237]

- Kountable, a primarily Rwanda/East African crowdfunding platform where an algorithm determines an SME and entrepreneur's business value from its "social media, email and text

---

[234] Nsehe, M. (2011, August 2). *The Best African Mobile Apps: iCow. Forbes.* Retrieved May 2016 from http://www.forbes.com/sites/mfonobongnsehe/2011/08/02/the-best-african-mobile-apps-icow/#58d5c8161934

[235] Shekhtman, L. *A Mobile Money Revolution in the Developing World.* (2012, November 2). Triple Pundit – People, Planet, Profit. Retrieved May 2016 from http://www.triplepundit.com/2012/11/mobile-money-revolution-developing-world

[236] *Safaricom. M-Pesa.* (n.d.). Retrieved May 28, 2016 from http://www.safaricom.co.ke/personal/m-pesa

[237] Shekhtman, L. A Mobile Money Revolution in the Developing World. (2012, November 2). Triple Pundit – People, Planet, Profit. Retrieved May 2016 from http://www.triplepundit.com/2012/11/mobile-money-revolution-developing-world

message networks" referred to as "social capital" and is given a "kscore," which a potential investor can factor into its determination of the investment potential of a company.[238]

- Zoona allows people to securely store savings on their phones, get insurance payouts, and receive and repay loans in Zambia, Zimbabwe, Mozambique, and Malawi.[239]

- Suba, Ghana's award-winning app, provides localized group photo storage and streaming, and Kenya's Safari Tales by AfroKidz Limited is an app featuring African books in different local languages. [240] [241]

---

[238] *Kountable.* (2016). Our Mission. Retrieved September 28, 2016 from http://www.kountable.com/about/

[239] Ibid.

[240] *Suba.* (2015). Home Page. Retrieved July 2, 2016 from http://www.subaapp.com/index.html, Suba also won the 2015 Mobile West Africa App Competition held in Lagos.

[241] *Safari Tales.* (2013). Home Page. Retrieved July 2, 2016 from http://safaritales.mobi/

On the e-health front, creative apps and tools have been developed to a range of health issues such as HIV/AIDS, Ebola, and pre-natal and daily care. Apps range from those helping remind HIV/AIDS patients to take their medicine, and assisting expectant mothers with pre-natal medication to those that helped with surveillance during the 2014-2015 West African Ebola crises, when apps and mobile phones (many in partnership with international donors) played a big role in sharing diagnostic and monitoring information. Examples of Africa-designed apps and tools, including those working with partners, to address health issues include the following:

- Hello Doctor, operating in about 11 African countries providing general health information and direction to the nearest doctor.

- Find-a-Med, a Nigeria-based app for locating a physician and tracking personal health.

- Kids First Aid, operating in Kenya, Nigeria, South Africa, and Tanzania, helping mothers with emergency issues for their children, and mHero, which surveyed and polled Ebola-affected communities.[242] [243] [244]

- Rapidpro, which helped with Ebola education, prevention, and communication campaigns.[245] (NB: The latter two were done in partnership with foreign donors, but the goal is to highlight the Africa-designed and supported ones done in conjunction with local partners.)

- SYROP, a Ugandan exact medicine dosage dispenser and bottle to assist mothers with providing the correct amount of medication to their children created by a Ugandan entrepreneur, working in the sector, who wanted

---

242 *Hello Doctor.* (2016). Who We Are. 2016 Hello Doctor. Retrieved July 2, 2016 from https://www.hellodoctor.co.za/app/

243 *Top 10 Healthcare Apps for Africa.* (2015, August 19). Features, Healthcare, Top Stories. *IT News Africa.* Retrieved July 2, 2016 from

http://www.itnewsafrica.com/2015/07/top-mobile-apps-made-in-africa/

244 Bremmen, N. *[Nine] 9 of South Africa's Best Mobile Apps.* (2013, August). Mobile/Mobile Apps. Memeburn. Retrieved July 5, 2016 from http://memeburn.com/2013/08/9-of-south-africas-best-mobile-apps/

245 United States Agency for International Development. (2014, November). *Use of Technology in the Ebola Response in West Africa: Technical Brief.* Retrieved May 28, 2016 from https://www.msh.org/sites/msh.org/files/technology_and_ebola_response_in_west_africa_technical_brief_final.pdf

to find a solution to address what he saw was a major problem in the country.[246]

The interesting Ah-ha Moment solutions that can be developed by Africa SMEs and entrepreneurs are endless given the vast technology-based possibilities and the fact that new technology uses are constantly coming online – drones, robots, etc. Africa is one of the most mobile-connected continents in the world as was mentioned earlier; thus, we can only expect apps,

---

[246] (2016, December 2). Global Business. [Television broadcast, 1:30 p.m.]. China Global Television Network.

innovations and solutions by Africa small businesses to grow even more over the next decades.[247] [248] [249] [250]

But what about other challenges where high-tech or "*disruptive*" apps just do not do the trick?[251] [252] Even

---

[247] *Mobile Phone Users Worldwide* 2013-2019. (2016). The Statistical Portal. Statista. Retrieved July 2, 2016 from

http://www.statista.com/statistics/274774/forecast-of-mobile-phone-users-worldwide/

[248] Qureshi, R. *Ericsson Mobility Report.* (1996-2016). Data and Forecast Page. Ericsson. Retrieved July 2, 2016 from https://www.ericsson.com/mobility-report#section_1

Also, the Data and Forecast page notes that the number of mobile devices is expected to reach 28 billion and users are expected to reach 9 billion in 2021.

[249] FYI: The difference in the 2016 number of worldwide devices of 6 billion, and worldwide users of 4.7 billion is likely a result of many people having more than one mobile device (phone, tablet, laptop), as I do. According to Statistic, 25 percent of the world population in 2016 with mobile devices had more than one device.

See: *Multiple Mobile Device Ownership.* (2016). The Statistical Portal. Statista. Retrieved July 2, 106 from http://www.statista.com/statistics/245501/multiple-mobile-device-ownership-worldwide/

[250] Piejko, P. *[Sixteen] Mobile Market Statistics You Should Know in 2016.* (2016, May 18). Mobiforge. Retrieved July 2, 2016 from https://mobiforge.com/news-comment/16-mobile-market-statistics-you-should-know-in-2016

[251] Christensen, C.M. *The Innovator's Dilemma.* (2003). First published 1997. *HarperBusiness Essentials.* HarperCollins Publishers. New York: New York.

[252] Harvard Business School professor Clayton M. Christensen is credited with coming up with the term "disruptive technology." His point was that technology falls into two categories. They are either sustainable or disruptive. Information on his book can also be found at http://whatis.techtarget.com/definition/disruptive-technology

in the non-tech area, African small businesses and entrepreneurs are thriving, by either reverting back to traditional solutions, revamping or creating new ones, or addressing everyday development challenges with non-high-tech responses. Therefore, let's take a look at some of these *non-disruptive* solutions being designed by Africa SMEs and social enterprises today, along with a possible new donor player in the SME space. I will then transition to discussing what some of the older donors are doing new and differently and what some of the newer donors are up to as both step up their assistance to Africa small businesses and entrepreneurs.

CHAPTER FIVE:
THE SME SPACE - MORE TOOLS, NEW MEANINGS

Part 1 highlighted the time it took for many donors, African and foreign governments, the UN, international and regional bodies such as the AU, African Capacity Building Foundation (ACBF), the REC economic communities, many NGOs, and the private sector to completely turn the corner, amp up their interest in Africa SMEs, and see them as important change-agents, as contributors to development, and more recently as worthy investment vehicles.

After Technology Got Us Here

As mentioned, young African nationals trying to find solutions to their job needs and living conditions wanted more than just project assistance, they not only responded to the challenges more creatively, but also did things differently to become self-sustaining. Meanwhile, the Africa Diaspora living outside of the region also was seeking to help with development issues back home or reconnect through business, historical, or family ties. I already discussed the significant role that the new technologies (especially by-products like social media) played in the impact of this convergence in the early-to-mid 2000s. But it was also the *timing* of when social media began to become more pervasive which fortuitously coincided with Africa's young adults finding new solutions to economic issues and creating their own SMEs as a response which cannot be overlooked. Many of the social media products first emerged in the early-to-mid 2000s and then caught on as global phenomena. This includes

- Facebook® (launched 2004, begins to reach mobile users in 2006, opens first international office October 2008);

- LinkedIn® (founded 2002, launched 2004, goes global 2008);

- Twitter® (launched 2006, took off in 2010);

- Snapchat/Snap Inc.® (launched 2011, took off in 2012, name change 2016); and the billions of other *how did we live without these before apps* and other common tech tools, concurrent with their mass utilization and reach.[253] [254]

All of these tools added to the extent to which Africa SMEs were propelled forward, allowing global access and the unprecedented knowledge management that we see today. African small businesses, along with their tech-savvy creativeness, have also remembered about traditions and are also using non-disruptive solutions to help with the region's transformation.

---

[253] *Facebook.* (2016). Company Info. Facebook News Room. Facebook. Retrieved July 6, 2016 from http://newsroom.fb.com/company-info/. The site also notes that 84.5 percent of Facebook users do not reside in the US or Canada. Facebook opened its international office in Dublin in October 2008. Additional Background: South Africa has the second largest number of Facebook users in SSAfrica at 5.5 million, which makes it the 32nd largest in the world, while Nigeria has the third largest number of users in the region with 5.35 million users, making it the 36th largest globally.

Adepetun, A. *Africa's Mobile Phone Penetration Now 67%.* (2015, June 17). Technology. *The Guardian.* Retrieved August 8, 2016 from http://guardian.ng/technology/africas-mobile-phone-penetration-now-67/

[254] *LinkedIn.* (2016). Our Story. LinkedIn. Retrieved July 6, 2015 from http://ourstory.linkedin.com/

The Real History of Twitter. (2016). About Us. 2016. AboutTech. Retrieved July 6, 2016 from http://twitter.about.com/od/Twitter-Basics/a/The-Real-History-Of-Twitter-In-Brief.htm

Crook, J., & Escher, A. (2015, October 15). *A Brief History of Snapchat.* TechCrunch. Retrieved July 6, 2016 from https://techcrunch.com/gallery/a-brief-history-of-snapchat/slide/12/

Snapchat changes name, rolls out video-recording spectacles (2016, September 26). *CBSNews.* Retrieved September 28, 2016 from http://www.cbsnews.com/news/snapchat-snap-video-recording-spectacles/

Enter – Appropriate Technology

We understand how Africa SMEs got where they are today by using technology-based solutions, mobile platforms, social media, and knowledge management to respond to job creation needs, on top of the desire to generate their own income, and help with economic development issues. But what about the things (yes, there are some things!) that technology could not answer, or at least not in certain environments?

Enter...more adaptation and use by Africa SMEs and social enterprises of *appropriate technology* solutions for 21st century economic development problems or income needs. There are lots of definitions of appropriate technology, but for me, this simple one is best: *technology that is suitable to the social and economic conditions of the geographic area in which it is to be applied, is environmentally sound, and promotes self-sufficiency on the part of those using it.*[255] While the goal of using appropriate technology is to "increase

[255] Appropriate Technology. Definition. Merriam-Webster. Retrieved September 27, 2016 from http://www.merriam-webster.com/dictionary/appropriate%20technology

the standard of living for the developing world without condescension, complication, or environmental damage. Inventions [can be] more labor intensive, [but] require fewer resources and use low cost or readily available materials wherever possible with special attention paid to the social, cultural, and ethical aspects of the communities."[256]

Many times, but not always, appropriate technology used by entrepreneurs manifests itself in the creative arts and climate change efforts such as waste material completely being repurposed for a different use other than the original. It also includes apps for agriculture (and for me new agricultural avenues for small holder farmers), or reverting back to ancestral traditional methods to respond to water, sanitation or a range of agricultural challenges.

Africa entrepreneurs have taken appropriate technology to a whole new level. I have seen old, rusted, abandoned car parts used for things as far ranging as:

---

256 Xilebat. "*10 Cases of Appropriate Technology.*" (2010, June 12). Technology. Listverse. Retrieved August 19, 2016 from http://listverse.com/2010/06/12/10-cases-of-appropriate-technology

- Steering wheels as turn handle mechanisms on locally-fashioned agricultural equipment used to shuck corn;
- Scrap metal refashioned as wheelbarrows or parts for manual tractors;
- Tools redesigned for local carpenters and mechanics and fan belts or chains to create pulleys;
- Plastic waste from bottles (including from the never-ending plastic bags that litter African streets and villages) refashioned into plastic pellets for making containers, bowls, and plates;
- Garbage converted to fertilizer;
- Unique or traditional methods of irrigation;
- New methods of organic farming.

Turning practically anything into something else that is climate smart or that makes using it more appropriate and sustainable within the African context, and responds to development needs with a local solution, for me, falls into the appropriate technology category. I have seen Africa SMEs and social enterprises doing all these things! They are designing non-tech equipment, devices, and products or providing services that are not contingent upon foreign assistance, foreign talent, or imported spare parts – in many cases harking back to or revamping old cultural traditions. These repurposed, redesigned, or, in some cases, former traditional approaches are not just more *appropriate* in the environment where they are being used, but simply put, *make more sense* in addressing the needs in a local context.

I remember in the early-to-mid 2000s, before technology and mobile platforms were as pervasive as they are today, out-of-date desktop computers, mostly shipped to the region from well-intentioned Western donors, were refitted (voltage change, script adaptations for language differences, reordered keyboards) for use in schools and other places in SSAfrica. Many of these modified computers were considered both "appropriate" (because they were repurposed) and because of that "green," but they were anything but and would not meet the current or future COP22 (Conference of Parties on Climate Change) climate change standards of green by any stretch of the imagination.[257] [258] The thought that these computers were appropriate didn't last long with me once I saw in Lagos, Nigeria, how exposed young Africans were to the dangerous toxic parts when the sealed hard drives and monitors were opened to execute the adaptations. (NB: I am not talking about the earlier, smaller solar-powered laptops that were introduced in the region around the same time.) Luckily, mobile phones, iPads®, and tablets finally

---

[257] Climate Change refers to the negative impact that human actions are having on the planet which in turn is affecting both climate and weather patterns. See: United States Environmental Protection Agency. (2016, June 14). *Climate Change.* Basic Information. Retrieved July 9, 2016 from https://www3.epa.gov/climatechange/basics/

Additional Background: The international community has been trying to work to addresses these issues for decades under different international conferences, or Conference of Parties, more commonly called COP. In December 2015, 195 countries in Paris attended and adopt the first universally legally binding Agreement, which is to enter into force in 2020. See: European Union Commission. (2016, July, 8). *Climate Negotiations Paris.* Climate Acton. Retrieved July 9, 2016 from http://ec.europa.eu/clima/policies/international/negotiations/paris/index_en.htm

[258] In 2016 COP 22 was held in New York, and COP 23 in Asia. See: *UNFCCC COP 24.* (1990-2016). Events. IISD Reporting Services. IISD. Retrieved July 9, 2016 from http://climate-l.iisd.org/events/unfccc-cop-24/

superseded all these efforts.[259] Today, parts of mobile devices and their plastic casings are recycled to make some of the newer tablets and laptops. Companies like Dell are trying to do this with its zero-waste efforts; I look forward to Africa SMEs moving fully into the zero-waste space and recycling the plastic parts from mobile device waste, which is increasingly becoming an issue given the number of mobile devices in the region.[260]

Appropriate technology can be complex or simple, creative, artistic, mechanical, non-mechanical, or a mixture of all. The material source origin can be metal, plastic, clay, paper, or anything really, including scraps, glass, cans, bottle caps, trash, old shoes, leather, material, and clothes. I have samples in my home today of many things made in SSAfrica from most of these materials. A few of my favorite things

---

[259] iPad® is a brand name of a tablet by Apple® Computers. See: *iPad.* 2016. Apple Inc. Retrieved July 7, 2016 from http://www.apple.com/

[260] *Dell's Commitment to Zero Waste Packaging.* (2016). About Us. Reducing Our Impact. Dell. Retrieved August 19, 2016 from http://www.dell.com/learn/us/en/uscorp1/corp-comm/cr-earth-reduce-reuse-recycle

made from a number of these materials by young creative African entrepreneurs are:

- A piece of jewelry made from recycled newspapers rolled into tiny cone shapes, that one drapes completely over a dress in very narrow strips like an American-style accordion blind or to use an African analogy, triple thin raffia strips.[261]

- Kenyan place card holders and napkin rings made from scrap metal from abandoned cars.

- A purse made from recycled plastic by an HIV-orphaned young male entrepreneur; I never met him, but his story touched me.

Of the many countries that I have traveled to in the region, I have found entrepreneurs in Kenya, Rwanda, Uganda and South Africa to be the most creative in

---

[261] Accordion blinds are either cloth or plastic whose purpose is to block out light or view and appear like the musical instrument the accordion, hence the name. Raffia is a natural plant which is used in a number of African countries on a number of things from artifacts to traditional clothes, jewelery and art work.

using recycled materials for decorative arts, with Ghana and Nigeria not far behind.

The Republic of Benin's Songhai climate smart food and environment project I mentioned in Chapters 2 and 4 that trains farmer-entrepreneurs does an excellent job of using scrap metal, recycled waste and plastics to create its own brand of agricultural equipment and tools for its farmer-entrepreneurs, and a range of water conservation and irrigation methods from gravity-based drip to natural infrared processes from recycled plastic sheathing.[262] [263]

Here are other samplings of appropriate technology using traditional methods, or new areas for small farm holders, developed mostly by Africa SMEs or social enterprises in partnership with others that I like:

---

[262] Songhai Centre is a model development program and natural laboratory providing sustainable socio-economic solutions. Songhai is headquartered in Porto-Novo (Benin Republic) under the incredible leadership of Director Father Godfrey Nzamujo, author of *Songhaï: When Africa lifts Up Its Head*. Sanders is on the board and worked with Songhai both during her diplomatic career and since creating FEEEDS in 2013.

[263] *The Songhai Centre*. (n.d.). About Us. Retrieved May 27, 2016 from http://www.songhai.org/index.php/en/home-en

- Pot-in-Pot Refrigerator – a simple refrigeration method helpful in rural areas using evaporation as the cooling method with moist sand between one smaller pot inside a larger pot.[264]

- Hippo Water Roller – a 90-liter rolling container that helps rural women and children collect water easily and provides for clean and filtered water through the use of a specially designed "utility cap." The "cap-in-cap" helps the hippo water roller serve dual purposes – collecting water and assisting in drip irrigation.[265]

- Climate Smart Affordable Housing – Homes made from recycled plastic bottles, or use "green technology" for house frames, and schools such as Lagos, Nigeria's former *Makoko* Floating School, which was the 2014-2016 Aga Khan award-winning open-air structure made of

---

264 *Rolex Awards for Enterprise.* (2005). Ancient Technology Preserves Food. Retrieved from http://www.rolexawards.com/profiles/laureates/mohammed_bah_abba/project

265 *Hippo Water Roller Project. Improving Water Access, Food Security and Income Generation.* Retrieved May 27, 2016 from http://www.hipporoller.org/solutions/

bamboo and plastics but suffered severe weather damage in June 2016.[266] [267]

- Climate Smart Small Holder Farms – new small farms, including fish farms and aquaculture projects raising produce or seafood not usually well-known in their communities such as the SME *Imbaza*, a black-owned floating mussel farm in South Africa, or the hydroponic produce shipping container farms by *Fresh Direct.*[268]

---

[266] In Kaduna in 2011 small affordable housing using recycled plastic bottles were being built to combat the high housing deficit, which many other African countries will increasingly face as urban population figures continue to rise. See: Laylin, T. *Africa's First Plastic Bottle House Rises in Nigeria.* (2011, July 11). Inhabitat. Retrieved August 19, 2016 from http://inhabitat.com/africas-first-plastic-bottle-house-rises-in-nigeria/nigeria-bottle-house-1/

I work with an affordable housing project in Nigeria using the light gauge steel made from green technology. As part of full disclosure, the green technology light gauge steel itself is imported in coils then local content labor is used to refashion the coils into beams and support structures with the rest of the local needed materials such as cement, etc.

[267] Makoko Floating School 2014-2016 Award Cycle. (n.d.). Aga Khan Award for Architecture. Retrieved December 1, 2016 from http://www.akdn.org/architecture/project/makoko-floating-school

The Makoko school was decommissioned in summer 2016. Since then the empty structure faced heavy rain damaged and collapsed.

[268] Imbaza Mussels. (n.d.). Retrieved December 1, 2016 from http://www.companies-southafrica.com/imbaza-mussels-hgui/

Fresh Direct. (n.d.). Retrieved December 1, 2016 from http://www.freshdirect.ng/about-us/

Fresh Direct was created by Angele Adelaja and is based in Nigeria.

When I think of things "appropriate" for the SSAfrica context, particularly with a climate change component, I include non-GMO hybrid seeds that combat drought and disease but increase yields, like the Lagos, Nigeria small business cooperative that repurposed cassava to make carbonation for soda, a project supported by the U.S. Embassy during my time as Ambassador there.[269] [270]

In my view, Africa SMEs have done the most not only in leading and actually turning policy into practice by using technology – appropriate or otherwise – to address job creation needs, but also in developing creative and innovative responses to economic transformation and poverty alleviation. Everyone else (donors and national governments) picked up on their cue, slowly at first, but now supporting them with a vengeance.

When I think back on my time as a diplomat, listening to what young African nationals and Diaspora

---

[269] Xilebat. "*10 Cases of Appropriate Technology.*" (2010, June 12). Technology. Listverse. Retrieved August 19, 2016 from http://listverse.com/2010/06/12/10-cases-of-appropriate-technology

[270] Terms "GMO" and "non-GMO" were previously cited in Chapter 2.

adults said they wanted for themselves and their children, as well as working with them, it is good to see these transformations, particularly as SMEs and social enterprises bring back traditional methods or repurpose 21st century waste into something useful.

Keeping the principles of mutual understanding, human cultural communication, and the importance of the study of sociology, ethnography, phenomenology, and the human experience in mind as anthropologists Edward T. Hall, Clifford Geertz and social scientist Goffman would note to do: I both observed and participated in these transitions over the years.[271] It's really been uplifting to not only see and experience the shift that has taken place, but also see the rapid pace and changes by donors and the private sector to focus their support on Africa SMEs and entrepreneurs. It was interesting for me, interacting at the grassroots

[271] Both Ernest Hall and Clifford Geertz were noted anthropologists and observers of culture through ethnographic means. It was their work in great measure that inspired me to write my first book about my cultural experience with a Nigerian communication expression called Uli. See Hall, E.T. (1977). *Beyond Culture.* New York: Anchor Books and Geertz, C. (1973). *The Interpretation of Culture* (2000 ed.). New York: Basic Books

Sanders, R. R. (2013). The Legendary Uli Women of Nigeria. Bloomington, Indiana: Xlibris Books.

level, to see these transitions take place: *SMEs pushing the envelope and donors taking notice, reacting, and supporting.*

What I am describing is what I experienced on the ground, in policy circles, participating in international donor meetings, leading two U.S. Embassies, serving as Permanent Representative to ECOWAS, serving twice as a Director for Africa at the NSC at the White House, or running the State Department's first Africa Office of Public Diplomacy.

Remember, it was not as if there was a *single light bulb* moment among the youth and young adults that ignited these changes or highlighted the insufficiencies of the previous donor aid models and/or national government job creation efforts, but I believe the convergent factors mentioned in Chapter 1. Quick recap:

- Growing populations.
- Shrinking donor financial budgets for development assistance.

- Wanting but not finding sufficiently strong institutional capacity in Africa to respond to social and economic hardships.

- Needing more job creation opportunities outside of the government civil service.

- Burgeoning, but at times fragile, evolving African democracies, in many nations, which opened up the regulatory environment on technology and mobile phone services.

- Dovetailing with the advent and growth of the then new technologies and the by-products of knowledge management, mobility and social media.

- Awakening. Noting that after 40 years or more of post-African independence, that donor assistance from 1960 to 2000 and nearly $US3.5 trillion spent, not a lot had changed to reduce large scale poverty, improve overall development or meet the jobs needs.[272]

---

[272] Shah, A. *Foreign Aid for Development Assistance.* (2014, September 28). *Global Issues.* Retrieved April 13, 2016, http://www.globalissues.org/article/35/foreign-aid-development-assistance

Enter – Sustainability

Africa SMEs demonstrated that what they wanted was sustainability above all else. The international community also realized this eventually which is what led to the MDGs by 189 countries in 2000, then *boldly* getting there on the importance of *sustainability* with the 2015-2030 SDGs adopted by 194 countries in New York during the September 2015 UN General Assembly (UNGA).[273]

Entrepreneurial Africans in the late 1990s and early 2000s who were already finding their own way by starting small businesses then might not have put all these points explicitly together, but they were way ahead of the development, government, and donor

---

[273] Discussion on the MDGs, or Millennium Development Goals, and SDGs, or Sustainable Development Goals and what they mean were extensively covered in Chapter 1 with their citations.

An additional citation on MDG monitoring can be found at: *Millennium Development Goals (MDG) Monitoring.* (2014, December 31). Statistics and Monitoring. UNICEF. Retrieved July 9, 2016 from http://www.unicef.org/statistics/index_24304.html

As noted earlier in the book, the MDGs didn't hit their stride in many UN countries for a long time (particularly connecting programs and budgets), but one could see a real effort in the last 5 years of the MDGs, as the end date in 2015 drew near, by many more nations to step up their work to better meet many of the targets, but most of SSAfrica fell short.

communities, even though some skills training was provided. The early Africa SMEs and entrepreneurs were addressing sustainability even if they didn't know or call it that at that time. Think about it. When did you really start hearing regularly the word "sustainability" in the layman's world? When did sustainability really enter the centerpiece of the development nomenclature? When did it finally become core to the mission of economic development? And when did we begin to see sustainability play out on the ground in Africa, with donors and African governments channeling their development dollars in that direction? Well, there are different dates or international frameworks which responded, in some measure, to all of these questions. The short story on the definition of the word *sustainability* explains why Africa SMEs were ahead of the game as their actions helped add to what the term means to all of us today. The word was first reportedly coined in 1980, by the International Union for Conservation of Nature in the World Conservation Strategy report, then in 1987 the *World Commission on Environment and Development,* chaired by then-Norwegian Prime Minister Gro Harlem Brundtland, is credited with rekindling the term "sustainability" in the Commission's *Brundtland Report.*[274] [275]

After that, it was used with different meanings and objectives at other international fora, from the 1992 UN Rio de Janeiro Earth Summit *Agenda 21* conference to the 1999 Council on Sustainable Development for America by then-U.S. President Bill Clinton, followed by the 2002 World Summit on Sustainable Development convened by then-South African President Thabo Mbeki. (NB: The Development Land Initiative's 2010 report provides a historical perspective on the

[274] The Brundtland Report was a 300-page report by the World Conservation Commission of 1987. Report on the World Commission on Environment and Development: Our Common Future. (1987). Report to United Nations General Assembly. United Nations.

[275] The term "sustainable" reportedly was first used in the international arena in 1980 after the conference by the International Union for the Conservation of Nature. See: *International Union for the Conservation of Nature* (1980). World Conservation Strategy. Retrieved May 2016 from http://www.triplepundit.com/2010/08/origin-of-sustainability-movement-leads-to-current-challenges/#

evolution of the use of sustainability.)[276] [277] Despite the word's usage during these global meetings, there was little to no success with it *catching on* in a global sense for more than a decade by the public, donors, governments, and the private sector. Today, there are a lot of definitions of sustainability. But the definition I like goes back to Brundtland's 1987 report:

> *"...development that meets the needs of the present without compromising the ability of future generations to meet their own needs."*[278]

My point is that many of the early Africa SMEs were focused on meeting the needs of the present without compromising the future as this is reflective in their

[276] The Agenda 21 Report from the United Nations 1992 Rio de Janeiro Earth Summit was a 900-page report with 120 goals to achieve sustainable development. See: United Nations Sustainable Development. (1992, June 3-14). *Agenda 21*. United Nations Conference on Environment & Development, Rio de Janeiro, Brazil. Retrieved June 27, 2016 from https://sustainabledevelopment.un.org/outcomedocuments/agenda21

[277] Moore, C. Sustainable Development Land Initiative. *Origin of Sustainability Movement Leads to Current Challenges – Historical Perspective*. (2010, August, 2). Triple Pundit: People, Planet, Profit. Republished from the February, 2009, issue of Sustainable Land Development Today Magazine. Retrieved May 2016 from http://www.triplepundit.com/2010/08/origin-of-sustainability-movement-leads-to-current-challenges/#

[278] World Bank Group. (2001). *What is Sustainable Development. DepWeb*. Retrieved July 9, 2016 from http://www.worldbank.org/depweb/english/sd.html

work today. They contribute to the international universality and respect for the role and importance of sustainability, sustainable projects, and sustainable jobs even if SMEs are not explicitly inscribed in the overarching framework or goals of the new 2015-2030 SDGs. (I would be surprised if at the next big SDG review there is not a modification to explicitly note the role of SMEs in achieving the goals of the SDGs.)

There is certainly an "*SME-awareness*" at the UN and within the international community, that they are critical to the progress of the region. All the performance indicators, goals, and budget linkages to the SDGs now give many of us hope.

Everything said previously applies also to the African and international private sectors, many who have changed their Corporate Social Responsibility (CSR) portfolios to include sustainability as part of their mantras to support projects and programs and most have some level of focus on the Africa SMEs and entrepreneurs as a result.[279]

[279] Corporate social responsibility (CSR) is the term used by many corporations that applies to both the office in the company and the action of providing grants, training, and other resources used in the

What is even more important is that young adults, as they continue to expand their SME and entrepreneurial efforts, will continue to move their businesses on the Continent in the right direction, even if donors and governments falter. I do not think they will, but there is always the possibility that governments will face shrinking budgets and may not be able to keep pace with current efforts. Africa SMEs grew up in an age of voids in development, therefore, I would suspect that will still continue to move forward even if governments and donors regress because of difficult economic environments.

In the meantime, the importance of sustainability in the Africa SME story, will be important and African governments, commercial banks, and businesses as well as donors need continue to support them and see them as one of the main partners to achieve sustainable development.

---

assistance to country development efforts. Ft.com provides the following definition: Corporate social responsibility (CSR) is a business approach that contributes to sustainable development by delivering economic, social and environmental benefits for all stakeholders. See: Corporate Social Responsibility. (n.d.). Definition. *Financial Times. Ft.com* Retrieved October 8, 2016 from http://lexicon.ft.com/Term?term=corporate-social-responsibility--(CSR)

In addition, fair and transparent African governments committed to social contracts with their nationals are going to want their development dollars, coupled with their national budgets, to produce real results that can survive past the life of any aid, grant, or loan. As a result, many African governments now see supporting SME development and entrepreneurship as an additional way to honor the social contract with their citizens. They also now realize that SMEs and entrepreneurs have *an enterprising development* role to play in nation-building, modernizing their societies, and helping grow their middle class (In a 2011 HuffPost article I wrote about the nation-building and enterprising development role of Africa SMEs.)[280] However, despite this realization, not enough SSAfrican governments are providing level playing fields for their SMEs – many examples already cited

---

[280] Sanders, Ambassador R. R. *Importance of SME Development in Africa: They Will Produce Africa's Middle Class.* (2011, July 1). Worldpost. [Blog post]. *Huffington Post.* Retrieved August 3, 2016 from http://www.huffingtonpost.com/amb-robin-renee-sanders/importance-of-sme-develop_b_888407.html

Sanders, R. R. *SMEs Development Enterprise Role in National Building: Recognizing the Valuable Role of SMEs in National Development.* (2011, June 22). FEEEDS® [Blog post]. Blogitrrs.blogspot.com. Retrieved August 3, 2016 from http://blogitrrs.blogspot.com/2011/06/smes-development-enterprise-role-in.html

in earlier chapters – but worth mentioning again such as providing: financing guarantees, support services, international and regional trade export opportunities and creating agencies like an SBA whose sole mission is to support them.

Africa's commercial banks, many which have SME funding guarantees by their central banks or international institutions like the AfDB also, have to continue to be more creative in finding non-traditional ways to provide financing and credit to Africa's small businesses. More tools like *warehouse-financing* (banks use warehoused products as collateral for financing) or the AfDB or central banks further limiting the number of basis points commercial banks can add to their funds given to commercial banks for SME support; right now, it can run as high as 10 points.

Kenya, Rwanda, Tanzania, and Uganda in the east, Ghana in the west, and South Africa are good showcases where such efforts already exist, but even they still need to expand; other African countries need to do much more.[281] [282] [283] Rwanda offers loans to registered SMEs and also has a particular loan program focused on women called *The Women's Guarantee Fund*. It also has a system of rural cooperative banks called *U-SACCOs,* which addresses financial inclusion

[281] African national governments and regional banks range from Development Bank of Kenya (DBK), the East African Development Bank (EADB), which includes Kenya, Tanzania, Uganda and Rwanda, the Cooperative Bank of Kenya, Kenya Commercial Bank, Consolidated Bank, and Kenya Women Finance Trust (KWFT). See: *Financing SMEs in Kenya.* (2012, April 12). Key Resources. Entrepreneur's Tool Kit: For Social and Environmental Entrepreneurs. Retrieved July 31, 2016 from http://www.entrepreneurstoolkit.org/index.php?title=Financing_SMEs_in_Kenya

[282] *Ghana Boosts Financial Support for SME Development.* (2014, January). Ghana-Economic Update. Oxford Business Group. Retrieved August 1, 2016 from http://www.oxfordbusinessgroup.com/news/ghana-boosts-financial-support-sme-development

[283] *Funding Agencies in South Africa.* (2015). Funding Connection. Retrieved August 1, 2016 from https://fundingconnection.co.za/funding-agencies-in-south-africa

and credit issues for SMEs and others, again with an emphasis on women.[284] [285] [286] [287] [288]

Other good Africa-backed financing examples worth noting are in Ghana and South Africa where SMEs also can obtain access to credit and financial guarantees. Despite tough economic times in 2016 and into 2017, Ghana has a government-backed funding program called the *SME Support Fund*, linked to local credit guarantors (e.g. EximGuaranty) as well as a system of rural banks coordinated by its National

---

[284] Martin, X. *Rwanda: A Country Finding Its Path to Financial Inclusion.* (2014, May). FinclusionLab. Retrieved July 31, 2016 from http://finclusionlab.org/blog/rwanda-country-finding-its-path-financial-inclusion

[285] Ibid.

[286] Blaire, C. *Rwanda's Gender Gap: Banks Must Stop Failing Female Entrepreneurs.* (2015, August 25). Africa. *The Guardian US Edition. The Guardian.* Retrieved July 31, 2016 from https://www.theguardian.com/global-development-professionals-network/2015/aug/25/rwanda-gender-gap-banks-failing-female-entrepreneurs

[287] Twahirwa, A., & Makome, K. *Rwanda: Women Win by Formalising Businesses.* (2010, June 8). Inter Press News Agency. Retrieved August 1, 2016 from http://www.ipsnews.net/2010/06/rwanda-women-win-by-formalising-businesses/

[288] FYI: Thirty-five percent of Rwandan women have a bank account, whereas, worldwide, 55 percent of women do not.

Board for Small-Scale Industry, which seeks to "unify [SME] funding and capacity building initiatives."[289]

The South African Government, on the other hand, has a combination of at least ten funds and several agencies which support and provide grants, loans, and financing to segments of the SME sector from youth to women. Its Small Enterprise Financing Agency (SEFA), established in 2012, is the closest I have seen to the comprehensive role that SBA plays in the US – offering a full range of loan options, financing facilities, and guarantees to SMEs, social enterprises, and cooperatives. In addition, its Trade and Industry Minister, Rob Davies, said during a private breakfast held on the margins of the US-Africa September 2016 AGOA Ministerial that his government had plans to create a Small Business Ministry in 2017; Liberia noted during the same session that it was drafting an SME Procurement Act that would provide 5 percent set

[289] *Ghana Boosts Financial Support for SME Development.* (2014, January). Ghana-Economic Update. Oxford Business Group. Retrieved August 1, 2016 from http://www.oxfordbusinessgroup.com/news/ghana-boosts-financial-support-sme-development

asides for small businesses in government contracts; we will need to see whether both things happen.[290]

East Africa and South Africa have a good head start, but West and Central Africa lag behind in their financing options, range of services and a sole agencies or ministry dedicated to SMEs in a one-stop shopping framework (exception is Republic of Congo which already has an SME Ministry, while Nigeria has the Bank of Industry, but no SME ministry).[291]

A reduction in Africa's regional trade barriers cannot be emphasized enough as regards to helping the sustainability of small businesses since by doing so, it will open up more markets and growth opportunities that in turn can become the platform for SMEs to develop into much larger companies, along with the positive ripple effects that go with that. The AU, the RECs of SADC,

[290] As a member of the United States Trade Representative's Trade Advisory Committee on Africa (TACA), I attended both the breakfast for South African Trade Minister Davies where he discussed this, and the September 2016 US-Africa AGOA Ministerial SME workshop where Liberia's Trade Minister discussed his country's plans to institute an SME Procurement Act.

[291] *Funding Agencies in South Africa.* (2015). Funding Connection. Retrieved August 1, 2016 from https://fundingconnection.co.za/funding-agencies-in-south-africa

EAC, COMESA and ECOWAS, and African governments all have a role in reducing these age-old barriers (e.g. taxes, tariffs, customs, market access, etc.), which have kept regional trade at 10-12 percent.[292] [293] In addition, if the entire Africa region finally moves forward on having its own 54-country Continental Trade Market (CTM) that has been batted about for years, CTM would also shore up the sustainability of not only SMEs but the region's own industrialization agenda. UNCTAD's Secretary-General noted at the October 2016 World Trade Organization meeting that the CTM would have a combined GDP of $US3.4 trillion; African leaders are now planning to launch the CTM in 2018.[294]

---

[292] Tafirenyika, M. *Intra-Africa Trade: Going Beyond Political Commitments.* (2014, April). *Africa Renewal* Online. United Nations Africa Renewal. Retrieved August 8, 2016, and July 6, 2016 from http://www.un.org/africarenewal/magazine/august-2014/intra-africa-trade-going-beyond-political-commitments

Ancharaz, V., Mbekeani, K., & Brixiova, Z. *Impediments to Regional Trade Integration in Africa.* (2011, September). AfDB Economist Complex. Africa Economic Brief. 2:11. African Development Bank. p. 2. Retrieved August 8, 2016 from http://www.afdb.org/fileadmin/uploads/afdb/Documents/Publications/AEB%20VOL%202%20Issue%2011_AEB%20VOL%202%20Issue%2011.pdf

[293] Africa regional trade figures previously cited in Chapter 2. Also, see (2016, May 11). *Global Business.* [Television broadcast, 2 p.m.]. China Global Television Network.

[294] Discussion for an African Continental free trade area (ACFTA) was raised again at the 27th African Union meetings in July 2016 in Kigali, Rwanda, and would include the entire region of 54 countries – not just the

Internal country economic regulatory and macroeconomic structural environments would be the other pillars needing improvement not only to help with the sustainability of Africa SMEs and entrepreneurs but also for the region writ large, so that international trade export facilities such as the European-Africa Economic Partnership Agreements (EPAs), Regional Trade Agreements associated with RECs, the U.S. AGOA facility, all can be better utilized, along with expanding in other foreign markets like

47 in SSAfrica. As envisioned and noted in the discussions, ACFTA would be functional by 2018, and according to the Washington Post, CGTN, and other sources. If implemented it would become the world's largest mega market, with the largest number of people by 2050, representing a GDP (based on 2016 estimates) of more than $US3.4 trillion. Also, see: Kenny, P. (2016). (2016, October 10). Africa makes progress on trade and economic integration. *Allafrica.com.* Retrieved October 14, 2016 from http://allafrica.com/stories/201610100001.html?aa_source=nwsltr-nigeria-en

China, India, and other South-South countries.[295] [296] (NB: There is some research stating that the few EPAs that have been signed do not favor SSAfrican exports that much, and the EU still has to pay some duties. On AGOA, there is also ample evidence that many African countries still are not taking full advantage of the facility, on top of some countries wondering how effective it is. It also will remain to be seen what emphasis will be placed on AGOA or if it will be maintained under the Trump Administration we will have to see how much emphasis is put on the AGOA trade facility. I hope it will be seen more as a business opportunity for the US economy (e.g., procurement, and

[295] EPAs are the European Partnership Agreements with several African countries, mostly in countries where there were past colonial ties. The EPAs give preferential trade treatment of goods and services between European and African markets where there is a signed EPA agreement. You will see these agreements referred to both ways with either the word "European" appearing first or the word "Africa" appearing first. In this book, they are referenced under Africa. The RECs were cited earlier in Chapter 4.

See: Africa-European Union Partnership. (n.d.). *Africa-EU Partnership Priority Areas for Sustainable and Inclusive Development and Growth and Continental Integration.* Retrieved May 9, 2016 from http://www.africa-eu-partnership.org/en/priority-areas/sustainable-and-inclusive-development-and-growth-and-continental-integration-6

Africa-European Union Partnership. (2013-2015). About us. Retrieved May 9, 2016 from http://www.africa-eu-partnership.org/en

[296] AGOA was already mentioned and explained in Chapter 6.

sales), along with being a trade facility for Africa SME products (which also helps US sales.) [297] [298]

What is most intriguing is the question of where other resources might come from that could potentially enter the Africa SME space and expand their potential for success and sustainability. One such potential funder is the New Development Bank (NDB) in Shanghai, China, and what further impact it will have as a donor since it started approving projects, providing resources in local currency (which neither the IMF or World Bank do), and expanding its operational mission.[299] Its involvement in the SME space writ large is something we all need to watch over the next decade, and

[297] World Bank. (2016, January). *Sub-Saharan Africa Analysis. Global Economic Prospects 2016.* Retrieved August 9, 2016 from https://www.worldbank.org/content/dam/Worldbank/GEP/GEP2016a/Global-Economic-Prospects-January-2016-Sub-Saharan-Africa-analysis.pdf

[298] Njiraini, J. *AGOA: The US–Africa Trade Dilemma.* (2014, December). United Nations. Africa Renewal Online. Retrieved August 11, 2016 from http://www.un.org/africarenewal/magazine/december-2014/agoa-us%E2%80%93africa-trade-dilemma

[299] *New Development Bank.* (n.d.). Retrieved June 30, 2016 from http://ndbbrics.org/

Global Business: Brics Summit 2016. (2016 October 17). [Television Broadcast]. China Global Television Network.

something I strongly hope it does do, in fact I would be surprised if it did not.

A Closer Look at the New Development Bank – Will It Help Africa SMEs?

It certainly will be interesting to see whether SMEs and entrepreneurs will become a focal point for the NDB (formerly known as the BRICS Development Bank).[300] [301] The NDB, which entered into force in July 2015, has an initial capital of $US50 billion in funding underwritten from the founding country members of Brazil, Russia, India, China, and South Africa (hence the BRICS acronym. I prefer to use all caps,

---

[300] Ibid.

[301] BRICS is the acronym for the mostly economic relationship among Brazil, Russian, India, China, and South Africa. See: *New Development Bank*. (n.d.). Agreement on the new development bank. Retrieved June 30, 2016 from http://ndbbrics.org/agreement.html

The term "BRIC" was reportedly first used by former Goldman Sachs Executive Jim O'Neill in 2001, with the "s" being added later for South Africa.

Olijnyk, Z. *Jim O'Neill: The Man Who Coined the Term BRIC.* (2014, October 2014). *BNN International.* Retrieved June 30, 2017 from http://www.bnn.ca/News/2013/10/24/Jim-ONeill-The-Man-Who-Coined-The-Term-BRIC.aspx

Information About BRICS. (n.d.). Home. Ministry of External Relations Brazil. Retrieved June 30, 2016 from http://brics.itamaraty.gov.br/about-brics/information-about-brics

although initially it was written as BRICs). The BRICS members hold 55 percent ownership in the NDB, and the member countries combined represent 42 percent of world's population. The BRICS nations have said that they are also open to other countries becoming members of the NDB.[302]

The NDB's current mission is to respond to the $US1 trillion needed to support "critical infrastructure" and renewable energy projects for its members -- two key areas on my TEL list (Chapter 4) where Africa small businesses can play a role.[303] The NDB's regional branch is based in Johannesburg, South Africa, which is scheduled to start dispensing financing in 2017. I think it likely that given the NDB's stated mission of supporting sustainable infrastructure and transformative projects of emerging nations that it will

---

302 (2016, July 8). *Africa Live* [Television broadcast, 1 p.m.] China Global Television Network. *New Development Bank*. (n.d.). Retrieved June 30, 2016 from http://ndbbrics.org/

BRICS Countries Launch New Development Bank in Shanghai. (2015, July 21). Business. *BBC News*. Retrieved July 9, 2016 from http://www.bbc.com/news/33605230

303 *New Development Bank*. (n.d.). Retrieved June 30, 2016 from http://ndbbrics.org/

see Africa SMEs as important to that goal and include them in its financing portfolio.

The original drive to create the NDB by the BRICS countries was to provide an alternative to the established, traditional, and primarily Western-controlled international financial institutions, such as the agencies which make up the World Bank Group. Some in the developing world believed (others may argue differently) that they were disadvantaged in project approvals, and that their country was expected to reach unrealistic macroeconomic goals in order to receive funds.[304] These issues were coupled with the massive amounts of money needed to finance infrastructure projects in the developing world. The creation of the NDB was in respond to these concerns. As of this writing, and highlighted during the BRICS October 2016 Summit held in India, the NDB has approved $US911 million in loans to finance clean energy projects for its member countries, stated it

[304] World Bank Group refers to all five of the international financial institutions of the World Bank such as International Monetary Fund (IMF), International Finance Corporation (IFC), etc., and the parent entity, the World Bank.

would establish a credit agency, announced plans to focus on agriculture and tax evasion, and noted that it (for the first time) held a joint session with the South Asia and Southeast Asia economic grouping called BIMSTEC.[305] [306] But, what I would like to see is the NDB, and its regional branch in Johannesburg, establish a "special SME window" addressing access to finance and credit issues for SMEs even if it is only for SMEs in infrastructure, renewable energy or other climate change areas. However, I also feel and hope they expand to include support to industrial or manufacturing centers for Africa small business development. I believe these are must-dos.

Although I am highlighting the NDB as a possible new donor for SMEs in certain sectors, I would be remiss if I did not provide a little background on the term and

---

[305] The New Development Bank: Its Role in Achieving BRICS Renewable Energy Targets. (2016, October). Institute for Energy Economic and Finance Analysis (IEEFA). Retrieved November 26, 2016 from http://ieefa.org/wp-content/uploads/2016/10/New-Development-Bank-and-Role-in-BRICS-Renewable-Energy-Targets-October-2016.pdf

[306] BIMSTEC is the acronym for the Bay of Bengal Initiative for Multi-Sectorial Technical and Economic Cooperation, and its seven member countries are from South Asia and Southeast Asia (India, Myanmar, Nepal, Bangladesh, Sri Lanka, Bhutan, Thailand).

country-grouping known first as BRIC, when the term entered the economic scene in 2001 (without South Africa), and then changing in 2010 to BRICs, to include South Africa.[307] All country members in BRICS in 2010 were riding high on their economic growth records, trade flows, commodity sales, and/or foreign direct investments (FDI).[308] Since late 2014 through early 2016, not unlike many nations around the world, Brazil, Russia and South Africa have taken huge economic hits, leading some, as noted in an *Economist* 2015 article, to wonder if these countries were still worthy of being members of the "BRICS club."[309] India is the exception; China's GDP is hovering around 6.9 percent,

---

[307] Olijnyk, Z. *Jim O'Neill: The Man Who Coined the Term BRIC* (2014, October). *BNN International.* Retrieved June 30, 2017 from http://www.bnn.ca/News/2013/10/24/Jim-ONeill-The-Man-Who-Coined-The-Term-BRIC.aspx

Crowe, P. *The Economist Who Coined the Term 'BRIC' Thinks Brazil and Russia Could Get Kicked Out of The Club.* (2015, January 8). *Business Insider.* Retrieved April 20, 2016 from http://www.businessinsider.com/the-brics-could-ditch-russia-and-brazil-2015-1

[308] Seria, N. *South Africa to Join BRIC to Boost Emerging Markets.* (2010, December) *Bloomberg Markets.* Retrieved April 20, 2016 from http://www.bloomberg.com/news/articles/2010-12-24/south-africa-asked-to-join-bric-to-boost-cooperation-with-emerging-markets

[309] Crowe, P. *The Economist Who Coined the Term 'BRIC' Thinks Brazil and Russia Could Get Kicked Out of The Club.* (2015, January 8). *Business Insider.* Retrieved April 20, 2016 from http://www.businessinsider.com/the-brics-could-ditch-russia-and-brazil-2015-1

still incredibly respectable, but down substantially from its six straight years of record high GDPs of 7 to 9 percent.[310] [311] Russia's and Brazil's economies have been hit with both lower currency values and oil prices (their major commodity), contributing to their financial woes, along with corruption and political scandals. South Africa always tended to be on the lower end of the 2009-early 2015 Africa economic boom but has slid further downwards economically from about 4.5 in the boom years to a negative 1.2 percent (-1.2%) in the first quarter of 2016 and hovered in the 1-2 per cent range into 2017 (an possibly into early 2018 as well), not yet meeting the expectation or the "resilience" noted by Trade Minister Davies at the 2016 AGOA Ministerial of possibly reaching 3.5 percent in the near term.[312]

---

[310] Chang, S. *China's First-Quarter GDP Growth Likely Slowed to a Seven-Year Low.* (2016, April 13). Markets. Market Watch. Retrieved July 7, 2016 from http://www.marketwatch.com/story/chinas-first-quarter-gdp-growth-likely-slowed-to-a-seven-year-low-2016-04-12

[311] Magnier, M. *China's Economic Growth in 2015 Is Slowest in 25 Years.* (2016, January 19). World. *Wall Street Journal.* Retrieved July 7, 2016 from http://www.wsj.com/articles/china-economic-growth-slows-to-6-9-on-year-in-2015-1453169398

[312] South Africa, in the list of 7-10 African countries cited during the 2011-to-early-2015 economic boom for Africa, South Africa was always at the lower end of the boom.

See: *South Africa Unemployment Rate 1993-2016.* (2016). Trading Economics. Retrieved May 14, 2016 from http://www.tradingeconomics.

[313] [314] South Africa also looks to be entering a period of some political ups and downs during 2016-2018, as its population begins to show signs of disenchantment within the ruling political party, the African National Congress (ANC), which could affect its near and medium-term economic outlook, particularly as international rating agencies have it on their watch list to downgrade.

The 2017 economic picture for three of the BRICS members still appears shaky, and for Brazil and South Africa, their financial challenges are coupled with high unemployment rates, at respectively 11.2 percent and 26.7 percent.[315] [316] Russia, so far, despite other

---

com/south-africa/gdp-growth

[313] *Bulging in the Middle: A Boom in Sub-Saharan Africa Is Attracting Business Talent from The Rich World.* (2012, October 20). *The Economist.* Retrieved May 2016 from http://www.economist.com/news/middle-east-and-africa/21564856-boom-sub-saharan-africa-attracting-business-talent-rich-world?zid=304&ah=e5690753dc78ce91909083042ad12e30.

[314] I attend the briefing given by South African Finance Minister Rob Davies on the margins of the US-Africa AGOA Ministerial.

[315] *Brazil Unemployment Rate 2012-2016.* (2016). [data set]. Trading Economics, Retrieved June 30, 2016 from http://www.tradingeconomics.com/brazil/unemployment-rate

[316] Holodny, E. (2016, May 9). *South Africa's Unemployment Rate Just Surged to a 12-year High.* Retrieved May 25, 2016 from http://www.businessinsider.com/south-africa-unemployment-rate-rises-2016-5

economic troubles, reported its 2016 second quarter unemployment at 5.6 percent, which is not (if true) that bad and about a point higher than the United States at 4.7 percent for the same period in 2016.[317] [318] [319]

Thus, we will need to see how Brazil, Russia, and South Africa fare economically going forward and how their financial situations impact their interaction and monetary ability to advance the NDB's mission. Clearly, China is by no means in the same economic situation; its economy is just slowing down to its new normal, and the world must become accustomed to its new economic reality. However, we still need to watch how it delivers on its financial commitments to the NDB, the impact its manufacturing slowdown has on SSAfrica – although I opined earlier, that China's manufacturing

317 *Russia Unemployment Rate* 1993-2016. (2016). [data set]. *Trading Economics*. Retrieved June 30, 2016 from http://www.tradingeconomics.com/russia/unemployment-rate

318 *How Far Do EU-US Sanctions on Russia Go*? (2014, September 15). Europe. *BBC News*. Retrieved July 7, 2016 from http://www.bbc.com/news/world-europe-28400218

319 United States Unemployment Rate 1948-2016. (2016). [data set]. *Trading Economics*. Retrieved June 30, 2016 from http://www.tradingeconomics.com/united-states/unemployment-rate

slowdown could be a win for region and Africa small businesses if they are able to pick up the slack.[320]

BRICS member India is interesting on all fronts. It had a 2016 GDP growth rate of 7.6 percent, is home to a technology center in Mumbai, the country's own version of Silicon Valley; and also in 2016 claimed the title of the "world's fastest growing major economy." India economic and business ties with SSAfrica have been growing since 2010.[321] India is also the only founding member of the BRICS group that remains relatively close to its 2010-2015 growth rates AND the only BRICS member whose economy is mostly on an upswing, despite several *hiccups* with the government's late 2016 decision to remove from circulation one of the primary monetary notes for every day Indians with little notice.[322]

---

[320] Chang, S. *China's First-Quarter GDP Growth Likely Slowed to A Seven-Year Low.* (2016, April 13). Markets. Market Watch. Retrieved July 7, 2016 from http://www.marketwatch.com/story/chinas-first-quarter-gdp-growth-likely-slowed-to-a-seven-year-low-2016-04-12

[321] Bengali, S. *What's Like to Live in the World's Fastest Growing Major Economy.* (2016, June 6). *Los Angeles Times.* Retrieved June 30, 2016 from http://www.latimes.com/world/la-fg-india-economy-20160606-snap-story.html

[322] (2016, July 6). *Global Business.* [Television broadcast, 2 p.m.] China Global Television Network.

Its current Prime Minister, Narenda Modi, visited Africa in summer 2016 to drum up additional India-SSAfrica business and economic ties.[323] There are similarities between the Africa Region today and where India was ten years ago, when its SMEs helped drive its growth and transformation through new technologies. India's good news SME story of a decade ago is synergistic with the Africa SME good news story of today.

Worth mentioning at this juncture is *Brexit,* and what people anticipated would be its possible impact on the Africa region as a result of the departure of the United Kingdom (UK) from the European Union (EU) on June 23, 2016.[324] Thus, far Brexit has not had substantial impact on the SSAfrica Region, but its ripple effect, not just in Africa or its SMES, but also in the rest of the world, may take several years to fully materialize as both the UK and the EU feel their way through the economic divorce process.[325] But it is also possible that

---

[323] Ibid.

[324] Brexit. (n.d.). Definition. *Investopedia.* Retrieved June 30, 2015 from http://www.investopedia.com/terms/b/brexit.asp

[325] On June 23, 2016, I watched the news (in my case on CNN International while in The Hague, Netherlands). I went to bed at midnight on June 23, 2016, sure Britain was in, woke up on June 24, and was in shock that it

as the UK looks for other markets and trading partners in a post-Brexit world, Africa could be its alternative "go-to" region and Africa SMEs their go-to investment group.

There is one last point I want to make on the entire term "BRICS" as a country grouping: I was neither a *fan* nor *fond* of the term. Most likely, I fell into a minority group of people who were not enamored with the term when it was introduced and at the height of its usage. I never thought BRICS captured or gave credit to the high GDPs of the other African economies in 2009-early 2015 that were much higher than South Africa's.[326] Interestingly enough in 2011 and again in 2013, I suggested in a HuffPost article, on my blog, and on Africa.com to change the acronym from BRICS to *BRICA*, which would have been a more inclusive representation of the Sub-Saharan Africa economic

---

was out. I listened in disbelief that the United Kingdom voters had decided to leave the European Union and that the Brexit decision had prevailed. The democratic process has spoken but we will all have to see what this means for economies around the world, particularly Africa, as colonial ties remain strong with many nations on the Continent. World stock markets and the British pound took a beating for the first couple of weeks, but things have begun to settle after the initial global shock.

[326] My view of time period where there was high usage of the term "BRICS."

boom years of 2009-early 2015.[327] [328] [329] The "A" in the term "BRICA" was meant to reflect the region's economic boom more broadly, as opposed to the "S" representing only South Africa. The positives in the region at that time were not (and still are not) limited to just one nation. For instance, Nigeria, Angola, Ghana, Mozambique, Rwanda, and Tanzania all had higher growth rates during those boom years than South Africa.[330] (NB: Nigeria and South Africa are playing tag-teamed over the title of *largest SSAfrican economy;* in 2014 Nigeria gained the title from South Africa, but lost

---

[327] Sanders, Ambassador R. R. *Coining the Acronym BRICA -- Adding Africa's Name to World Regions and Economies in Economic Boom!* (2011, May 31). [Blog post] *Huffington Post.* Retrieved July 1, 2016 from http://www.huffingtonpost.com/amb-robin-renee-sanders/coining-the-acronym-brica_b_868649.html

Sanders, R. R. *Coining the Acronym BRICA – Adding Africa's Name to World Regions & Economies in Economic Boom! (2011,* May 26). FEEEDS® Series [Blog post]. http://blogitrrs.blogspot.com/2011/05/coining-acronym-brica-adding-africas.html

[328] Sanders, R. R. *Coining a New Acronym: BRICA: Adding Africa's Name to World Regions & Economies in Economic Boom – Part One.* (2011). News. [Blog post]. *Africa.com.* Retrieved July 7, 2016 from http://www.africa.com/coining_a_new_acronym_brica_adding_africa8242s_name_to_world_regionseconomies_in_economic_boom_8211_/

[329] Sanders, Ambassador R. R., *The 5th BRICS Summit: Lessons for the "Developed' World."* (2012) Updated 2013, June 2). [Blog post]. *Huffington Post.* http://www.huffingtonpost.com/amb-robin-renee-sanders/the-5th-brics-summit-less_b_2995658.html

[330] Ibid.

it in August 2016 when South Africa regained the top spot. Both countries are having their various economic woes that are expected to last until 2018, but just in different macro areas than the other.)[331]

Now, let's take a deep dive into what the range of donors are doing in the Africa small business space, including how they have doubled down to help.

In Part 3 we will:

- Take an illustrative look (consider them my favorite examples) of the good catch-up game by donors, governments, the private sector, and philanthropists as they step up their engagement with Africa SMEs;

- Discuss what is being done by African female SMEs and what still needs to be done to further advance women entrepreneurs; and

---

[331] (2016, August 11). *Africa News.* [Television broadcast, 6:30 p.m.] China Global Television Network.

- Highlight the other tangible and intangible contributions of SMEs such as lending their voice to opening up the governance, transparency, and economic space on the Continent.[332]

[332] The phrase "catch-up game" is a US idiomatic expression meaning someone or something was behind in an area, a subject, or in reacting or responding but has since caught up.

Part Three: Doubling Down by Old and New Players

"Africa Diaspora SMEs have the possibility to do it all, establish and grow their businesses in the U.S., leverage that success to play a role back home through investments and exports which can in turn support the Continent's growth and development."

—Ngozi Bell, Region III Advocate, U.S. Small Business Administration (SBA), 2009-2016

Chapter Six:
The More, The Merrier

From 2008 to 2009, one could really see the shift-change and proliferation of engagement and interest in Africa with the increase in the number of foreign players from a variety of non-governmental organizations (both international and national), to the international private sector and an array of foreign countries not involved previously in the region.

During this same period, foreign direct investment (FDI) began to increase, and it more than doubled for the region in the 2008-2009 period, jumping from $US8 billion to $US32-39 billion.[333] [334] [335] The 2015 FDI

---

[333] World Bank. (2013, January). *Sub-Saharan Africa Region.* Global Economic Prospects. Site Resources. pp. 3-4. Retrieved August 15, 2016 from http://siteresources.worldbank.org/INTPROSPECTS/Resources/334934-1322593305595/8287139-1358278153255/GEP13aSSARegionalAnnex.pdf

Ezeoha, A.E., & Cattaneo, N. (2011). *Economic Development in Africa.* Department of Economics & Economic History. Rhodes University, Grahamstown, South Africa. p. 2. Retrieved August 15, 2016 from http://www.csae.ox.ac.uk/conferences/2011-edia/papers/294-ezeoha.pdf

[334] World Bank. (2013, January). *Sub-Saharan Africa Region.* Global Economic Prospects. Site Resources. pp. 3-4. Retrieved August 15, 2016 from http://siteresources.worldbank.org/INTPROSPECTS/Resources/334934-1322593305595/8287139-1358278153255/GEP13aSSARegionalAnnex.pdf

[335] Ibid.

for the Sub-Saharan Africa Region per *fDi Intelligence* (a branch of the *Financial Times)* was $US61 billion, up from the 2014 UNCTAD number of $US54 billion.[336] [337] [338] The point is that these numbers – $US54 billion and $US61 billion – were big increases in FDI for the region over the previous two decades when the average FDIs (as reported by UNCTAD and UNIDO) were $US11.9

[336] fDi Intelligence, Division of Financial Times. (2015). *Foreign direct investment for Sub-Saharan Africa report.* Retrieved April 17, 2016 from http://www.ft.com/cms/s/0/79ee41b6-fd84-11e4-b824-00144feabdc0.html#axzz4HRlWalVD

[337] Fingar, C. *Foreign Direct Investment in Africa Surges.* (2015, May 10). Emerging Markets. *Financial Times.* Retrieved August 15, 2016 from http://www.ft.com/cms/s/0/79ee41b6-fd84-11e4-b824-00144feabdc0.html#axzz4HRlWalVD.

[338] *UNCTAD 2014/2015 Annual Report.* (2015). UNCTAD. Retrieved August 15, 2016 from http://unctad.org/en/PublicationsLibrary/wir2015_en.pdf.

billion (1995-1999), $US8.7 billion (2000), and $US18 billion (2005).[339] [340]

Even though there was not a huge growth in FDI between 2014 and 2015 because the economic environment on the Continent tightened, Sub-Saharan Africa still was considered an attractive destination for FDI, and levels continue to remain well above any we saw before 2008-2009 when the big shift took place, and the interest in the region increased – bringing with

---

[339] United Nations Industrial and Development Organization. (2008, August). *Foreign Direct Investment in Sub-Saharan Africa: Determinants and Location Decisions*. Research and Statistic Branch. Working Paper. p. 6. Retrieved August 16, 2016 from http://www.unido.org//fileadmin/user_media/Publications/Research_and_statistics/Branch_publications/Research_and_Policy/Files/Working_Papers/2008/WP082008%20Foreign%20Direct%20Investment%20in%20Sub-Saharan%20Africa%20-%20Determinants%20and%20Location%20Decisions.pdf

United Nations Conference on Trade and Development. (2005). *Economic Development in Africa*. Report. United Nations. p. 12. Retrieved August 15, 2016 from http://unctad.org/en/docs/tdr2005_en.pdf

Mijiyama, A.G. *What Drives Foreign Direct Investment in Africa*? (n.d.) An Empirical Investigation with Panel Data. African Center for Economic Transformation. African Development Bank. Accra, Ghana. Retrieved August 15, 2016 from http://www.afdb.org/fileadmin/uploads/afdb/Documents/Knowledge/What%20Drives%20Foreign%20Direct%20Investments%20in%20Africa%20An%20Empirical%20Investigation%20with%20Panel%20Data.pdf

[340] United Nations Industrial Development Organization. (2009). *Annual Report 2009*. Vienna: United Nations. p. 1. Retrieved May 2016 from https://www.unido.org/fileadmin/user_media/Publications/Annual_Report/2009/10-50277_Ebookb.pdf

it an array of international investors, many who remain there today.[341]

To begin the discussion on the doubling down that began with foundations, philanthropists and investors in the 2008-2009 timeframe, we will be looking at some of the old donors that expanded their activity during this time frame, the new donors who became interested in Africa, and the new investors who entered the region – all coinciding with the timing of the economic boom, and the surge in the growth of Africa SMEs.

This doubling down by old players and entrance of new players was also part of the *convergence* I mentioned earlier as Africa transitioned from the *Renaissance* phase to the *Rising* phase.

Whatever the reasons (technology, population as a future market, growing development needs) that sparked a foreign country, philanthropist, investor,

---

[341] *EY's Attractiveness Survey 2015.* (2015). Making Choices. Summary. Ernst & Young. Retrieved June 30, 2016 from http://www.ey.com/Publication/vwLUAssets/EY-africa-attractiveness-survey-june-2015-americas/$FILE/EY-africa-attractiveness-survey-june-2015-americas.pdf

equity firm, or private sector company to double down on either their interest or their investment also transferred to recognizing the ever-increasing importance of Africa SMEs and entrepreneurs to the Continent's economic transformation. This is still the case today despite the economic tightening in some African countries.

In addition, African countries that were becoming evolving or nascent democracies that sought to do better by their citizens, coupled with a few older African leaders passing on, helped advance this doubling down. Granted, not all of these democracy efforts were successful; not all of the new leaders then in office were truly committed to democratic change in practice, but there were enough glimmers of hope in 2008-2009 in places like Benin, Botswana (solidifying its democracy well before 2008), Ghana, Mozambique, Namibia, Senegal, and South Africa, to name a few, that encouraged donors and investors to do more.
In fact, an earlier 2000-2006 poll by Afrobarometer showed that 71 percent of Africa nationals said that "democracy was the best path for their countries to

take."[342] Hence, as we began to move into the end of the first decade of the 21st century, more African nations in 2009-2015 were beginning to meet some of the democracy-building requirements of many organizations and governments, at least on the U. S. AGOA facility than before, with some 37 of the 47 nations in the region making the cut.[343] [344] [345] Some

---

[342] On African elections during the 2000-2006 periods, *The Afrobarometer*, which conducted surveys during this period, highlights the trend of African citizens seeing democracy as the right path for governance in their country. Their surveys also highlight those countries that were those that had already moved in the right direction such as Ghana, and those that had not done so at that time such as Tanzania, Zambia, Zimbabwe, Nigeria, Malawi, and several others. The poll focused on how 8 African nationals feel about foreign investment, globalization, and such things as whether they favorably viewed the US. In general, nationals in this poll did not feel they were being treated fairly in trade negotiations.

See: *Study 2003-2004*. (2003-2004). Funded by World Bank and Royal Africa Society. Poll conducted by Globescan. http://www.afrobarometer.org/data, and http://www.worldpublicopinion.org/pipa/articles/brafricara/209.php?lb=braf.

[343] International Trade Administration. (2001-2009). Summary of AGOA I. Retrieved August 17, 2016 from http://trade.gov/agoa/legislation/index.asp.

[344] During the first signing of the African Growth and Opportunity Act (AGOA), I had the honor to be invited to the White House Rose Garden Ceremony when then-President Clinton signed the legislation. I also had the honor to attend then President Obama's White House event celebrating the renewal of the legislation in 2015. AGOA is the trade framework that the U.S. has established for duty-free exports of some 6,800 products from SSAfrica to the United States. In order to be eligible, countries have to meet performance indicators on many democracy pillars such as human rights, elections, and press freedoms. The AGOA legislation was renewed in June 2015 for a new 10-year period.

[345] Both the World Bank and the U.S. Government use 47 as the number of Sub-Saharan Africa countries. See: http://web.worldbank.org/WBSITE/EXTERNAL/COUNTRIES/AFRICAEXT/

African nations also were able to meet the even tougher U.S. Government democracy standards required by one of my favorite programs the Millennium Challenge Corporation (MCC), created under the Bush Administration.[346] MCC's standards included countries having *score cards* based on indicators from third-party institutions such as *Freedom House, World Bank, Brookings Institution, Afrobarometer, Transparency International, World Economic Forum Global Competitiveness Report, Gallup World Poll,* and

---

0,,contentMDK:20226042~menuPK:258664~pagePK:146736~piPK:226340~theSitePK:258644,00.html

[346] Millennium Challenge Corporation. (n.d.) Home Page. United States Government. Retrieved August 17, 2016 from http://www.mcc.gov

many others (see full list at www.mcc.gov.)[347] [348] [349] (NB: There has been some backsliding on the democracy front in 2015-2016, but more on this in Chapter 9.)[350]

What I found fascinating in this transition from *Renaissance-to-Rising*, along with the doubling

---

[347] Full List of groups from which MCC determines its indicators can be found at: Millennium Challenge Corporation. (2014, October 9). Report Guide to Indicators. Retrieved May 17, 2016 from https://www.mcc.gov/resources/doc/report-guide-to-the-indicators-and-the-selection-process-fy-2015. Those cited here are illustrative of what is on the MCC site: http://www.mcc.gov

Background: MCC is a program I really admire (although as of 2016 it is under funding pressure from the U.S. Congress). It was created under the Administration of President George W. Bush, who supported a number of great signature programs with his Assistant Secretary of State for Africa Jendayi Frazer and her team that helped the region, particularly with such well-known initiatives as PEPFAR to combat HIV/AIDS, and revamping the Africa Education Initiative (AEI) (of which the precursor was the Education for Democracy and Development Initiative, EDDI, launched by the Clinton Administration during his 1998 Africa trip.)

[348] *Jendayi E. Frazer, Ph.D. - CIPI Director and Distinguished Public Service Professor. (n.d.)* Center for International Policy and Innovation. Carnegie Mellon University. Retrieved August 17, 2016 from http://www.cmu.edu/cipi/people/frazer-jendayi.html

[349] The White House. (2007). *Africa Education Initiative.* Background. National Security Council. Retrieved August 17, 2016 from http://agsp.worlded.org/background.htm

The White House. (1998). *Promoting Peace and Democracy.* Ghana Speech. National Security Council. Retrieved April 26 & August 17, 2016 from http://clinton5.nara.gov/WH/EOP/NSC/html/nsc-01.html

[350] I know think tanks, donor governments, FEEEDS, and other activists are concerned about this trend by the new crop of leaders to also remain in power past the existing Constitutional mandate or change their Constitutions to accommodate this desire. Burundi, Democratic Republic of Congo, Republic of Congo, and Rwanda are 2016 examples of this.

down by old and new donors and investors was the increase in the number of African and non-African philanthropic involvement in the Africa SME space. Older philanthropic organizations ballooned in their contributions, and newer ones also came on line with a solid focus on job creation, training, and support for entrepreneurs.

Philanthropists, Foundations, Awards, Donors, and Equity Funds

It is worth noting that some of those early, primarily or solely Africa-focused philanthropic entities were founded by Africans. I think we tend to forget this and see today's Western, European, or Asian name-driven organizations as the main ones doing the early *giving* to African projects and programs. But they were not. Older, more internationally-recognized foundations such as Ford and MacArthur, (which I highly respect and had great working relationships with throughout my diplomatic career), and many other Western, European and Asian groups provided then and provide now great assistance around the world, and have certainly done so in Africa.[351] But this book is about highlighting African nationals and Diaspora entrepreneurs leading the way – so that donors and investors began to see SMEs as critical to SSAfrica's development.

Foundations *founded and funded* by African nationals that primarily focused on Africa date as far back as the mid-1990s before many of the newer ones became active in the region. However, since the 2008-2009 shift-change when there was an uptick in interest in Africa – no matter when these foundations were created –they all have turned a laser-like focus on the Africa SME sector.

First, I want to highlight the timelines for some of the early Africa founded and financed foundations particularly since it is rarely noted just how early Africa foundations had a role in the development of the

---

[351] *Ford Foundation*. Home Page. Retrieved August 3, 2016 from https://www.fordfoundation.org/

MacArthur Foundation. Home Page. Retrieved August 3, 2016 from https://www.google.com/search?q=macarthur+foundation&rls=com.microsoft:en-US:IE-Address&ie=UTF-8&oe=UTF-8&sourceid=ie7&rlz=1I7ADFA_enUS478&gws_rd=ssl

Continent and then discuss what some of them as well as others are doing to assist SMEs and entrepreneurs. Here are a few of the Africa philanthropic foundations which played early roles in development and are still extremely involved and active today such as the Dangote Foundation (1994, Aliko Dangote, based in Nigeria), Masiyiwa Family Foundations/Capernaum Trust (1996, Strive Masiyiwa, based in Zimbabwe), and the Sawiris Foundation (2001, Onsi Sawiris, based in Egypt).[352] [353] [354]

Samples of others that followed these early groups included both African and non-African-led organizations:

---

[352] *Aliko Dangote: A Lesson for African Entrepreneurs.* (2014, March 22). *Vanguard Newspaper.* Retrieved March 30, 2016 from http://www.vanguardngr.com/2014/03/aliko-dangote-lesson-african-entrepreneurs/

[353] Mfonobong, N. (2011, November 29). *The Philanthropy of Africa's 40 Richest. Forbes.* Retrieved, March 3, 2016 from http://www.forbes.com/sites/mfonobongnsehe/2011/11/29/the-philanthropy-of-africas-40-richest/#78c4dc8740a0

[354] Egypt falls outside of the prime focus of this book, which is on the 47 nations in the Sub-Saharan Africa Region, but I thought it was important to include the Sawiris Foundation as it was one of the earlier *giving* organizations created by a national of an African country to further underscore that Africans themselves were involved in giving back to both their countries and the region.

- 2002 – The William J. Clinton Foundation Africa programs, the earlier 1997 version of the organization was called the Clinton Foundation (without the first name) and was solely focused on Arkansas. As of 2013, the organization is called the Bill, Hillary and Chelsea Clinton Foundation.[355]

- 2003 – Safricom Foundation, which is affiliated with Kenya's Safricom Limited, the owner of *M-PESA,* the largest mobile money transfer business in Africa. (There is a 60/40 ownership of Safricom with British telecom company Vodafone.)[356]

---

[355] The Clinton Foundation. (n.d.). The Clinton Foundation History. Retrieved May 10, 2016 from https://www.clintonfoundation.org/about/clinton-foundation-history

The Inside Story: How the Clintons Built a Two Billion Global Empire. (2015, June 2). *The Washington Post.* Retrieved April 13 and May 15, 2016 from https://www.washingtonpost.com/politics/the-inside-story-of-how-the-clintons-built-a-2-billion-global-empire/2015/06/02/b6eab638-0957-11e5-a7ad-b430fc1d3f5c_story.html

[356] *Safaricom Foundation.* (n.d.) Home Page. Retrieved May 14, 2016 from http://www.safaricomfoundation.org

- 2005 – The Lundin Foundation, based in Vancouver, with regional offices in Kenya, and Ghana.[357]

- 2006 – The Mo Ibrahim Foundation, Mo Ibrahim founder, based in Senegal and London.[358]

- 2006 – Gates Foundation's Africa programs, although the Foundation itself was created in 2000.[359]

- 2009 – The MTN Foundation, founded by the South African-owned *Mobile Telephone Network*, better known as MTN, one of the largest mobile telephone companies in SSAfrica.[360]

---

[357] *Lundin Foundation.* (n.d.) Portfolio Manager. Retrieved May 30, 2016 from http://www.lundinfoundation.org/i/pdf/lundingfoundation_portfoliomanager.pdf

[358] *Mo Ibrahim Foundation.* (n.d.) Home Page. Retrieved June 23, 2016 from http://mo.ibrahim.foundation/

Mo Ibrahim Biography. (n.d.) Retrieved April 19, 2016 from https://en.wikipedia.org/wiki/Mo_Ibrahim_Foundation

[359] *Gates Foundation.* (2013). Who We Are. Profiles. Retrieved April 18, 2016 from http://www.gatesfoundation.org/How-We-Work/Resources/Grantee-Profiles and, *Gates Foundation.* (2010-2013). How We Work. Retrieved May 12, 2016 from http://www.gatesfoundation.org/Who-We-Are/General-Information/History

[360] *MTN SA Foundation.* (2009). *Entrepreneurship.* Mobile Telephone Network (MTN). Retrieved May 11, 2016 from http://services.mtn.co.za/mtnfoundation/Entrepreneurship.html

- 2009 – The Africa Innovation Foundation.[361]

- 2010 – The Elumelu Foundation, founded by Tony Elumelu.[362]

Certainly, there are many other foundations working in Africa; however, these particular ones are illustrative and noted because they all have a huge focus on African SMEs and entrepreneurship. The Dangote Foundation in 2012 contributed approximately $US252 million to a joint revolving fund managed by Nigeria's BOI for the development and training of Nigeria's small and medium size businesses.[363] [364] In 2014, the

[361] *African Innovation Foundation* (n.d.) [Blog]. Retrieved May 6, 2016 from http://www.africaninnovation.org/, and, http://www.africaninnovationfoundation.org/blog

[362] *Tony Elumelu Foundation.* (2016). *Elumelu Entrepreneurs Program 2016.* Startups. Retrieved June 17, 2016 from http://tonyelumelufoundation.org/teep/startups/elumelu-entrepreneurship-programme/

Tony Elumelu Foundation. (n.d.) Retrieved March 30, 2016 from https://en.wikipedia.org/wiki/The_Tony_Elumelu_Foundation

[363] Dangote, A. *38th Pre-Convocation Lecture.* (2016, January). Speech. Amadou Bello University. Nigeria: Zaira.

[364] Reflects 2016 exchange rate of Nigeria's currency the naira to US dollars. BOI is Nigeria's Bank of Industry which was mentioned earlier in the book.

Foundation also received a $US1.25 billion endowment from its founder, Aliko Dangote.[365]

The Mo Ibrahim Foundation, in addition to focusing on governance and leadership, supports SMEs through its strengthening and capacity-building programs, particularly those working in the agricultural and climate change sectors.[366] While the Elumelu Foundation holds an annual entrepreneurship competition which encourages investment in African small businesses and has helped advance the development of 1,000 entrepreneurs per year since the creation of the Foundation's $100 million flagship competition in 2014.[367] The 2016 Elumelu competition highlight another round of innovative

---

[365] *TBY talks to Aliko Dangote, Chairman of Dangote Group, On Rising Profits, listing on International Stock Markets, and Plans for the Year Ahead.* (2016) Solid Bet. *The Business Year.* Retrieved March 28, 2016 from https://www.thebusinessyear.com/nigeria-2016/solid-bet/interview. FYI: Nigeria Bank of Industry or BOI was cited earlier in Chapter 2 as a partner in the BOI-Western Union-FEEEDS-ADM SME training programs.

[366] *Mo Ibrahim Will Participate in EU-Africa Business Forum.* (2014). Latest News. Mo Ibrahim Foundation. Retrieved June 17, 2016 from http://mo.ibrahim.foundation/news/2014/mo-ibrahim-will-participate-in-eu-africa-business-forum/

[367] *Tony Elumelu Foundation.* (2016). Elumelu Entrepreneurs Program 2016. Startups. Retrieved June 17, 2016 from http://tonyelumelufoundation.org/teep/startups/elumelu-entrepreneurship-programme/

startups and help more established SMEs with an infusion of investment. The Lundin, Safricom, and MTN Foundations, all mentioned above, have similar programs and support a combination of entrepreneurship training, mentorship, and financial assistance to startups.

In addition to the doubling down by philanthropists, there was also a surge in yearly events and award-based competitions for Africa SMEs held by a variety of organizations and governments. Some examples follow.

From the US end, there is the Global Entrepreneurship Summit (GES), heavily supported by the U.S. Government, brings together a range of SMEs and social enterprise organizations, at all stages of development working in every conceivable sector. (In 2016 GES was held in Silicon, Valley, California, and in 2015 in Kenya.)[368] GES receives substantial requests to participate in its Summits from Africa SME businesses and accepts attendance applications

---

[368] *Global Entrepreneurship Summit* (GES). (n.d.). Home Page. Retrieved June 17, 2016 from http://www.ges2016.org/

from proof of concepts to startups to more established small companies. Other U.S. Government SME-related programs are USAID's ADM competition, the Development Innovation Venture Program (DIV) that offers three grant stages for SMEs and functions in a venture capital-like manner, the Africa Women's Entrepreneurship Program (AWEP), and the Africa Trade Hubs which provide resources and information to assist Africa SMEs.[369]

The AfDB has its program entitled the African Guarantee Fund for Small and Medium-Sized Enterprises, and the International Finance Corporation (IFC) has the Aureos Africa Fund, LLC – both provide

[369] United States Agency for International Development. (2016). *Africa Diaspora Marketplace.* Retrieved August 7, 2016 from http://www.diasporamarketplace.org/

United States Agency for International Development. (2016, July 26). *USAID Development Innovation Venture (DIV).* Retrieved June 2016 from https://www.usaid.gov/div

USAID Trade Hubs in Africa. (n.d.) U.S. Department of State. Retrieved August 7, 2016 from http://www.state.gov/p/af/rt/awep/196204.htm

United States Department of State. (n.d.). *African Women's Entrepreneurship Program.* (AWEP). Retrieved August 7, 2016 from http://www.state.gov/p/af/rt/awep/index.htm

extensive funding and broader financing facilities for SMEs.[370]

On award programs for Africa SMEs, here too there is a variety of organizations that offer prizes to innovative African small businesses. Examples are:

- *Anzisha* Prize by the South Africa-based African Leadership Academy, or ALA (ALA's overall education approach will be highlighted more later);

- *SEED Award* for entrepreneurs with offices in Berlin, London, and Pretoria;

- *African Entrepreneurship Award* supported by BMCE Bank of Africa;

- *Innovation Prize for Africa* (IPA) by the Innovation Foundation, supporting creative entrepreneur-innovators (its 2015 SME winner created an

---

[370] African Development Bank. (2013). *African Guarantee Fund for Small and Medium Sized Enterprises.* Retrieved May 14, 2016 from http://www.afdb.org/en/topics-and-sectors/initiatives-partnerships/african-guarantee-fund-for-small-and-medium-sized-enterprises/

International Finance Corporation. (2016). *Aureos Africa Fund L.L.C.* Retrieved May 4, 2016 from http://ifcext.ifc.org/ifcext/spiwebsite1.nsf/ProjectDisplay/SPI_DP26992

agri-business platform for investors interested in the region's agricultural sector);

- *Demo Africa* in Johannesburg, which picks five innovative winners, usually in tech, who get an opportunity to seek funding and mentors from companies in Silicon Valley; and [371] [372] [373] [374]

---

[371] African Leadership Academy. (n.d.). Our Programs. *The Anzisha Prize.* Retrieved April 20, 2016 from http://www.africanleadershipacademy.org/our-programs/anzisha-prize/

SEED. (n.d.) Home Page. Retrieved May 15, 2016 from https://www.seed.uno/about/who.html

BMCE Bank of Africa is a Moroccan-based international bank. Although Morocco falls out of the SSAfrica focus of this book, it is mentioned because its *African Entrepreneurship Award* is a pan-African one and entrepreneurs and SMEs from around SSAfrica participate. See: *African Entrepreneurship Awards.* (2015 Edition). BMCE Bank of Africa. Retrieved August 3, 2016 from https://africanentrepreneurshipaward.com/

[372] *African Innovation Foundation* (n.d.) [Blog]. Innovation Prize for Africa. Retrieved May 6, 2016 from https://africaninnovationfoundation.org/blog

Afterblixen. (2015, November 30). *10 Great Funding Opportunities for African Entrepreneurs.* Afterblixen.com. Retrieved August 3, 2016 from https://afterblixen.com/2015/11/30/10-great-funding-opportunities-for-african-entrepreneurs/

[373] One of the 2015 winners for the *Innovation Prize for Africa* was Alex Mwaura Muriu from Kenya. His "Farm Capital Africa" an agri-business funding model to attract investors to the sector in Africa, which also gives investors a share in the farming profits. The Innovation Foundation has offices in Switzerland and Angola and offers an annual prize to creative entrepreneurs with new ideas to address Africa's economic development or poverty issue. The Foundation was created in 2009 by Swiss businessman Jean-Claude Bastos De Morais. See: *Innovation Prize for Africa.* (n.d.). Home Page. Innovation Prize for Africa. Retrieved May 6, 2016 from http://innovationprizeforafrica.org

[374] *Demo Africa.* (2016, August 29). *Africa Live.* [Television broadcast, 1 p.m.] China Global Television Network. The 2016 winners and participants were *ConnectMed, Mediabox, Soltice Energy, RadioVybe, and SORTD.*

- *Diaspora Demo Summit* in Washington, D.C., a gathering, which showcases startups, entrepreneurs and includes angel investors and venture capital companies.[375]

Countries such as Great Britain through its Department for International Development (DFID), as well as by participating in a compendium called the *Africa Enterprise Challenge Fund* (AECF), which includes funding from Australia, Denmark, Netherlands, and Sweden, provides annual competitive grants to support innovative Africa small business ideas in several economic development sectors.[376]

The Swedish International Development Agency (SIDA) has also done great work to assist social enterprises and business cooperatives beginning earlier in the

[375] Diaspora Demo Summit. (n.d.). Diaspora Demo. Retrieved November 27, 2016 from http://diasporademo.com/

[376] Africa Enterprise Challenge Fund. (2016) Overview. Retrieved April 27, 2016 from http://www.aecfafrica.org/

region than most in places like Zambia (2000) with SME training programs in agri-business.[377] [378]

While the European Union began by first focusing on building Africa SME and entrepreneurial capacity and technology skills and later in 2008 targeted SMEs involved in small scale-manufacturing as part of its support to the sustainable development pillar of the EU-Africa Partnership.[379]

---

[377] Open Aid Data. (2014, May 28). Open Aid. Retrieved May 7, 2016 from http://www.openaiddata.org/purpose/288/321/10/

Open Aid Data. (2014, May 28). Zambia. Open Aid. Retrieved May 7, 2016 from http://www.openaiddata.org/purpose/288/321/918/

[378] Africa Union-European Union Partnership group was formalized in 2007 and provides a strategic framework under which the Africa Union and the European Union work together on a range of policy and development issues. Its current strategic plan runs from 2014 to 2017 and has five priority areas of which sustainable development is one, which is where their efforts on Africa's SME sector falls. Their last Summit, called the 4th Africa-EU Summit, was in 2014 in Brussels, Belgium. See: http://www.africa-eu-partnership.org/en/priority-areas/sustainable-and-inclusive-development-and-growth-and-continental-integration-6

[379] *European Union Africa.* (n.d.) About Us. EU-Africa Infrastructure Trust Fund. Retrieved May 9, 2016 from http://www.eu-africa-infrastructure-tf.net, also at http://www.eu-africa-infrastructure-tf.net/attachments/library/ica-presentation-2008-02-15%20.pdf

EU-Africa Partnership. (2013-2015). *Africa-EU Partnership Priority Areas for Sustainable and Inclusive Development and Growth and Continental Integration.* Retrieved May 9, 2016 from http://www.africa-eu-partnership.org/en/priority-areas/sustainable-and-inclusive-development-and-growth-and-continental-integration-6

Africa-European Partnership. (2013-2015). *Africa-European Union Partnership.* About Us. Retrieved May 9, 2016 from http://www.africa-eu-partnership.org/en

The Chinese Government, through its Johannesburg branch of the China Construction Bank Corporation, assists more established African companies with loans and trade finance, which has advanced China-Africa trade. For SMEs, it sponsors the *China-Africa SME Convention* in Shanghai, in conjunction with the AU's Trade and Industry Commission. The convention also includes training sessions for Africa's small businesses and helps link them to other Chinese SMEs and larger firms. More recently the *Guangzhou Africa Investment Forum* was created, offering Africa SMEs investment and partnerships opportunities.[380] [381]

Other Asian countries such as Japan have also begun to see Africa's SMEs as the right development approach to growing the Continent's private sector. In fact, Japan

---

[380] Matthee, M. & Finaughty, E. (2010, March 18-19). *Trade with China: How to Support African SMEs*. The 7th African Finance Journal Conference. Paper. Spier Wine Estate, Stellenbosch, South Africa.

China Construction Bank Corporation Johannesburg Branch. (n.d.). About Us. China Construction Bank Corporation. Retrieved August 17, 2016 from http://za.ccb.com/johannesburg/en/gywm.html

[381] *China-Africa SME Convention*. (2016, June 7-10). Reliconn. Retrieved May 5, 2016 from https://www.reliconn.com/presentation

Second Guangzhou Africa Investment Forum. (2016, September 7-8). News Guangzhou. Retrieved September 7, 2016 from http://www.newsgd.com/news/2016-09/07/content_155386819.htm

"welcomed" and called its 2000 Asia-Africa Business meeting, which included UNDP and UNCTAD, the "Year of the SME," but nothing substantive happened with their efforts until much later during the shift-change years that I am talking about (2008-2009) in this chapter.[382] Japan's big support for Africa SMEs came in earnest when it made a $US1 million contribution in 2009 to AfDB's African Training and Management Services Project (ATMS), and later when its International Cooperation Agency, JICA, helped finance a 2011 World Bank study examining the impact of Africa SMEs on development as part of Japan's support for the MDGs.[383] [384] This important study also focused

---

[382] Ministry of Foreign Affairs, Government of Japan. (2014). *Japan's New Assistance Program for Africa in-line with TICAD II Agenda for Action.* Retrieved May 11, 2016 from http://www.mofa.go.jp/region/africa/ticad2/agenda_n.html

[383] African Development Bank. (2009, October 6). *Japan and African Development Bank Commit USD one million technical assistance grant for SME capacity building in Africa.* Retrieved May 10, 2016 from http://www.afdb.org/en/news-and-events/article/japan-and-afdb-commit-usd-1-million-technical-assistance-grant-for-sme-capacity-building-in-africa-5156

The Foundation for Advanced Studies on International Development (FASID) was part of the joint partnership to produce this study. FASID is a Japanese non-profit organization. See: FASID. Home Page. Foundation for Advanced Studies on International Development. Retrieved August 4, 2016 from http://www.fasid.or.jp/e_about/

[384] Japan International Cooperation Agency. (2011, March-April). *JICA, the World Bank, and FASID Publish a Study on Industrial Clusters and SME*

on the contribution of SMEs to Africa's GDP, their training needs, and whether they would benefit from industrial clusters.[385]

Even though Japan began engaging in a more comprehensive way with Africa SMEs during the same time as most everyone else, it, like China, was more forward thinking on the diplomatic front, and preceded other donors in holding comprehensive meetings with African Heads of State way ahead of the West. Japan's first *Tokyo International Conference on African Development* or TICAD was held in 1993, followed afterward in 5-year increments, 1998, 2003, 2008, 2013, with the most recent one in Kenya in August 2016, the first ever held in Sub-Saharan in the 20-year history of the event. The latter meeting in Kenya demonstrating, in my view, how mature Africa's relationship has become with its Japanese partner

---

Growth in Africa. Newsletter. Retrieved May 5 and August 4, 2016 from http://www.jica.go.jp/usa/english/office/others/newsletter/2011/1103_04_08.html

385 Ibid.

and on the Japanese end, how important it views its engagement in the region.[386]

South-South nations like India, Turkey, and Brazil either began or expanded their involvement in the region during this time and also included a focus on Africa small businesses in their efforts by providing funding to several AfDB SME financing facilities such as:

- The Fund for African Private Sector Assistance (India);
- AfDB's Trust Fund (Brazil); and
- The African Development Fund (Turkey); Turkey joined AfDB in 2013 and holds a Turkey-Africa Summit.[387]

---

[386] Ministry of Foreign Affairs, Government of Japan. (2014). *Japan's New Assistance Program for Africa in-line with TICAD II Agenda for Action.* Retrieved May 11, 2016 from http://www.mofa.go.jp/region/africa/ticad2/agenda_n.html

United Nations. (n.d.). *Tokyo International Conference of African Development (TICAD).* Partnerships. Office of the Special Advisor for Africa. Retrieved August 4, 2016 from http://www.un.org/en/africa/osaa/partnerships/ticad.shtml

TICAD VI Summit Nairobi. (2016). United Nations. Retrieved August 4, 2016 from https://ticad6.net/

[387] African Development Bank. (2015, May 25). *India Signs Replenishment Agreement with African Development Bank.* Retrieved May 10, 2016

In addition to the various AfDB funds already mentioned *(Africa Small and Medium Enterprises Program* and *African Guarantee Fund for Small and Medium-Sized Enterprises)*, it also provides a range of technical assistance, management training, internships, and credit to Africa SMEs.[388] [389] [390] [391]

---

from http://www.afdb.org/en/news-and-events/article/india-signs-replenishment-of-technical-cooperation-agreement-with-african-development-bank-group-14266/

African Development Bank. (2011, March 9). *African Development Bank Sets-up New Trust Fund with Brazil.* Retrieved May 10, 2016 from http://www.afdb.org/en/news-and-events/article/afdb-sets-up-new-trust-fund-with-brazil-7803/

African Development Bank. (2015, September 22). *Ambassador of Turkey Pays Courtesy Visit.* African Development Bank. Retrieved May 10, 2016 from http://www.afdb.org/en/news-and-events/article/ambassador-of-turkey-pays-courtesy-visit-to-president-adesina-14704/

African Development Bank. (2013, December 9). *Republic of Turkey Joins African Development Bank Group.* Retrieved May 10, 2016 from http://www.afdb.org/en/news-and-events/article/the-republic-of-turkey-joins-african-development-bank-group-12660/

[388] African Development Bank. (2014). *Building Capacity for Private Sector Development.* Fund for Africa Private Sector Assistance. Retrieved August 17, 2016 from http://www.afdb.org/en/topics-and-sectors/initiatives-partnerships/fund-for-african-private-sector-assistance/

[389] African Development Bank. (2013, July 22). *African Development Bank SME Program Approval Boosting Inclusive Growth in Africa.* Retrieved March 10, 2016 from http://www.afdb.org/en/news-and-events/article/the-afdb-sme-program-approval-boosting-inclusive-growth-in-africa-12135/

[390] African Development Bank. (2013). *African Guarantee Fund for Small and Medium Sized Enterprises.* Retrieved May 14, 2016 from http://www.afdb.org/en/topics-and-sectors/initiatives-partnerships/african-guarantee-fund-for-small-and-medium-sized-enterprises/

[391] African Development Bank. (2014). Annual Report. *Fund for Africa Private Sector Assistance.* Retrieved May 10, 2016 from http://www.afdb

All of these – awards, competitions, conferences, donors, foundations, funds, governments, international institutions, and summits discussed above – are just illustrative (not meant to be comprehensive as there are many more), but they provide a picture of the doubling down that old players (e.g., governments and foundations) and the engagement of many new players who have really *tuned in and turned up* their support for Africa small businesses from 2008 onward.

On the private sector side, the big new private sector players, which rapidly increased their involvement during 2008-2009, were Africa-focused venture capital funds and private equity firms, growing to more than 200 by 2011. Estimates in 2016 are that these firms have more than doubled their activity in the region with investments reaching $US8.1 billion in 2014 and 2015. Samplings of these funds are: Helios, Carlyle Group, Emerging Capital Partners, Development Partners International, Blackstone's Black Rhino Unit,

---

org/fileadmin/uploads/afdb/Documents/Generic-Documents/FAPA_Annual_Report_2014.pdf/

and many others.[392] [393] [394] [395] [396] Among those that are heavily focused on Africa small businesses are those such as the Africa Agriculture Fund (AAF), raising $US30 million at first close on its Small-Medium Enterprises sub-vehicle, and then $US36 million in its second round.[397] [398] Others in the SME space are the following: AfricInvest; the various Aureos-named funds such as Aureos Africa Health Fund and Aureos

---

[392] See *Home* or *About Us* webpages for the funds listed: http://www.heliosinvestment.com/, https://www.carlyle.com/about-carlyle, http://www.ecpinvestments.com/, http://www.dpi-llp.com/, and http://blackrhinogroup.com/

[393] Africa Assets Data Base. (2016). Home Page. http://www.africa-assets.com/data.

[394] Delevingne, L. *Private Investors Pile into Africa.* (2015). NetNet. *CNBC.* Retrieved July 12, 2016 from http://www.cnbc.com/2015/03/17/private-equity-investors-pile-into-africa.html

[395] Southern Africa Venture Capital and Private Equity Association (SAVCA). (2015). *Africa Private Equity Confidence Survey.* Deloitte. http://www2.deloitte.com/content/dam/Deloitte/na/Documents/finance/na_za_private_equity_confidence_survey_may2015.pdf

[396] *African Private Equity and Venture Capital Association.* (2016). Home Page. ACVA. Retrieved August 4, 2016 from http://www.avca-africa.org/

[397] *The Africa Fund.* (2016). About Us. What Is TAF. The Africa Fund. Retrieved November 12, 2012 and also on August 4, 2016 from http://www.aaftaf.org/en/about-us/

Welcome to The AAF's Technical Assistance Facility. (2016). Phatsia Fund Managers. Retrieved August 4, 2016 from http://www.aaftaf.org/en/

[398] Sanders, Ambassador R. R. It's the Economics: Refocusing & Reframing Africa, Part One. (2012, November 12). [Blog post]. Huffington Post. Retrieved May 2016 from http://www.huffingtonpost.com/amb-robin-renee-sanders/its-the-economics-africa_b_2084087.html

Capital's West Africa Fund; the UK Government's CDC Group; Norfund's various funds; IFHA Fund; 4Di Capital; Africa Media Ventures Fund; Annona Sustainable Impact Fund; Jacana Partners; TBL Mirror Fund; and the Mara Launch Uganda Fund.[399] Some of these funds are also listed on the VC4 Africa (Venture Capital 4 Africa) website (www.vc4a.com).[400]

The interest in the region by venture capital funds and private equity firms concentered around the same time as large private corporations operating in Africa

399 The paragraph citations for either the *Home* or *About US* webpages for companies and institutions are listed below in order of appearance in the paragraph. Many were also cited in my 2012 comprehensive HuffPost and blog articles on the growth of venture capital and private equity funds in Africa:

http://blogitrrs.blogspot.com/2012/11/its-economics-refocusing-reframing.html, http://www.africinvest.com/the-firm/, http://www.abraaj.com/news-and-insight/news/aureos-africa-fund-completes-10m-investment-in-leading-ghanaian-bank/, http://www.cdcgroup.com/Who-we-are/Key-Facts/, http://www.norfund.no/sme-funds/category316.html, http://www.ifhafund.com/,

http://www.4dicapital.com/, http://www.amvf.nl/, http://www.kit.nl/sed/project/annona-sustainable-investment-fund/, http://agtech.partneringforinnovation.org/community/funding/blog/2014/04/04/jacana-partners-funding, http://www.tblmirrorfund.com/, and http://www.mara-foundation.org/

400 *Connecting Innovators with Capital: Meet 40 Investor from the VC4Africa Investor Network*. (2013). Venture Capital for Africa (VC4Africa). Retrieved May 13, 2016 from https://vc4a.com/blog/2013/03/14/connecting-innovators-with-capital-meet-40-investors-from-the-vc4africa-investor-network/

pivoted toward SMEs. Large private companies began to view Africa's small businesses as a good sector to invest their CSR dollars and to help with the region's sustainability. On the US end, companies like Chevron and Exxon come to mind as I worked with both of them in the region as they turned their CSR focus to supporting more SME and entrepreneurial training. In addition, many African firms and banks also began to do the same such as the Pan-Africa Ecobank, which today is in 36 African countries and has $US 1.2 billion in financing available for SMEs.[401] [402]

What we see today is a singular effort in the SME sector by all these investment players, and their role and support is just as important as any government, national or foreign. In many cases, their investment dollars in the sector match or, in many cases, surpass African governments' investment dollars in their small businesses.

---

[401] CSR was already defined in Chapter 5.

[402] The 1.2 billion figure is based on the comments by head of Ecobank-Ghana SME Scale Enterprises, Abdulai Abdul-Rahman, during the September 2016 US-Africa AGOA Ministerial which I attended as part of the United States Trade Representative's Trade Advisory Committee on Africa.

Meanwhile, what is important about this dovetailing of venture capital, private equity, and private sector CSR funding for entrepreneurs are that several African governments such as Botswana, Cape Verde, Congo-Brazzaville, Cote d'Ivoire, Ghana, Ethiopia, Kenya, Mozambique, Nigeria, Rwanda, Senegal, South Africa, Tanzania, and Uganda also *began* to value their SME sectors during this shift-change period (2008-2009).

Today SMEs have become the "sector of choice" for many more (certainly not all) African national governments as they have recognized and appreciated their value-added to GDP, trade, sales and jobs.[403]

Don't Forget Local-level African Governments and Administrations

One other supporter of the SME sector I would like to highlight a bit more is the creative role that some African local, municipal, and village governments are playing in assisting their local entrepreneurs. Many

[403] Mali had a coup attempt, which has been followed by subsequent 2012-2016 internal conflicts and terrorist attacks, and as of 2016 still had a UN peacekeeping force in-county to combat extremists given the fragile security environment.

of these sub-sovereign administrations in nations like Benin, Botswana, Cape Verde, Ghana, Kenya, Mozambique, Namibia, Nigeria, Rwanda, Senegal, South Africa, Tanzania, and Uganda (even if some of them are facing tough economic times), are trying to help, but of course, there are still many countries where this is not the case. Again, those that are not supporting SMEs and can need to step up and do better.

Some sub-sovereign administrations are using new, atypical approaches to local development projects by better connecting planning needs with training for their entrepreneurs in specific vocational areas linked to the needs of the local community – including using budgetary resources symbiotically with resources from donor partners. For example, in Nigeria's Kaduna State (unfortunately the state faced problematic ethnic and religious tensions at end of 2016 and into early 2017), Governor Mallam Ahmed Nasir el-Rufai has begun to use this approach – working with funding partners, such as the World Bank, to help train entrepreneurs and vocational specialists in key development sectors needed in the state such as housing.[404] [405] [406] One program I am familiar with is his early efforts to address Kaduna's affordable housing deficit using the model described above, providing skills training to entrepreneurs in the sector (e.g. carpentry, masonry, painting, construction, etc.), so they can help reduce the state's housing deficit, which is anecdotally estimated at somewhere between 5 and 6 million.[407] Overall, Nigeria has an overall 17 million+ housing shortfall, and many African countries suffer from

---

[404] Link to best bio found on el-Rufai: https://en.wikipedia.org/wiki/Nasir_Ahmad_el-Rufai.

[405] I met Governor el-Rufai following his term as FCT Minister, and have respect for his views. He participated in a program to discuss the Nigerian 2011 elections that I co-chaired as Africare's International Affairs Advisor, along with the Atlantic Council. Atlantic Council is a conservative think tank, based in Washington, D.C. In addition to holding timely events of key issues in Africa and around the world, it also publishes a monthly online newsletter and can be found at http://www.atlanticcouncil.org/. Africare is one of the oldest African American led NGOs operating in Africa and was founded in the 1960s by two African American ex-Peace Corps Volunteers, C. Payne Lucas and Dr. Joseph Kennedy, and can be found at https://www.africare.org/who-we-are/

[406]

[407] Marshall, I. & Onyekachi, O. *Funding Housing Deficit in Nigeria: A Review of the Efforts and The Way Forward. 2014.* (2014, December). International Journal of Business and Social Science. Vol 5:13. Center for Promoting Ideas: USA. Retrieved July 9, 2016 from http://ijbssnet.com/journals/Vol_5_No_13_December_2014/22.pdf

Sani, K. S., & Gbadegesin, J. T. (2015). *A Study of Private Rental Housing Market in Kaduna Metropolis, Nigeria.* Journal of Resources Development and Management, 11.

similar housing challenges, which is why the sector is noted on the TEL. (NB: FEEEDS has participated in Nigeria's housing stakeholder committee meetings and has been working in the sector since 2012.)[408]

There are other good examples of sub-sovereign administrations in places like Kenya and Rwanda where municipal, county or local area governments are supporting efforts to train and support their entrepreneurs. In Kenya's Nakuru County, Deputy Governor Joseph Ruto and County Executive of Lands, Physical Planning, and Housing Rachel Maina told me during our 2015 UN Sustainable Development Goals Africa panel how their county and municipal governments have joined forces to support SME skills training in the areas of housing and planning.[409] In

---

[408] Figure also used by former Nigerian Finance Minister, Ngozi Okonjo-Iweala, at session in New York in 2014 attended by Ambassador Sanders at the Harvard Club hosted by Kuramo Capital Management. See *Kuramo Capital.* (2016). Retrieved June 16, 2016 from https://kuramocapital.com/

Anecdotal estimates in 2016 are that Nigeria's housing deficit has reached 20 million.

[409] Kenyan Revenue Authority. (2015, September, 2). iTax System Is Now Easier Than Ever. Retrieved June 23, 2016 from http://www.nakuru.go.ke/2015/09/02/deputy-governor-ruto-welcomes-itax-support-centre-to-nakuru-county/

Nakuru County. (n.d.) About Us. Retrieved June 24, 2016 from http://www.

addition, they help their local small businesses take better advantage of the Kenyan Government's overall effort to provide technology-based tools that assist SMEs through the creation of such web apps as the *iTax system.*[410] The *iTax system* is a government one-stop shop for a variety of services, helping to ease some of the financial management challenges, particularly paying the right amount of business tax transparently that SMEs, as well as the local population writ large, might face. (For me Ghana, Kenya, Rwanda, Tanzania, Senegal, and South Africa lead the way in their SME and entrepreneurial programs.)[411]

Before leaving the discussion about doubling down, it is important to give credit to local and international NGOs that supported SMEs and entrepreneurs in the

---

nakuru.go.ke/about/

Africa Economy: Kenya's County Enhances Economic Relations with Chinese Investors. (2015, August 21). China.org.cn. Retrieved June 24, 2016 from http://china.org.cn/world/Off_the_Wire/2015-08/21/content_36369519.htm

Direct biography on Joseph Ruto & Rachel Mania could not be found, but Ruto is referenced in the two links above.

[410] The *iTax* system in Kenya allows business and individuals to research and pay the taxes owed. This has helped alleviate some of the paperwork burden on SMEs in the country to be compliant as a registered SME. http://www.kra.go.ke/

[411] Ibid.

early years when neither interest nor funding for them were not as prevalent as they are today. Organizations like Startup Africa (works in the East Africa Region and the US), ORT-South Africa, Development Workshop-Angola, and *Kickstart* in the East Africa all are good examples.[412] Others like Operation Hope (OH), headquartered in the US, with offices in South Africa, supports entrepreneurship and economic empowerment through its *Business in a Box* and *Banking on Our Future* programs.[413] [414]

On the social enterprise end, *Nike Okundaye's Arts and Cultural Centers* fosters, teaches, trains, and supports female entrepreneurs in the arts as well as helps them sell their creations from ceramics to furniture to wearable art made via traditional methods.[415] Then there is Nigeria's Foundation for Skills Development (FSD), which since 2003 provides SME and vocational

---

412 See Home or About Us web pages for footnotes 403-405: http://www.ortsa.org.za/, http://startupafrica.org/conference/, http://www.dw.angonet.org/, and http://kickstart.org/about-us/

413 https://www.operationhope.org/

414 https://www.operationhope.org/banking-on-our-future-south-africa

415 *Nike Centre for Arts and Culture.* (n.d.). *Nike Art.com.* Retrieved August 20, 2016 from http://www.nikeart.com/

training to both young and older adults.[416] FSD also trains individual who were formerly displaced by the extremist group Boko Haram (some from the Chibok area where 270 young girls were abducted in 2014), as well as those who may not want to be a business proprietor but still want vocational in-demand skills (mechanic, computer repair, brick layer, etc.) in order to earn a living.[417]

It is clear that the SME space will continue to grow, and more support will be needed for the sector. That support can be in many forms (other than financial) and be as simple as allowing SMEs and entrepreneurs just to be. . .grow. . .and thrive. The space – *to be, to grow, to thrive* – is ever so important for the Africa female entrepreneur.

---

[416] Foundation for Skills Development Nigeria (FSD), a prominent NGO and social enterprise group, provides a variety of training skills for SMEs and those interested in vocational training. FSD is headquartered in Lagos, Nigeria, but does programming throughout the country. See: http://www.foundationforskillsdevelopment.com/about-index/

[417] In April 2014 240-270 (figures have ranged) girls were abducted from their school in the Northern State of Borno, Nigeria. The village was decimated and many who lived there relocated to other areas of the country. Some participated in various training programs for internally displaced person and FSD has trained some of these.

Of the many challenges that African SME female nationals on the Continent, sometimes face is their mere existence in traditional cultural spaces that can, more than not, be an additional challenge for them to work around or overcome. Diaspora women also have challenges, but for those that work on the Continent there are added hurdles. Therefore, special attention needs to be paid to female small businesses operating in the region. African women are known as the *workers and backbone* of the Continent. This comes with – in many cases – little to no recognition, extremely poor wages or none at all, and struggles to feed their families, on top of many living in fragile security areas. I have found this personally to be true in *practice, purpose, and policy* – meaning that women need to be better respected, protected, supported, and more tools (especially in financing) need to be created to help them in business.

Given that African women on the Continent represent just over 50 percent of the region's overall population, it is important to take a closer look at their current circumstances in the small business sector. There are some good news stories, but challenges do remain.

Since the AU declared 2010-2020 the *Decade of the African Woman,* let's take a look at what women small businesses are doing (the good news stories), as well as what is being done (and not being done) on the policy front to ensure that female SMEs move ahead just as fast and substantially as male-owned and operated small businesses in the region.[418] [419]

---

[418] *Population-Female (Percent of Total) In Sub-Saharan Africa.* (2016). TradingEconomics. Retrieved July 9, 2016 from http://www.tradingeconomics.com/sub-saharan-africa/population-female-percent-of-total-wb-data.html

[419] Ernst & Young. (2014). *Women of Africa – A Powerful Untapped Economic Force for the Continent.* Retrieved July 10, 2016 from http://www.ey.com/Publication/vwLUAssets/Women_of_Africa/$FILE/Women%20of%20Africa%20final.pdf

Chapter Seven:
It's the Time...It Is the Decade of the African Woman!

Given that females represent slightly over half (50.1% to %50.2%) of Africa's burgeoning population, women-owned and operated small businesses in the region need to grow much more in this all-important AU *Decade of the African Woman* (2010-2020).[420] [421] [422]

In 2010, the AU announced a 10-year plan to "address gender equality across all sectors and walks of life for women and girls," which includes helping female small business owners and entrepreneurs.[423] In 2013, the AU further added its emphasis on women under its *Agenda 2063* program, a 50-year strategic development plan for

[420] *Population-Female (% of total) in Sub-Saharan Africa.* (2014). Trading Economics. Retrieved August 17, 2017, from http://www.tradingeconomics.com/sub-saharan-africa/population-female-percent-of-total-wb-data.html

[421] AU is explained in detail in Chapter 1.

[422] The period of 2010-2020 is described as the "Decade of the African Woman." See: http://pages.au.int/carmma/documents/african-womens-decade

The Africa Women Development and Communication Network (FEMNET). (2016, February, 19). *African Women's Decade 2010–2020.* Campaigns. Women's Rights. Retrieved July 9, 2016 from http://femnet.co/2016/02/19/african-womens-decade-2010-2020/

[423] Ibid.

the Continent, which includes an additional focus on gender parity and equality.[424] So what needs to be done to achieve this for African female small businesses? I would put financing and credit at the top of the list, along with the cultural space to thrive. Although these are big issues for the entire Africa SME community, they are especially more acute for female business owners, startups and entrepreneurs.

According to the World Bank, only about a third of formal SMEs worldwide are run by women, and about 70 percent of those are "underserved," by all global and local financial institutions.[425] This represents a gap in the financing need for female SMEs of about $US285 billion.[426] As early as 2011 and 2013, the IFC began to highlight how critical the worldwide finance and credit

[424] African Union. (n.d.). *African Union Agenda 2063.* Retrieved May 11, 2016 from http://agenda2063.au.int/en/about

[425] World Bank. (2015). *Financing Women Entrepreneurs in Ethiopia.* News. Retrieved May 13, 2016 from http://www.worldbank.org/en/news/feature/2015/11/16/financing-women-entrepreneurs-in-ethiopia

[426] Ibid.

gaps were for female SMEs and entrepreneurs.[427] [428] Hopefully venture capitalists are paying attention to this investment opportunity as women businesses, historically, are known to have positive repayment track records. The Copenhagen Business School, as cited in a *TradeMark East Africa* report, said that for "each $US1.00 spent on improving women's access to economic opportunity returns $US7.00 worth of impact."[429] (I mentioned earlier my own experience in

---

[427] World Bank Group. (2014). *Women-Owned SMEs: A Business Opportunity for Financial Institutions, International Finance Corporation, McKinsey & Company Report*. p. 11.

[428] International Finance Corporation. (2013). *Closing the Credit Gap for Formal and Informal, Micro, Small and Medium Enterprises*. IFC Advisory Services. Access to Finance. Retrieved August 17, 2016 from http://www.ifc.org/wps/wcm/connect/4d6e6400416896c09494b79e78015671/Closing+the+Credit+Gap+Report-FinalLatest.pdf?MOD=AJPERES

International Finance Corporation. (2011, October). Strengthening Access to Finance for Women-Owned SMEs in Developing Countries. Retrieved August 17, 2016 from http://www.ifc.org/wps/wcm/connect/a4774a004a3f66539f0f9f8969adcc27/G20_Women_Report.pdf?MOD=AJPERES

[429] The original report by the Copenhagen Business School could not be found. Therefore, this reference is from a 2015 blog article by *TradeMark East Africa*, which references the business school's report.

See: Asiimwe, A. (2015, November 30). Investing in women's ability to do business makes sense. *Trademark East Africa*. Retrieved May 15, 2016 from https://www.trademarkea.com/blog/investing-in-womens-ability-to-do-business-makes-sense

TradeMark East Africa is a regional program focused on assisting and training East African women traders to be more knowledgeable as well as help them to better access opportunities within the East African Community (EAC), which is one of the 5 regional economic communities

Congo with Congolese women businesses having good repayment records.)

Some financing programs for female SMEs do exist, but they are not enough, and certainly nowhere close to the need. A program example is the *Women's Entrepreneurship Development Project* (WEDP), a $US50 million global lending facility solely focused on women small businesses. WEDP falls under the World Bank's International Development Association (IDA) and seeks to address the financing gap, but $US50 million only puts a small dent in need.[430] [431] IFC, AfDB, AU, and Africa Capacity Building Foundation (ACBF) are all stepping up their efforts to assist Africa's female SMEs and entrepreneurs in both financing and training.[432] However, more needs to be

(RECs) in SSAfrica. The RECs organizations were discussed in Chapter 5. See: https://www.trademarkea.com/

430 World Bank. (2015, November 16). *Financing Women Entrepreneurs in Ethiopia.* Retrieved May 13, 2016 from http://www.worldbank.org/en/news/feature/2015/11/16/financing-women-entrepreneurs-in-ethiopia

431 World Bank/IRBD-IDA. (2016). *Women Entrepreneurship Development Project.* Project & Operation. Overview. Retrieved July 10, 2016 from http://www.worldbank.org/projects/P122764/women-entrepreneurship-development-project?lang=en

432 African Union. (2015, December 12). *African Union Commission Coaches SME Women.* Retrieved March 10, 2016 from http://www.au.int/en/

done by all players given how great the financing gap is.

The fact that SME female businesses worldwide, particularly Africa female businesses, are underserved by financial institutions (and I would add also by donor and African governments) is not surprising when one takes into account that in SSAfrica women in senior business or political positions are not well represented. For instance, African women represent only 5 percent of the private sector and 29 percent of its managers (consider what this means for the banking sector), hold only 22 percent of cabinet positions, and 24 percent of African parliamentary seats, although strides have

---

pressreleases/19485/african-union-commission-coaches-sme-women-trade-fair-and-agro-value-chain

African Development Bank. (2016). *African Women in Business Initiative.* Retrieved March 10, 2016 from http://www.afdb.org/en/topics-and-sectors/initiatives-partnerships/african-women-in-business-initiative/

Investment Climate Facility for Africa. (2014, April 8). North African Women and SMEs: An Opportunity Hiding in Plain View. News. Retrieved March 10, 2016 from http://www.icfafrica.org/news/north-african-women-and-smes-an-opportunity-hiding-in-plain-view

Africa Capacity Building Fund. (n.d.) Africa Capacity Report 2015: Overview. Retrieved March 10, 2016 from http://www.acbf-pact.org/sites/default/files/ACR%202015%20Overview.pdf

been made to increase female representation in the latter two – one can take a look at McKinsey and Company's 2016 *Women Matter Report* on these stats that highlights the full details of where the gaps are for African women.[433] How these low percentages, on the number of African women in the private sector and in senior management positions, translate to me, is that in practice it is unlikely (but not impossible) that a female entrepreneur will be seated across the table from a female banker, manager or executive when they seek a loan or credit for their business. That is a tough reality when you think about and can be intimidating to some female business women starting out.

So think also about this: With the current number of African women representing just over 50 percent of SSAfrica's population; the growing number of young girls that are part of the African youth bulge; and the fact that by 2020, some 600 million jobs will be needed on the Continent of which females will represent the

[433] Moodley, J., Holt, T., Leke, A., & Desvaux, G. *Women Matter. Africa.* (2016, August). McKinsey & Company. Retrieved August 18, 2016 from http://www.mckinsey.com/global-themes/women-matter/women-matter-africa

biggest part of that demand at all levels, there clearly needs to be more assistance, training and financing for Africa female SMEs as well as more female bankers, managers and executives.[434] [435] [436]

What then might be some of the sectors where women businesses can grow, where young girls coming up can be encouraged and trained, and where financing can be directed to help them?

First of all, to be clear, I would never discourage any woman, or young girl, in any way from anywhere, from entering any SME sector she chooses or is passionate about or that helps improve her quality of life of that of her family. But I do believe there are niche opportunities and/or innovative approaches

---

434 UN Women. (n.d.). *Africa – Where We Are*. Retrieved July 10, 2016 from http://www.unwomen.org/en/where-we-are/africa

435 United Nations Industrial Development Organization (UNIDO). (2000). *Annual Report 1999*. Vienna: United Nations. United Nations Industrial Development Organization (UNIDO). (2015). *Annual Report 2014*. Vienna: United Nations.

436 Abor, J., & Quarterly, P. (2010). *Issues in SME Development in Ghana and South Africa*. International Research Journal of Finance and Economics. Euro Publishing (39), 218-226. Retrieved May 2, 2016 from http://www.smmeresearch.co.za/SMME%20Research%20General/Journal%20Articles/Issues%20in%20SME%20development%20in%20Ghana%20and%20SA.pdf

to sectors not traditionally thought of for women, presenting unique advantages for the Africa female small business. The business doesn't have to be anything complex to be unique, although complex is also good, but no idea should be shied away from by women or young girls in pursuit of their entrepreneurial goals.

Africa female SMEs should be involved in every possible sector from fashion to beauty; small manufacturing to food processing; construction to services (e.g., tourism); and any other *STEM, STEAM* and *STREAM* opportunities they wish (NB: STEM is science, technology, engineering, and mathematics; the two newer terms are STEAM and STREAM, which include the words *activism* and *reading and activism*, hence the "A's" and the "R".) However, I would like to encourage female entrepreneurs to *think niche*, as an additional way to go.

Take for example in Butare, Rwanda, the *Inzozi Nziza* (in the country's Kinyarwanda language) or *Sweet Dreams* in English, a social enterprise women-owned and operated ice cream shop.[437] [438] It is one of my favorite business stories not only because it's a success and it's about women, but mostly because ice cream has turned out to be a niche area in Rwanda. The women who work at Inzozi Nziza manage the shop, make the ice cream, learn skills, and have stable incomes. It is the kind of niche entrepreneurial business for women that I am talking about when I highlighted my three "I's" in Chapter 2 (*innovative, imaginative, and insta-impact*). Prior to the arrival of Inzozi Nziza *or Sweet Dreams,* home-made ice cream or eating ice cream (especially cones) was not a well-known indulgence in Butare.[439] Walking down the

[437] There are lots of definitions of what a social enterprise is, but the one I like and that fits best with the groups I have worked with and that underscores the business elements of an entity like Sweet Dreams is by the Social Enterprise Coalition of the UK. They define it as follows: "Social enterprises are businesses that are changing the world for the better. Social enterprises trade to tackle social problems, improve communities, people's life chances, or the environment. They make their money from selling goods and services in the open market, but they reinvest their profits back into the business or the local community." See: Social Enterprise UK. (n.d.). *About Social Enterprise.* Retrieved July 10, 2016 from http://www.socialenterprise.org.uk/about/about-social-enterprise

[438] *How Rwanda's Only Ice Cream Shop Challenges Cultural Taboos.* (2014, April 10). National Public Radio NPR Retrieved March 21, 2016 from http://www.npr.org/sections/parallels/2014/04/10/301414587/how-rwandas-only-ice-cream-shop-challenges-cultural-taboos

[439] Ibid.

street eating ice cream or licking an ice cream cone also was not something initially culturally acceptable to do. The idea for the project was introduced by Odile Gakire Katese.[440] Katese met Alexis Miesen and Jennie Dundas, co-founders of Blue Marble Ice Cream in Brooklyn, New York, and formed a partnership to open the shop in Butare in 2010.[441] Since then, the Butare business has become a huge success and has made eating and making ice cream a community tradition. Similarly, and just starting out is *Nelwa's Gelato,* located in Tanzania's capital Dar es Salaam, owned by Mercy Kitomari that is a niche homemade ice cream business in the city expanding its customer base,

---

[440] *Sweet Dreams - Rwanda Women Ice Cream Business.* (2014, April 26). *The Guardian.* Retrieved March 21, 2016 from http://www.theguardian.com/global-development/2014/apr/26/rwanda-women-ice-cream-business-sweet-dreams

Fallon, A. (2014, April 26). Sweet Dreams: *Rwanda Women Whip Up Popular Ice Cream Business. The Guardian.* Retrieved March 21, 2016 from http://www.theguardian.com/global-development/2014/apr/26/rwanda-women-ice-cream-business-sweet-dreams

[441] The owners of Blue Marble Ice Cream, Alexis Miesen and Jennie Dundas held shares in Sweet Dreams with the cooperative staff for 18 months. Once the group of Rwandan women easily proved their skills, talent, organization and business credentials Miesen and Dundas transferred their shares to the women. The cooperative is reportedly 60-women strong at the time of this writing. See: *Blue Marble Ice Cream.* Home Page. Retrieved May 3, 2016 from http://www.bluemarbleicecream.com/

creating its own supply chain, and providing training to other women.[442]

Again. . .women small businesses, like Inzozi Nziza and Nelwa's Gelato, which are--*a new social enterprise, or cooperative business, in a niche sector, can be successful, sustainable, and able to generate-income, just as much as a business in a traditional area.* In addition, many of the women who work in the Inzozi Nziza shop also participate in a drum and dance group connected to the business. These activities may not be called marketing, but that is exactly what they are. If you have not seen the film *Sweet Dreams* about Inzozi Nziza, do so!

Africa SME Women – What & How They Are Doing

In looking at other niche female SMEs or new spins on traditional businesses, another favorite of mine is *XChem Chemicals PTY* in South Africa, a woman-owned SME which exports its sealants, adhesives and detergents to other places in Africa. It is also developing

---

442 *Nelwa's Gelato.* (n.d.). Nelwa's Gelato. Facebook. Retrieved November 28, 2016 from https://www.facebook.com/NelwasGelato/

environmentally-friendly versions of its products and is the brainchild of the owner and founder Angela Pitsi.[443] Others niche businesses include cooperative *Organic Farms Group* that focuses on self-employment opportunities to empower women, as well as men, in organic farming.[444] African women are the main farmers on the Continent, but not necessarily in organic farming. Organic Farms addresses this, but the niche spin is that it is helping to *repurpose skills* for women who have lost their manufacturing jobs, teaching them organic farming which they turn into income for themselves. I tweeted about Organic Farms in early 2016 after I saw an interview of an older woman talking about losing her manufacturing job, as South Africa's economy slows. Organic Farms provided her with a whole new set of skills in addition to a way to have an independent way to earn a living and generate-income.

443 XChem Chemicals (PTY) LTD. (n.d.). Retrieved November 28, 2016 from http://www.xchem.co.za/index.html and http://www.wbs.ac.za/search-results/?q=angela+pitsi

444 *Organic Farms*. (2016). Home Page. Retrieved May 14, 2016 from http://www.organicfarmsgroup.com/

I like what Organic Farms, and others like it, are doing in countries like South Africa where the economic situation has affected the manufacturing sector, impacting women significantly more, since in recent years many factory workers in cities like Johannesburg are female. South African women laid off from their manufacturing jobs have found themselves struggling to find jobs, adding to the country's already staggering 2016 unemployment rate (26.7 percent, a 12-year high); the country's young people are also greatly affected by the economic woes, along with the country's troubled mining sector.[445] Other niche female small businesses that are cropping up in South Africa are women-owned vegan restaurants like *Addis Cape Town* and *Plant* – full service vegetarian, non-dairy commercial restaurants. Restaurant and food services are traditional businesses, but being a vegan business is what is unique as each is the only one in their respective city at the moment.[446]

---

[445] Holodny, E. (2016, May 9). *South Africa's Unemployment Rate Just Surged to a 12-year High. Business Insider.* Retrieved May 25, 2016 from http://www.businessinsider.com/south-africa-unemployment-rate-rises-2016-5

[446] *Addis in Capetown.* (2016). About Us. Retrieved August 20, 2016 from http://www.addisincape.co.za/

To this day, I smile when I think of the very creative mature biochemist Muslim woman from Kaduna, Nigeria, who participated in one of the SME access to finance programs I worked on in 2013 as part of the *BOI-WU-FEEEDS-ADM* training programs.[447] She had developed her own line of natural cosmetics using her science degree. I just loved her because she broke all possible stereotypes that might be out there for mature women. I consider her business niche for several reasons – being located in a conservative community where there were not similar businesses, using her STEM skills to create her own cosmetic line, and having her own small manufacturing setup. She was just great – talented, creative, in the STEM field, and had super business and financial management skills. Since her business was successful and moving in the

---

Plant. (n.d.). Home Page. Retrieved August 20, 2016 from http://www.plantcafe.co.za/

[447] The BOI-WU-FEEEDS-ADM SME programs were initially mentioned in Chapter 4 and will be described in more detail in Chapters 8 which highlights additional good examples of SME businesses and programs. A recap: BOI is Nigeria's Bank of Industry, WU is Western Union, FEEEDS is Sanders' advocacy initiative, and ADM is USAID's Africa Diaspora Marketplace program. The international company Western Union is known for its global money services and partnered with BOI, FEEEDS Advocacy Initiative, and USAID's ADM program to hold Pan-African SME programs in Nigeria.

right direction; she was looking for additional capital to expand at the *BOI-WU-FEEEDS-ADM* sessions.

It is clear that assisting African female entrepreneurs will be one of the keys to the success of the Continent's economic development. As their numbers grow, and their income-earning potential increases, women tend to also use their additional resources to help improve their communities, but equally as important, the lives of their children. Most income-earning women will ensure that their girl children are educated and possibly not succumb to or be forced into a childhood marriage in countries where that is still prevalent.

In addition to the difficult financing issues facing female entrepreneurs, the other big hurdles are helping women in the informal sector transition to the formal sector, and assisting formal female businesses with more access to export buyers and regional trade opportunities (these points also apply to male-owned businesses as well, but are greater issues for women.)

Starting with the informal sector, I have already noted that most of the stats on Africa female entrepreneurship, come from information on the formal sector. But anyone who knows SSAfrica well, particularly at the grassroots level, recognizes that many African women work in the informal sector, and whatever can be done to better capture their information will be important. I included the informal sector in my critical mass group of SMEs needing much more assistance, support, and credit, which also means *affordable* steps to their growth so neither they nor their businesses end up with unsustainable debt. The IFC's 2014 report on SMEs noted that "registered" (formal sector) African female-owned small businesses are roughly 24 percent of SME private companies.[448] [449] We know that the percentage figure

---

[448] World Bank Group. (2014). *Women-Owned SMEs: A Business Opportunity for Financial Institutions, International Finance Corporation, McKinsey & Company Report.* p. 11.

[449] International Finance Corporation. (2013). *Closing the Credit Gap for Formal and Informal, Micro, Small and Medium Enterprises.* IFC Advisory Services. Access to Finance. Retrieved August 17, 2016 from http://www.ifc.org/wps/wcm/connect/4d6e6400416896c09494b79e78015671/Closing+the+Credit+Gap+Report-FinalLatest.pdf?MOD=AJPERES

International Finance Corporation. (2014, February 26). *Expanding Women's Access to Financial Services.* Retrieved August 17, 2016 from http://www.worldbank.org/en/results/2013/04/01/banking-on-women-extending-womens-access-to-financial-services

International Finance Corporation. (2011, October). *Strengthening Access to Finance for Women-Owned SMEs in Developing Countries.* Retrieved August 17, 2016 from http://www.ifc.org/wps/wcm/

on the number of female-owned businesses would move much higher if the informal sector numbers were included in these assessments, on top of being able to capture their contributions to GDP. In 2016, this 24 percent figure might be slightly higher, but even if it is, the problems outlined on access to finance, credit, exporters, better counting the female informal sector, and increasing the number of female-owned small business all remain. Women and young girls must have more of an opportunity to own, be party to a small business cooperative/social enterprise, and qualify more for credit and financing. There will be no substantial dent in job creation needs, unemployment, poverty or economic development on the Continent without tripling the efforts to help Africa's females and exposing young girls more to the opportunities and idea of running their own companies.[450]

On exporting special efforts need to be made for Africa female businesses. At The 2016 World Economic Forum

---

connect/a4774a004a3f66539f0f9f8969adcc27/G20_Women_Report.pdf?MOD=AJPERES

[450] This is a 2014 figure which was the most recent primary source figure that could be found.

(WEF), held in Rwanda's capital Kigali, there were substantial discussions about helping Africa SME women with access to export buyers, internationally as well as within the Africa region. A May 12, 2016, *Allafrica.com* news article on the Kigali WEF session focused on an event organized on the margins of the conference by the International Trade Center (ITC), the Rwandan Government, and the German global delivery service DHL for entrepreneurs and traders.[451] Female-owned businesses, like Rwandan handicraft company Gahaya Links, for example, underscored during the event the difficulty for Africa women small businesses in reaching foreign buyers with their products and services.[452] [453]

As difficult as it is for women to break into exporting, there are success stories. Zena Exotic Fruits – a Senegalese exporting firm co-owned by a woman that

---

[451] DHL is a German global logistics company, and the abbreviation stands for Dalsey, Hillblom and Lynn, which are the surnames of the founders. For more on DHL see: http://www.dhl.com/en.html.

[452] Tumwebaze, P. (2016, May 12.) *Rwanda: SMEs Urged to Embrace E-Commerce.* Interview. *Allafrica.com.* Retrieved June 30, 2016 from http://allafrica.com/stories/201605120051.html

[453] *Gahayalinks Rwanda Handicraft Company.* Home. Retrieved June 19, 2016 from http://gahayalinks.com/

employs nearly 90 percent women – is a good example of the positive return that comes from assisting women to export their products. Zena Exotic Fruits started exporting its array of exotic fruit juices to Europe in 2007 and, in 2013, began exporting to the US as the "first Senegalese business to take advantage of the U.S. Government's AGOA program," the previously mentioned US duty-free preferential trade facility. Zena also now exports to the Middle East and Canada.[454] XChem Chemicals PTY in South Africa, mentioned earlier is a good example of regional exporting as their products are found in Ghana and Zimbabwe. More common are female textiles and clothing export businesses, like one of the first SME women I helped in Nigeria to take advantage of AGOA in to manufacture her own line of clothing called *Patience Please*; Patience was the sole female at my very first U.S. Embassy AGOA event in Lagos in 2008. Today her clothing designs are marketed both in the US and back home in Nigeria, and she has participated in a fashion

[454] Date of Zena's first AGOA entry products by co-owner of Zena Exotic Fruits, Randa Filfil, via email to me Sanders on May 18. 2016. See: http://www.zenaexoticfruits.com/en/about

show at the Smithsonian National Museum of African Art in Washington, D.C., which I attended in 2015. Cosmetic businesses, particularly shea butter not on my TEL, is another export success for Africa females, but women owners on the manufacturing end of the industry tend to be in the minority, although they are the biggest users of the product, and their companies tend to be on the sales end.

Let's also not forget about the cut flower export industry, mostly in East Africa, that is a predominately women-employed industry. There are the (well-known to me) Ugandan women cut flower industry that harks back to the original cooperative groups with some (not all) starting as part of the old donor income-generation model in the early 1990s. Today, the cut flower industry is about a $US40 million export business for Uganda, encompassing an entrepreneurial framework; in 2008-2010, its export value reached upwards to $US60 million.[455]

---

[455] Cunningham, E. *Uganda: Good Labor Practices Bloom in Flower Industry.* (2007, August 23). *Interpress News Agency.* Retrieved August 18, 2015 from http://www.ipsnews.net/2007/08/uganda-good-labour-practices-bloom-in-flower-industry/

I remember one of the early leading Ugandan cut flower women cooperatives in 1998 being a project the NSC team I was part wanted then-President Clinton to visit during his Africa trip (which he did).[456]

Although Kenya, Zimbabwe, Tanzania, and Ethiopia have larger horticulture export industries than Uganda today, the point is this industry is niche for women employees as it is a reliable sector to provide them with stable incomes, that also contributes significantly to a country's GDP's, has future investment and growth potential, and, over the years, has forced the implementation of better country-wide labor practices. What we need to see more of, however, is women-owned horticulture export businesses, particularly because the industry is such a big employer of women. There may be one in the East Africa group of horticulture countries, but I could not find one during the course

International Trade Center. (2016, March 10). *Ugandan Flower Exporters Facing Tough Times*. Retrieved August 18, 2016 from http://www.intracen.org/blog/Ugandan-flower-exporters-facing-tough-times/

[456] Wilson, J. (2004). *The Politics of Truth: Inside the Lies that Led to War and Betrayed My Wife's CIA Identity*. New York, New York: Carroll & Graf. 2004. I mentioned earlier that I was part of the White House NSC team that planned then-President Clinton's firs Africa trip.

of the research for this book. The additional niche opportunity for women in this industry is for them to create employment agencies that train and provide female workers for the lucrative industry.

Where one lives in the region can also present a different set of challenges for the female entrepreneur. Females, as we know, even in the developing world, face different hardships, especially economic. But worldwide women and girls are the most affected by poverty, income disparity, discrimination, conflict, ethnic strife, rape as a weapon of war, human rights abuses, and education and economic disadvantages – all of which usually have a life-long impact. For Africa, these hardships can be even more acute.

However, I have also found that even in conflict and post-conflict zones where women bear the brunt of these devastating issues – projects which generate-income for women, by far, can have one of the greatest impacts on development. One of the best 2016 examples of the *resilience and leadership* of women SMEs in post-conflict or fragile security environments is Somalia where women entrepreneurs have really taken off, providing the commerce in shops and kiosks, running small residential hotels and services, and selling everything from clothes to crafts, food and textiles. The polling data from Somali nationals that you will see in Chapter 11 shows that there is a strong sense, particularly among Somali females and youth, that the country is a good place to start a business, despite it being a post-conflict country.

My personal experience with women entrepreneurs in fragile post-conflict environments comes from the Central African Republic (CAR), which I visited in mid-2015, in the Republic of Congo (talk about earlier), and in the old Sudan (before the country was divided).

In the case of CAR, I was invited to look at UNDP's projects on job creation as a peace-building tool for the previously warring groups of anti-balaka and ex-Seleka that had contributed to the devastating violence, civil war, and continued security challenges in the CAR for more than three years (2012-2015), as a result of the coup by the Seleka in 2012.[457]

By April 2016, there were positive signs in CAR that the main violence was finally over as a result of a fairly decent January 2016 election – moving the country into a fragile post-conflict period. The transfer of power from President Catherine Samba-Panza, who oversaw the transition, to the new President Faustin Touadéra was peaceful and there is optimism, as he starts his tenure. Touadéra has noted that he will be focusing on rebuilding, reconciliation, and job creation – and assisting and supporting entrepreneurial ventures will be an important part of his job creation efforts.

---

[457] The location of the session is intentionally left out as part of the Chatham House rules of the meeting.

Background note: During 2012-2015 the Central Africa Republic experienced a devastating civil war followed by ongoing instability brought on by years of misrule, dire economic and social conditions, and the historic tactic by successive governments to pit ethnic groups against each other. A Muslim militia coalition group called the Seleka led a coup in December 2012, which in turn spurred the anti-balaka, made up of primarily Christian militia, to both counter attack and instigate attacks. Both groups were violent and committed human rights atrocities-- leaving the capital in ruins and segregating the country into Muslim and Christian enclaves. The country maintained a fragile security environment for two years, under UN-peacekeeping troops, with UNDP and other foreign governments assisting, and a transitional president, leading up to a January 2016 successful election.

I asked outgoing President Samba-Panza (a business woman herself) in February 2016, at a private session in the United States, what she thought was the most important thing for CAR's continued stability; she highlighted job creation and entrepreneurial training as top things on her list, noting that these can only come with an enabling environment of peace and political stability.[458]

While I was in CAR in 2015, I spoke with anti-balaka young girls and women, who were small-scale entrepreneurs involved in a range of things from making craft-textiles to basket weaving, garden-farming, and digging water wells. They all talked about how important it was to work for themselves and that they feared *idleness* more than anything else. Idleness in their view was the biggest threat to CAR's fragile peace. It is not by coincidence that the very dynamic and committed UNDP team in CAR was led by Mr.

[458] The January 2016 elections were deemed free and fair by international and local observers, and a new president, Faustin Touadéra, was elected. As of this writing, things remain calm in CAR and Africa watchers following the issues there will be closely monitoring the progress. I testified on CAR issues before the United States Congress House of Representative, Africa and Global Health Subcommittee in June 2014.

Agbénonci, my former PPP partner from the UNDP-U.S. Embassy MERC project in Congo-Brazzaville.[459]

Also during my post-conflict days in the Republic of Congo in 2003-2005, my small Embassy team and I worked with a number of women – young and older – who had been traumatized by the devastating civil war and the nearly 10-year post-conflict period. They were affected by all or a combination of the horrific things I mentioned above (human rights abuses, rape as a weapon of war, conscripted into fighting as combatants, etc.). We helped a number of them start beauty parlors, hair salons, bakeries, juice stores, and clothing design shops (seamstresses) with small stipends and loans. But no matter, the women SMEs and business cooperatives thrived, with all of them paying back or renewing their loans, but of course not really becoming self-sustaining or an investment vehicle as the SMEs model would call for today. There were two types of businesses that were my favorites – the bakeries and

[459] Mr. Agbénonci, while in CAR, as cited earlier in Chapter 2 was UN Resident Coordinator, UNDP Resident Representative, and Deputy Special Representative for the UN Multidimensional Integrated Stabilization Mission in CAR. As of early 2016, he is the Minister of Foreign Affairs and Cooperation for Benin Republic.

the local exotic juice store for a number of reasons. Yes, of course creating a small income was important, but these projects allowed for what I thought of then as a *community of economic purpose*, but today this would be called a social enterprise. For many of the women, the strength and support, particularly in post-conflict Congo, they found in a cooperative provided them with the safety of always being together and gave them confidence. These elements are so important for women in post-conflict environments.[460]

What also came with the community of economic purpose, which I liked a lot, and what I never thought the U.S. Government did enough of before or possibly now, is vocational training. In the case of the exotic juice store – as the women learned how to better pasteurize and refrigerate – they also learned vocational skills such as how to use, clean, and maintain the new industrial juicer; fix equipment; sanitize their bottles; and recycle for the first time

[460] Community of Economic Purpose – Sanders' expression used to describe a variety of innovative economic development solutions done by one or more people.This would be similar to what is called a social enterprise today, but in this case, she was specifically directing this phrase to women coming out of post-conflict environments.

(remember, 2003-2005 was early for *thinking green* in SSAfrica), on top of managing their business and doing financial plans for at least a year. The exotic juice store reminds me a bit of the Rwandan *Sweet Dreams* Ice Cream Shop story today, where a cooperative business: provides vocational training; offers a train-the-trainer component; develops as a niche business for a community; helps women earn a living; and becomes an enjoyable experience for the members.

For the previous female combatants wanting to learn sewing or become seamstresses in Congo, we did similar project of providing them with small loans, stipends and vocational training. Once finished, the women were supplied with sewing machines to be able to work for an existing tailor or setup their own businesses. These loans and stipends were part of a U.S. Government-funded humanitarian assistance program run by the US NGO International Partnership for Human Development, or IPHD. When I went back to Congo in 2015, I traveled to what was the war-torn southeast when I was there as Ambassador with the Minister of Small and Medium Size Enterprises,

Minister Madame Yvonne Adeläide Mougany.[461] We looked at farmlands to start a Songhai farmer-entrepreneur project in the region, which would include women and unemployed youth.

These are just some examples of the good news stories, challenges, and what more needs to be done to assist female SMEs, entrepreneurs, social enterprises, and business cooperatives. It is also paramount that we provide entrepreneurial and vocational training for young girls (8-15-years old) as early as possible; girls in this age group needs to be higher on everyone's agenda – philanthropists, foundations, African and foreign governments and other institutions – as one with which to begin early entrepreneurial training.

In some places in the region, opportunities are improving for young girls. One can follow these changes for girls on *Save the Children's Girls Opportunity Index*, which showed in 2016 that

---

[461] Minister Mougany provides comments in the book's opening scene setter. Bio related info on the Minister can be found at: *EntreCongo*. (2016, July 15). *Yvonne Mougany, And Still the Passion of Cargolight*. Retrieved August 20, 2016 from http://www.entrecongolais.com/adelaide-mougany-la-passionnee-des-produits-eclaircissants

opportunities for girls in Rwanda continue to improve with a current world ranking of 49 out of 144 countries. The US ranks 32; the top four spots on the index went respectively to Sweden, Finland, Norway, and Netherlands.[462] Most of Sub-Saharan Africa did not fare well on the index, with only two countries ranking 100 or above, Kenya (97) and Ghana (100); the entire bottom tier of 20 countries on the list of 144 were in SSAfrican, with Niger logging in at 144th.[463]

Although African governments, the AU, AfDB, ACBF, philanthropists, and the Africa and international private sectors are much more involved today in the Africa SME space than they were at the start of the millennium, which of course is a good thing. Assistance to women and girls, as the stats show, still lag very far behind. So, in reality doubling or tripling down to help African female nationals and their small businesses as well as young girls would simply mean, in many ways, just catching up.

[462] Save the Children. (2016, October 10). *Girls Opportunity Index.* Retrieved October 15, 2016 from https://assets.savethechildren.ch/downloads/index_only_every_last_girl_print_version_inside_pages_3_10_16_3_.pdf

[463] Ibid.

Cannot Say Enough – ICT Power Equals Power for Women

There are also whole sectors that need to have more Africa female representation. I, for one, given my information system and communications (ICT) academic background, have an unabashed bias in wanting to see many more women and girls involved in ICT or (at minimum) becoming more ICT savvy. This could include being web developers, analysts, designers, app-creators, and code writers or at least understanding enough code to be able to have some oversight over their business website and social media presence. There are efforts in places like Uganda (Hive CoLab), Zambia (BongoHub, Ghana (MEST), South Africa (Smart XChange), Kenya (iHub), Botswana, and Nigeria (Co-Creation Hub) and other countries which have in some cases (not all) cyber-training solely to assist women and girls with these ICT skills.[464] There are approximately 90 ICT hubs across Sub-Saharan

---

[464] World Bank Group. (2014, April 30). *Tech Hubs Across Africa Which Will Be Legacy Makers.* [Blog post]. Retrieved May 15, 2016 from

http://blogs.worldbank.org/ic4d/tech-hubs-across-africa-which-will-be-legacy-makers

Africa, with many of them helping women and girls with a range of ICT skills including coding and web development.[465] One of my favorite ICT programs that focuses on elementary school girls in disadvantaged areas is a Ghanaian afterschool girls program that is teaching coding and other ICT skills, an initiative that not only needs to be replicated elsewhere, but also better supported with resources (the Ghana program's limited resources require 10 girls to use one laptop.)[466]

One also sees more and more conferences such as the *SheHives* that I tweeted about throughout 2016, which held several events in various global cities organized by *She.Leads.Africa,* connecting young female entrepreneurs, including in the ICT sector.[467]

The general point about giving Africa female SMEs (particularly those in the region) the space just *to be,*

[465] (2016, September 13). *Global Business.* [Television broadcast, 2p.m.] China Global Television Network.

[466] Ibid.

[467] For information on She.Leads.Africa and its SheHive events see: http://sheleadsafrica.org/, http://sheleadsafrica.org/shehive-new-york/ or http://sheleadsafrica.org/shehive-london/. In addition to SheHive events in New York and London. They have also been held in South Africa and Kenya.

to grow, to thrive, is not just about cultural instances where it may be difficult for women entrepreneurs, but also in some sectors, like ICT, where at times it can be a challenging environment for both young girls to learn ICT skills and for women ICT businesses to enter the sector. Thus, female-focused ICT hubs and other safe spaces for women and girls in the technology field are so important – removing any intimidation or as many challenges as possible. SSAfrica is not an exception on having the ICT sector dominated by males, either in SMEs or big businesses. Most everywhere in the world this is a challenge, including in the United States, Europe and Asia. Male dominance in ICT is changing very slowly, and we have seen good examples within the last 5 years with female tech CEOs, COOs and other executive-level positions such as Facebook's Sheryl Sandberg (who is number one on Forbes list of women leading tech companies).[468] Other ICT female notables include CEOs Susan Wojcicki (YouTube), Virginia "Ginni" Rometty (IBM), Meg Whitman (HP

---

[468] Vinton, K. & Forbes Staff. (2015, May 25). The Most Powerful Women in Tech. *Forbes Tech. Forbes.* Retrieved August 5, 2016 from http://www.forbes.com/sites/katevinton/2015/05/26/the-most-powerful-women-in-tech-2015/#133a1642cab6

CEO), Marissa Mayer (Yahoo!), Safra Catz (Oracle), and Apple's Senior VP Angela Ahrendts.[469] I highlight women's role in tech not only because it is an important sector for women globally because of the contributions they can make, but there is also a historical connection. Remember, Ada Lovelace? It was Lovelace who is credited with foreseeing the "multi-functionality of the modern-day computer" as far back as the mid-1800s, noting that "any piece of content including music, text, pictures, and sound could be translated into digital form and manipulated by machine." And, the seven unsung women – Katherine Johnson, Mary Jackson, Dorothy Vaughan, Kathryn Peddrew, Sue Wilder, Eunice Smith and Barbara Holley – many who were brought to light in the 2017 film *Hidden Figures,* who were mathematicians computing (really, they were human computers) for the US space agency NASA in the 1960s. They demonstrate another extraordinary example of the role women have and can play in any STEM field.[470] Thus, with that history

[469] Ibid.

[470] Henry Ford Innovation Nation. (2016, April 2). [Television broadcast] *Columbia Broadcast System* (*CBS*).

of the role of women in ICT and STEM, it would be great to see more senior executive females in ICT and particularly an Africa female ICTer on the list of top 10 world tech leaders or CEOs – MTN, Safricom?

All in all, this shows that the glass ceiling for women in this field is not close to being *vaporized,* and a lot more women worldwide need to make it into the CEO or senior ranks in ICT. ICT is big on my list for Africa female entrepreneurs to consider and as a sector in which to focus training and opportunities. When I worked with W.TEC-Nigeria in 2013 and 2014, we created a separate ICT training component for the Pan-African women who had attended the BOI-WU-FEEEDS-ADM access to credit SME programs. What we saw in the overall training was a dearth in the ICT skills. The goal with the separate sessions for women was to spark an interest in ICT for those who had not

---

Klein, C. (2015, December 15). 10 Things You Didn't Know About Ada Lovelace. History in the Headlines. Retrieved November 21, 2016 from http://www.history.com/news/10-things-you-may-not-know-about-ada-lovelace

Hidden Figures. How Black Women Did the Math That Put Men on the Moon. 2016, September 25). Author Interviews. *NPR News*. Retrieved January 5, 2017 from http://www.npr.org/2016/09/25/495179824/hidden-figures-how-black-women-did-the-math-that-put-men-on-the-moon

yet embrace all the things the new order can provide, but also to help demonstrate how technology can help their companies or become a business itself.[471] These separate ICT workshops were a direct outgrowth from the successful BOI-WU-FEEEDS-ADM Pan-Africa SME programs, which included the participation and sponsorship of some 10-14 Nigerian Banks. The BOI-WU-FEEEDS-ADM sessions were based on a partnership that included Nigeria's BOI, led at that time by its Managing Director Ms. Evelyn Oputu; Western Union (WU), with the dedicated commitment and involvement of its Regional Vice President for Africa Aida Diarra and Vice President for Global Public

---

[471] *W.TEC Nigeria Africa SME Women's ICT Training Session.* (2014) Final Report. 2014. W-TEC. Lagos, Nigeria. The report can be found on the *FEEEDS'* cloud at: www.bit.ly/W-TEC-FEEEDS-ICT-Female-SMEs. The 2014 TCT training session was funded by Diamond Bank, Plc. More on W.TEC-Nigeria can be found at http://www.w-teconline.org/

Affairs Barbara Span; the FEEEDS Advocacy Initiative; and USAID's ADM and AWEP programs.[472] [473] [474] [475]

Given all of these issues affecting women SMEs--financing, access to credit, insurance, export opportunities, entering male-dominated sectors like ICT, and needing more outreach to female informal businesses that I have mentioned – I would add

---

[472] USAID's ADM or Africa Diaspora Marketplace and AWEP or African Women's Entrepreneurship programs were noted earlier in Chapter 6. Oputu and Span provide comments in the book's scene setter. Links to bios for Ms. Oputu, Ms. Diarra and Ms. Span follow and can be found at links below & on reference page:

Oputu - http://www.bloomberg.com/research/stocks/private/person.asp?personId=207764043&privcapId=20376911

Diarra – http://www.africatopsuccess.com/en/2014/04/22/aida-diarra-western-union-africa-vice-president-the-continent-financier/

Span - https://www.chatham.edu/cwe/networking/thinkbig/2013/span.cfm.

[473] YouTube link with highlights of the 2012 & 2013 BOI-WU-FEEEDS SME event can be found on the FEEEDS Cloud at http://bit.ly/1Ytb3OF

[474] FEEEDS' report on the 2012 2-day BOI-WU event can be found on the FEEEDS Cloud at www.bit.ly/BOI-WU-FEEEDS2012, and Information on the FEEEDS Advocacy Initiative can be found at http://blogitrrs.blogspot.com/p/feeeds.html. And FEEEDS' report on the 2012 2-day BOI-WU event can be found on the FEEEDS Cloud at www.bit.ly/BOI-WU-FEEEDS2012, and Information on the FEEEDS Advocacy Initiative can be found at http://blogitrrs.blogspot.com/p/feeeds.html

[475] W.TEC Nigeria 2013 Final Report on Africa Female SME Special ICT Training Session at BOI-WU-FEEEDS-ADM Event can be found on the FEEEDs' cloud at: bit.ly/W-TEC-ICTSpecialSession and W.TEC-Nigeria-FEEEDS Nigeria Executive Summary for standalone Africa Female 2014 ICT Training Program can be found on cloud at www.bit.ly/W-TEC-FEEEDS-ICT-Female-SMEs

leadership to that list. Organizations like *SME Women South Africa* and *WimBiz Nigeria* specialize in mentoring women entrepreneurs in their country, and Pan-Africa women's groups like *New Faces New Voices* assists female SMEs in a range of areas are all responding to the issue of leadership.[476] [477] [478] *New Voices New Faces* does a great job of helping female entrepreneurs with leadership, mentorship, and networking.[479] Venture Capital for Africa (VC4A) in its 2011 report highlighted a comment by *New Voices New Faces* Executive Director Nomsa Daniels that encompasses a lot of points that are critical to Africa female SME development: "African women and girls represent 52 percent of the Continent's population and are responsible for the majority of its agricultural work

---

[476] *WIMBIZ.* (2016). Home Page. Retrieved August 5, 2016 from http://wimbiz.org/

SME Women. (2016). Women in Business. SME South Retrieved August 18, 2016 from http://www.smesouthafrica.co.za/SME-Women/

[477] *New Faces New Voices.* (n.d.) Home Page. Retrieved August 5, 2016 from http://www.nfnv.org/

[478] White, B. (2011, October 31). *Female Entrepreneurs a Driving Force in African SMEs.* VC4A. Venture Capital for Africa. Retrieved April 2016 from https://vc4a.com/blog/2011/10/31/female-entrepreneurs-a-driving-force-in-african-smes/

[479] Ibid.

and food production, but make less than 10 percent of the region's income and own barely 1 percent of its assets."[480] [481]

Daniels' comments sum up the challenges very well, not just for Africa's women, but emphasize the struggle for women SMEs everywhere. Take a look at the "Story Exchange-1000+ Stories"– where women from all over the world discuss their road to entrepreneurship and business – it really provides the worldwide perspective on the positives and challenges that today's small business women face, particularly in the emerging markets in the developing world.[482]

---

[480] According to a Venture Capital for Africa report, Nomsa Daniels, the Executive Director of New Faces New Voices, an African organization of women in business and finance whose mission is to accelerate the economic empowerment of African women, said this statement at a recent AfDB conference. See: White, B. (2011, October 31). *Female Entrepreneurs a Driving Force in African SMEs*. VC4A. Venture Capital for Africa. Retrieved April 2016 from https://vc4a.com/blog/2011/10/31/female-entrepreneurs-a-driving-force-in-african-smes/

[481] Nomsa Daniels (n.d.). LinkedIn. Retrieved April 2016 from https://za.linkedin.com/in/nomsa-daniels-ba2b6439

[482] *Story Exchange-1000+ Stories*. (n.d.). The Story Exchange. Retrieved April 2016 from http://thestoryexchange.org/1000-stories-women-business/?gclid=COeZta2AvcsCFdcagQodftYLyw

Chapter Eight: Entrepreneurship and New Educational Approaches

I would be remiss if I didn't add *Education, Education, and Education* to the mix of skills development needed for those in the region wanting to be entrepreneurs. This means, though, that there needs to be more innovation and tools in the education field, including basic, higher, tertiary education, and diploma-based training programs, providing new approaches to traditional formats that will help further Africa's next generation of entrepreneurs and SMEs, including their exposure to new business solutions.

On the academic front, there are a number of really good signs and new innovative approaches putting entrepreneurial spins on traditional education formats, along with adding leadership training. These will help build a cadre of next-generation leaders versed in entrepreneurship and skills for small business. One of my favorites innovative educational institutions is the African Leadership Academy (ALA) (I mentioned its Anzisha Entrepreneur Prize in Chapter 6), the brain-child of Fred Swaniker, Chris Bradford and others, which is supported by a number of organizations and individuals, including such leading philanthropists as Myma Belo-Osaige and Hakeem Belo-Osaige.[483] ALA has a number of partnerships with leading tertiary institutions in the United States, the United Kingdom and elsewhere.[484] It was the entrepreneurial efforts of the ALA founders that really put this concept on the map and turned it into a unique educational, training, and leadership platform for African nationals and Africa Diaspora students, along with having a big focus on females. In addition to the general academics, it provides a range of skills development and has an entrepreneurial *21st century* curriculum that better meets the needs of the Continent, including having a big emphasis on Pan-African Cooperation. ALA is a very good example of what the Pan-African innovative and collaborative

[483] African Leadership Academy (n.d.). About Us. Retrieved April 2016 from http://www.africanleadershipacademy.org/about/founders-story/

[484] African Leadership Academy. (n.d.). Our Founding Beliefs. Retrieved May 12, 2016 from http://www.africanleadershipacademy.org/about/our-founding-beliefs/

spirit is all about, underscored by one of ALA's stated mission pillars – the *Power of One*.

There also is Ghana's Asheshi University whose total approach to education is from an entrepreneurial perspective.[485] Many of Asheshi graduates were selected to be part of former President Obama's YALI program which I referred to earlier that began in 2014. The YALI program was created to provide internships for young African nationals at businesses or universities around the United States. There were 500 YALI Fellows in 2014 and 1,000 in 2016.[486] I didn't go to all the previous YALI-connected events in Washington, D.C., in 2014 and 2016, but I did have opportunities to interact with many of them at the U.S. Congress, U.S. Chamber of Commerce, and during a lecture I gave to a segment of the group on the Africa youth bulge at the Institute for International Education (IIE). I was always blown away by the SMEs, NGOs, and social enterprises whose

---

[485] *Ashesi University*. (n.d.). Home Page. Retrieved May 10, 2016 from http://www.ashesi.edu.gh/

[486] United States Department of State. (n.d.). *President's Young African Leaders Initiative*. Retrieved July 11, 2016 from https://yali.state.gov/washington-fellowship/

CEOs were trained at Asheshi.[487] The YALI program is one I would think the Trump Administration should want to keep as part of a longer-term strategy for the United States in its efforts to have a generation of good business partners with which to work and for American companies to engage. Any program that does that is a positive sum game for the US and its economy.

Other examples of new educational platforms are *Edutech*, created by the innovative SME Venture Garden Group, which responds to the critical university *seat-space* issue in many African countries for qualified tertiary students.[488] Millions of talented and qualified students are excluded from tertiary education opportunities because many African

---

[487] International Institute for Education (IIE) is a well-respected programming entity that manages a number of U.S. Government education and cultural programs. I have worked with them while a U.S. diplomat, but also since then as CEO-FEEEDS Advocacy Initiative giving lectures to their International Visitors Leadership Groups as well as special training of legislative staff of the Nigerian National Assembly. See: *International Institute for Education.* (2016). Home Page. Retrieved May 9, 2016 from http://www.iie.org/

[488] I serve on the board of Venture Garden Group (VGG) because it is such a unique approach to addressing the tertiary space issue, it provides transparency in university payments, and it is an innovative ICT company. See: *Venture Garden Group.* (2016). Home Page. Retrieved May 2, 2016 from www.venturegradengroup.com

universities already are overcrowded. Nigeria is an example. Edutech addresses the seat-space issue through its proprietary software created in conjunction with the universities and their accreditation bodies. It also provides for transparency in student registration and school-fee payments. Edutech is one of those new entrepreneurial twists on how to address traditional education needs and challenges. There are numerous examples of new educational approaches with more of an entrepreneurial approach and that have a heavy ICT focus growing daily on the SSAfrica region.

Always, always more needs, and should be done so that the Continent can continue its lock-step efforts toward economic progress. Increasing the number of innovative SMEs, helping female small businesses (especially those in the informal sector), training more young girls and creating new entrepreneurial approaches to traditional educational formats can all help advance development and transformation.

Chapter Nine:
SMEs: Lending Voice to Economic Transparency

In addition to the fundamentals of job creation, spurring the growth of Africa's middle class, and helping to increase the Continent's GDP, there are other benefits that SMEs and entrepreneurs are contributing to encourage positive changes in the region: *lending voice* and *having a voice* on the broader spectrum of socio-economic governance. These important aspects do not get highlighted as often, but for me, they are the other big pluses that come with the growth of Africa SMEs and entrepreneurs. We all know that with growing economic influence come other positives that can impact policy and governance. Entrepreneurs have helped, to some extent, open up the regulatory environment and competition in the technology sector. Their increased demand for mobile phones and platforms has in turn helped expand the choices of mobile phone providers. There are certainly more African-owned or partially-owned mobile providers than there was a decade ago in Sub-Saharan Africa. There are numerous instances of

Africa small businesses using social media not only as tools for their business, but also for voicing their views on business constraints and hurdles, addressing the gap between good governance and development needs, demanding better economic governance at the federal and legislative levels, and also insisting on more economic transparency of government resources in the business sector. Chapter 11 that highlights the data in *@The FEEEDS Index* will show that on aggregate 70-75 percent of all African citizens polled see corruption in government and corruption in business as two of the major issues in their country. Africa's small businesses have voiced their concerns about corruption in business practices as well as what they view as the lack of a level playing field and transparency in offers for African government contracts and procurements.[489] The activism of SMEs has helped move countries forward on improving economic governance, pushing to change legislation and demanding better labor

489 @The FEEEDS Index, powered by Gallup Analytics, is an index published by the FEEDS Advocacy Initiative which focuses on polling data based on views of actual African citizens polled in their country.

practices – the cut flower and shea butter industries are good examples.

Moreover, this also means that if there is a minimum of democracy in a country where SMEs are operating, they can play a role in supporting transparent candidates, fair elections, and positive changes in leadership. South Africa's 2016 municipal elections serve as a good demonstration of this as many of the voters in the two opposition parties which gained ground were young, dynamic South Africans, many small business owners, activists or academics voting their displeasure at the ballot box over corruption in government and in business. Gabon's presidential election in August 2016 reflected similar sentiments on top of concerns about transparency in the election process amidst accusations of voter intimidation.

Governance and Transparency

Clearly governance and transparency remain an overall challenge for the region, although there have been some positive gains on the democracy front since the turn of the millennium, making the region attractive to investors and the foreign private sector, which already has been highlighted. Unfortunately, there has been some backsliding and slippage recently on the democracy front in a few countries that many us thought were on the right path, while in other cases, there has been no movement in the right direction since or just after independence (e.g., Cameroon, Chad, Uganda, and Zimbabwe). Particularly in 2015-2016, the region has faced conflicts (South Sudan, Northern Nigeria), questionable elections (Uganda and Gabon), and constitutional changes (Rwanda, Burundi, Congo-Brazzaville) to allow presidential third terms or reluctant political opposition compromises (DRC) to allow a year extension of power for an incumbent who doesn't wish to depart that have African nationals, and the Diaspora, particularly activists and small businesses, as well as die-hard African activists like myself closely watching.

Although Rwanda's presidential third term appears to be very much a citizen-supported decision, we will need to watch to ensure transparency in the 2017 elections and afterwards. We also need to see what happens with the direction of the democratically-elected leadership in Tanzania as there has been some lack of inclusiveness, while Zambia's close election on August 11, 2016, kept the political environment there initially uneasy, but it seems the country has turned the corner on the hotly contested election. Both of these countries had decent elections respectively in 2014 and 2015.[490] The positive solidifications in democratic processes have happened in countries like Benin, Botswana, Ghana and Namibia, all which have held several successful elections (I served in Namibia as a junior diplomat during its transition to independence from South Africa); Senegal (where I served as chief of the political section at the U.S. Embassy); Nigeria, and Tanzania – all which have had mature elections in recent years exemplifying the concept of free and fair. There are still leaders-for-life in the region (Angola, Cameroon, Chad, etc.), although forced populist changes took place in Burkina Faso, removing its 30-year president, Blaise Compaoré, in October 2014. But then there are twists like the Gambia, which first ushered in an

[490] Congos - refers to the Democratic Republic of the Congo and Republic of Congo.

unexpected peaceful political change with the defeat and initially magnanimous concession from President Yahya Jammeh, who had ruled fairly ruthlessly for 22 years, which swiftly became a regional crisis when Jammeh did a head spinning about-face withdrawing his concession and declaring voter irregularities. On January 20, 2017, Jammeh finally agreed to depart the Gambia following political and military pressure from ECOWAS and the swearing in of President Adama Barrow in Senegal. Barrow's arrival in Gambia on January 26, 2017, to jubilant crowds to begin his mandate, which is seen as a victory for SSAfrican democracy.

Meanwhile, Ghana continued its democratic traditions by holding yet another peaceful election in 2016 which ushered in a new leader (Nana Akufo-Addo), and removed an incumbent further underscoring the sophistication of its voters, many Millennials, wanting to see both political and economic change.

The point here is that regardless of the challenges that exist in a particular country, they have not impeded the growth of a vibrant SME and entrepreneur sector from still emerging. (NB: @ *The FEEEDS Index®* in Chapter 11 will show that nationals in places like the Congos, Chad, Somalia, and Zimbabwe and other unexpected places rated their ability to start a new business very high, at 65 percent or above.)[491]

The Central Africa sub-region, made up of some eight countries, lags behind all other sub-regions as it has less transparent investment opportunities and political and economic freedoms and closed regulatory environments. The region also is conflict-prone, home to some (not all) of the Continent's lowest human index indicators, and some of the higher (not the highest though) income inequality figures. (NB: Chapter 2 discussed in detail income disparities in SSAfrica.)[492] But even with these

---

491 Smith, D. *Power Struggle in Burkina Faso After Blaise Compaoré Resigns as President.* (2014, November 1). *The Guardian.* Retrieved May 2016 from http://www.theguardian.com/world/2014/oct/31/burkina-faso-president-blaise-compaore-ousted-says-army

492 Pasquali, V. (2011, August 22). *Income Inequality and Wealth Distribution by Country.* Project Coordinator Denise Bedell. *Global Finance.* Retrieved July 1, 2016 from https://www.gfmag.com/global-data/economic-data/wealth-distribution-income-inequality

challenges, their SME sectors are doing well, particularly in Congo-Brazzaville which was rated high by its nationals as a good place to start a business in the polling data on *@The FEEEDS Index* that will be discussed in Chapter 11.

I also would be remiss if I did not highlight that security does plague some countries in what I have called the *Sahel Extremism Belt* that runs from Mali, Niger, Chad, Cameroon, Nigeria's northeast, and Cote d'Ivoire, over to Tanzania, Kenya, and Somalia. Security has and will continue to have an impact on business, particularly SMEs in the tourist industry. I have talked about the stark stats on education, energy, food security, housing, and potable water – all things that do need realpolitik analyses and solutions. The challenges, however, neither change nor diminish the overall good news story on Sub-Saharan Africa's SMEs—what they are doing, how they are doing it, and their impact and contribution to the Continent's development, economy, job creation, and middle

---

Earlier retrieved April 14, 2014 from http://www.gfmag.com/tools/global-database/economic-data/11944-wealth-distribution-income-inequality.html#axzz2x0eRLqkL

class – all things giving them voice in economic governance and transparency and adding to political transformation in the region.

A Recap of the Africa SME Contribution – The Economics of It All!

We know that on the GDP front, Africa small businesses are estimated today to contribute more than 33 percent to the region's overall economy on top of the 43 percent contribution to job creation as noted in Chapter 2. However, the goal is to help them get those numbers up even higher.[493] We have seen examples all over the world that show that as the number of SMEs increase, they raise GDP, job creation levels, trade, and sales numbers (the latter does not get highlighted as much) right along with their growth. It is this same group – SMEs – by comparison, which we know drives economies like the U.S., China, India and others.

---

[493] *African Development Bank SME Program Approval Boosting Inclusive Growth in Africa.* (2013, July 22). African Development Bank. (Retrieved March 10, 2016 from http://www.afdb.org/en/news-and-events/article/the-afdb-sme-program-approval-boosting-inclusive-growth-in-africa-12135/

The U. S. SBA (reminder: this is U.S. Small Business Administration) notes that the 28 million SMEs in the US account for 54 percent of all US sales and 55 percent of all US jobs.[494] American SMEs have had this type of impact throughout the economic history of the United States, as well as being the centerpiece of the US middle class. US SMEs and entrepreneurs have also ensured that their voices are heard on key political and economic policy issues; we saw this play out in the US 2016 election as the needs of small businesses and America's middle class were front and center in the campaigning and afterwards.

SSAfrica's SMEs are playing all these same roles today in the region and will likely do so more in the decades ahead. I mentioned that I have a strong emphasis on the phrase "job creation" and less on the word "employment" (as for me the latter conjures up a 9 a.m.to 5 p.m. workday, advancing someone else's wealth). My perspective is the latter will come with the former, but it will be different, as the Africa SME owner will be in control of his or her own destiny. It

[494] United States Small Business Administration. (n.d.). *Small Business Trends Impact*. Retrieved March 9, 2016_from https://www.sba.gov/content/small-business-trends-impact

is this *controlling one's own destiny* that makes the group of Africa Generation-Xers and Millennials so impressive for the depth and range of the creative small businesses they lead or seek to lead, underscoring that they will also have a future impact on economic policy and legislation on top of their direct economic impact.

I talked extensively about how uncertain the information is on the actual number of Africa SMEs there are in the region in Chapters 2 and 3 since no research document for 2015-2016 provided good figures of the current number of registered or unregistered small businesses.[495] If we go as far back as the 2010 IFC Report by Kushnir, Mirmulstein, and Ramalho, SSAfrica only hosted about 13 million registered SMEs.[496] This

---

[495] World Bank Group/IBRD-IDA. (2015, September 1). *Small and Medium Enterprises (SMEs) Finance. Finance Brief.* [Blog post] p. 8 Retrieved July 5, 2016 from http://www.worldbank.org/en/topic/financialsector/brief/smes-finance

Other key figures on SMEs in emerging markets (Asia, Africa, and Latin America) in this same study are: "365-445 million micro, small and medium enterprises (MSMEs) in emerging markets: 25-30 million are formal SMEs; 55-70 million are formal micro enterprises; and, 285-345 million are informal enterprises."

[496] Kushnir, K., Mirmulstein, M.L., & Ramalho, R. (2010). *Micro, Small, and Medium Enterprises Around the World: How Many Are There, And What Affects the Count.* pp. 1-9. World Bank/International Finance Corporation. Retrieved March 5, 2016 from http://www.ifc.org/wps/wcm/connect/9ae1dd80495860d6a482b519583b6d16/MSME-CI-AnalysisNote.

report was six years ago; so, we know this figure is much higher today. As I mentioned, current anecdotal evidence supports a global SSAfrica SME figure of 30-35 million (registered and unregistered), which I use, with caution, as my 2016 benchmark.[497]

But the main point at this juncture is that it is certainly conceivable with 30-35 million Africa SMEs, and as their number continues to increase, the sector could reach the threshold of providing more than 45-50 percent of the region's jobs, sales, trade, and growth over the next several decades – as the sector has done for other countries. This path would be similar to the SME impact in upmarket emerging nations such as (in impact order):

1.) China (the most recent numbers are from 2014), where SMEs contribute 60 percent to GDP, and 80 percent of urban jobs;

---

pdf?MOD=AJPERES

[497] As noted in earlier chapters the figure of 30 million was mentioned by former Nigeria Finance Minister Okonjo-Iweala highlighted in New York in September 2014 when speaking at a McKinsey & Company event on margins of the 2014 session of the United Nations General Assembly.

2.) India (the most recent numbers are from 2015 to 2016), where SMEs add 8-22 percent to GDP, but more significantly contribute nearly a billion jobs, 45 percent to manufacturing, and 40 percent to exports); and

3.) Brazil (The most recent numbers are from 2014), where SMEs contribute 20 percent to GDP, provide 54 percent of jobs, and 43 percent of all wages), although the country current economic challenges have brought these figures lower, SMEs still have played a big role there. [498] [499] [500] [501]

Examples in the West where SMEs have made similar or greater contributions in some of the same areas (GDP, jobs, trade, etc.) are the US (39 percent to GDP),

---

[498] Sham, T., & Pang, I. (2014, September). *China's SME Development.* OCBC Wing Hang Bank Monthly Newsletter. OCBC Wing Hang Bank. Retrieved July 11, 2016 from http://www.ocbcwhhk.com/webpages_cms/files/Investment%20Newsletter/English/Investment%20Newsletter_Sep_e(1).pdf

An earlier 2012 World Trade Organization Report stated then that China SMEs contributed 75 percent to urban employment and 60 percent to GDP. Therefore, the 60 percent figure to GDP appears to be the prevailing view among economists, institutional organizations, and businesses. It stands to reason that by 2014 China SMEs' contribution to urban growth could reach 80 percent. See: Zhang, L., & Xia, W. (n.d.). *Small and Medium-Sized Enterprises into Global Trade Flows: The Case of China.* Chapter 3. World Trade Organization. Retrieved July 11, 2016 from https://www.wto.org/english/res_e/booksp_e/cmark_chap3_e.pdf

[499] Small and Medium Business Development Chamber. (2016, February). *About MSMEs in India.* Empowering SMEs for Global Competitiveness. Retrieved August 6, 2016 from http://www.smechamberofindia.com/about_msmes.aspx

Salunkhe, C. (2016, February 17). Micro and Macro Developments Will Help SMEs Expand. *The Times of India.* Retrieved August 6, 2016 from http://www.smechamberofindia.com/MediaCoverage/timesofindia_feb2016.pdf

[500] Office of Evaluation and Oversight (OVE). Inter-American Development Bank. (2014, October). *A Comparative Analysis of IDB Approaches Supporting SMEs: Assessing Results in the Brazilian Manufacturing Sector.* Retrieved August 5, 2016 from https://publications.iadb.org/bitstream/handle/11319/6683/SME_BRIK_English.pdf?sequence=1

[501] Katura, T.N. (2014, December). *The Role of SMEs in Employment Creation and Economic Growth in Several Countries.* Catholic University of Eastern Africa Lecturer. Vol 2:12. International Journal of Education and Research. Retrieved August 18, 2016 from http://www.ijern.com/journal/2014/December-2014/39.pdf

UK (49.8 percent to GDP, but post-Brexit impact undetermined), Germany (75 percent to GDP), and many of the Nordic countries fall in-between.[502] [503] Africa SMEs could become even more significant for the region in these same areas (GDP, jobs, trade, sales) if their current numbers keep pace or surpass the job creation needs of the region (18 million per year) that I talked about in Chapter 1.[504] Furthermore, when

---

502 *Four Global Experiences to Support SME Development.* (2016). SME Cooperation Forum. Global Alliance of SMEs/Consultative Status with UNIDO. Retrieved August 6, 2016 from http://www.globalsmes.org/news/index.php?func=detail&lan=en&detailid=945&catalog=03

Ward, M., & Rhodes C. *Small Business and the UK Economy.* (2014, December 9). Economic Policy and Statistics. House of Commons. Stand Note: SN/EP 6078. Retrieved August 6, 2016 from http://researchbriefings.files.parliament.uk/documents/SN06078/SN06078.pdf

Department for Business Innovation and Skills Innovation. (2015, October 14). Statistical Release. National Statistics. Government of the United Kingdom/URN15/92. Retrieved August 6, 2016 from https://www.gov.uk/government/uploads/system/uploads/attachment_data/file/467443/bpe_2015_statistical_release.pdf

503 Airaksinen, A., & Luomaranta, H. (Statistics Finland), P. Alajääskö, and A. Roodhuijzen. *Dependent and Independent SMEs And Large Enterprises.* (2015). Site Modified June 29, 2016. Statistics on Small and Medium-Sized Enterprises. Eurostat Statistics Explained. European Union. Retrieved August 6, 2016 from http://ec.europa.eu/eurostat/statistics-explained/index.php/Statistics_on_small_and_medium-sized_enterprises

Kelly, D., Singer, S., Herrington, M., & The Entrepreneurship Research Association (GERA). (2015-2016). *Global Entrepreneurship Monitor 2015-2016 Global Report.* Global Entrepreneurship Monitor. Retrieved August 6, 2016 from http://www.gemconsortium.org/report

504 International Labour Organization. (2015). *Global Employment Trends for Youth 2015: Scaling Up Investment for Descent Job for Youth.* Document, p. 9. Geneva: Switzerland. *ILO.org.* Retrieved July 5, 2016 from http://

economic environments in African countries tighten, and larger Africa companies down-size to achieve better economies of scale, then Africa small businesses also can step into that gap (gladly so!).

To me all of these potential opportunities add to the broader benefits of *Africa Rising*, whereas sometimes for many in the West, and possibly the East, they think the phrase is about business or investment deals for them as opposed to the systemic change on the Continent (although China has a better handle on the intangibles in their relationship with SSAfrica than the U.S., at least for now). Africa Rising is really about a different future for Africa, by Africans, including the Africa Diaspora. All are contributing to the creative ideas we see in the region from Malawi's solar tents for drying fish for market women, to mobile phone

---

www.ilo.org/wcmsp5/groups/public/---dgreports/---dcomm/---publ/documents/publication/wcms_412015.pdf

African Union Youth Division. (n.d.). *Welcome to the Youth Division of African Union Commission*. Department of Human Resources, Science, and Technology. Retrieved July 30, 2016 from http://www.africa-youth.org/

International Monetary Fund. (2015, April). *Sub-Saharan Africa-Navigating Headwinds. Regional Economic Outlook*, p. 36. Retrieved July 24, 2016 from https://www.imf.org/external/pubs/ft/reo/2015/afr/eng/pdf/sreo0415.pdf

charging shoes by a young Kenyan technology guru, to a child's solar-charging school backpack created by an Ivorian entrepreneur.[505] [506] And, who is to say, how the break through experiment by the young South African scientist, Sandile Ngcobo, of the first digital laser at Pretoria's Center for Scientific and Industrial Research (CSIR) will further change the region and the world and be used by SMEs.[507]

As we take a look at other illustrative innovations (or new spins on old ways) in the Africa SME and

---

[505] Chimjeka, R., & Chiwaula, L. (Unima). (2015, October 1). *Unima Invents Solar Fish Dryer.* The University of Malawi. *The Nation.* Retrieved from http://mwnation.com/unima-invents-solar-fish-dryer-equipment/

These dryers assist market women sell dried fish better and provide a more sanitized environment for the process. The dryers are faster than air drying and allow the women to process more fish, and thus have more sales. Also, reported at: Amondo, K. *Solar Fish Dryers.* (2016, August 5). *Africa live newscast.* [Television broadcast, 1 p.m.] China Global Television Network.

[506] *Technology: A Young Kenyan Invents Charger Shoes!* (2014, December 8). Kenya. They Make Africa. Africa Top Success. Retrieved August 6, 2016 from http://www.africatopsuccess.com/en/2014/12/08/technology-a-young-kenyan-invents-charger-shoes/.

[507] Alexander, M. A. *'Disruptive' Technology: Sandile Ngcobo's World-First Digital Laser.* (2014, July 15). Media Club South Africa. Retrieved August 7, 2016 from http://www.mediaclubsouthafrica.com/tech/3932-a-disruptive-technology-sandile-ngcobo-s-world-first-digital-laser#ixzz4Gc2Sahup

South African Scientists Develops the World's First Digital Laser. September 13, 2013. *CSIR Media Release.* Center for Scientific and Industrial Research. Retrieved August 6, 2016 from http://ntwwl.csir.co.za/plsql/ptl0002/PTL0002_PGE157_MEDIA_REL?MEDIA_RELEASE_NO=7525990

entrepreneurial space, you will see and understand just how dynamic the environment is on the Continent today.

Chapter Ten: The Sweet Spots: Success Belongs to Africa and Africa SMEs

This Chapter will be short and sweet – as the point is to further underscore how the greater Africa SME Community is working together for the *right-kind* of business and economic development for the Continent, something I have talked a lot during my diplomatic career and as part of my FEEEDS Advocacy Initiative. But the sweet spot is really the *dynamism* in the Africa SME space from inventions to innovations to investments to the role of other financial institutions, not usually thought of, that are providing additional exposure and opportunities to the region's SMEs--what I am talking about are African stock markets. African stock markets probably are not traditionally the first financial institution that comes to mind as an important partner in the Africa SME space, but they are, and they are playing their role in the sector just as other groups like venture capital and equity firms are playing theirs. Many of Africa's stock markets have special programs and exchanges just for Africa SMEs.

Unique Role of African Stock Markets – Doing Their Part

I didn't include African Stock Markets in the chapter on *new players* because they play a different role, and their support provides a unique platform from which SMEs can raise capital.[508] Therefore, the dynamism in the Africa SME space is not only about the *uniqueness* of the *right-kind* of development services that Africa SMEs are creating, but also about where the *distinctiveness* of additional exposure and international market-learning experience is coming from that can help put SMEs on the path to becoming a bigger business with a larger reach. In addition, this kind of exposure can have the attendant benefit of further helping Africa small businesses enter the middle-class or million-dollar club. African stock markets across the Continent have made a good effort to help the SME sector as special exchanges exist

[508] *Africa Assets.* (2015) Home Page. Retrieved July 12, 2016 from http://www.africa-assets.com/data

Southern Africa Venture Capital and Private Equity Association (SAVCA). (2015, May). *Africa Private Equity Confidence Survey.* Deloitte. Retrieved July 12, 2016 from http://www2.deloitte.com/content/dam/Deloitte/na/Documents/finance/na_za_private_equity_confidence_survey_may2015.pdf

in Botswana (Venture Capital Board); East Africa Stock Market Exchange (based in Rwanda); Ghana (GAX); smaller exchanges in Malawi, Mauritius (DEM), and Tanzania; and the region's three largest exchanges in Johannesburg, South Africa (JSE), in Nairobi, Kenya (NSE), and in Lagos, Nigeria (Nigerian Stock Exchange).[509] [510] [511] [512] The interest by African stock exchanges in SMEs underscores that they too understand and want to capitalize on the growth and

---

[509] Minney, T. (2016, May 5). *Exchanges Give SMEs a Helping Hand. Africa Business Times.* Retrieved July 12, 2016 from http://africanbusinessmagazine.com/african-banker/exchanges-give-smes-helping-hand/

[510] *Stock Exchanges for Small and Medium Enterprises.* (2016, July 13). *Africa Strictly Business.* Retrieved March 10 and July 12, 2016 from http://www.africastrictlybusiness.com/lists/stock-exchanges-small-and-medium-enterprises

[511] East *African Stock Exchange: East African Stock Exchange in The Works to Merge Buoyant. Business.* (2013, July 9). International Business Times. *IBTimes. IBT Media.* Retrieved July 12, 2016 from http://www.ibtimes.com/east-african-stock-exchange-works-merge-buoyant-profitable-markets-1338415

Understanding the East African Stock Markets. (2016, July 3). *AFK Insider.* Retrieved July 12, 2016 from http://afkinsider.com/129044/understanding-east-african-stock-markets/

Stock Exchange of Mauritius. (n.d.). Investor Education. Retrieved December 4, 2016 from http://www.stockexchangeofmauritius.com/faqs-listingon-dem

[512] *Stock Exchanges for Small and Medium Enterprises.* (2016, July 13). *Africa Strictly Business.* Retrieved July 12, 2016 from http://www.africastrictlybusiness.com/lists/stock-exchanges-small-and-medium-enterprises

market potential that they represent. Most African stock markets began looking at SMEs in earnest in 2013, according to *African Business Times*, when several of the exchanges established "specialized trading or growth board" for Africa SMEs.[513] NSE in Nairobi has the *Growth and Enterprise Market Segment*, or GEMS for SMEs, while the Nigerian Stock Exchange has the *Alternative Securities Exchange Market* (AseM), which helps measure SME performance and gives SMEs the opportunity to raise low-cost capital. Earlier than others, the JSE in 2003 (the oldest and largest of SSAfrica's exchanges) launched the *Alternative Public Equity Exchange* (AltTX) strictly focused on small businesses, and also hosted a female SME day at the exchange on International Women's Day 2016 (which I tweeted about then).[514] In March 2016, an over-the-counter

---

[513] Minney, T. *Exchanges Give SMEs a Helping Hand.* (2016, May 5). *Africa Business Times.* Retrieved July 12, 2016 from http://africanbusinessmagazine.com/african-banker/exchanges-give-smes-helping-hand/

[514] Sources for Africa Stock Exchanges mentioned in this paragraph:

NSE in Nairobi, Kenya:

Nairobi Securities Exchange (NSE) Launches the Growth Enterprise Market Segment (GEMS). (2013, January 22). *Press Release.* Nairobi Securities Exchange Limited. Retrieved July 12, 2016 from https://www.nse.co.ke/

(OTC) license was granted to *ZAR-X* in Johannesburg; it will be interesting to see if it begins offering special opportunities for the Africa SME sector.[515] [516] It also is worth mentioning that not many females hold the most senior positions in African stock markets, but there are a few such as Director of the JSE's Capital Markets (Donna Oosthuyse), and the Managing Partner of the East Africa Exchange (Jendayi

---

media-center/press-release.html?download=6259%3Apress-release-launch-of-the-growth-enterprise-market-segment, and also found at www.nse.co.ke

Nigerian Stock Exchange in Lagos, Nigeria:

Alternative Securities Market. (2016) Issuers. Nigerian Stock Exchange. Retrieved July 12, 2016 from http://www.nse.com.ng/Issuers-section/listing-your-company/asem, and also see http://www.nse.com.

JSE in Johannesburg, South Africa:

Johannesburg Stock Exchange: JSE Overview. (2013) History. Retrieved July 12, 2016 from https://www.jse.co.za/about/history-company-overview

Donna Oosthuyse, Director of Capital Markets, Johannesburg Stock Exchange: Interview. South Africa/Economy. (2016, June 15). Oxford Business Group. Retrieved July 12, 2016 from http://www.oxfordbusinessgroup.com/interview/going-strong-obg-talks-donna-oosthuyse-director-capital-markets-johannesburg-stock-exchange-jse

515 *New Rival to JSE On Cards as ZAR X Granted Licence.* (2016, March 31). Africa News Network. Retrieved July 12, 2016 from http://www.ann7.com/new-rival-to-jse-on-cards-as-zar-x-granted-licence/

516 There is also the West Africa Stock Market (usually recognized using the French abbreviation/symbol BVRM), which is located in Abidjan, the capital of Cote d'Ivoire and has eight members. Research did not show that it specially has a board for SMEs, but its members are Benin, Burkina Faso, Guinea Bissau, Cote d'Ivoire, Mali, Niger, Senegal, and Togo. See: *BRVM.* (2009) About Us. BRVM. Retrieved July 12, 2016 from http://www.brvm.org/Accueil/tabid/36/language/en-US/Default.aspx

Frazer).[517] Today there are numerous bi-Continental and global connections which links African nationals, African immigrants, and the Africa Diaspora in some way through family, through culture, through friendship, through self-definition, and now through SME businesses – be they on the Continent, trading and exporting off, vice versa, or using specialized, unique fund raising and investment platforms such as *Homestrings,* which encourages the Africa Diaspora to participate in investment opportunities "back home."[518]

SMEs – The Soft Power of Smart Business-Aiding-Development Ideas

What has really taken off and is part of the sweet spot discussion is the *smart*

---

[517] *Donna Oosthuyse, Director of Capital Markets, Johannesburg Stock Exchange: Interview.* South Africa/Economy. (2016, June 15). Oxford Business Group. Retrieved July 12, 2016 from http://www.oxfordbusinessgroup.com/interview/going-strong-obg-talks-donna-oosthuyse-director-capital-markets-johannesburg-stock-exchange-jse

Jendayi E. Frazer, Ph.D. - CIPI Director and Distinguished Public Service Professor. (n.d.). Center for International Policy and Innovation. Carnegie Mellon University. Retrieved August 17, 2016 from http://www.cmu.edu/cipi/people/frazer-jendayi.html

[518] *Homestrings.* (2016) Home Page. https://www.homestrings.com/

business-aiding-development companies that many Africa SMEs and entrepreneurs have created. They have becoming *a bloc of innovators* who are not only doing good business, but also are fundamentally contributing to the forward movement of the region. I have already shared some of these examples in the earlier chapters where these small businesses have helped to change things and brought new innovative ideas to the fore, but here are a few other examples worth noting as they are illustrative of not only the success of SMEs, but of the smart business-aiding-development solutions they have created. It also is interesting to see that many of them are using the latest technology – drones – to engage. Take for instance small drone usage in Ghana by the SME *Aeroshutter*, a company that began using drones to assist other firms in their advertising and promotions but transformed the business to focus on important development challenges such as providing agricultural land surveys for water resource management and geological analysis for housing construction site surveys.[519] In Rwanda, drones started in August 2016 (tweeted about this in June 2016) to deliver medical supplies to hard-to-reach rural areas as part of a Government of Rwanda PPP with the US company *Zipline*, working with local Rwandan partners and health providers (The Rwandan Government, of course is not an SME, but this shows the creativeness of African government with new development ideas).[520] *DroneAfrica*, of *Will & Brothers* Consulting Company winner of Cameroon's June 2016 *Digital Thursdays (DT's) Competition*, measures pollution levels and maps key resources from land to water (NB: also tweeted about this in June 2016).[521] The company is looking now to

---

[519] Aeroshutter also says on its website, as of March 2016, that it is the first commercial drone operation in Ghana. *Aeroshuttergh.* (2015) Home Page. Retrieved March 5, 2016 from http://www.aeroshuttergh.com/aeroshutter.html

[520] *Zipline.* (n.d.) Zipline. Retrieved August 17, 2016 from http://flyzipline.com/product/

[521] The Will & Bill Consulting Company, of which DroneAfrica is a part, develops innovative technology ideas and usages. Drone Africa promotes the use of drones for business services and civil defence tools such as mapping.

See: *William Elong: Africa's and Cameroon's Promising Entrepreneur.* (2016, June 27). *TechCrunch Africa Growth Hacker.* People/Startups. June 27, 2016. TechCrunch. Retrieved July 12, 2016 from http://techcrunch-africa.com/people/william-elong-africas/

move into small-scale manufacturing (on my TEL list) of a 4-propeller drone called in the industry a *quadcopter*, which flies at 500-meter altitudes loaded with a high-definition camera that would capture land and geological compositions in more detail.[522] [523] [524] And in Kenya, an *octocopter* drone (drone with eight rotors) developed for mapping the country's all-important potato farms was manufactured by a young entrepreneur there producing all the parts through 3-D printing, making the drone inexpensive to create at around $US1000.[525] (Potential of 3-D

Will & Brothers Consulting. (n.d.) Home Page. Will & Brothers. Retrieved July 12, 2016 from http://will-brothers.com/

522 Ibid.

523 TEL is my Top Eight List for sector and niche areas for Africa SMEs referred to and first discussed in Chapter 4.

524 *Quadcopter.* (2016). Oxford Dictionary. Retrieved June 24, 2016 from http://www.oxforddictionaries.com/us/definition/american_english/quadcopter

Oxford Dictionary.com defines quadcopter as: "An unmanned helicopter having four rotors: a quadcopter which flies autonomously using only the computing power of a smartphone." See: http://www.oxforddictionaries.com/us/definition/american_english/quadcopter

Dictionary.com defines high definition as: "a system for screen display of images that are sharper and more detailed than normal, having many more than the standard number of scanning lines per frame." See: http://www.dictionary.com/browse/high-definition

525 Global Business: *Octocopter.* (2016, August 180. [Television broadcast, 2 p.m.] China Global Television Network.

printing to change the face of small manufacturing in the region was mentioned earlier). On a larger scale, smart business-aiding-development ideas that help Africa SMEs include the previously discussed industrial *Special Economic Zones* (SEZs), but some examples of where they are actually providing that kind of assistance to SMEs come from China (in its donor-partner-business roles). China has helped countries like Ghana, Kenya, Tanzania, and Zambia create SEZs where training, innovation, technology, processing, manufacturing, and services have all come together in one location, along with support services linking SMEs to larger businesses and internal or export markets.[526] [527] [528] China has also

---

Octocopter. (2016) Oxford Dictionaries. Retrieved August 18, 2016 from http://www.oxforddictionaries.com/us/definition/american_english/octocopter

[526] Schiere, R., Ndikumana, L., & Walkenhorst, P. (Eds.). (2011). *China and Africa: An Emerging Partnership for Development?* African Development Bank Group. Retrieved June 24, 2016 from http://www.afdb.org/fileadmin/uploads/afdb/Documents/Publications/Anglaischina.pdf

[527] Zeng, D. *Global Experiences with Special Economic Zones with a Focus on China and Africa.* (2015). Trade and Global Competitiveness Practice. World Bank. Retrieved June 24, 2016 from http://www.worldbank.org/content/dam/Worldbank/Event/Africa/Investing%20in%20Africa%20Forum/2015/investing-in-africa-forum-global-experiences-with-special-economic-zones-with-a-focus-on-china-and-africa.pdf

[528] *Special Economic Zone. Investment Opportunity. Government of Tanzania.* Retrieved June 24, 2016 from http://www.epza.go.tz/invest.php?p=232

entered into discussion with Zimbabwe in November 2016 to build three economic zones in three cities with a focus also on assisting the SME sector.

Also, Aliko Dangote (Africa's leading businessman, who began as an entrepreneur and remains a strong advocate of entrepreneurs) has often called for the establishment of more industrial clusters for SMEs, which he highlights in the *Foreword*, because these centers can help SMEs learn, thrive, and receive training. His advocacy for entrepreneurship I also feel is further emphasized in one of his company's key adverts which calls "For an Empowered Africa," reflecting both his support for the region, the sector and his focus on providing and creating jobs that will help Africa's overall economic development. Dangote has been recognized by numerous organizations for his support to SMEs and as a leading Africa entrepreneur and businessman, including from the Africa-America Institute (AAI) on the margins of the 2016 UN session

(See Photograph 5, AAI 2016 Awards event.) [529] [530]

[531] Smart business-aiding-development solutions mentioned throughout the book demonstrate the range of innovation and creativity being delivered by Africa SMEs, or suggested by a number of other forward thinkers and African countries, along with their foreign partners.

Certainly, it is evident that SSAfrica's SMEs are playing numerous roles that are moving the Continent forward, both in tangible and intangible ways. I have provided my TEL list of what sectors I believe are prime targets for Africa SMEs and emphasized what more African governments, donors and investors can do to help them thrive, expand and become more sustainable.

---

[529] Dangote is listed in Forbes Magazine as the 51st wealthiest person in the world. One of the Dangote Group's advertisements on CNN international, which also appears on the company letterhead, is "For an Empowered Africa." See: http://www.aaionline.org/ and http://www.aaionline.org/news-and-events/aai-awards-gala/ for information on the Africa-America Institute and its award events.

See: *Aliko Dangote #51.* (2016) Rankings. The World's Billionaires. August 7, 2016. Forbes Magazine. Retrieved August 7, 2016 from http://www.forbes.com/profile/aliko-dangote/

[530] *Aliko Dangote.* (2016, January 2016). Speech. *38th Pre-Convocation Lecture.* Amadou Bello University, Zaira, Nigeria.

[531] Dangote – Entrepreneurs. (2016). Famous Entrepreneurs. Retrieved August 7, 2016 from http://www.famous-entrepreneurs.com/aliko-dangote

SMEs are already working in a lot of sectors, but other examples with my TEL (climate change and tourism) could be tapped further as opportunities. A short review of tangible and intangible SME contributions:

- Job Creation
- Growth of Africa's middle class
- Growth of GDP
- Contribution to foreign trade, sales, and exports
- Smart business-aiding-development solutions
- Development work around solutions
- Creative technology use, particularly apps, drones, and 3-D printing
- Pursuit of new technologies to address economic development
- Contribution to regional integration or inter Africa trade

- Voice for good economic governance and transparency

- *Innovation* and *Inimitability.*

If I had to sum all this up, on the sweet spots on Africa's SMEs, I would say they are several things, the "Power of Pan-Africanism," the "Power of Cooperation," the "Power of Innovation," and the "Power of Inimitability" – all working together to serve the SSAfrica Region well.

You will see in the next chapter on the special *@The FEEEDS Index* on the environment in which Africa SMEs operate, responses from African nationals on overarching themes that impact the sector in at least 31-32 countries where polling was done. Despite the challenges that exist or may arise, you will see that Africa small businesses, with their entrepreneurial spirit, remain hopeful and find ways to manage or work around the on-ground challenges. It is not easy, of course, but they are getting it done, and they see their role as a small business as the best way to fundamentally change things. The prevailing sentiment and my take-away:

Young adults, no matter where they are living on the Continent or off, prefer to work for themselves and have their own SME or entrepreneurial business. For them, this is the best way to change their quality of life, the inequalities that may exist in their home country or country to which they have an affinity, with the desire to improve the overall economic governance and transparency in the region, and help move Sub Saharan Africa forward.

Part Four: Africa's Nationals: Polling Their Views

"Ambassador Sanders believes that data is vital to understanding the priorities, attitudes, and wellbeing of more than 1 billion people in Sub-Saharan Africa. The data-driven analysis which follows below looks at Africa's economic and business environments for SMEs continue in this vain. @ The FEEEDS Index, powered by Gallup Analytics®, reveals an Africa keen on entrepreneurship and well-disposed to the private sector.

The data reveals that many view entrepreneurship and having their own small and medium size businesses not only as a means to their own job creation, but as a preference to traditional employment. The in-depth look at the state of SMEs in Africa and their potential role in the continent's growth and development provide important implications for policymakers, investors, and the wider development community."

—Jay Loschky, Africa Director Gallup World Poll

Chapter Eleven: @The FEEEDS® Index

The FEEEDS Advocacy Initiative publishes *@The FEEEDS Index,* which is powered by Gallup Analytics. The yearly *Index* polls views (including breakdowns between youth and gender) on a range of policy and economic development issues on what African nationals have to say about:

- Their governments;
- Their national militaries and police;
- Whether people feel they have had enough food to eat (are people hungry or in fear of being hungry, talked about extensively in Chapter 1);
- Whether they have adequate shelter (affordable housing);
- Whether they have access to adequate health care and educational opportunities; and

- Whether they have a sense of *wellbeing* – a measure that was discussed in Chapter 1, which several organizations like the UN, World Bank, Gallup, OECD, WEF, and countries such as the United Kingdom see as an important indicator on how people feel in general about where they live and work.

In *@The FEEEDS Index,* there is a human systems or *human cultural communications* approach in seeking to understand, show, and reflect in the *DataGraphs* how African nationals feel about key issues that affect their lives (governments, food, shelter, education, etc.) – basically, are they *thriving or just surviving*? The *Index* seeks to capture the mission behind the acronym FEEEDS (Food security, Education, Energy-Environment, Economics, Development, and Self-Help/ Wellbeing).[532] FEEEDS has created a special *@The FEEEDS Index* of polling data from Africa on themes

[532] Human cultural communication is a concept, a focus, and a signature lecture theme of the author highlighted in her first book, *The Legendary Uli Women of Nigeria*, and in her dissertation. It means seeking to better understand and respect what and how cultures communicate based on what is impacting the lives of those in the culture, including both verbal and non-verbal cues and communication expressions of signs and symbols and what they express in a culture.

that are relevant and have an impact on the Africa SME operating environment in at least 31-32 countries where polling was done. Explanation of the overarching themes that have an impact on the Africa SME sector, the data analysis, and the actual DataGraphs of the special *@The FEEEDS Index* follow below.

<u>What African Nationals Have to Say</u>

In the special *@The FEEEDS Index,* each overarching theme highlights the aggregate responses in the region, providing a slice or reflection of the overall sentiment in SSAfrica, followed by the specific responses in each country where polling was done. The questions polled for the special *@The FEEEDS Index* were as follows:

1. Is it easy or hard to start a small business in the country you live in?

2. Are the economic conditions good or bad?

3. Is the level of corruption in government and business widespread?

4. Is there confidence in the national government?

5. Is there is a sense of wellbeing (thriving in at least three of the five elements of purpose, social, financial, community or physical environment)?

The headings on each of the DataGraphs for the questions above are:

- *Starting a Business*, with youth (15-29 years), and female breakdowns;
- *Economic Conditions*;
- *Corruption in Business & Corruption in Government*
- *Confidence in National Government; and*
- *Wellbeing.*

The polling on *starting a new business* does not distinguish between a registered or unregistered (informal sector) business, which I believe is a good thing, since the informal sector is equally as important in the SSAfrican context to African economies as registered SMEs, particularly for female businesses, and especially since the informal sector can be the primary means of survival or life line for many families.

PowerHouse Nations and Key Data Take-Aways

The *Index* also drills down to look at polling data for what FEEEDS® calls the *PowerHouse Nations* in the region – Angola, Democratic Republic of the Congo (DRC), Ethiopia, Ghana, Kenya, Nigeria, Rwanda, South Africa, and Tanzania. PowerHouse Nations is a FEEEDS designation (which some may or may not agree with), based on my the on-ground and professional experiences over many years on the Continent as a: political and economic officer/ analyst; U.S. Ambassador, staff member participating in U.S. Africa policy circles from the White House to the State Department to U.S. Congress; executive of The FEEEDS Advocacy Initiative coupled with the analysis by the FEEEDS' team. The idea behind the category PowerHouse Nations is these countries can impact (positively or problematically) their sub-regions' stability, their political and socio-economic environments, excluding (not surprisingly) regional integration. (NB: Research by the World Bank suggest country economic conditions do not affect regional integration that much; I am presuming this is because regional integration figures are so low.)[533] [534]

FEEEDS sees these PowerHouse Nations as bellwethers for how the Continent is doing overall as well as how each sub-region (Central, East, West, and South) is faring on the FEEEDS pillars of *Food security, Education, Energy-Environment, Economics, and Self-Help/Wellbeing,* and their attendant subthemes of good governance, corruption, security, small business, housing, and sustainability.

The PowerHouse Nations can and will change over time as internal country and regional dynamics vary, along with variables impacting a country's economic growth,

---

[533] World Bank. (2016, January). *Sub-Saharan Africa Analysis. Global Economic Prospects 2016.* Retrieved August 9, 2016 from https://www.worldbank.org/content/dam/Worldbank/GEP/GEP2016a/Global-Economic-Prospects-January-2016-Sub-Saharan-Africa-analysis.pdf

[534] This report from the World Bank notes that there is a "negligible" impact that most countries have on regional integration since it is currently so low. The exception may be South Africa since it does export many of its good and services to other countries in its region.

governance, development, security, stability, and interaction within its sub-region.

Specifically, turning to the key *take-aways* on the enabling environment for Africa SMEs in the region, the news is fivefold:

- Positive on starting a new business;
- Concerns about economic conditions;
- Concerns about the prevalence of corruption in business and in government;
- Positive direction on confidence in the national government; but surprisingly
- Low on wellbeing.

It was interesting to see in the data that despite African nationals seeing corruption in government and in business as widespread, they noted improvements in their confidence in their national governments from 2014 to 2015. One of the big concerns for FEEEDS that came out of the data was the overall low sense of wellbeing (only 10 percent of the people in most countries said they were thriving in three of five elements); perhaps the tough facts and stats noted in Chapters 1-2 could be factors reflected in the negative responses by those polled.

However, the real positive nugget in all the data is that although economic conditions, corruption, and wellbeing polled poorly, the majority of Africans were still positive that where they lived was a good place to start a new business in spite of these challenges. The polled respondents were overwhelmingly positive on the theme of starting a new business, including the region's youth (15-29 years) and female populations. The positive poll responses from African females on this theme is particularly encouraging given some of the special challenges for them discussed in Chapter 7. These responses underscore why Africa SMEs and entrepreneur numbers are growing so fast and why they are playing such key roles in the Continent's job creation, GDP growth, and spurring the middle class.

Given the emphasis on the environment in which Africa SMEs and entrepreneurs operate, it is important to consider some possibilities regarding what factors might have played a role in how respondent answered the question about whether where they lived was a good place to start a new business. In FEEEDS' analysis factors which could have played a role in their responses included:

- Were they a registered or unregistered business;
- Were inspired to start a new business because they could not find a formal job, had a great innovative idea, or had a strong business-aiding-development desire to address a social-economic need for their country;[535]
- Benefitted from an award or innovation prize;
- Needed access to credit or financing; and

[535] A Gallup World Poll analysis of 2016, during the FEEEDS-Gallup 3rd annual Africa on the topic of Africa SMEs, showed that there was a strong preference by African citizens in the countries polled to be in the private sector as opposed to working in the public sector for the government. The Gallup World Poll graph can be seen on the FEEEDS cloud for the FEEEDS-Gallup 2016 event: www.bit.ly/FEEEDS-GALLUP7-14-16

- Had connections to organizations/institutions that had an SME training/mentor program or other special platforms for SMEs (e.g. NGOs, private sector companies, or stock exchanges with small business boards).

The above responses are some of the main ones I have heard over the years. In addition, having worked a lot with Africa SMEs, many also have told me that it is usually a story of survival, perseverance, but especially or the *activist/good global citizen* desire to give back and make a difference, while also generating-income – *the business-aiding-development approach* (mentioned in Chapter 9).

@The FEEEDS Index – An Analysis of the Polling Data

The 2015 DataGraphs reflect the responses for SSAfrica on *Aggregate, By-Country,* and for the *PowerHouse Nations* on the five overarching themes included in the special *@The FEEEDS Index* about the environment in which SSAfrica SMEs and entrepreneurs operate. The data in Figures 1-30 is analyzed in detail below followed by the actual DataGraphs. The polling is from the most recent polling year, 2015, except for one theme, *confidence in national government,* as the data from 2014 and 2015 is included to show the year-to-year improvement. Given the number of countries polled (31-32 depending on the theme), all *By-Country DataGraphs* are divided by alpha order into two parts: Benin-Malawi and Mali-Zimbabwe.

Figure 1: *Starting a Business Aggregate*: On Starting a Business-Aggregate, 71 percent of those polled said that *where they lived was a good place to start a new business.* This data underscores the good news I have been discussing about SMEs and is also reflective of why African SMEs are growing, despite the economic conditions, concerns about corruption, or any other challenge they may face, e.g., regulatory, registration, and access to capital. On aggregate, only 25 percent of those polled said where they lived was not a good place to start a business.

Figures 2-3: *Starting a Business By-Country*: As one can see in the two By-Country DataGraphs, the positive sentiments on this theme for nearly all of the countries polled showed highly favorable responses. Even those on the lower end of the graph did not fall below 56 percent. The countries with the highest number of nationals saying they thought their country was a good place to start a new business were Congo-Brazzaville (86%), Kenya (84%), Mali (83%), Tanzania (81%), Malawi (80%), followed by Mozambique, Somalia, and Uganda (78%). Even in countries thought of to have difficult economic environments such as DRC, Nigeria, or Somalia, the responses were all well above 60 percent. I mentioned in Chapter 7 that countries with fragile security environments also are still good places for Africa SMEs, and the polling data bears this out with the positive results from countries like Mali and Somalia which are facing security challenges.

Figures 4-5: *Starting a Business Youth (15-29 years)*: I talked extensively about the size of Africa's young population in Chapters 1-2. Thus, taking a look at how Africa's youth view starting a business where they live is extremely important, regardless of the challenges (economic conditions, corruption, access to capital, etc.). The DataGraphs show that the majority of the African youth polled were very positive about beginning businesses where they live. All countries scored above 55 percent. The top nine were Congo-Brazzaville (86%), Kenya (84%), Mali (83%), Tanzania (81%), Uganda (78%), Somalia (76%), Nigeria (73%), Senegal (72%), and South Africa (67%).[536] [537] This certainly is borne out in the discussions above. Africa's young people continue to see working for themselves as one of the best avenues for their own job creation, and to generate their own income.

Figures 6-7: ***Starting a Business African Females:*** For African females, their deliverables were also high on whether where they lived was a good place to start a new business. We know that females face many more obstacles, hardships, and sometimes cultural impediments in certain countries (many which have been outlined in the chapters above). But despite or in spite of these issues, African females polled positive

[536] Females in the 15-29 age range are also included in the comprehensive youth graph. The author thought it was important to also show a breakdown for females overall on ease of doing business.

[537] Since @The FEEEDS Index is powered by Gallup Analytics®, the DataGraph on Africa's youth is reflective of 15-29-year age group.

on this theme. In some countries, their positive polling numbers were higher than the overall youth responses in the same countries. For example, female scores were higher in Congo-Brazzaville (87%), Kenya (83%), Nigeria and Malawi (80%), Tanzania (79%), and Somalia (78%). The other top country responses for females came from Liberia and Chad (77%), Uganda and Mozambique (76%), and Senegal (72%). Somalia is particularly interesting as regards to the earlier discussion and my own experiences with post-conflict countries being good places for new businesses to begin, particularly so for women. Even though security in Somalia is still an issue, today's fragile environment is still better than it was over the last 30 years or more of serious clan-based internal conflict. Thus, small businesses are cropping up in areas from food and hotel services to fashion design and textile stores, mostly all run by women. Youth figures in those same countries, respectively, were still very good, and just a few points off from the female responses. The youth figures again were Congo-Brazzaville (85%), Nigeria (73%), Somalia (76%), and Senegal (72%).

Figure 8: ***Starting a Business PowerHouse Nations:*** As noted earlier, PowerHouse Nations is a FEEEDS® designation which examines the impact (positively or problematically) that these nine nations (Angola, DRC, Ethiopia, Ghana, Kenya, Nigeria, Rwanda, South Africa, and Tanzania) have on their sub-regions. No polling was done for any of the themes in 2015 for Angola, but the other eight PowerHouse Nations didn't fair badly on how their nationals felt about starting a business in these countries. All the nations in this category scored above 63 percent, with Kenya on the high end at 84 percent, Tanzania at 81 percent, followed by Nigeria and South Africa at 68 percent – all in all, not bad.

Figure 9: ***Economic Conditions Aggregate:*** The SSAfrica Region scored poorly with their nationals as regards to economic conditions. Only 21 percent of those polled said they thought economic conditions in their country were *good or favorable*, while 42 percent deemed the economic conditions *only fair*, and 30 percent saying conditions in their country were *poor*. This sentiment could underscore the overall macro-economic issues and challenges that many SSAfrica nations face today that were discussed in the above chapters from currency fluctuations, low commodity prices, high food costs, challenges with affordable housing, and so on.[538] The everyday economic environment for most Africans is tough, even during the economic boom days of 2011-early 2015; trickle-down economic benefits did not reach the masses despite the region's economic growth numbers. As of mid-2016, several countries, like South Africa, have and are facing 1-3 percent GDP growth rates over the 2017-2018 period and high unemployment. Thus, this low aggregate figure of only 21 percent of respondents saying that economic conditions in their country are good is not surprising.

---

[538] Gallup Africa Director Rheault's at the FEEEDS-Gallup July 2016 program highlighted an August 2016 2016 Gallup World Poll article which showed an improvement in the aggregate sentiment for the region on economic conditions with 38 percent feeling it was good, 39 feeling it was fair, and 22 percent saying they saw no difference from previous years. Rheault's presentation on this can be found on the FEEEDS-Gallup July 14, 2016 event cloud at: www.bit.ly/FEEEDS-GALLUP7-14-16

Also, see Gallup World Poll at: Gallup World Poll. Topics. Gallup World Poll. Retrieved August 7, 2016 from http://www.gallup.com/services/170945/world-poll.aspx

Figures 10-11: ***Economic Conditions By-Country:*** The two By-Country DataGraphs mirror the pessimistic view noted in the aggregate data on the region. Of the countries polled, most scored poorly, with only a negligible segment of their populations saying they thought the economic conditions in their country were excellent. There were a few countries where their nationals said conditions were good, but only one country, surprisingly Somalia, scoring at 51 percent. This was followed by Rwanda (44%), then a big drop off before the next group which included Mozambique (33%), Ethiopia (32%), and Kenya (30%). The bulk of the countries received an *only fair* rating by those polled, examples include Senegal (61%), Burkina Faso (56%), Gabon (53%), Mali (53%), Botswana (49%), Congo-Brazzaville (46%), and Nigeria (41%). Several countries also received *poor* as a rating on their economic conditions, but the highest negatives came from the nationals of Liberia (62%), Ghana (57%), South Sudan (58%), Zambia (57%), and Zimbabwe (54%), followed by Sierra Leone (41%) and Nigeria (33%). It is worth highlighting that Rwanda's nationals were close to being evenly split between those who said conditions were *good* (44%) and those that said things were *only fair* (49%).

Figure 12: ***Economic Conditions PowerHouse Nations:*** The PowerHouse Nations followed the trends in the region with a negligible number of respondents per country saying things were *excellent*. Only two countries, Rwanda (44%), and a distant second, Ethiopia (32%), received respectable numbers from their nationals that economic conditions were *good*. Most responses from nationals in the PowerHouse Nations fell into the *only fair* category such as South Africa (47%), Kenya (46%), and Tanzania (46%). Those nations that received the highest negative scores on having *poor* economic conditions were DRC (52%), Ghana (53%), and Nigeria (33%).

Figure 13: ***Corruption in Business Aggregate*****:** For the SSAfrica Region, 72 percent of African nationals said that corruption in business was a problem in their country. Only 18 percent of respondents said they didn't see corruption in business as a problem with the other 2 percent saying they didn't know or they did not respond.

Figures 14-15: *Corruption in Business By-Country:* Here the two DataGraphs show that nationals in nearly all countries polled felt strongly that corruption in the business sector was high in their respective countries. The nationals of the following countries in 2015 had the highest number of their nationals saying corruption was a problem: Nigeria (87%), Ghana (86%), Tanzania (84%), Kenya (80%), and South Africa (78%). The exceptions were Rwanda with 84 percent of its nationals responding that corruption in business was not a problem, followed by Somalia at 61 percent. (NB: Rwanda, with a population of 11.8 million, has continually had high marks for its low level of corruption and is generally internationally recognized by the international community for low overall corruption levels.)[539] [540]

[539] *Rwanda Population.* (n.d.). WorldOMeters. Retrieved June 15, 2016 from http://www.worldometers.info/world-population/rwanda-population/

[540] *Corruption Perception Index.* (2015). Transparency International. Retrieved September 30, 2016 http://www.transparency.org/cpi2015?gclid=CNfvjKeQuM8CFYY7gQodxm0Ghw

Figure 16: *Corruption in Business PowerHouse Nations*: Results for the PowerHouse Nations fared no differently than the aggregate or by-country responses as these nations also had high negatives on corruption in business with the following at the top of the leader board: Nigeria (87%), Ghana (86%), Tanzania (84%), Kenya (80%), South Africa (78%), and DRC (74%). Exception, as noted above, was Rwanda, with 84 percent of its nationals saying corruption in business was not a problem there.

Figures 17-19: *Corruption in Government Aggregate and By-Country*: The DataGraphs in this category had staggering numbers. Corruption was universally high for most all the countries polled with ratings at 75 percent reflecting the concerns of respondents that corruption in government was widespread in their country. The SSAfrica aggregate DataGraph shows 75 percent; the two by-country DataGraphs reflect the high levels per country. The countries with the highest levels in alpha order were Nigeria (95%), Ghana (91%), Tanzania (90%), South Africa (88%), Chad (87%), South Africa (88%), Kenya (86%), Uganda (84%), and Malawi

(82%). On the extreme lower end, again is Rwanda, as it bested every other nation with only a small 7 percent of those polled saying corruption in government in the country was a problem, while the majority (88%) gives the government high marks with having low corruption.

It is important to highlight that the polling shows that for most African nationals, corruption in *governments and corruption in business* were the two most pervasive and challenging issues in their country.

Figure 20: ***Corruption in Government PowerHouse Nations:*** With the exception of Rwanda, these nations followed the trend seen in the aggregate data for SSAfrica with high negatives responses from those polled saying that corruption in government was widespread. The countries with the highest levels of negative responses from their nationals were Nigeria (95%), Ghana (91%), Tanzania (90%), South Africa (88%), Kenya (80%), and DRC/ Congo-Kinshasa (75%). Rwanda as noted above had low levels of corruption (7%).

Figures 21-22: ***Confidence in National Governments Aggregate 2015 and 2014:*** Confidence in National Government Aggregate for 2015 showed 56 percent of those polled in the SSAfrica Region said they didn't have confidence in their national government. As mentioned earlier, this is an improvement over the earlier 2014 aggregate data for the region on confidence in national government, which was at 50 percent. This change represents a 6 percent improvement on this theme in the region from 2014 to 2015 with more Africans having confidence in their national governments; FEEEDS' analysis is that this change is attributable to some of the changing leadership in the region as a result of elections held in 2015.[541]

Figures 23-26: ***Confidence in National Government By-Country 2015 and 2014:*** Some countries that

---

[541] Rheault, M. & McCarthy, J. (2016, June 13). *In Busy Election Year, African Leaders Enjoy High Approvals.* Gallup World Poll. Retrieved June 14, 2016 from http://www.gallup.com/poll/192584/busy-election-year-african-leaders-enjoyed-high-approval.aspx?utm_source=genericbutton&utm_medium=organic&utm_campaign=sharing

This data was also presented at the annual FEEEDS-Gallup July 14, 2016, event by Gallup's Africa Regional Director Magali Rheault and her presentation is on the FEEEDS-Gallup July 14, 2016 event cloud at: www.bit.ly/FEEEDS-GALLUP7-14-16

were on the lower end of the scale in 2014 improved in 2015. Botswana, Burkina Faso, Ethiopia, Ghana, Kenya, Nigeria, Sierra Leone, and Somalia were the top eight countries that improved significantly (10% or more) from 2014 to 2015, while others like DRC/ Congo-Kinshasa had significant drops in confidence between 2014 and 2015. Examples of detailed year-to-year changes were in the following countries: Nigeria improved from only 29 percent of those polled in 2014 saying they had confidence in the national government to 41 percent in 2015; Ethiopia jumped from 68 percent in 2014 to 83 percent in 2015 (but this is likely going to be much lower in 2016 and going forward given recent big protests and demands to open up its closed political process, improve human rights and allow freedom of expression); Kenya had a positive change from 64 percent in 2014 to 75 percent in 2015; Sierra Leone had 59 percent of its nationals having confidence in the national government in 2014, but that rose to 65 percent in 2015; and Somalia, which had improved polling data in almost all the overarching themes in the special *@The FEEEDS Index*, improved from 66 percent in 2014 to 78 percent of its nationals in 2015 saying they had confidence in the national government. There are two By-Country DataGraphs for both 2015 and 2014.

Figure 27: *Wellbeing Aggregate*: To restate, wellbeing addresses whether those polled believe they were thriving in at least three of the following five areas: purpose, social, financial, community, and physical environment. The news here is not good as only 10 percent of those polled on aggregate for the region in 2015 said they were thriving in at least three of these areas. This means that, with the exception of a few countries that roughly 80-90 percent of people in SSAfrica do not feel they are thriving in the core wellbeing elements. These results are an overall challenge for the region, African governments and societies to address. FEEEDS' analysis is these responses are likely a reflection of the tough *facts and stats* on unemployment, food security, health and living conditions, etc., for the majority of the people in the region that were highlighted in Chapters 1-2 as well as the gaps between good governance and these development needs, and concerns about corruption. Examples already mentioned above for 2016 and into 2017 where African nationals riled against governments not addressing these tough quality of life issues either through the ballot box (South Africa) or through protests (Burundi, Chad, DRC, Ethiopia, Gabon, Zambia, and Zimbabwe). Addressing these tough facts and stats, along with efforts on the SDGs, must become the order of the day for governments, donors, and investors in order to impact and change this trend on wellbeing.

However, what I also want to stress is that in spite of this negative result on wellbeing there still is a *resilience* by Africa SMEs and entrepreneurs borne out by the polling data in the *starting a new business* theme above regardless of the environmental or wellbeing challenges. SME and entrepreneur numbers are still growing, they are still creating great business-aiding-development solutions, and they are still helping make small dents in increasing middle-class numbers. The challenges have not deterred them; uphill battles have not dampened their resolve. The polling data above on starting a new business supports this.

Figures 28-29: ***Wellbeing By-Country***: The two *By-Country Wellbeing* DataGraphs are similarly negative, with a flat 10 percent for nearly all countries, except with a slight positive spike to 30 percent for Sierra Leone and Somalia, and 20 percent for Ethiopia, Mauritania and Senegal. But even with these small increases, this is still not a great showing for the region, as 70-90 percent of Africans in the countries polled feel they are not thriving in at least three of the five elements of wellbeing. Sierra Leone's civil war ended in 2002, and it has moved past the post-conflict period and held several democratic elections since then, and Somalia's security environment (although still fragile) has drastically improved in the last several years. These transitions could explain the slightly higher positive responses in these two countries over the average for the region.

Figure 30: ***Wellbeing PowerHouse Nations*:** The results here also are not good, and the PowerHouse

Nations followed the negative trend. They too had only 10 percent of their nationals saying they were thriving or feeling positive about any three of the five elements included in the analysis of wellbeing. It is important to highlight that even in countries like Rwanda which had good ratings from its national as regards to high marks on having low corruption in government (7%) and in business (12%) and had better responses than most countries on economic conditions (44% said good, 49% said only fair), its nationals still said they were not thriving in three of the five wellbeing elements. It too received the same low 10 percent rating evident overall for the region. Contrarily, Ethiopia had a slightly higher result of 20 percent of its nationals saying they were thriving in three of the five elements of wellbeing, but received high negatives on corruption in government (40%) and in business (45%).

The Polling DataGraphs: The Africa SME Operating Environment

Below in Figures 1-30 are the DataGraphs on which the analyses above are based. When "dk/rf" appears on a graph, it means the respondent did not know or preferred not to answer; the percentage of respondents in the dk/rf category for each of the overarching themes is extremely small.

FEEEDS®

The Special @The FEEEDS Index:

The Africa SME Operating Environment

The DataGraphs[542]

[542] All DataGraphs are copyrighted and permission to use must be given by FEEEDS® or Gallup®.

Information on polling methodology can be found at http://www.gallup.com/178685/methodology-center.aspx or http://www.gallup.com/178667/gallup-world-poll-work.aspx

Highlights Starting a Business Aggregate 2015
High Positive Level: 71% of those polled said where they lived was a good place to start a business.

Figure 1

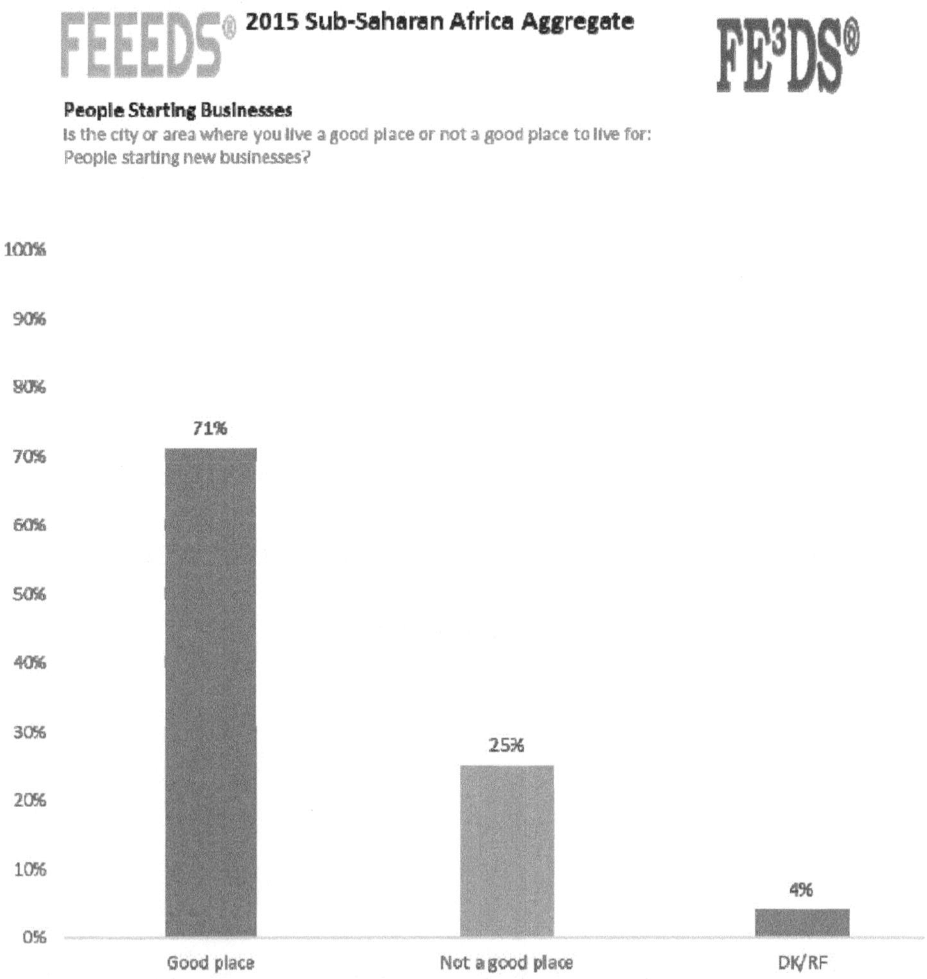

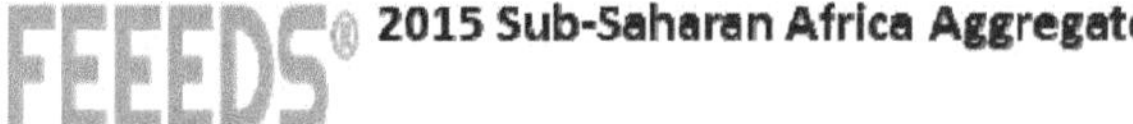

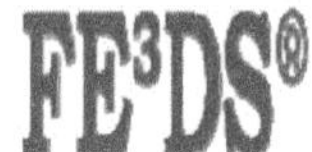

FEEEDS® 2015 Sub-Saharan Africa Aggregate
FE3DS®
People Starting Businesses
Is the city or area where you live a good place or not a good place to live for:
People starting new businesses?
100%
90%
80%
70%
60%
50%
40%
30%
20%
10%
0%
71%
25%
4%
Good place
Not a good place
DK/RF

Part One: **Highlights Starting a Business By-Country: Benin-Malawi**
Highest Positive Levels: Congo-Brazzaville (86%), Kenya (84%), Mali (83%).

Figure 2

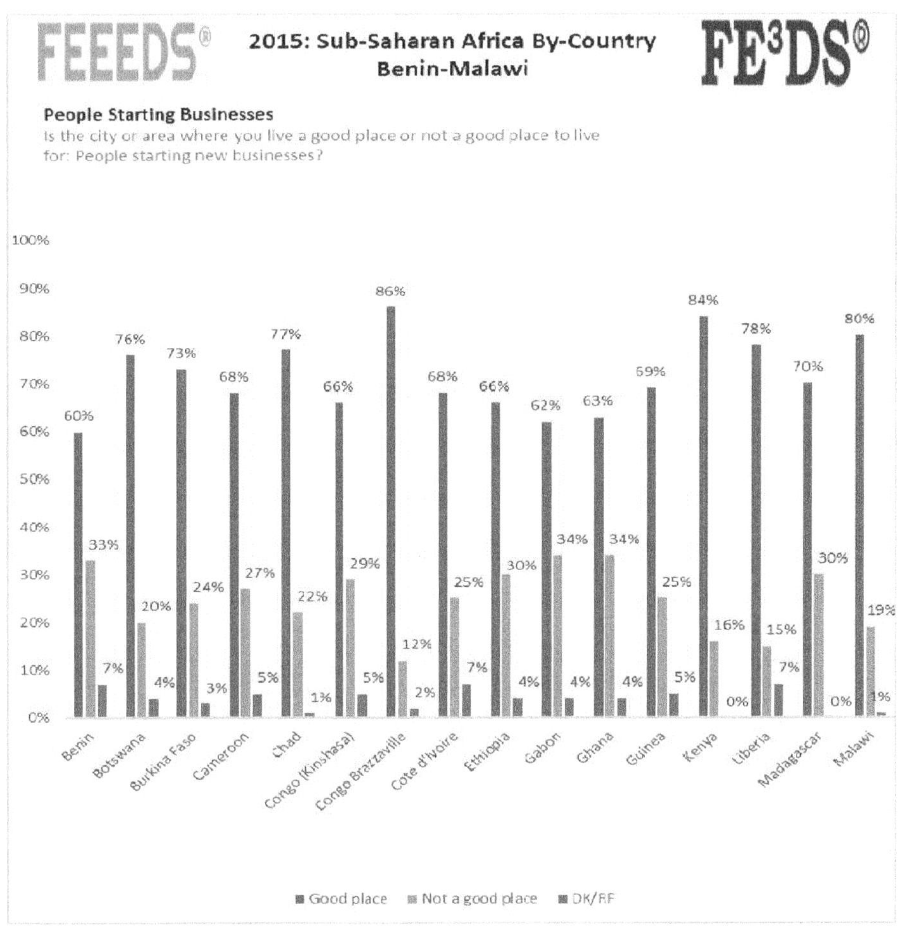

Part Two: Highlights Starting a Business By-Country: Mali-Zimbabwe
Highest Positive Levels: Mali (81%); Tanzania (81%); Mozambique, Somalia, and Uganda (78%); Nigeria (73%); and Senegal (71%).

Figure 3

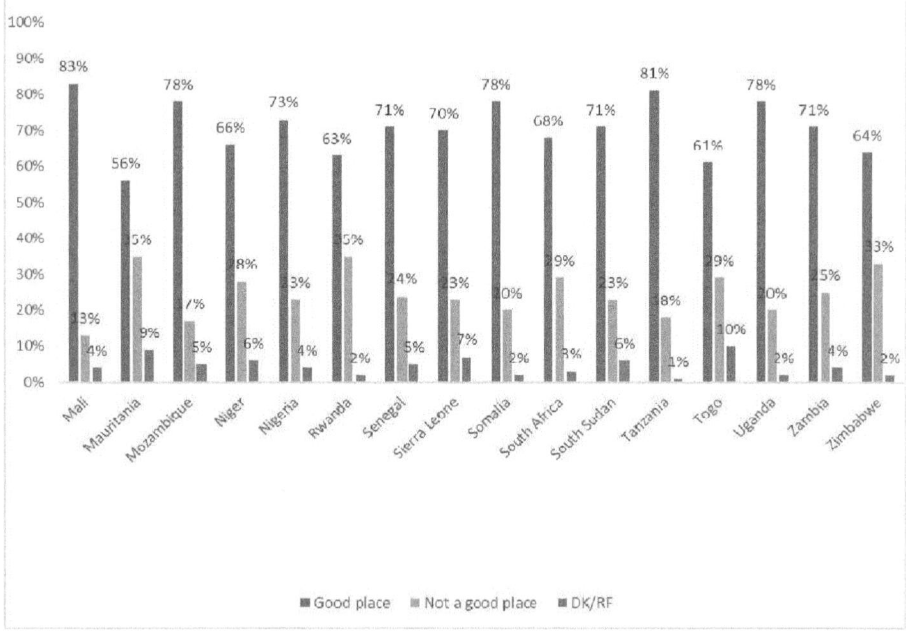

***Part One:* Highlights Starting a Business By-Country Youth (15-29 yrs): Benin-Malawi**

Highest Positive Levels: Congo-Brazzaville (85%); Kenya (84%), Chad and Malawi (78%); Liberia (77%); Botswana and Burkina Faso (74%); and Madagascar (71%).

Figure 4

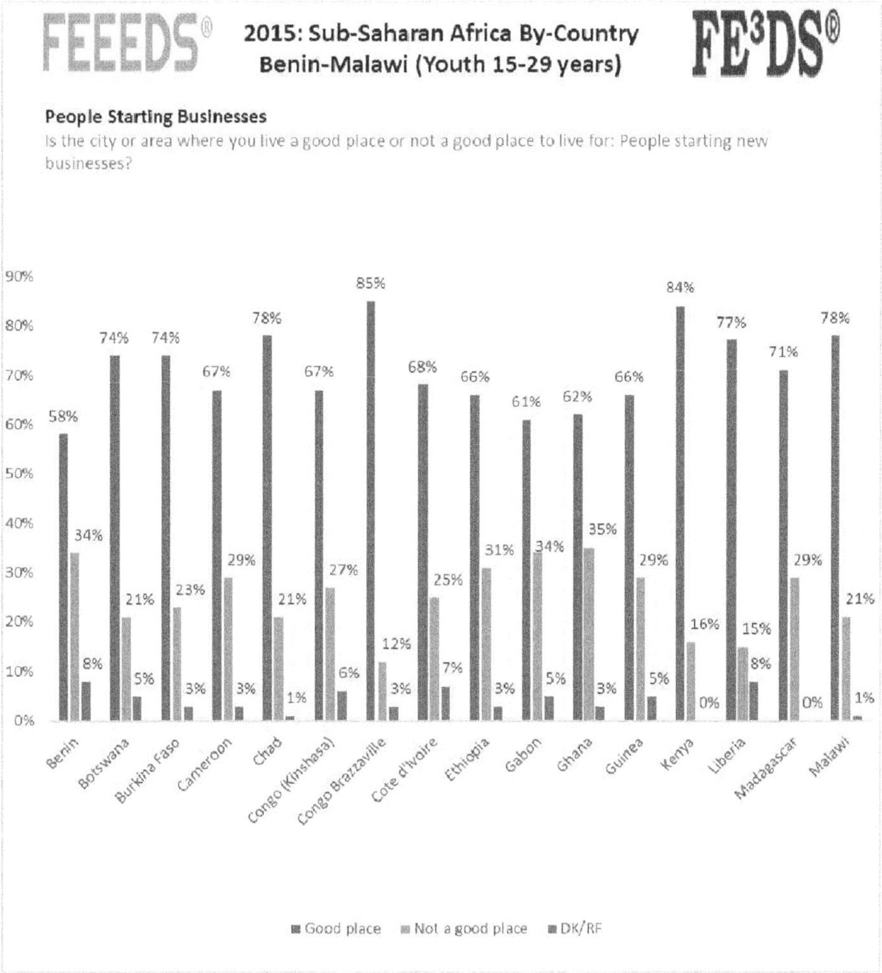

2015: Sub-Saharan Africa By-Country
Benin-Malawi (Youth 15-29 years)

People Starting Businesses

Is the city or area where you live a good place or not a good place to live for: People starting new businesses?

	Good place	Not a good place	DK/RF
Benin	58%	34%	8%
Botswana	74%	21%	5%
Burkina Faso	74%	23%	3%
Cameroon	67%	29%	3%
Chad	78%	21%	1%
Congo (Kinshasa)	67%	27%	6%
Congo Brazzaville	85%	12%	3%
Cote d'Ivoire	68%	25%	7%
Ethiopia	66%	31%	3%
Gabon	61%	34%	5%
Ghana	62%	35%	3%
Guinea	66%	29%	5%
Kenya	84%	16%	0%
Liberia	77%	15%	8%
Madagascar	71%	29%	0%
Malawi	78%	21%	1%

Part Two: **Highlights Starting a Business Youth (15-29yrs): Mali-Zimbabwe**
Highest Positive Levels: Tanzania (80%); Mozambique (78%); Uganda (77%); Somalia (76%); Nigeria (73%); and Senegal (68%).

Figure 5

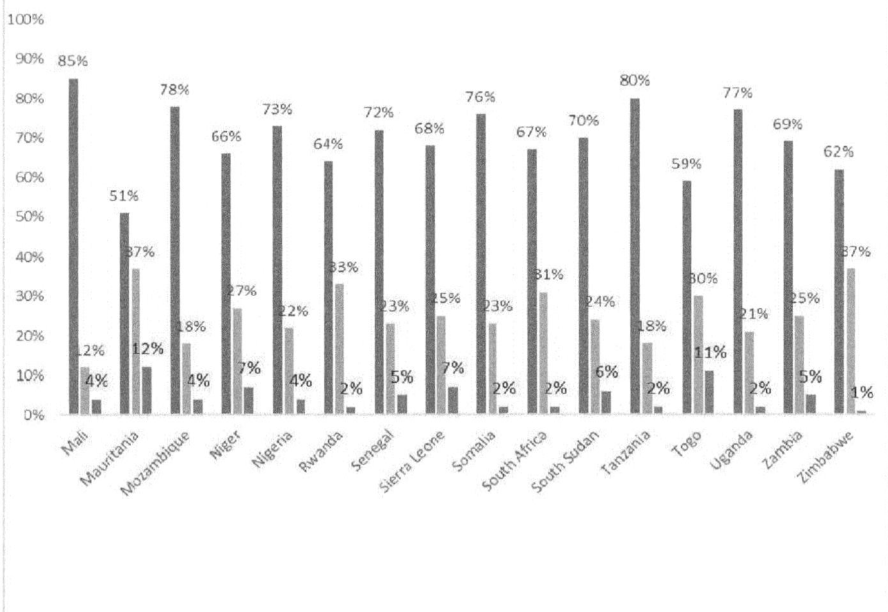

***Part One:* Highlights Starting a Business Female: Benin-Malawi**

Highlights Positive Levels: Congo-Brazzaville (87%); Kenya (83%); Malawi (80%); Liberia and Chad (77%).

Figure 6

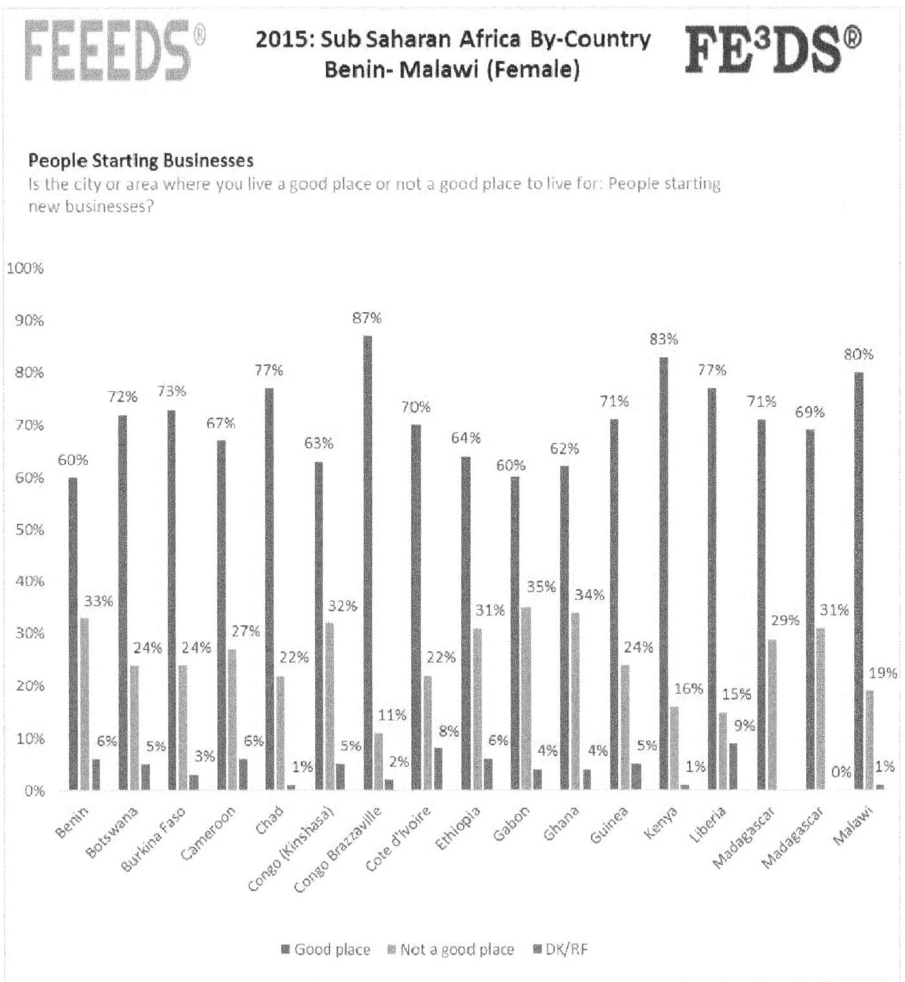

***Part Two:* Highlights of Starting a Business Female: Mali-Zimbabwe**

Highlights Levels: Nigeria (80%); Tanzania (79%); Somalia (78%); Uganda and Mozambique (76%); and Senegal (72%).

Figure 7

2015: Sub-Saharan Africa By-Country
Mali-Zimbabwe (Female)

People Starting Businesses

Is the city or area where you live a good place or not a good place to live for: People starting new businesses?

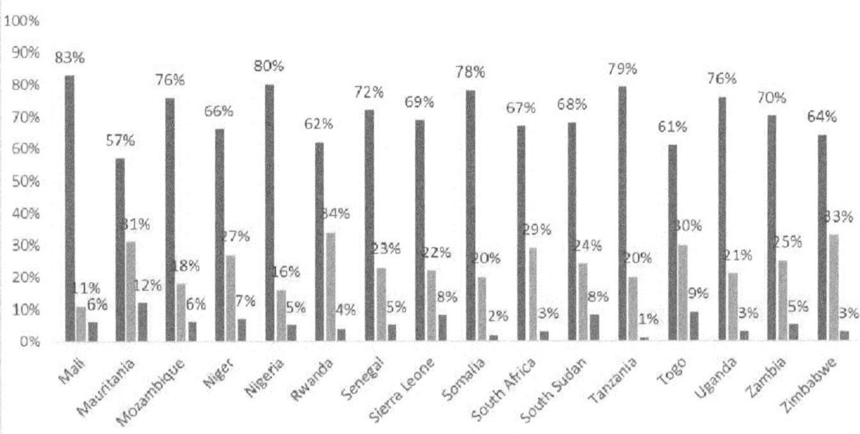

Highlights Starting a Business PowerHouse Nations

Highest Levels: Kenya (84%); Tanzania (81%); Nigeria (73%); South Africa (68%); DRC/Congo-Kinshasa and Ethiopia (66%); and Ghana (63%).

Figure 8

2015: FEEEDS PowerHouse Nations

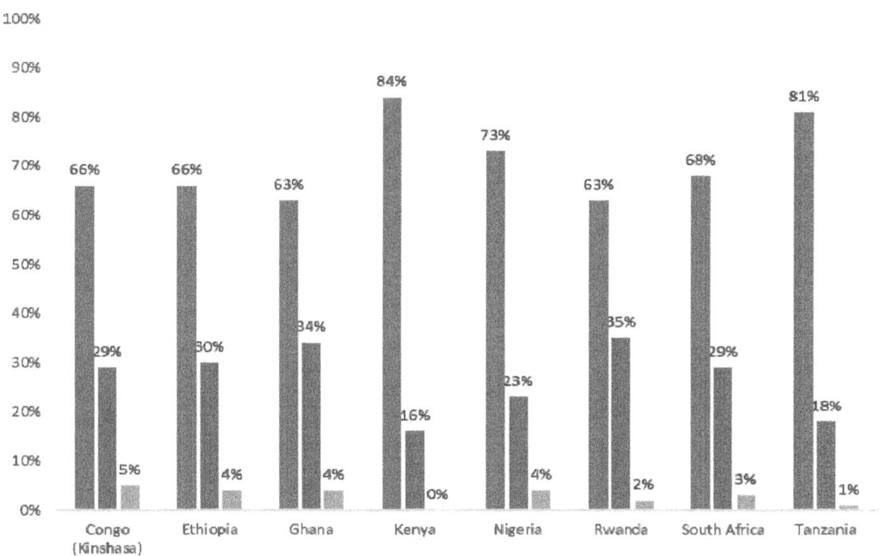

Highlights Economic Conditions Aggregate 2015
Excellent: 4% of SSAfrica nationals said economic conditions were excellent.
Good: 21 %. Only Fair: 42%. Poor 30%.

Figure 9

2015: Economic Conditions
Sub-Saharan Africa Aggregate

How would you rate economic conditions in this country today as excellent, good, only fair, or poor?

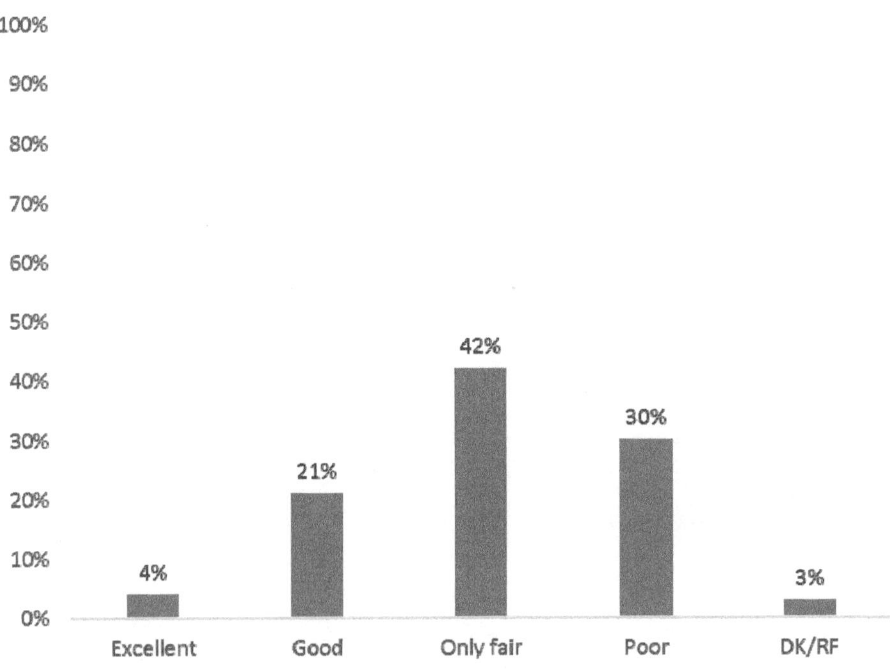

Part One: Highlights Economic Conditions By-Country: Benin-Malawi
Excellent: Negligible. Good Highest Levels: Ethiopia (32%); Kenya (30%).
Only Fair Highest Levels: Burkina Faso (56%); Gabon (53%); Congo-Brazzaville (46%); and Ethiopia (45%).
Poor Highest Levels: Liberia (62%); Ghana (57%); and DRC/Congo-Kinshasa (52%).

Figure 10

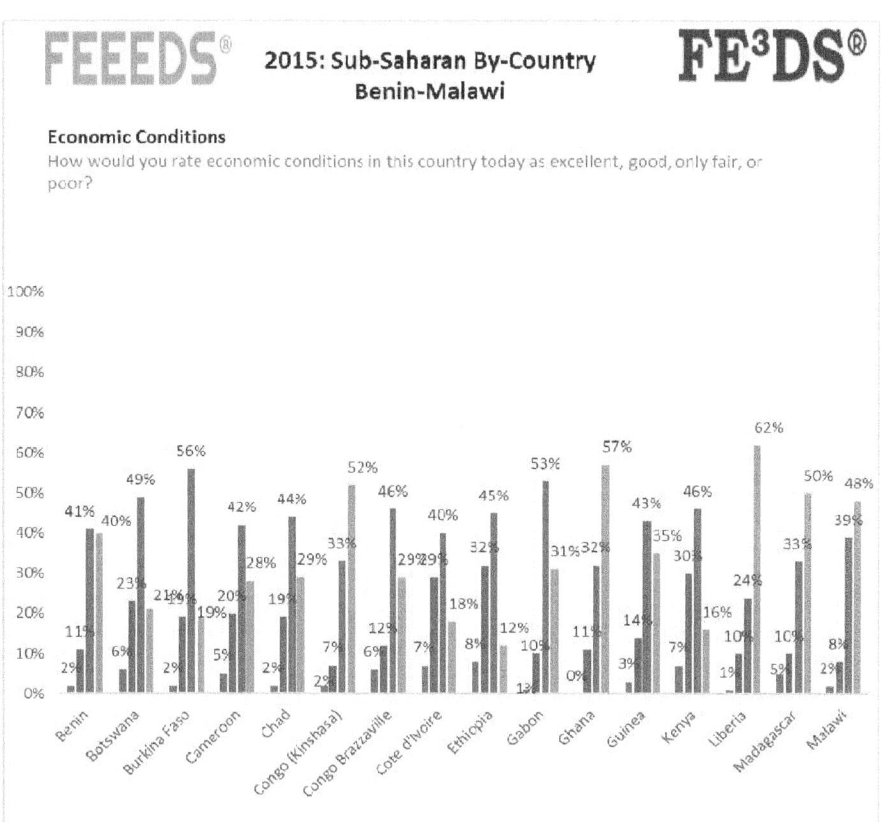

***Part Two:* Highlights of Economic Conditions By-Country: Mali-Zimbabwe**

Excellent: Negligible for all countries.

Good Highest Levels: Somalia (51%) and Rwanda (44%). Only Fair: Senegal (61%); Mauritania (56%); Togo (49%); and South Africa (47%).

Poor Highest Levels: South Sudan (58%); Zambia (57%); Zimbabwe (54%); Nigeria and Sierra Leone (41%).

Figure 11

2015: Sub-Saharan By-Country Mali-Zimbabwe

Economic Conditions

How would you rate economic conditions in this country today as excellent, good, only fair, or poor?

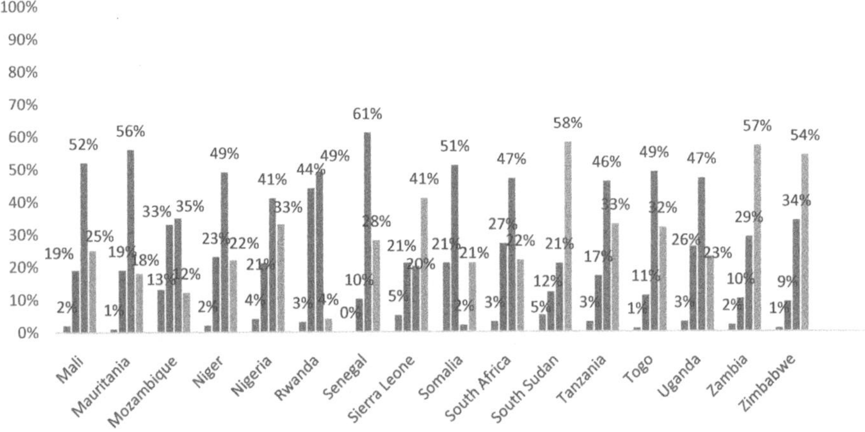

Highlights Economic Conditions PowerHouse Nations
Excellent: Negligible.
Good Highest Levels: Rwanda (44%); Ethiopia a distance second (32%).
Only Fair Highest Levels: Rwanda (49%); South Africa (47%); Kenya and Tanzania (46%).
Poor Highest Levels: DRC (52%); Ghana (53%); Nigeria and Tanzania (33%).
Rwanda's population is almost evenly divided for those saying *good* or *only fair.*

Figure 12

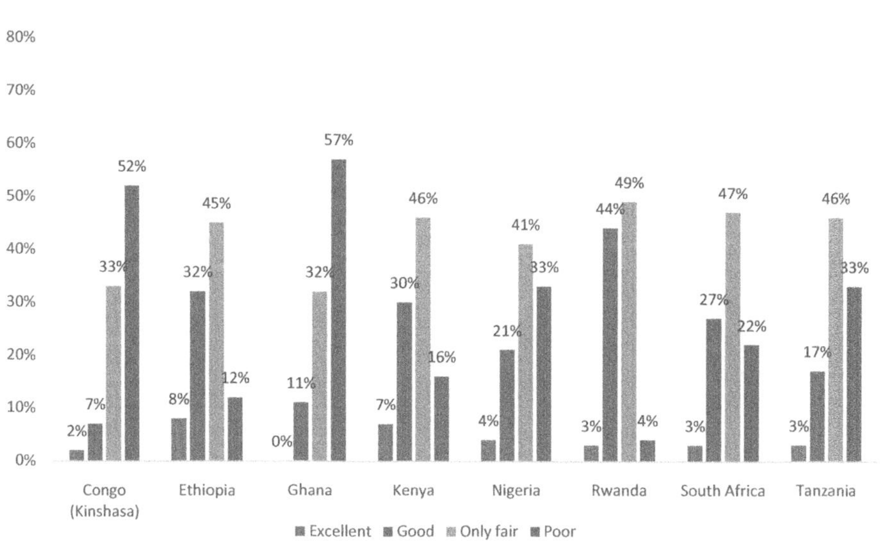

Highlights Corruption in Business Aggregate 2015

72% of African nationals polled felt corruption in business in their country was high; only 18% said they did not see it as a problem.

Figure 13

2015: Sub-Saharan Africa Aggregate

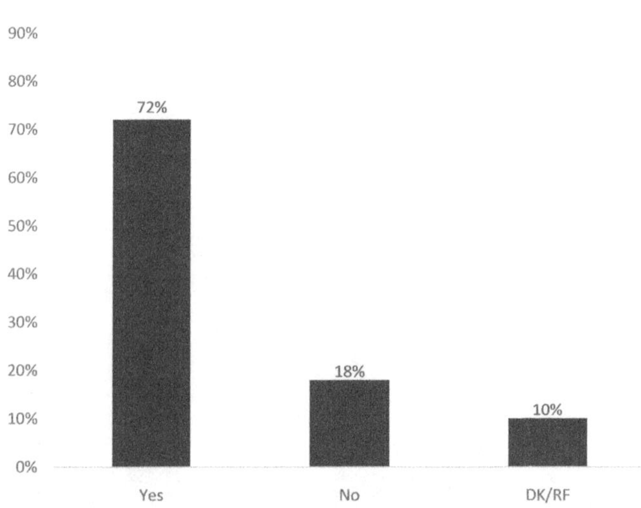

***Part One*: Highlights Corruption in Business By-Country: Benin-Malawi**

Highest levels: Ghana (86%); Kenya (80%); South Africa (78%); and DRC/Congo-Kinshasa (74%).

Figure 14

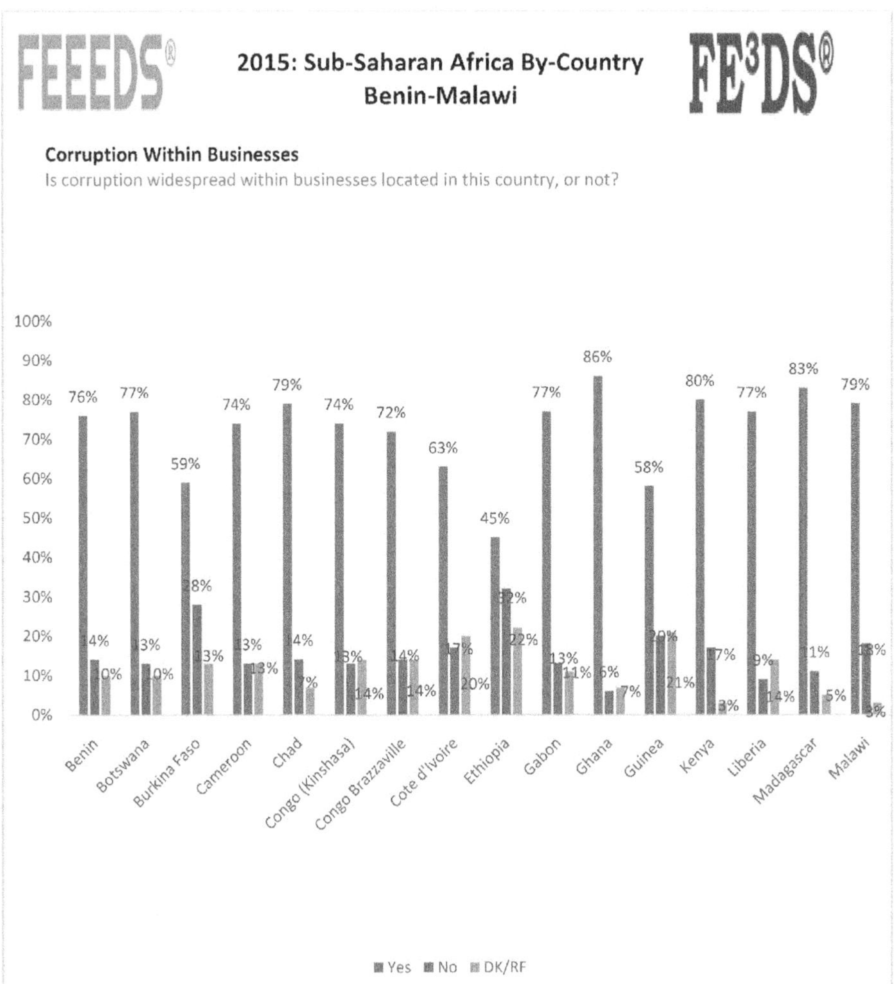

Part Two: **Highlights Corruption in Business By-Country: Mali-Zimbabwe**
Highest Levels: Nigeria (87%); Tanzania (84%); and South Africa (78%).
Exceptions: Rwandans (84%) polled believed there is no corruption in business; Somalia (61%) was not too far behind.

Figure 15

FEEEDS® **2015: Sub-Saharan Africa By-Country Mali-Zimbabwe** FE³DS®

Corruption Within Businesses

Is corruption widespread within businesses located in this country, or not?

100%

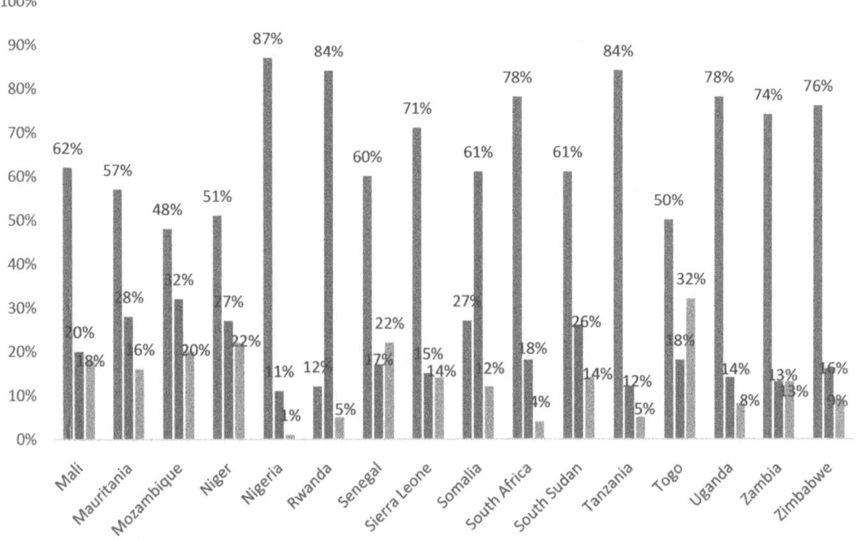

■ Yes ■ No ■ DK/RF

Highlights of Corruption in Business PowerHouse Nations

Highest Levels: Nigeria (87%); Ghana (86%); Kenya (80%); Tanzania (78%); and South Africa and DRC (74%).

Exception: Rwandans (84%) polled believed there is no corruption in business.

Figure 16

2015: FEEEDS PowerHouse Nations

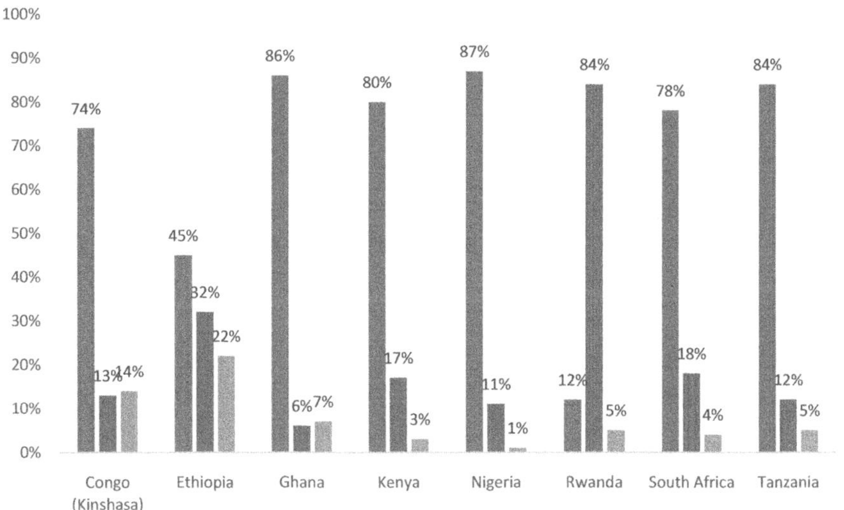

Highlights Corruption in Government Aggregate 2015

75% of African nationals in countries polled saw corruption in government as widespread in their country.

Figure 17

2015: Sub-Saharan Africa Aggregate

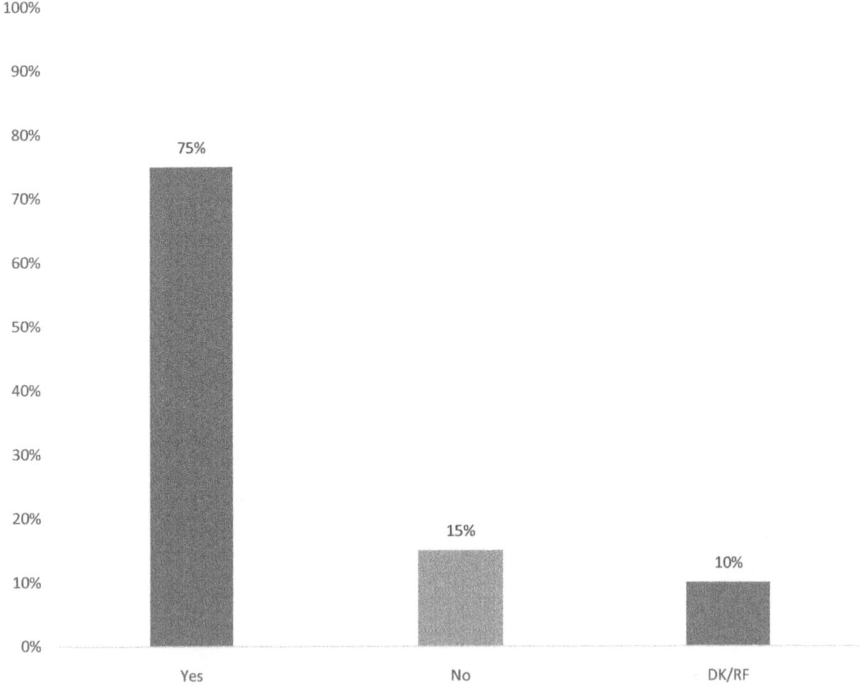

***Part One*: Highlights of Corruption in Government By-Country: Benin-Malawi**
All countries had high levels, but these had highest: Ghana (91%); Chad (87%); Kenya (86%); Malawi (82%); Madagascar (79%); Botswana and Liberia (77%); and Benin (76%).

Figure 18

FEEEDS

2015: Sub-Saharan Africa By-Country Benin-Malawi

FE³DS©

Corruption in Government

Is corruption widespread throughout the government in this country, or not?

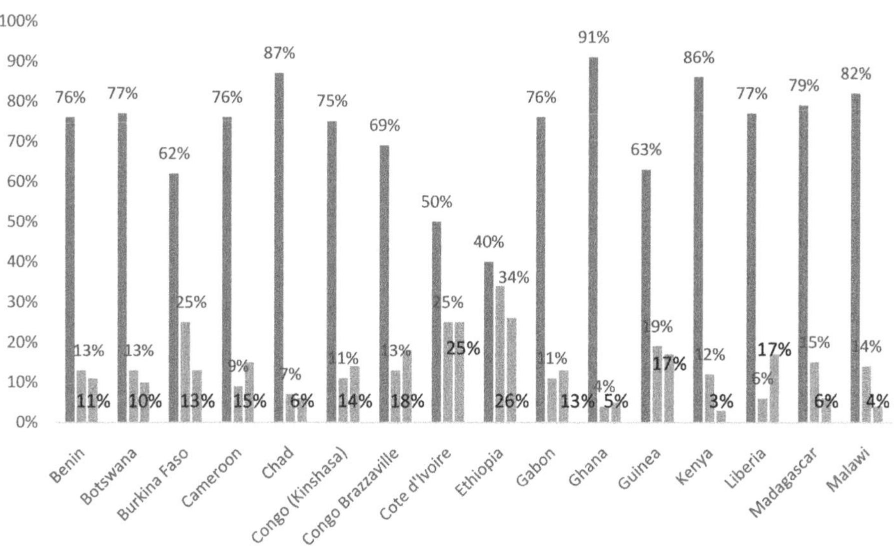

■ Yes ■ No ■ DK/RF

Part Two: Highlights of Corruption in Government By-Country: Mali-Zimbabwe
All countries had high levels, but these had the highest: Mali (78%); Nigeria (95%); South Africa (88%); Tanzania (90%); Uganda (84%); and Zimbabwe (69%).
Exception: Rwanda had low levels (7%), with most nationals saying corruption wasn't a problem (88%).

Figure 19

FEEEDS®

2015: Sub-Subaran Africa By-Country Mali-Zimbabwe

FE³DS®

Corruption in Government

Is corruption widespread throughout the government in this country, or not?

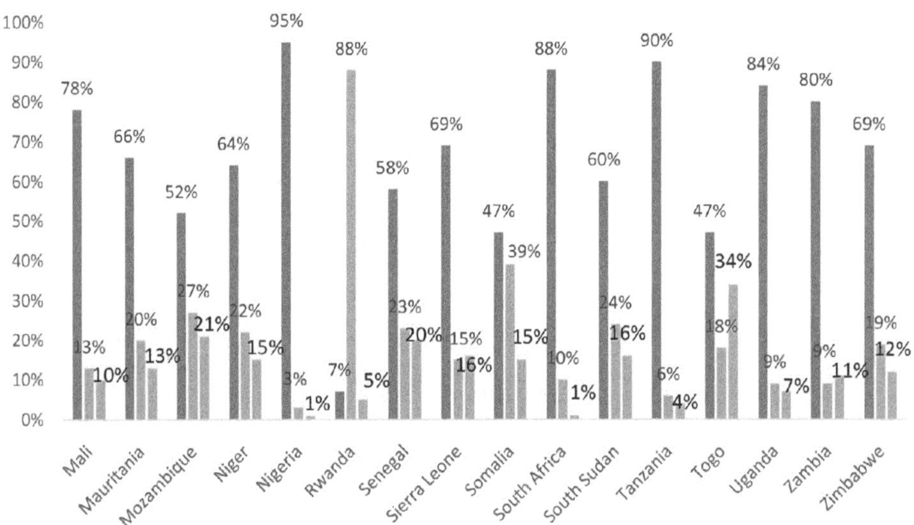

■ Yes ■ No ■ DK/RF

Highlights Corruption in Government PowerHouse Nations

Highest levels: Nigeria (95%); Ghana (91%); Tanzania (90%); South Africa (88%); Kenya (80%); and DRC/Congo-Kinshasa (75%).

Exception: Rwandan nationals (88%) said there was no corruption in government; Ethiopians where the closest second (34%).

Figure 20

FEEEDS® **2015 FEEEDS PowerHouse Nations**

Corruption in Government

Is corruption widespread throughout the government in this country, or not?

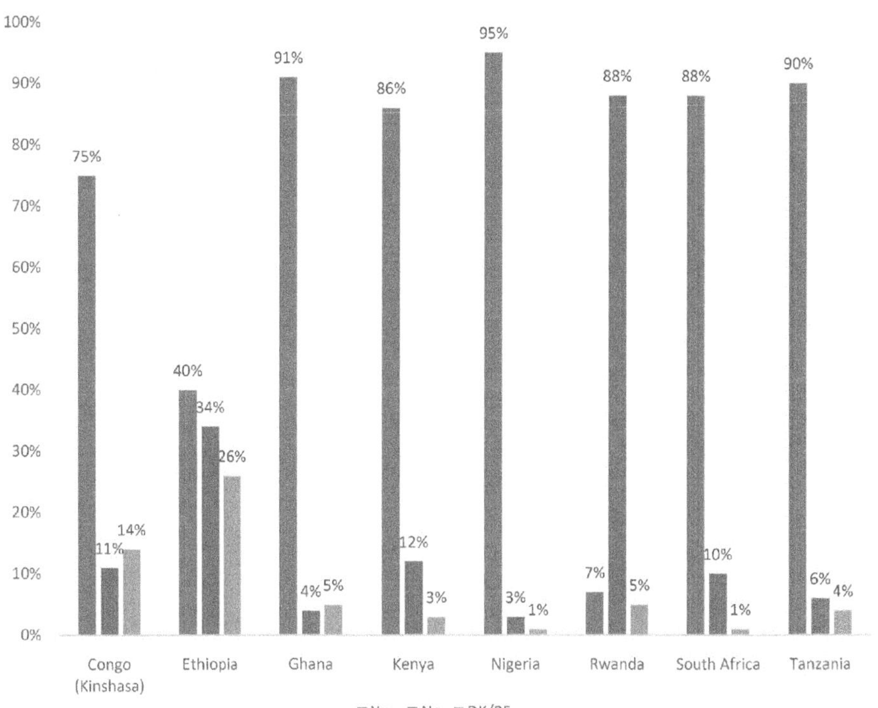

Highlights Confidence in National Government Aggregate 2015

56 % of SSAfrican countries polled had confidence in their governments, up from 2014. This is likely as a result of the number of countries in the region that had descent elections and new leaders in 2015.

June 23, 2016, Gallup World Poll® article noted that SSAfrican nationals polled were pleased with the performance of their leaders in 2015. See footnote.[2]

Figure 21

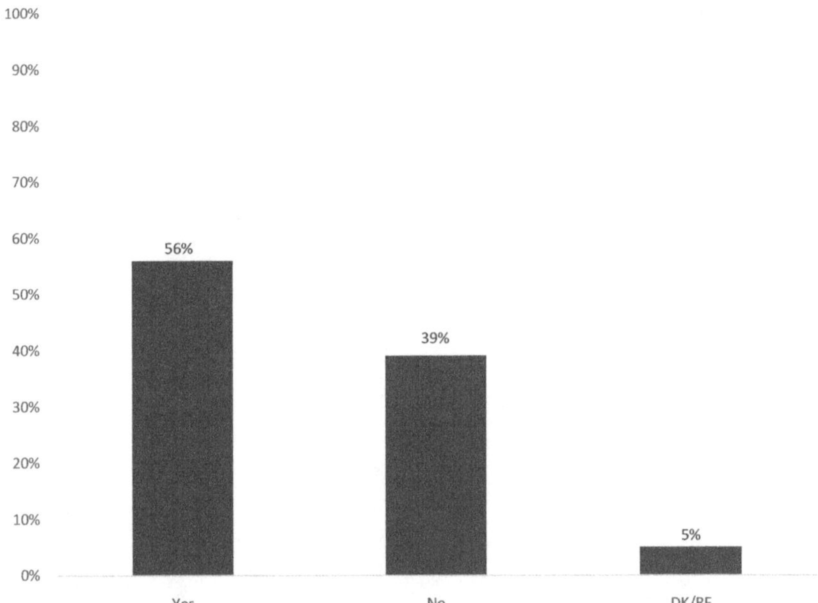

[2] Rheault, M. & J. McCarthy. *In Busy Election Year, African Leaders Enjoy High Approvals.* Gallup World Poll. Retrieved June 14, 2016 from http://www.gallup.com/poll/192584/busy-election-year-african-leaders-enjoyed-high-approval.aspx?utm_source=genericbutton&utm_medium=organic&utm_campaign=sharing

Highlights Confidence in National Government Aggregate 2014
50% of SSAfrica nationals polled said they had confidence in their national government in 2014. This improved in 2015 to 56% (See previous DataGraph).

Figure 22

2014: Sub-Saharan Africa Aggregate

Confidence in National Government

How about national government?

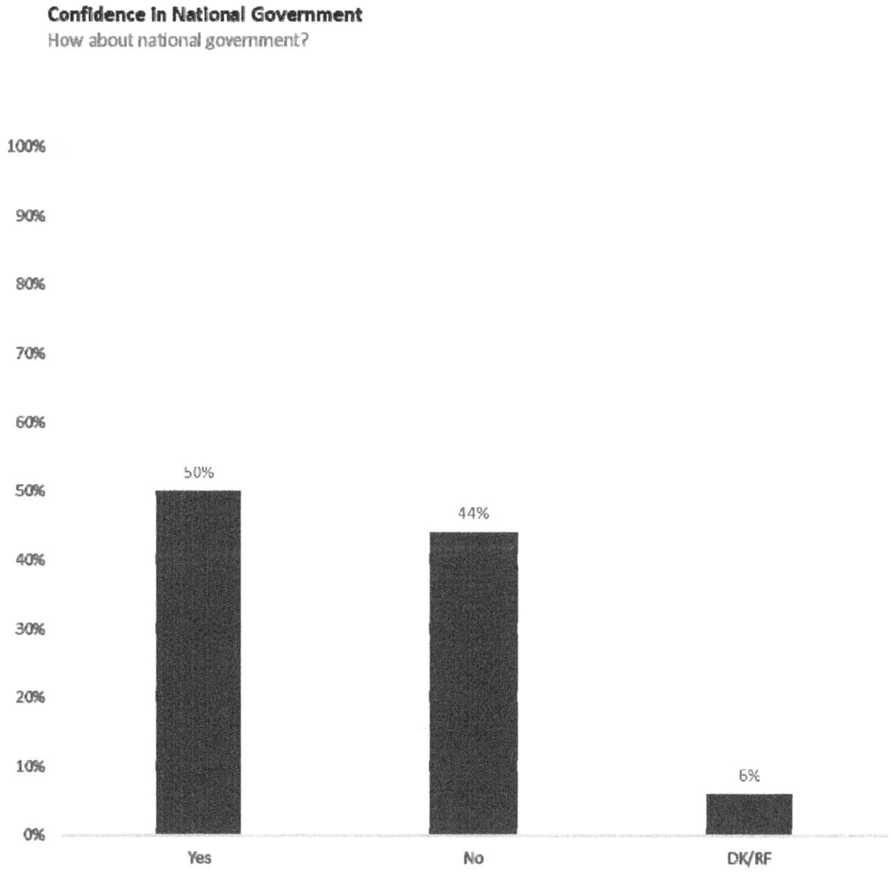

***Part One:* Confidence in National Government By-Country 2015: Benin-Malawi**

Highest positive responses: Ethiopia (83%); Botswana (82%); Kenya (75%); Burkina Faso (67%); and Cote d'Ivoire (64%).

Ethiopia, Botswana, Kenya, and Burkina Faso are in the group of the top eight countries that had big improvements (10% or more) in this theme from 2014 to 2015.

Figure 23

2015: Sub-Saharan Africa (By-Country) Benin-Malawi

Confidence in National Government

In this country, do you have confidence in each of the following, or not? How about national government?

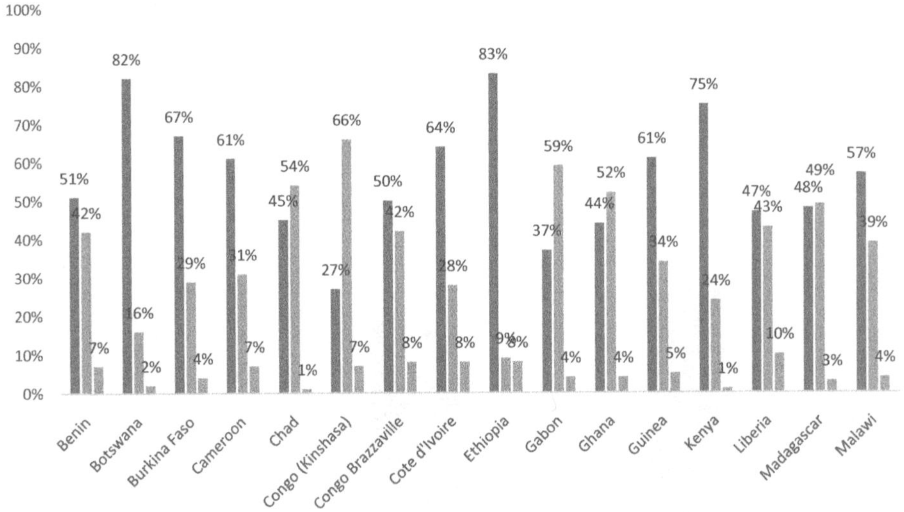

Part Two: **Confidence in National Government By-Country 2015: Mali-Zimbabwe**

Highest positives responses: Mozambique (71%); Somalia (78%); Tanzania (68%); Sierra Leone (65%); and Senegal (62%).

Nigeria, Somalia and Sierra Leone are in the group of the top eight countries that had big improvements (10% or more) in this theme from 2014 to 2015.

Figure 24

2015:Sub-Saharan Africa (By-Country)
Mali-Zimbabwe

Confidence in National Government

In this country, do you have confidence in each of the following, or not? How about national government?

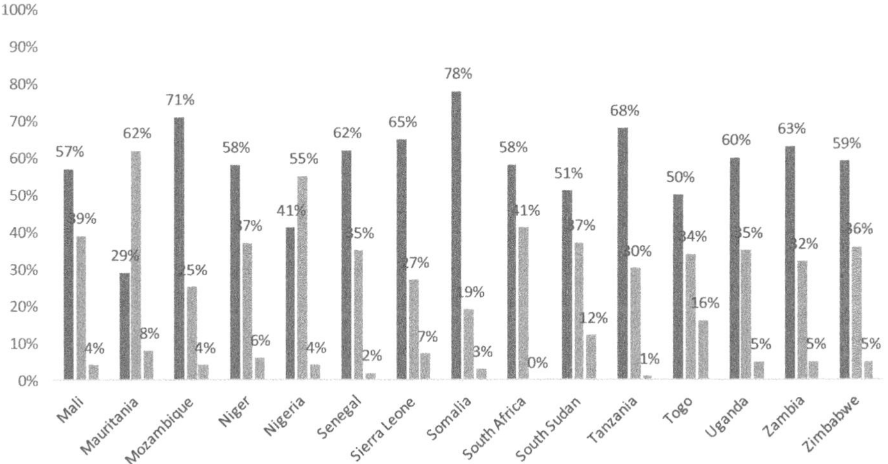

Part One: **Confidence in National Government By-Country 2014: Benin-Malawi**

Highest positive responses: Botswana (71%); Ethiopia (68%); Kenya (64%); Cote d'Ivoire (63%); and Malawi (62%).

Botswana, Burkina Faso, Ethiopia, Ghana, and Kenya are in the group of the top eight countries that had big improvements (10% or more) in this theme from 2014 to 2015.

Figure 25

FEEEDS FE3DS®

2014: Sub- Saharan Africa (By-Country)
Benin-Malawi

Confidence in National Government

In this country, do you have confidence in each of the following, or not? How about national government?

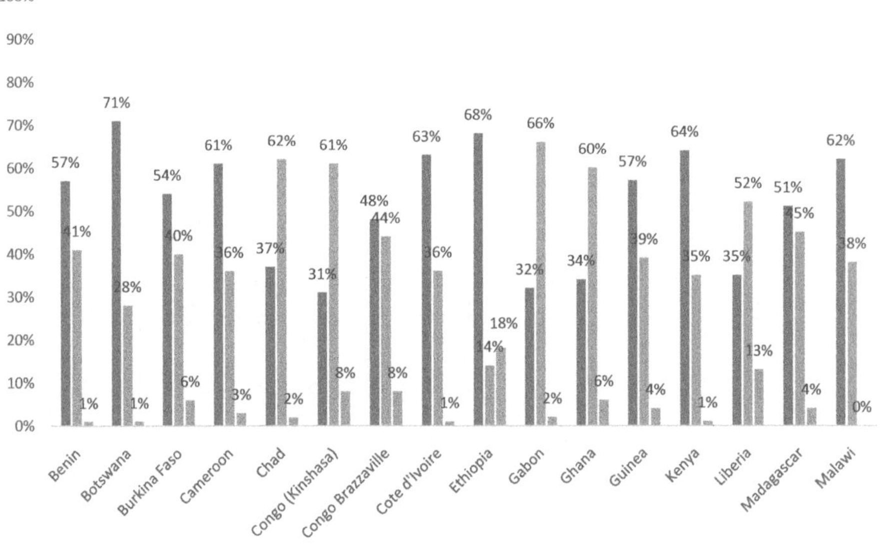

■ Yes ■ No ■ DK/RF

> ***Part Two:* Confidence in National Government By-Country 2014: Mali-Zimbabwe**
>
> **Highest positive responses: Namibia (78%); Senegal (66%); Tanzania 65%); Somalia (63%); and Mali (63%).**
>
> **Nigeria, Sierra Leone and Somalia are in the group of the top eight countries that had big improvements (10% or more) in this theme from 2014 to 2015.**

Figure 26

2014: Sub-Saharan Africa (By-Country)
Mali-Zimbabwe

Confidence in National Government

In this country, do you have confidence in each of the following, or not? How about national government?

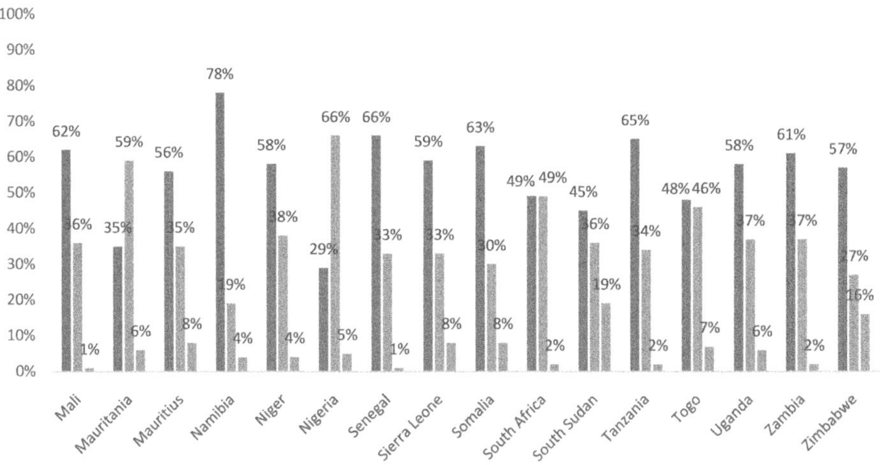

■ Yes ■ No ■ DK/RF

Sub-Saharan Africa Wellbeing Aggregate 2015
Only 10% of African nationals polled said they were thriving on at least three elements of wellbeing: purpose, social, financial, community and physical environments.   **Possibly reflects the staggering socio-economic *facts & stats* highlighted in Chapter 1-2.**

Figure 27

FEEEDS© **2015 Sub-Saharan Africa Aggregate** FE³DS®

Global Wellbeing Index

Percentage of residents thriving in three or more of the five elements of wellbeing (purpose, social, financial, community and physical).

40%
35%
30%
25%
20%
15%
10%
5%
0%

10%

Value

***Part One:* Sub-Saharan Africa Wellbeing By-Country: Benin-Malawi**

Most countries fell within the weak 10% showing on three of the five elements of wellbeing. Exception was Ethiopia, with slightly higher response of 20%. DRC/Congo-Kinshasa and Malawi both had 0%.

Possibly reflects the staggering socio-economic *"facts & stats"* highlighted in Chapter 1-2.

Figure 28

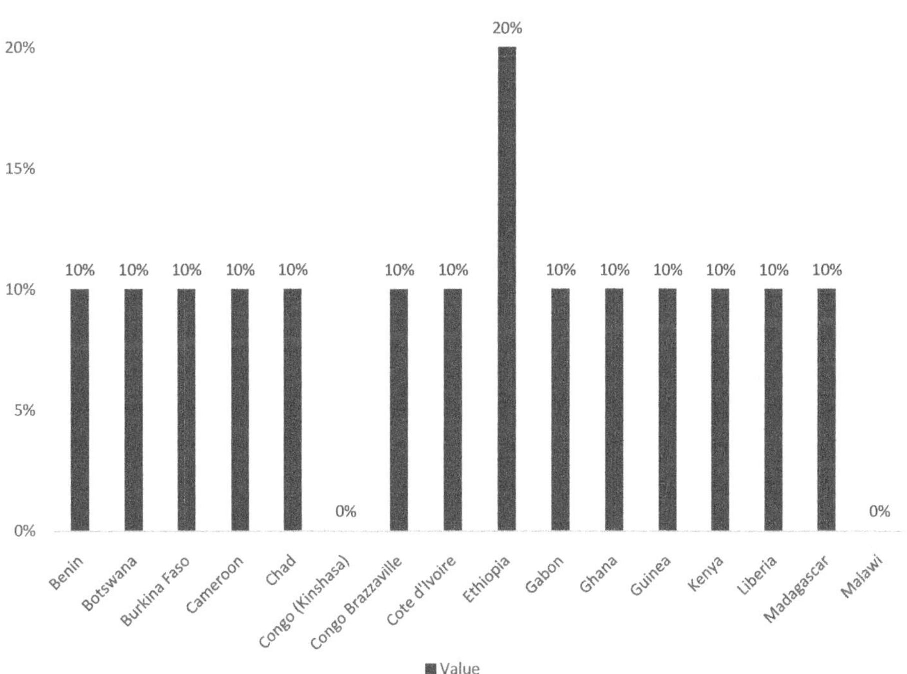

Part Two: **Sub-Saharan Africa Wellbeing By-Country: Mali-Zimbabwe**

Most countries fell within the weak 10% showing on three of five elements in wellbeing. Exceptions were: Sierra Leone & Somalia (30%); Senegal and Mauritania

Figure 29

2015: Sub-Saharan Africa By-Country Mali-Zimbabwe

Global Wellbeing Index

Percentage of residents thriving in three or more of the five elements of wellbeing (purpose, social, financial, community and physical).

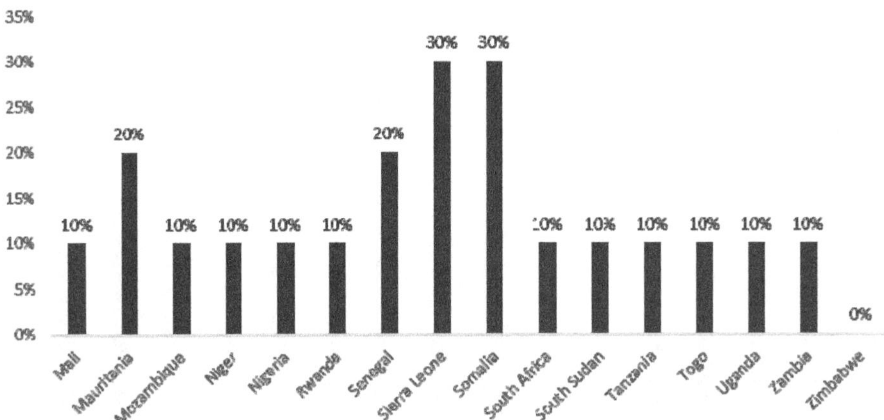

Sub-Saharan Africa Wellbeing PowerHouse Nations

Highest Positive Level: Ethiopia at 20%, but still not a great showing.

Others countries follow the SSAfrica regional trend of 10% of their nationals saying that they were not thriving in at least three of the wellbeing elements: purpose, social, financial, community and physical environment.

Possibly reflects the staggering socio-economic *facts & stats* highlighted in Chapter 1-2.

Figure 30

2015: FEEEDS PowerHouse Nations

FE³DS©

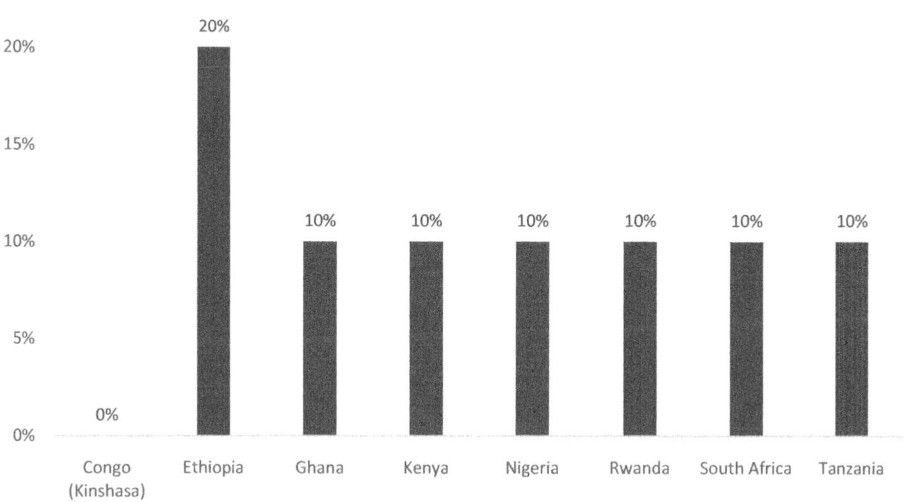

Part Five: Wrapping It Up: The Closing Comments

"As a social enterprise organization, Foundation for Skills Development (FSD) has worked since 2003 – way before today's focus on small and medium size enterprises (SMEs) was viewed by leaders of the private and government sectors as important to development – to provide a center to encourage people to create small businesses and also provide them with skills training to do so.

What we also did then and continue to do today is to focus on vocational and technical training which is equally as important as our support to SMEs. Ambassador Sanders was one of the few people in those early days that immediately understood the importance and value of our work, particularly on vocational training, and encouraged our work at FSD by attending our programs, encouraging our trainees and supporting the FSD leadership. She did that as a senior U.S. diplomat and continues to do so today as CEO-FEEEDS."

—Omowale Ogunrinde, Founder, President of Foundation for Skills Development

Chapter Twelve: Opportunities, Forecasts, and Recommendations

This book is all about giving credit where credit is due:

> *The success of the Africa SME and entrepreneur sector is more a testament to the resilience of many African nationals and the Diaspora, wanting to find a better path to changing the 40-year development model that had not fundamentally reduced poverty, provided sustainable jobs, or created strong institutions. They wanted to interact at home, in countries of affinity, and with the world differently – using their creativity and taking advantage of the unlimited possibilities that both technology and mobility offered.*

Certainly, donors, African governments and institutions, philanthropists, the private sector, venture capitalists, private equity firms, and African stock markets have all played a role in this shift-change and focus on Africa SMEs and entrepreneurs. But it was the young African nationals and the

Diaspora who got the ball rolling and helped move the development conversation and donor-recipient paradigm from *income-generating to generating-income.* Along with this shift-change, Generation-Xers and Millennials underscored the importance of DIY (do-it-yourself) in finding ways to support themselves, using technology and its mobility in the process, many creating business-aiding-development companies, and, contributing to either their countries of birth, that of their parents, or to an African nation where they have an ancestral link, affinity or interest.[543] [544] [545]

Being on the ground in Africa or working in policy circles in Washington, and experiencing how U.S. Government agencies; the foreign and national private sectors and investors; as well as other countries and

---

543 *Do-it-Yourself.* (n.d.). DIY. Retrieved June 17, 2016 from https://en.wikipedia.org/wiki/Do_it_yourself.

544 *Do-it-Yourself (DIY)* (n.d.). Home Page. Geiger Counter. Retrieved June 17, 2016 from http://ocw.mit.edu/courses/nuclear-engineering/22-s902-do-it-yourself-diy-geiger-counters-january-iap-2015/.

545 The term "DIY," although having been around since 1912, according to Wikipedia, previously referred only to self-home improvement projects but is used more colloquially now to mean some self-initiative to address, fix, create (particularly apps) a solution to a problem, or respond to request that go unanswered. The DIY term is being used in sectors as wide ranging as nuclear science and engineering. The DIY term now covers a wide range of skill sets.

political groupings from the UK, China, Japan, India, Turkey, Brazil, Indonesia, the European Union, several Nordic countries, and today, several Gulf States (e.g., United Arab Emirates) – have all now developed their own economic framework for working with the Continent. This all has all been fascinating to be a direct part of or observe in real time.[546]

Areas where venture capitalists, private equity firms, and the private sector should look to do more is certainly with female SMEs and women and girls writ large since they represent over 50 percent of the region's population now and growing. Without helping women and girls more, there will be no long-term changes on the stark numbers on poverty, job creation needs or development.

In addition, I have highlighted extensively how important it is to better assist and count informal Africa SMEs and

---

[546] *Gulf Cooperation Council* (GCC). (2015, June 9) Membership. International Organization. Encyclopædia Britannica. Retrieved August 7, 2016 from https://www.britannica.com/topic/Gulf-Cooperation-Council

Gulf Cooperation Council. (2016) About GCC. Organizational Structure. Gulf Cooperation Council. Retrieved August 7, 2016 from http://www.gcc-sg.org/en-us/AboutGCC/Pages/OrganizationalStructure.aspx.

help that all-important critical mass group, which I believe is where the bulk of Africa SMEs and entrepreneurs are today – making $US10,000-$US250,000 per year – along with developing more creative solutions on access to finance and credit, and providing more security for the fragile or floating middle class.

The China Factor?

This brings me to discussing China a bit more and what the future relationship between China and Africa might look like given the quadruple role China is playing as an emerging global market leader, Africa's single biggest trading partner (about 40 percent of its market), becoming the second largest economy in the world (as of June 2016), and heading toward becoming the world's largest net credit lending country – the importance of this latter point cannot be underestimated. (NB: China is also the US's biggest trading partner).[547]

---

[547] *The Heat.* (2016, June 17). News Magazine. [Television broadcast, 12:30 p.m.] China Global Television Network.

Comments made at the August 2016 U.S.-Africa AGOA Ministerial program attended by me as a member of the U.S. Trade Advisory Committee on Africa (TACA).

China has an ever-changing relationship with the Continent which will be important to watch, particularly as China's manufacturing base shrinks, and SSAfrica, hopefully, picks up the slack. Or, alternatively, Chinese companies moving some of their manufacturing to SSAfrica to take advantage of lower production and labor costs, which one sees in Ethiopia (shoe factories), Republic of Congo (proposed car manufacturing), and with plans in other countries like Kenya, South Africa and Tanzania.

Because of these reasons, other nations (yes, the United States included) need to still do much more for and with Africa SMEs so that these small businesses going forward know that there is equally as much opportunity elsewhere and with other countries as with China. Clearly with China, there are other issues of concern as to how it historically has operated in the region such as lack of skills transfers (which they are doing a lot better on these days), lack of what the West would view as good governance and transparency requirements on transactions, fairness in business practices, and on occasion subtle or sometimes not so subtle racial overtones. Other countries and regions

(US, post-Brexit UK, European Union, Japan, and India, to name a few) of course have a role, but they will likely have to work harder to balance out China's influence over the next decade. In addition, as China establishes itself as the biggest credit lending country in the world, along with its influential role in the NDB (New Development Bank) mentioned in Chapter 5, then it could provide more opportunities for SSAfrica SMEs not only in creating solutions, sourcing materials, exporting manufactured goods, and expanding their efforts in building infrastructure (new efforts in roads, bridges, and railways like in Ethiopia, Tanzania and Zambia) but also for responding to the Africa SME access to finance issues, more than any other nation. This of course remains to be seen, but these dynamics are something I would forecast to pay much more attention to in the coming years, particularly if there is a desire to counterbalance or just balance. Furthermore, on top of China's role in the NDB, the China Development Bank and China Export-Import Bank are also big lending institutions to emerging regions like SSAfrica. China also seeks to play an ever- increasing global role on just about everything from development and climate change to engaging more on world issues. Thus, it is hosting an "International Cooperation Summit" in May 2017 announced by President Xi Jinping at the 2017 World Economic Forum.

All of this does not mean that what Western or other South-South countries (especially India) have to offer will not be welcomed; of course it will, but if it is simply a numbers game of money, access to credit, resources, opportunities, and flat out continued comprehensive high-level engagement – then China could have the longer-term leg up, giving where it is starting from today. These are not negative sum game comments against other nations, or China, just a realization of where the trends seem to be going from the vantage point of 2016-2018.[548]

[548] Chang, S. (2016, April 13). *China's First-Quarter GDP Growth Likely Slowed to a Seven-Year Low.* Markets. Market Watch. Retrieved July 7, 2016 from http://www.marketwatch.com/story/chinas-first-quarter-gdp-growth-likely-slowed-to-a-seven-year-low-2016-04-12.

The US-Africa Relationship: 2017 and Beyond

For the United States, we have an opportunity going forward in 2017 and beyond to both keep and tweak some of the good existing program that we have put in place over years, and also especially create new positive ones. SSAfrica will not be able to be ignored by the US (and should not be) just by virtue of its shear population growth (2.4 billion by 2050), and because that population is young (more than half under 35 years old) and mostly female.

Thus, here are my recommendations for the US over the coming years as to how it can engage more, even if that engagement is different than before. Let's look at the baseline today and see what else can be done to enhance those existing programs and where I recommend we create new programs, keeping budget issues in mind as well as the message that the US viewpoint on trade facilities may change in several directions over the coming years.

First there is AGOA (started under former President Clinton, and reauthorized under successive administrations of former Presidents George W. Bush and Obama – I worked for all three administrations to support it), which has already been discussed in several chapters above. But if it remains something that the Trump Administration supports over the next four years and beyond until its 2025 expiration date, then it needs to be shored up a lot more with technical assistance (TA) and capacity building in order to ensure that new African trade ministers and SMEs utilize its benefits more, particularly adding phytosanitary training on Federal Drug Administration (FDA) guidelines to increase African agricultural exports (something I have advocated for over a number of years) as well as having a better list or data base of trade-capable SMEs. Right now, for instance, on the US end, there is no clear or singular comprehensive data base of what Africa-based companies are taking advantage of the AGOA facility; U.S. Embassies do as much as they can to follow these connections, but there should be a central data base where all this information can be fed in Washington. We know many, but certainly not all, and it is not systematically followed or recorded so that information can populate a data base. These TA and capacity building programs can be done as part of a PPP or 4-P model as opposed to a strictly development aid model. This allows for business and trade partnerships to gather steam and develop, be they SMEs or larger businesses on the Continent.

MCC, PEPFAR, the *expanded* International Visitor Leaders (IVLP, as prior it was called the IV program) and AEI programs (created under former President George W. Bush), and YALI (already discussed) are also important to Africa SMEs. Africa small businesses can be important partners on key MCC areas such as infrastructure development and as subcontractors on construction projects as mentioned on the TEL in Chapter 4. On PEPFAR we have already seen the role creative SMEs are playing in the African health sector from apps to appropriate technology. The Trump Administration has already said it plans to keep PEPFAR. The Bush Administration in 2000 both changed the name and expanded the IV program to become the International Visitors Leadership Program

(IVLP), enhancing its training-focus and including more emphasis on entrepreneurship; YALI has taken all this a step further. AEI, led by the late Dr. Sarah E. Moten, focused on scholarships for elementary and secondary school girls, paid for school fees, books and supplies, and was a wonderful program that helped address the huge problem of both getting and keeping African girls in school (NB: The precursor to AEI was the former president Clinton's EDDI mentioned earlier in Chapter 6.)[549] I have highlighted a number of innovative educational approaches that Africa SMEs are doing now in education in Chapter 8, and certainly their role in reducing gender inequality as called for by the UN SDGs and the AU will continue to be important. Therefore, the US can take the lead on helping women SMEers more and assisting with the capacity of young girls (8-15 years) to be trained early on as entrepreneurs or with vocational skills, similarly through PPP or 4-P models.

---

[549] Sarah E. Moten. (2013). George Bush Presidential Center. Retrieved December 4, 2016 from http://www.bushcenter.org/people/sarah-e-moten.html

Power Africa and USAID's DIV grants (created under former President Obama and discussed in Chapter 8) also are SME-friendly programs as they support TA training, addressed energy needs, and offered access to grants for SMEs. These too are good programs and still can meet the stated changes the US new administration wants institute because they provide opportunities for US businesses, marketing of US manufactured goods, and for good partnerships with Africa SMEs who can then build more links back to the Continent. I have worked for all three of these administrations as a U.S. diplomat, and have first-hand experience on the impact and effectiveness of these programs and how they can assist Africa SMEs, but also more importantly, how they all contribute to the US economy.

Therefore, the U.S. Government can build, tweak, expand and create new positive programs to reach out to this all-important group of future business leaders in the region. SSAfrica's business potential is as evident as is its future market potential for US goods and services which can be a complement to a growing

Africa manufacturing sector. US business leaders in senior private and public positions in 2017 and going forward will likely see and want to engage both the SME sector and the region overall for these basic business reasons. At least I am going to anticipate now that they will see the value of doing so, particularly viewing SMEs as businesses that can procure US goods and services useful and complementary to SSAfrica's needs, especially from the potentially reinvigorated "Rust Belt" manufacturing states of the US Midwest.[550]

This would also argue for keeping the U.S. Export-Import Bank that allows for loan financing guarantees that help the US economy and US manufacturers. Remember the US will need markets for a renewed manufacturing sector, and as mentioned SSAfrica will have the world's largest population in 2050. Neither point diminishes SSAfrica stepping up its own capacity to manufacture. And, I do not see either – SSAfrica stepping up its manufacturing and US having an

[550] Rust Belt is a term referring to an area of the US covering the Great Lakes Region, most of the Midwest and parts of Appalachia which in the past served as the heart of the US manufacturing sector.

additional large market for its goods and services as a negative sum game.

Also, in my recommendation basket is a suggestion that the UN's 2015-2030 SDGs and the AU's 2063 program put more of an explicit emphasis on Africa SMEs as one of the best practices in responding to poverty, job creation, human capacity building, and economic development, especially since small businesses are not now specifically mentioned (although implied) in the 17 goals or 169 targets of the SDGs or in the AU 2063 Agenda.[551] [552]

However, I must at least give the UN and AU credit for beginning to work more with SMEs. Even if SMEs are not specifically mentioned (yet), it is clear that they recognize, like everyone else, that Africa SMEs are important to the region's growth. For me, the role of

---

[551] García de Alba, M. V. (2016, January 10). A small player with a big footprint... SMEs, CSR and the SDGs. Retrieved July 17, 2016 from http://www.eoi.es/blogs/imsd/a-small-player-with-a-big-footprint-smes-csr-and-the-sdgs/

[552] International Labour Organization. (1996-2016). *Decent Work and the 2030 Agenda for Sustainable Development.* Topics. Goal #8: Decent Work and Economic Growth. Retrieved July 17, 2016 from http://www.ilo.org/global/topics/sdg-2030/lang--en/index.htm.

SMEs best fit under the UN SDG Goal #8 – *Promote sustained, inclusive and sustainable economic growth; full and productive employment; and decent work for all.* Therefore, SMEs should at least be explicitly mentioned under this goal.[553]

The question will be how the UN and AU, particularly the AU with it new chairperson) measure not only SME successes, but outlining in more detail in what areas they advance sustainable development outside of job creation. Moreover, it will be important within the SDG framework and other studies by international organizations on the SME sector to find better ways to count and include the contributions made by Africa's large informal sector. There are already signs that the UN and AU are beginning to look to the SME sector more. I tweeted on June 13, 2016, about the proceedings I was following that day of a collaborative program of the UN, AU, member countries, and

[553] Ibid.

United Nations. (n.d.). *Sustainable development goal 8: promote sustained, inclusive and sustainable economic growth, full and productive employment and descent work for all.* Sustainable Knowledge Platform. Retrieved October 11, 2016 from https://sustainabledevelopment.un.org/sdg8

NGOs that emphasize and the SDG-entrepreneurship connection, particularly for youth and women.[554] What I liked most about the event, reading through the discussions, was the view (synergistic with mine) that for the SDGs to succeed, SME and entrepreneurship have to be included more. The event was hosted by the UN's Office of the Special Advisor on Africa (OSAA), and included a variety of other prominent AU commissioners, country representatives from Kenya and Ghana, and several other important UN offices such as UN Women, and the Office of the Secretary General's Envoy on Youth. The E4Impact Foundation, private sector companies, and other civil society groups also attended.[555] [556] [557]

---

554 *UNESCO and E4IMPACT to Develop Cultural and Education Entrepreneurship in Africa.* (2016, February 2). United Nations Education and Cultural Organization. http://www.unesco.org/new/en/media-services/single-view/news/unesco_and_e4impact_to_develop_cultural_and_education_entrepreneurship_in_africa/#.V23b3I9OIic.

555 Ibid.

556 United Nations. (2016, June 13). *The High-Level Event on Women and Youth Entrepreneurship in Africa: The Impact of Entrepreneurial Education on Development.* Office of the Special Advisor on Africa. Retrieved June 15, 2015 from http://www.un.org/en/africa/osaa/events/2016/entrepreneurship.shtml.

557 E4Impact Foundation. (2015, September 19). *A New Foundation Launched To Support Impact Entrepreneurship In Africa.* Lioness of Africa. Retrieved June 25 and August 18, 2016 from http://www.lionessesofafrica.com/blog/2015/9/19/a-new-foundation-launched-to-support-impact-

I am making the argument that both the UN and the AU under its new chairperson need to be more SME-centric. However, for the AU, in particular, a SME-centric focus is especially important for its 2063 plan to succeed. A few of the plan's key goals are to reduce overall unemployment by 25 percent, and reduce both female and youth unemployment by an additional 2 percent in the first 10 years of the 2063 plan. This means a reduction in unemployment of 27 percent for both women and youth. I worry that this 27 percent goal is too low given the current size of the female population; given that half the region's youth fall mostly in the prime working age years of 15-35; and given the looming reality that the region's working-age population will be more than the rest of the world combined by 2035 as cited earlier – the AU may be realizing this itself more and more since it declared 2017 as *The Year of Harnessing Demographic Dividend Through Youth.*[558]

---

entrepreneurship-in-africa

[558] African Union Agenda 2063. (n.d.). Retrieved May 11, 2016 and January 5, 2017 from http://agenda2063.au.int/en/about

International Monetary Fund. (2015, April). *Sub-Saharan Africa-Navigating Headwinds.* Regional Economic Outlook, p. 36. Retrieved July 24, 2016

For the UN and AU to be more strategic about the role Africa SMEs play and include them as being *fundamental* to any on-ground implementation of either the SDGs or the AU 2063 Plan they can modify their frameworks and state so.[559] Not overly hard to do. This will help with having a more accurate picture of the positive changes and role of Africa SMEs in reducing many of the stark statistics already discussed.

If you forgot any of those stark stats, here is an illustrative short recap, along with a few country-specific examples of the high unemployment figures many nations face:

- 15% is the average estimated unemployment rate in Africa, with some countries even higher. The high roller is South Africa with an overall unemployment rate in mid-2016 of 26.7 percent followed by other staggering numbers in places

from https://www.imf.org/external/pubs/ft/reo/2015/afr/eng/pdf/sreo0415.pdf.

559 Ibid.

like Kenya (17.4%), Nigeria (15.6%), DRC (11.9), and Angola (10.5); [560] [561]

- 60% of the people in SSAfrica's who are unemployed are young people; [562]

- 10-12% represents the overall small amount of regional trade for the Sub-Saharan African region; in East Africa, however, sub-regional trade has improved and now is closer to 26 percent;[563]

---

[560] Full citation earlier in Chapter 5. http://www.businessinsider.com/south-africa-unemployment-rate-rises-2016-5

[561] World Bank/IBRD-IDA. (2016). *Unemployment, Youth Total (% of Total Labor Force Ages 15-24).* Data. Retrieved July 17, 2016 from http://data.worldbank.org/indicator/SL.UEM.1524.ZS

[562] See checklist data box from: United Nations. (2016, June 13). *The High-Level Event on Women and Youth Entrepreneurship in Africa: The Impact of Entrepreneurial Education on Development.* Office of the Special Advisor on Africa. Retrieved June 15, 2015 from http://www.un.org/en/africa/osaa/events/2016/entrepreneurship.shtml.

[563] Tafirenyika, M. (2014, April). *Intra-Africa Trade: Going Beyond Political Commitments.* Africa Renewal Online. United Nations Africa Renewal. Retrieved August 8, 2016, and July 6, 2016 from http://www.un.org/africarenewal/magazine/august-2014/intra-africa-trade-going-beyond-political-commitments

Ancharaz, V., Mbekeani, K., & Brixiova, Z. (2011, September). *Impediments to Regional Trade Integration in Africa.* AfDB Economist Complex. Africa Economic Brief. Vol. 2: Issue 11. African Development Bank. p. 2. Retrieved August 8, 2016 from http://www.afdb.org/fileadmin/uploads/afdb/Documents/Publications/AEB%20VOL%202%20Issue%2011_AEB%20VOL%202%20Issue%2011.pdf

- 1.1 billion is the World Bank's and UN's 2015 population estimates for the region; [564]

- 2.4 billion is the region's expected population by 2050, if population growth rates remain at 2.55 percent;[565]

- 18 million is the yearly jobs which need to be created; and [566]

- Worth repeating, one of the most staggering stats to me is – Africa's working-age population

---

(2016, May 11). *Global Business.* [Television broadcast, 2 p.m.] China Global Television Network.

Kenny, P. (2016, October 10). Africa makes progress on trade and economic integration. *Allafrica.com.* Retrieved October 14, 2016 from http://allafrica.com/stories/201610100001.html?aa_source=nwsltr-nigeria-en

[564] United Nations. (2015). *World Population Prospects: Key findings and Advance Tables.* Revision. United Nations. Retrieved April 17, 2016 from http://esa.un.org/unpd/wpp/publications/files/key_findings_wpp_2015.pdf

World Bank/IBRD-IDA. (2015). *Sub-Saharan Africa Population.* [data set]. Retrieved August 15, 2016 from http://data.worldbank.org/region/sub-saharan-africa.

[565] Ibid.

[566] International Monetary Fund. (2015, April). *Sub-Saharan Africa-Navigating Headwinds. Regional Economic Outlook,* p. 36. Retrieved July 24, 2016 from https://www.imf.org/external/pubs/ft/reo/2015/afr/eng/pdf/sreo0415.pdf

is on course to supersede the world combined working-age population by 2035.[567]

So, my main questions for the region on which my forecasting comments will be based are as follows:

- What is next for SSAfrica if all of these things move in the direction predicted?

- What else does the region need to do to prepare for growth and development – if both move in a positive direction?

- How best to help informal SMEs move into the formal sector?

Certainly, there are unknown variables, and the role of security will play a part in the region. Any intended and unintended consequences that are linked to security issues, particularly for countries like Cote

---

[567] Ibid. This data also was presented at the FEEEDS-Gallup July 14, 2016 event by Gallup's Africa Regional Director Magali Rheault and her presentation is on the FEEEDS-Gallup July 14, 2016 event cloud at: www.bit.ly/FEEEDS-GALLUPSlides

Also, see: World Bank/IBRD-IDA. (2016). *Unemployment, Youth Total (% of Total Labor Force Ages 15-24).* [data set]. Retrieved July 17, 2016 from http://data.worldbank.org/indicator/SL.UEM.1524.ZS

d'Ivoire, Kenya, Mali, Niger, Nigeria, Somalia, South Sudan, and Tanzania and any other nation in the Sahel Extremism Belt, could impact different countries in the region, on top of new threats unforeseen today. Internal political and governance upheavals in a country can and will impact growth, development, investment and business. It is important to remember that during 2017-2018 there will be 17 elections in SSAfrica that we hope will go well, so that Africa's efforts to advance and strengthen democratic processes can continue. I already mentioned a few SSAfrica countries in 2016 that are on my watch list for 2017 and into 2018 because they:

- Had elections that worried the international community (Congo-Brazzaville, Gabon, Zambia).

- Had constitutional changes to allow presidential third terms (Burundi, Republic of Congo, and Rwanda), where political opposition had to compromise to allow an incumbent to remain a year past his term (DRC), or faced uncertain stability because an incumbent would not accept election results (Gambia).

- Faced popular demonstrations against closed regimes (Ethiopia, which also had spurts of banning social media and the press) or remained a closed regime (Angola, Cameroon, Chad, and Zimbabwe).

- Had uncertain, questionable governance or conflict (Equatorial Guinea, and South Sudan).

- Experienced changes through the ballot box against governments seen as not doing enough to fight corruption or reduce unemployment (South Africa), or countries which will have important elections in 2017 (Rwanda and Kenya).

In addition, the growing security issues can have an impact on any country's growth, but taking that into account, SSAfrica SMEs should still be able to manage their contributions to their country's economic sectors even if investors get scared off by security challenges. As in the end, it mostly likely will be the local investors and Africa SMEs that will not be afraid to continue their work and not be scared off by local challenges.

The challenges are how will all these things be managed, and can they be managed well? My goal in this book is to share some thinking on these issues and shed some light on what is being done now, and what more can be done in the near-term to support and advance the positive growth and role of the SSAfrica SMEs and entrepreneurs, despite the knowns and unknowns.

Creating an Africa SME Strategic Plan (Africa SSP)

So, how would this work – getting more of a handle on the sector and the impact of the knowns, plus scenarios on the possible outcomes and unknowns? Things like what countries are SMEs contributing the most to the middle class, GDP, trade, and job creation and why, and what African governments are doing the most to assist their small businesses are elements that are important on which to have better knowledge management. Rwanda and Senegal are noted a lot for support to their entrepreneurs, and South Africa is not far behind, particularly since it has several events as well as comprehensive institutions to assist their small businesses, and plans to establish an SME Ministry. Rwanda has a *Made in Rwanda Fridays*, started by a young entrepreneur there to raise awareness of local SME goods and services, and South African small businesses also have entrepreneurially pulled together to create an annual event called the *Makhelewane Festival*, a millennial approach to marketing where private township homes are turned into *business-stalls-for-a-day* to help entrepreneurs sell their wares from food to crafts to clothes.[568] As mentioned earlier, even in countries like Somalia which gets high marks from its nationals on having a conducive environment for its SMEs, the country has established an "Entrepreneur of the Year" award, which in early January 2017 went to Ilwad Elman, a dynamic Somali-Canadian born female entrepreneur and human rights activists in Mogadishu.[569]

---

[568] *Makhelewane Festival.* (2016). Retrieved December 2, 2016 from https://twitter.com/makhelwanefest

[569] Ilwad Elman – Leaders of Sustainable Development. (n.d.). Thomason Reuters. Retrieved January 6, 2017 from http://sustainability.thomsonreuters.com/women/authors/ilwad-elman/

Thus, then what would be useful as Africa small businesses continue to grow is more specific goals and data on the work African SMEs are doing in the SDG goal areas such as health, education, gender equality, food security (nutrition-focused agriculture), and shelter, as well as on key development sectors such as tourism, transportation, infrastructure, and manufacturing. Bottom line:

> *What I am calling for is* an Africa *SME Strategic Plan (SSP) – where all organizations, donor countries, foundations, and private sector entities have a universally agreed-upon approach to assist Africa's SMEs.*

Keeping in mind the OECD reports mentioned earlier that donors may pull back on their development budgets through 2018 (which we see already happening) an Africa SPP becomes even more important. And, on the US end, the new Trump Administration is seeking to do things differently, therefore the input from the US on the elements of an Africa SSP could be focused on the business and the data aspects of working with sustainable startups, SMEs and entrepreneurs in the SDG and critical development areas. Doing so would have a business-focus and business benefit. My suggestion for a strategic plan could include all of the things talked about thus far in this book, but linked together as a universal Africa SSP that also included:

1.) Longer Term mentoring program (2-3 years).

2.) Increased creative credit mechanisms such as warehouse financing, lower and tiered loan and insurance programs.

3.) Fixed partnerships with US businesses in similar sectors.

4.) Targeted regional and foreign export opportunities.

5.) Regionally based industry clusters/SEZs (a big center per REC area).

6.) Increased assistance to move more SMEs from the informal to the formal sector.

7.) Increased capacity building and training.

All of these suggestions help Africa's development, SME business growth and SDGs even if the relationship is business-centered. I have already talked about areas within the Africa SME sector which needs more and better data, so I would also include a data gathering aspect to the Africa SSP to include collecting and annually publishing information on the *State of SSAfrica's SMEs.* A State of SSAfrica's SMEs Report, as part of the Africa SSP, could provide growth numbers, sectoral emphasis, GDP and trade impact, country financial support to entrepreneurs, figures on startups per year, number of female-owned businesses per country, and better figures on registered and unregistered SMEs. My idea for an Africa SSP is something that could be produced by the UN and AU together, and connected to updates from the region on their progress on the SDGs. The *Kauffman Index on Entrepreneurship Growth Report* in 40 US cities is one example of what is done by some organizations in the US on trying to get a better handle on the *where and how* the current US entrepreneurship sector is impacting the US economy and employment. My idea of an Africa SSP goes along with my previous comments above that the UN's SDGs and AU's 2063 Agenda need to specifically list SMEs and entrepreneurs as core to the progress of both plans as well as to the success and economic development of the Sub-Saharan Africa Region.[570]

Furthermore, if the population growth we anticipate happens, the region must better prepare for it. In 2014, 54 percent of the world's population lived in urban areas, with Asia leading the way; urban dwellers are expected to grow to 66 percent by 2050.[571] In 2016, Asia and Latin America were home to 16 of the world's 28 most crowded cities.[572] But we know that Africa is going to catch up and catch up fast over the next three decades on these urban statistics as

---

[570] Kauffman Index on Growth Entrepreneurship. (2016). Retrieved December 2, 2016 from http://www.kauffman.org/microsites/kauffman-index/reports/growth-entrepreneurship

[571] United Nations DESA's Population Division. (2014). *World's Population Increasingly Urban with More Than Half Living in Urban Areas.* World Urbanization Prospects. Retrieved June 25, 2016 from http://www.un.org/en/development/desa/news/population/world-urbanization-prospects-2014.html.

[572] Ibid.

its population continues on the current trajectory of reaching 2.4 billion people. Indeed, if the predictions on population growth, job needs, and the increase in the size of the region's urban cities are at all accurate and converge, African nations will have to continually look at urban and rural infrastructure development, not isolated from, but connected to the demand for job creation and human capacity building. It appears to me that these two things – demand for job creation and infrastructure needs – are not necessarily being connected but talked about on separate tracks. In reality with all the push for jobs and African countries discussing their infrastructure needs for transport services, power, and housing, they will have to take into account, on top of current planning, just how much more will be required for urban and rural infrastructure.

At the July 2016, joint FEEEDS-Gallup event, with media partner Allafrica.com, on the *Importance of Africa SMEs Businesses*, there was ample discussion about Africa small businesses being the answer to many of the development challenges of the Continent but that they need to be included more in the big picture issues and discussions.[573] [574]

The program attended by some 180 Africa businesses and groups noted that more mainstream large businesses, intuitions, donors, and African governments need to further expand and redefine the role and involvement of Africa SMEs and entrepreneurs in big picture challenges and planning.

In the end, for me the overall news is still good, and although it has been a long time coming for Africa SMEs to have their rightful place and recognition serving as one of the key drivers of economic development and growth in the region – that is now happening apace, and can be further expanded with actions on the many suggestions provided in the chapters above and on creating an Africa SSP to ensure we get there. I am hoping, coupled with their current positive roles as this books cites (spurring

---

[573] Allafrica.com is a leading online daily publication featuring a range of political, business and economic news about Africa. See http://www.Allafrica.com

[574] Most who attended where African immigrants, and Africa Diaspora SMEs.

development, economies and growing the middle class) that my proposal for a universally-agreed Africa SSP can be developed (am ready and willing to volunteer) and linked in large measure to the consensus frameworks of the UN's SDGs and AU's 2063 agenda. An Africa SSP could be something accomplished fairly easily at the first 3 to 5-year review of the SDGs, which would be around 2018 or 2020, or by the AU at any of its yearly summits. I would hope both organizations will do so by 2018 or sooner. This will keep pressure on donors, foundations, NGOs, investors, and the private sectors to fundamentally see Africa SMEs and entrepreneurs as core to their missions. I know they will remain core to mine.

Key Dates

1870-1885	Europeans had trading control, missionary, and political influence in Sub-Saharan Africa before the 1884-1885 Berlin Conference, which formalized colonial control of certain territories by Britain, France, Germany, and Portugal.
1884-1885	Proposed by Portugal, the Berlin West Africa Conference (Nov. 15, 1884-Feb. 26, 1885) took place in Germany to negotiate which of the European imperialists including Britain, France and the host country would secure colonial rule. Portugal pursued control of the Congo estuary known as the Congo River basin but was overruled, resulting in a neutral territory, free for trade and shipping
1900s-1956 & 1956-1960s	Colonies, term mandates, and protectorates existed in Sub-Saharan Africa during this period until the wave of independence started in 1956 and running until the mid-1960s for most African nations. Some outliers received independence in the later years of 1975, 1976, 1990, and 1993 (respectively Angola, Seychelles and Djibouti, Namibia, and Eritrea)

1960- 2000	**The period when the donor community and governments spent nearly $US3.5 trillion on development assistance with relatively no long-term impact or shift-change in the lives of most citizens of African countries. See citation Chapter 1, p. 10. This realization precipitated the International Community coming together in September 2000 to launch the Millennium Development Goals (MDGs).**
1980	**International Union for the Conservation of Nature published the World Conservation Strategy**
1987	**1987 World Commission on Environment and Development chaired by then-Norwegian Prime Minister Gro Harlem Brundtland**
1991-1997	**Civil War in Congo**
1992	**UN Rio de Janeiro Earth Summit *Agenda 21***
1996	**Olympics in Atlanta, Georgia. Former Atlanta mayor, Ambassador Andrew Young, Jr., serving as the city's Co-Chair of the Atlanta Olympic Committee**
1997-2007	**Congo's Post-Civil War/Post-Conflict period of Transition and Rebuilding**
1998	**President William Jefferson Clinton's first visit to Africa**
1998 March	**President William Jefferson Clinton's historic speech in Independence Square, Accra, Ghana**

1998-1999	**Then South African President Thabo Mbeki mentions the term "African Renaissance" in two speeches**
1999	**Council on Sustainable Development for America**
2000	**First legislation passed by Congress of the African Growth and Opportunity Act better known as AGOA**
2000-2015	**Period of UN Millennium Development Goals (MDGs)**
2000-2006	**A turning point/transition period time frame, in the author's view, when various governments, the private sector, and other donors began to view Africa differently than in the past**
2002	**2002 World Summit on Sustainable Development**
2003-2005	**Ambassador Sanders serving as U.S. Ambassador to the Republic of Congo**
2003-2005	**Mobile phones are not that pervasive in this period in the Republic of Congo as they are today**
2003	**Sanders began texting on her mobile phone**
2003	**A turning point for Sanders in Congo on her perspective on how to link policy and practice by working with UNDP to start a PPP to help young Congolese address their desire to generate-income and learn English**

2005	**Opening of the UNDP-U.S.-MERC in Brazzaville, Congo, a PPP created between UNDP Brazzaville and the U.S. Embassy Brazzaville when Ambassador Sanders served there as U.S. Ambassador, and Mr. Aurelien Agbénonci was UNDP Resident Representative and UN Coordinator**
2007-2010	**Ambassador Sanders' tenure as U.S. Ambassador to Nigeria and U.S. Permanent Representative to West Africa's economic and political body called the Economic Community of West African States (ECOWAS)**
2008-2009	**Beginning of when the author saw a big shift in focus toward SSAfrica SMEs and entrepreneurship as important development tools**
2009	**Former president Barack Obama's speech in Ghana and Egypt on importance of democracy in Africa**
2010	**Sustainable Development Land 2010 Initiative & Report**
2010-early 2015	**Height of the use of the term "BRICS"**
2010-2020	**Decade of the African Woman, as declared by the African Union (AU)**
20012-2015	**Years of mass conflict and civil war in the Central African Republic precipitated by a 2012 coup d'état**
2013-2063	**The African Union declared period for its Agenda 2063 development plan to transform the Continent**
2011–early 2015	**SSAfrica "Economic Boom Period"**

2014	**OECD's Report on development financing from 2000 to 2014 and its report Global Outlook for Aid**
2014	**FEEEDS-Gallup Inaugural Africa Conference: Pre-event for US-Africa First Business Forum**
2015-2030	**Period of the UN Sustainable Development Goals (SDGs)**
2015	**FEEEDS-Gallup 2nd Africa Conference on African elections held in 2015**
2016	**April 2016 elections were held in the Central African Republic**
2016	**Exit of the United Kingdom for the European Union on June 23, 2016, under the Brexit Referendum**
2016	**FEEEDS-Gallup Third Annual Conference entitled *The Importance of Africa SMEs***
2016-2018	**Period of likely lower GDP growth for SSAfrica**
2035	**Estimated date Africa's working-age population will be larger than the rest of the world combined**

Glossary of Terms

A

AAF –	**Africa Agriculture Fund, a private equity investment fund**
AEI –	**Africa Education Initiative**
ACBF –	**African Capacity Building Foundation**
ACP –	**African Caribbean & Pacific Countries**
ADM –	**African Diaspora Marketplace Program by USAID**
AECF –	**Africa Enterprise Challenge Fund**
AfDB –	**African Development Bank**
AGOA –	**African Growth and Opportunity Act**
"A-ha Moment" –	**The author's term for unique, improved, or never-before-thought-of solutions that Africa SMEs are creating**
ANC –	**African National Congress - the ruling political party of South Africa as of 2016. The ANC has governed South Africa since 1999, when Nelson Mandela was first elected after the end of apartheid in the country.**
Africa Small and Medium Enterprises Program –	**An African Development Bank (AfDB) program**

Africa SSP -	**Sanders idea of a strategic plan focused on SSAfrica SMES which she would call the *Africa SME Strategic Plan***
Africa youth Bulge/Africa Youth -	**Various international institutions define differently the age range on Africa youth: AfDB 15-24 years, African Union 15-35 years, World Bank/ILO 15-24 years, Gallup 15-29 years, and OECD less than 15 years**
African National Congress -	**Ruling Party of South Africa from 1994 to present**
African Leadership Academy -	**Innovative educational institution in Johannesburg teaching academics, leadership and entrepreneurial skills**
ALA -	**African Leadership Academy which gives out the Anzisha Prize**
AltTX -	**Alternative Public Equity Exchange of the Johannesburg, South Africa Stock Exchange**
Ambassador's Self-Help Fund -	**The U.S Ambassador's Special Self-Help Program is part of U.S. Government Development Assistance funds, which are used to assist community-based, community-run projects in the local communities around the globe and are managed by U.S. Embassies. The goal of the Self-Help Program is to improve the basic economic and social conditions of a village or community and should benefit the greatest number of people possible.**

Anti-balaka –	**One of the militia groups which contributed to the devastating violence, civil war, and continued security challenges in the CAR for more than three years (2012-2015)**
App –	**Abbreviation for an Internet-based service-related or information tool which is downloadable as an application of a mobile device**
Appropriate Technology –	**Using or turning a resource, waste, or by-product into something that is refashioned or repurposed for use in response to a particular need or challenge**
ARS –	**U.S. Government's Africa Regional Service (ARS) office in Paris**
ASeM –	**Nigerian Stock Exchange's Alternative Stock Emerging Markets**
ATMS –	**African Training and Management Services Project under the African Development Bank's (AfDB) Fund for African Private Sector Assistance, which itself is abbreviated as FAPA**
AU –	**African Union**
AUC –	**African Union Commission**

B

BMCE –	**BMCE is the French acronym for the Commercial Bank of Morocco known better in English as BMCE Bank of Africa**
BOI –	**Nigeria's Bank of Industry**

BOI-WU-FEEEDS-ADM– Nigeria's Bank of Industry-Western Union-FEEEDS-Advocacy Initiative-Africa Diaspora Marketplace, a joint program over 2 years to help with access to finance for Pan-African SMEs. In 2014, Western Union-FEEEDS-W-TEC Nigeria held an ICT training program for women

Brexit – Brexit is a mashup of the words "Britain" and "exit" and used in connection with both the referendum leading up to the vote on whether the United Kingdom would depart the European Union (EU), the departure itself which was what the British people determined with their June 23, 2016 vote to leave the EU, and most things connected to the issue since the vote.

BRICA – Author's term used in HuffPost and blog articles in 2011 to be more inclusive of SSAfrican countries experiencing an economic boom, besides South Africa

BRICS – Acronym referring to the country grouping referring to Brazil, Russia, India, China, and South Africa

BRVM – The French acronym for the Regional Stock Exchange of West Africa, representing the eight countries of West Africa, and the Exchange is most known by its French acronym, BVRM, which in French stands for Bourse Régionale des Valeurs Mobilières

C

CAR –	**Central African Republic, a country in the Central Region of Africa**
CGTN –	**China Global Television Network**
China-Africa SME Convention –	**Annual Convention held in Shanghai, China**
China Construction Bank Corporation –	**Chinese Government institution and that provides loans and assistance on behalf of the Chinese government to projects in overseas countries, and it has several branch offices, including in Johannesburg, South Africa**
Colonial Influence & Colonial Era in Africa –	**Period when European countries controlled vast swaths of the African Continent, 1870-1960s**
COMESA –	**Common Market for East and Southern Africa**
Community of Economic Purpose –	**What the author called the groups of income-generating women working together in post-conflict Republic of Congo when she was there 2003-2005; phrasing was specifically directed to women coming out of post-conflict situations**
COP22 –	**Conference of Parties on climate change held in Paris, France, in 2015. Future *Conference of Parties* (COPs) will be COP23, COP24, and so on**

CSIR –	**Center for Scientific and Industrial Research in Pretoria, South Africa**
CSR –	**Corporate Social Responsibility (CSR) is the term used by many corporations that applies to both the office in the company and the action of providing grants, training, and other resources used in the assistance to development efforts**
CTM –	**Continental Trade Market, not established but discussed as SSAfrica having its own trade market like the European Union.**

D

DataGraph –	**The bar graphs in *@The FEEEDS Index***
Decade of The African Woman –	**Period from 2010 to 2020 as declared by the African Union**
DFID –	**International Development**
DHL –	**German global logistics company, with the abbreviation standing for Dalsey, Hillblom & Lynn, the surnames of the founders**
Disruptive/ Disruptive Technology –	**Term by Harvard Business School professor Clayton M. Christensen from his 1997 "The Innovator's Dilemma," which highlights that technology can be separated into two categories: sustaining and disruptive**
DIV –	**USAID's Development Innovation Venture Program**

E

EAC –	East African Community
ECOWAS –	Economic Community of West African States
EDDI –	Education for Democracy and Development Initiative
Embassy Brazza –	Shortened Version (and sometimes more commonly used) for the U.S. Embassy in Brazzaville, Republic of Congo
Embassy Brazzaville–	The U.S. Embassy in Brazzaville, the capital of the Republic of Congo
EPAs –	Economic Partnership Agreements between Europe and SSAfrica on trade and economic issues
E-empowerment Services –	Used in this book to mean any type of services provided to customers or the public through digital electronic means, usually on a mobile platform
EU –	European Union
EU-Africa Partnership –	African Union-European Union Partnership group was formalized in 2007 and provides a strategic framework under which the African Union and the European Union strategically work together on a range of policy and development issues

Ex-Seleka –	**Individuals who were members of the Seleka group that was responsible for initiating a coup which led to the devastating violence, civil war, and continued security challenges in the CAR for more than three years (2012-2015)**

F

FAPA –	**African Development Bank's Fund for African Private Sector Assistance, which hosts a number of monies for various programs and projects in Africa to encourage more private sector involvement, including with Africa SMEs**
FASID –	**Foundation for the Advancement of the Studies of International Development is a Japanese non-profit organization, which jointly worked on a 2011 World Bank Study with the Japanese Government to examine the value of SMEs on GDP, training needs in the sector, etc.**
FCT –	**Federal Capital Territory, the state area in Nigeria where its capitol, Abuja, is located**
FDI –	**Foreign Direct Investment**

FEEEDS Advocacy Initiative –	**Ambassador Sanders is Founder and CEO of the small advocacy group which focuses on economic development issues. FEEEDS is an acronym meaning Food security, Education, Energy-environment, Economics, Democracy and Self-help.**
FEEEDS-Gallup Event –	**FEEEDS Advocacy Initiative has partnered from 2013 to 2016 with Gallup and its Managing Partner Jon Clifton to host a data-driven event on key Africa issues from elections to business.**
FCT –	**Federal Capital Territory (FCT), better known as Abuja, the capital of Nigeria**
FDI –	**Foreign Direct Investment**
Framing Analysis –	**Theory of Canadian Sociologist Erving Goffman related to how one can provide a framework to discuss a range of things from behavior to culture, to economics to politics**
French24 –	**French 24/7 Media outlet**
FSD –	**Nigeria's Foundation for Skills Development**
Future-Morrow –	**Future-Morrow is a phrase used by the author meaning the future and tomorrow or in today's lingo a mashup of the words "future" and "tomorrow."**

G

G-77 –	**Group of 77 nations in the developing world and in the south-south tier of the globe**
GEMS –	**Nairobi Stock Exchange or NSE of Kenya's Special Growth Board for Africa SMEs**
Generation-Xers –	**Slang referring to those individuals born after 1960**
GES –	**Global Entrepreneurship Summit**
GDP –	**Gross Domestic Product**
GINI Coefficient –	**Statistic which measure income inequality**
GNI –	**Gross National Income**
GSM -	**Global System for Mobile Communications – more commonly referred to as GSM. It is the technology which has been adopted by most countries as a way to make a call on a mobile phone.**
GSMA –	**Abbreviation for GSMA Association, which is the professional association of mobile industry professionals and companies using or associated with the mobile communications system called GSM, or Global System for Mobile Communications**

H

High Definition –	**As defined by Merriam-Webster Dictionary: "being or relating to an often-digital television system that has twice as many scan lines per frame as a conventional system, a proportionally sharper image, and a wide-screen format" (See Reference list for source citation)**
HuffPost –	**Slang for the Huffington Post, which is an online news website**

I

IBRD –	**International Bank for Reconstruction and Development**
***iCow* –**	**An Internet application that assists rural farmers**
ICT –	**Information Systems (technology), Communications, and Telecommunication**
ICTers –	**Author uses the term to refer to people working in the ICT sector**
IDB –	**Inter-American Development Bank**
IDA –	**International Development Agency, part of the World Bank Group**
IFC –	**International Finance Corporation**
IIE –	**International Institute for Education**
IPA –	**Innovation Prize for Africa**
IPHD –	**International Partnership for Human Development, a US NGO**

IPPs – **Independent Power Plants, which are small targeted power supply options for a village, an economic zone, or neighborhoods**

ITC – **International Trade Center**

iTax – **Electronic tax application in Kenya for forms and filing**

J

JICA – **Japan's International Cooperation Agency, which is the Japanese Government's development arm**

JSE – **Johannesburg Stock Exchange**

K

Kaduna – **Considered the 4th largest city in Nigeria, located in the central region of the country**

Kiosk banks – **Kiosk or corrugated banks are small shops or stands where bills, recharge cards, and money transfer can be made**

M

m-Hero – **Internet-based health application**

M-Pesa – **The Kenyan money transfer payment system by Safaricom**

MCC – **Millennium Challenge Corporation**

MERC – **Multi-Education Resource Center**

Millennials –	**Person reaching adulthood around the year 2000**
MTN –	**Mobile Telephone Network, South Africa's largest mobile phone provider**

N

Naira –	**Name of Nigeria's currency**
NASA –	**National Aeronautics and Space Administration of the United States, is the U.S. Government civilian agency responsible for the US space program, as well as aeronautics and aerospace research**
New Development Bank (NDB) –	**Formerly known as the BRICs Development Bank entered into force in July 2015, with an initial pledge of $US50 billion, with capitalization up to $US100 billion**
NDB –	**New Development Bank, which was formed by the countries referred to as the BRICS – Brazil, Russian, India, China, and South Africa – that are founding members. NDB was formerly known as the BRICS Development Bank and entered into force in July 2015, with an initial pledge of $US50 billion from its founding members.**
NGOs –	**Non-governmental organizations**
Non-GMO –	**Food that has not been grown with a genetically-modified organism**

NSC –	**U.S. Government's National Security Council**
NSE –	**Nairobi Stock Exchange based om Kenya**
Nigerian Stock Exchange –	**Sometimes also referred to as NSE of Nigeria.**

O

OECD –	**Organization for Economic Cooperation and Development**
OH –	**Operation Hope, a non-profit organization with offices in the US and Johannesburg, South Africa**
OSAA –	**UN's Office of the Special Advisor on Africa**
OTC –	**Over-the-counter, referring to a manner (decentralized) in which one can purchase stocks, which are not listed on a stock market or derivative exchange**

P

PEPFAR –	**Well-known U.S. Government HIV/AIDS program known by this abbreviation, but the full name is The President's Emergency Plan for AIDS Relief**
PC –	**Personal Computers**
Pink Taxis –	**Company in Egypt of taxis painted pink driven by women, for women to help with safety issues**

Power Africa –	**Initiative began by former President Obama in 2013 to add 30,000 megawatts to the SSAfrica's electricity power output in response to the energy needs of the region**
PowerHouse Nations –	**A FEEEDS designation of Angola, Democratic Republic of the Congo (DRC), Ethiopia, Ghana, Kenya, Nigeria, Rwanda, South Africa, and Tanzania, which can have a positive or challenging effect on the sub-region in Africa where they are located**
PPP –	**Public private partnerships**
PPPP –	**The 4-P model Sanders suggests that cross-fertilizing public-to-public sector resources, connected to donors, private sector, and NGOS**

O

Octocopter –	**Drone with eight rotors**

Q

Quadcopter –	**An unmanned drone with four propellers, which can be controlled by a smartphone**

R

RECs –	**Refers to African Regional Economic Communities such as EAC, COMESA, ECOWAS, and SADC (these terms are also noted here in the glossary of terms)**
Resolution 2626 –	**40-year-old call to action by the UN for more commitment to aid and progress on development for the Africa region**
RPG –	**Rocket Propelled Grenade**

S

SA –	**South Africa**
SADC –	**Southern Africa Development Corporation**
Sahel Extremism Belt –	**Term used by Sanders to describe the region that runs like a belt across the top half of the Continent where either terrorist groups have taken a foothold or there are current terrorist activities (Tunisia-Libya-Mali-Niger-Nigeria-over to Kenya-Tanzania-Somalia)**
SAM-7s –	**Surface-to-air missiles**
SBA –	**U.S. Small Business Administration**
SDGs –	**Sustainable Development Goals**
Seleka –	**The group responsible for initiating a coup which led to the devastating violence, civil war, and continued security challenges in the CAR for more than three years (2012-2015)**

SEZ -	**Special Economic Zones**
SIDA -	**Swedish International Development Agency**
SMEs -	**Small and Medium Size Enterprises**
SMEers -	**Author's slang and upbeat term for SMEs**
SSAfrica/ SSAfrican -	**Sub-Saharan Africa/ Sub-Saharan-African**
State of Africa SME Report -	**A report and recommendation suggested in the book by Sanders to ensure better data and information on SSAfrica SMEs to improve support and assistance to them**
STEM, STEAM, & STREAM -	**STEM is science, technology, engineering, and mathematics; the two newer terms are STEAM and STREAM, which include both *activism* and *reading*, hence the "R" and the "A"**
Sustainability -	**Defined in 1987 Brundtland Report as "development" that meets the needs of the present without compromising the ability of future generations to meet their own needs**

T

Tech -	**Slang to mean technology**
TEL -	**TOP Eight List - author's top 8 sectors providing big opportunities for Africa SMEs**

TICAD – Tokyo International Conference on African Development, the comprehensive 5-year meetings with all African nations; the most recent was held with only 3 years in between in 2016 in Kenya

Tweet – Sending a message on the social media platform Twitter

Twitter – A social media platform to send messages of 140 characters or less

U

UN – United Nations

UNCTAD – United Nations Conference on Trade and Development

UNDP – United Nations Development Program

UNDP-U.S. Embassy MERC – The Multi-Educational Resource Center created and established as a public-private partnership between the United Nations Development Program (UNDP) and U.S. Embassy Brazzaville in the Republic of Congo under the vision and leadership of UNDP Resident Representative Aurelien Agbénonci and Ambassador Robin Sanders in 2004. The UNDP-U.S.-Embassy MERC was a 5-year PPP agreement.

UNEC – United Nations Economic Commission

UNEP – United Nations Environment Program

UNGA –	**United Nations General Assembly**
UNIDO –	**United Nations Industrial Development Organization**
UNWTO –	**United Nations World Tourism Organization**
UK –	**United Kingdom**
US –	**United States, meaning things, people, etc., in or connected to the American people or the country of the United States**
U.S. –	**Before any word or name means that entity is a United States Government institution or agency, e.g. U.S. Embassy, U.S. National Security Council, etc.**
USAID –	**U.S. Agency for International Development**
$US –	**Represent currency stated in U.S. dollars**
USDF –	**United States African Development Foundation**
USG –	**An abbreviation referring to the United States Government**

V

VC4 Africa –	**Venture Capital 4 Africa**

Villa Washington – A sister location of Embassy Brazzaville where "English Clubs" were established where Congolese could come to practice English, where English language materials, movies and programming were held during my time in Congo, and which have expanded and continue today under the leadership of many other U.S. Ambassadors since 2003

W

WB – World Bank

WEF – World Economic Forum

WEDP – Women's Entrepreneurship Development

WhatsApp – Internet application for sending messages worldwide

WiFi® – As per the website webopedia, WiFi is a registered trademark name owned by a company called WiFi Alliance and it refers to the technology itself that uses radio waves to connect devices to the Internet. The term is more commonly used today as to mean a slang referring to a device being connected to the Internet.

World Bank – World Bank is the parent institution of the World Bank Group

World Bank Group –	**World Bank Group refers to all five of the international financial institutions of the World Bank such as International Monetary Fund (IMF), International Finance Corporation (IFC), etc., and the parent entity, the World Bank.**
WU –	**Western Union, is a US Company operating around the globe to provide financial, payment and transfer services**

Y

YALI –	**Program created by former President Obama called the Young African Leaders Initiative, also called the Mandela Fellows**

Z

ZAR-X –	**Name of a licensed over-the-counter (OTC) market in Johannesburg, South Africa**

Photograph 1: Secretary Colin Powell & Ambassador Andrew Young before swearing-in Sanders as Ambassador to the Republic of Congo, Department of State.

Photograph 2: Ambassador Andrew Young with Sanders before her swearing-in ceremony as U.S. Ambassador to the Republic of Congo, Department of State.

Photograph 3: Congolese Foreign Minister Rodolphe Adada giving Sanders the medal of merit/honor or "Order Du Mérite Congolais, Le grade de Commandeur" award at the end of her official tour of duty as United States Ambassador to the Republic of Congo.

Photograph 4: Ambassador Andrew Young & Ambassador Sanders, Selfie 2016.

Photograph 5: Mr. Aliko Dangote President & CEO Dangote Group, Chairman Dangote Foundation & Ambassador Sanders, 2016 AAI Event.

Reference List*

(2016, December 2). Global business. [Television broadcast, 1:30 p.m.]. China Global Television.

(2016, November 1). Global business. [Television broadcast, 1 p.m.]. China Global Television.

(2016, September 13). Global business. [Television broadcast, 2 p.m.]. China Global Television.

(2016, August 11). *Africa live newscast.* [Television broadcast, 6:30 p.m.]. China Global Television.

(2016, July 8). *Africa live newscast.* [Television broadcast, 1 p.m.]. China Global Television.

(2016, June). *Global business Africa.* [Television broadcast, 2 p.m.]. China Global Television.

(2016, May 14). *Global business Africa.* [Television broadcast, 2 p.m.]. China Global Television.

(2016, May 11). *Global business Africa.* [Television broadcast, 2 p.m.]. China Global Television.

(2016, April 30). *Africa live newscast.* [Television broadcast, 1 p.m.]. China Global Television.

(2016, April 30). *Africa live newscast.* [Television broadcast, 1 p.m.]. China Global Television.

(2015, December 9). Africa live newscast. [Television broadcast, 12 p.m.]. China Global Television.

**There are a few website references which require direct pasting into a browser.*

4DI Capital: From Garage to Global. (n.d.). Retrieved May 12, 2016 from http://www.4dicapital.com

A chronological list of independence dates for Africa. (n.d.). In *About.com.* Retrieved July 30, 2016 from http://africanhistory.about.com/library/timelines/blIndependenceTime.htm

Abor, J., & Quartey, P. (2010). Issues in SME Development in Ghana and South Africa. *International Research Journal of Finance and Economics*, (39), 218-226. Retrieved May 2, 2016 from http://www.smmeresearch.co.za/SMME%20Research%20General/Journal%20Articles/Issues%20in%20SME%20development%20in%20Ghana%20and%20SA.pdf

Abraaj Group. (2010, November 16). Aureos Africa Fund completes 10 million investments in leading Ghanaian bank. Retrieved May 2, 2016 from http://www.abraaj.com/news-and-insight/news/aureos-africa-fund-completes-10m-investment-in-leading-ghanaian-bank/

Access to Water. (2000-2015). International Decade for Action 'Water for Life.' United Nations. Retrieved August 25, 2014 from http://www.un.org/waterforlifedecade/africa.shtml

Across Africa, 3 in 4 Countries Improve Business Environment. (2016, November 7). News. *This Is Africa Online.* Retrieved November 7, 2017 from http://www.thisisafricaonline.com/News/Across-Africa-3-in-4-countries-improve-business-environment?ct=true

Addis in Capetown. (2016). About Us. Retrieved August 20, 2016 from http://www.addisincape.co.za/

Adepetun, A. (2015, June 17). Africa's mobile phone penetration now 67%. The *Guardian.* Retrieved August 8, 2016 from http://guardian.ng/technology/africas-mobile-phone-penetration-now-67/

Aeroshuttergh. (n.d.). Retrieved March 5, 2016 from http://www.aeroshuttergh.com/aeroshutter.html

Africa-America Institute. (n.d.). http://www.aaionline.org/

Africa Assets. (2016). [Database]. Retrieved March 11, 2016 from http://www.africa-assets.com/data

Africa Economy: Kenya's county enhances economic relations with Chinese investors. (2015, August 21). Retrieved June 24, 2016 from http://china.org.cn/world/Off_the_Wire/2015-08/21/content_36369519.htm

Africa Enterprise Challenge Fund. (n.d.). Retrieved April 27, 2016 from http://www.aecfafrica.org/

Africa Investment Forum Addis Ababa. (2015, October 27-29). Africa Investment Forum. Retrieved September 7, 2016 from http://africainvestmentforum.net/

Africa Media Ventures Fund. (n.d.) Retrieved April 21, 2016 from http://www.amvf.nl

Africa Renewal Online. (n.d.). Retrieved July 6, 2016 from http://www.un.org/africarenewal/

Africa Top Success. (2014, April 22). Aida Diarra: Western Union Africa vice-president. The continent financier. Retrieved May 13, 2016 from http://www.africatopsuccess.com/en/2014/04/22/aida-diarra-western-union-africa-vice-president-the-continent-financier/

Africa-EU Partnership (2016). Priority areas-sustainable and inclusive development and growth and continental integration. Retrieved May 9, 2016 from http://www.africa-eu-partnership.org/en/priority-areas/sustainable-and-inclusive-development-and-growth-and-continental-integration-6

Africa-European Union Partnership (2013-2015). About us. Retrieved May 9, 2016 from http://www.africa-eu-partnership.org/en.

African Agriculture Fund. (n.d.). Retrieved from http://www.aaftaf.org/

African Capacity Building Fund. (n.d.) *Africa Capacity Report 2015: Overview.* Retrieved March 10, 2016 from http://www.acbf-pact.org/sites/default/files/ACR%202015%20Overview.pdf

African, Caribbean, and Pacific Group of States (ACP). (n.d.). Retrieved May 2016 from http://www.acp.int/content/secretariat-acp

African Development Bank Group. (2016). *Africa economic outlook reports.* (15th ed.). African Development Bank, Organization for Economic Development and Cooperation, and the United Nations Development Programme. Retrieved July 5, 2016 from

http://www.afdb.org/fileadmin/uploads/afdb/Documents/Publications/AEO_2016_Report_Full_English.pdf

African Development Bank Group. (2015). *Africa economic outlook.* African Development Bank, Organization for Economic Development and Cooperation, and the United Nations Development Programme. p. 13. Retrieved July 5, 2016 from

http://www.africaneconomicoutlook.org/fileadmin/uploads/aeo/2015/PDF_Chapters/Overview_AEO2015

African Development Bank Group. (2012). *Africa economic outlook.* African Development Bank, Organization for Economic Development and Cooperation, and the United Nations Development Programme. Retrieved July 5, 2016 from http://www.afdb.org/fileadmin/uploads/afdb/Documents/Publications/AEO_2016_Report_Full_English.pdf

African Development Bank Group. (2016). *Africa's recent MDG performance. 2016 report.* Retrieved July 24, 2016 from http://www.afdb.org/en/topics-and-sectors/topics/millennium-development-goals-mdgs/africa%e2%80%99s-recent-mdg-performance/

African Development Bank Group. (2016). Light up and power Africa – A new deal on energy for Africa. Retrieved July 30, 2016 from http://www.afdb.org/en/the-high-5/light-up-and-power-africa-%E2%80%93-a-new-deal-on-energy-for-africa/

African Development Bank Group. (2015, May 25). India signs replenishment agreement with African Development Bank. Retrieved May 10, 2016 from http://www.afdb.org/en/news-and-events/article/india-signs-replenishment-of-technical-cooperation-agreement-with-african-development-bank-group-14266/

African Development Bank Group. (2015). Africa tourism monitor 2015: Tourism in Africa is on the rise, but has not yet reached its full potential. Retrieved July 6, 2016 from http://www.afdb.org/en/news-and-events/article/africa-tourism-monitor-2015-tourism-in-africa-is-on-the-rise-but-has-not-yet-reached-its-full-potential-15284/

African Development Bank Group (2011, March 9). African Development Bank sets up new trust fund with Brazil. Retrieved May 10, 2016 from http://www.afdb.org/en/news-and-events/article/afdb-sets-up-new-trust-fund-with-brazil-7803

African Development Bank Group. (2013, July 22). African Development Bank SME program approval boosting inclusive growth in Africa. Retrieved March 10, 2016 from http://www.afdb.org/en/news-and-events/article/the-afdb-sme-program-approval-boosting-inclusive-growth-in-africa-12135/

African Development Bank Group. (2013, July 22). The AFDB SME program approval: Boosting inclusive growth in Africa. Retrieved May 10 and July 24, 2016 from http://www.afdb.org/en/news-and-events/article/the-afdb-sme-program-approval-boosting-inclusive-growth-in-africa-12135/

African Development Bank Group. (2013). African guarantee fund for small and medium sized enterprises. Retrieved May 14, 2016 from http://www.afdb.org/en/topics-and-sectors/initiatives-partnerships/african-guarantee-fund-for-small-and-medium-sized-enterprises/

African Development Bank Group. (2012). African Women in Business Initiative. Retrieved March 12, 2016 from http://www.afdb.org/en/topics-and-sectors/initiatives-partnerships/african-women-in-business-initiative/

African Development Bank Group. (2014). *Annual report 2014. Fund for African private sector assistance (FAPA). Building capacity for private sector development.* Retrieved August 17, 2016 from http://www.afdb.org/en/topics-and-sectors/initiatives-partnerships/fund-for-african-private-sector-assistance/

African Development Bank Group. (2011). *China and Africa: An emerging partnership for development?* R. Schiere, L. Ndikumana, & P. Walkenhorst (Eds.). Retrieved March 13, 2016 from http://www.afdb.org/fileadmin/uploads/afdb/Documents/Publications/Anglaischina.pdf

African Development Bank Group. (2009, October 6). Japan and African Development Bank Commit USD One Million Technical Assistance Grant for SME Capacity Building in Africa. Retrieved May 10, 2016 from http://www.afdb.org/en/news-and-events/article/japan-and-afdb-commit-usd-1-million-technical-assistance-grant-for-sme-capacity-building-in-africa-5156

African Development Bank Group. (2008). *Selected social statistics on African countries 2008.* Retrieved May 20, 2016 from http://www.afdb.org/en/documents/publications/selected-statistics-on-african-countries/

African Development Bank Group. (2013, December 9). Republic of Turkey joins African Development Bank Group. Retrieved May 10, 2016 from http://www.afdb.org/en/news-and-events/article/the-republic-of-turkey-joins-african-development-bank-group-12660/

African Development Bank Group. (2011, April 20). *The middle of the pyramid: Dynamics of the middle class in Africa*. Section 2.2, p. 2. Retrieved August 7, 2016 from http://www.afdb.org/fileadmin/uploads/afdb/Documents/Publications/The%20Middle%20of%20the%20Pyramid_The%20Middle%20of%20the%20Pyramid.pdf

African Economic Outlook. (2011, June 6). *Africa should embrace new economic giants and boost social inclusion, says African Economic Outlook*. Retrieved May 2016 from http://www.africaneconomicoutlook.org/en/news-events/article/africa-should-embrace-new-economic-giants-amd-boost-social-inclusion-says-african-economic-outlook-2011-72/

African Entrepreneurship Award. (2015). BMCE Bank of Africa. Retrieved August 3, 2016 from https://africanentrepreneurshipaward.com/

African Innovation Foundation (n.d.) [blog]. Retrieved May 6, 2016 from http://www.africaninnovationfoundation.org/blog

African Innovation Foundation. (n.d.). *Innovation Prize for Africa*. June 23, 2016 Retrieved from http://www.africaninnovation.org/

African leaders, China to meet on investment. (2006, November 1). *Washington Times*. Retrieved July 23, 2016 from http://www.washingtontimes.com/news/2006/nov/1/20061101-115934-5178r/

African Leadership Academy. (n.d.) Nomsa Daniels. Retrieved June 3, 2016 from http://www.africanleadershipacademy.org/profiles/nomsa-daniels/

African Leadership Academy. (n.d.) Our founding beliefs. Retrieved May 12, 2016 from http://www.africanleadershipacademy.org/about/our-founding-beliefs/

African Leadership Academy. (n.d.) Our programs. The Anzisha Prize. Retrieved April 20, 2016 from http://www.africanleadershipacademy.org/our-programs/anzisha-prize/

African Leadership Academy. (n.d.) The founders' story. Retrieved May 12, 2016 from http://www.africanleadershipacademy.org/about/founders-story/

African Private Equity and Venture Capital Association. (2016). ACVA Retrieved August 4, 2106 from http://www.avca-africa.org/

African Union Commission. (2006). *African youth charter.* Retrieved July 5, 2016 from http://www.un.org/en/africa/osaa/pdf/au/african_youth_charter_2006.pdf

African Union. (2015, December 12). African Union Commission coaches SME Women on trade fair and agro value chain. Retrieved March 10, 2016 from http://www.au.int/en/pressreleases/19485/african-union-commission-coaches-sme-women-trade-fair-and-agro-value-chain

African Union. (n.d.) About Agenda 2063. Retrieved May 11, 2016 from http://agenda2063.au.int/en/about

African Women's Entrepreneurship Program. (n.d.). U.S. Department of State. Retrieved August 7, 2016 from http://www.state.gov/p/af/rt/awep/index.htm

Africare. (2016). Retrieved June 23, 2016 from https://www.africare.org/who-we-are/

Africa's middle class - Few and far between. (2015, October 24). *The Economist.* Retrieved May 2016 from http://www.economist.com/news/middle-east-and-africa/21676774-africans-are-mainly-rich-or-poor-not-middle-class-should-worry

AfricInvest. (2016). Retrieved May 3, 2016 from http://www.africinvest.com/the-firm/

Afrobarometer. (2016) Retrieved May 7, 2016 from http://www.afrobarometer.org/

Afterblixen. (2015, November 30). 10 great funding opportunities for African entrepreneurs [blog post]. Retrieved August 3, 2016 from https://afterblixen.com/2015/11/30/10-great-funding-opportunities-for-african-entrepreneurs/

Airaksinen, A., Luomaranta, H., Alajääskö, P., & Roodhuijzen, A. (2015-2016). [modified June 29, 2016]. *Dependent and independent SMEs and large enterprises. Statistics on small and medium-sized enterprises. Eurostat statistics explained.* Retrieved August 6, 2016 from http://ec.europa.eu/eurostat/statistics-explained/index.php/Statistics_on_small_and_medium-sized_enterprises

Alexander, M. (2014, July 15). A 'disruptive' technology: Sandile Ngcobo's world-first digital laser. Media Club South Africa. Retrieved August 7, 2016 from http://www.mediaclubsouthafrica.com/tech/3932-a-disruptive-technology-sandile-ngcobo-s-world-first-digital-laser#ixzz4Gc2Sahup

Aliko Dangote: A lesson for African entrepreneurs. (2014, March 22). *Vanguard.* Retrieved March 30, 2016 from http://www.vanguardngr.com/2014/03/aliko-dangote-lesson-african-entrepreneurs/

Aliko Dangote #51 - The world's billionaires ranking. (2016, August 7). *Forbes Magazine.* Retrieved August 7, 2016 from http://www.forbes.com/profile/aliko-dangote/

Ambassador Andrew Young. (n.d.). *Biography.com.* Retrieved July 1, 2016 from http://www.biography.com/people/andrew-young-jr-9539326

Amondo, K. (Reporter). (2016, August 5). *Africa live: Solar fish dryers.* [Television broadcast]. China Global Television Network.

Ancharaz, V., Mbekeani, K., & Brixiova, Z. (2011). Impediments to regional trade integration in Africa. *Africa Economic Brief* 2(11), p. 2. Retrieved August 8, 2016 from http://www.afdb.org/fileadmin/uploads/afdb/Documents/Publications/AEB%20VOL%202%20Issue%2011_AEB%20VOL%202%20Issue%2011.pdf

Appropriate technology. (n.d.). In *Merriam-Webster Dictionary.* Retrieved July 6, 2016 from http://www.merriam-webster.com/dictionary/appropriate%20technology

Apps. (2016). Retrieved July 2, 2016 from http://www.dictionary.com/browse/app

Ashesi University. (n.d.). Home Page. Retrieved May 10, 2016 from http://www.ashesi.edu.gh/

Ashesi. (n.d.). About Us. Retrieved June 24, 2016 from http://www.ashesi.edu.gh/about.html

Asiimwe, A. (2015, November 30). Investing in women's ability to do business makes sense. *Trademark East Africa.* Retrieved May 15, 2016 from https://www.trademarkea.com/blog/investing-in-womens-ability-to-do-business-makes-sense

Atlantic Council. (n.d.). Retrieved June 23, 2016 from http://www.atlanticcouncil.org/

Badal, S. B. (2013). How large corporations can spur small business growth. Gallup.com. Retrieved July 1, 2016 from http://www.gallup.com/businessjournal/160109/large-corporations-spur-small-business-growth.aspx

Beal, V. *ISDN - Integrated Services Digital Network.* (n.d.). Term. Webopedia. Retrieved July 31, 2016 from http://www.webopedia.com/TERM/I/ISDN.html

Beal, V. (2010, July 14). Wi-Fi definition is not wireless fidelity. *Webopedia.* Retrieved July 8, 2016 from http://www.webopedia.com/DidYouKnow/Computer_Science/wifi_explained.asp

Bengali, S. (2016). What's it like to live in the world's fastest growing major economy? *Los Angeles Times.* Retrieved June 30, 2016 from http://www.latimes.com/world/la-fg-india-economy-20160606-snap-story.html

Berhe, H. (2014, April 4). Jacana partner funding. AgTech XChange. Retrieved June 15, 2016 from http://agtech.partneringforinnovation.org/community/funding/blog/2014/04/04/jacana-partners-funding

Berlin West Africa Conference. (n.d.). In *Encyclopædia Britannica Online*. Retrieved August 26, 2016 from http://www.britannica.com/event/Berlin-West-Africa-Conference

Blaire, C. (2015, August 25). Rwanda's gender gap: Banks must stop failing female entrepreneurs. *The Guardian* [U.S. ed.]. Retrieved July 31, 2016 from https://www.theguardian.com/global-development-professionals-network/2015/aug/25/rwanda-gender-gap-banks-failing-female-entrepreneurs

Blue Marble Ice Cream. (2016). Retrieved May 3, 2016 from http://www.bluemarbleicecream.com/

BOI-WU-FEEEDS SME [Video file]. (2013, November). FEEEDS Cloud. Retrieved from http://bit.ly/1Ytb3OF

Brazil unemployment rate 2012-2016. (2016). *Trading Economics*. Retrieved June 30, 2016 from http://www.tradingeconomics.com/brazil/unemployment-rate

BRCK Education. (2016). Retrieved May 17, 2016 from http://www.brck.com

Bremmen, N. (2013). 9 of South Africa's best mobile apps. Retrieved July 5, 2016 from http://memeburn.com/2013/08/9-of-south-africas-best-mobile-apps/

Brexit. (n.d.). Definition. *Investopedia*. Retrieved June 30, 2016 from http://www.investopedia.com/terms/b/brexit.asp

BRICS countries launch new development bank in Shanghai. (2015, July 21). BBC News. Retrieved July 9, 2016 rom http://www.bbc.com/news/33605230

BRVM. (n.d.). Retrieved July 12, 2016 from http://www.brvm.org/Accueil/tabid/36/language/en-US/Default.aspx

Bryant, J. H. (2014). How the poor can save capitalism: Rebuilding the path to the middle class. San Francisco, California: Berrett-Koehler.

Bulging in the middle: A boom in Sub-Saharan Africa is attracting business talent from the rich world. (2012, October 20). *The Economist.* Retrieved May 20, 2016 from http://www.economist.com/news/middle-east-and-africa/21564856-boom-sub-saharan-africa-attracting-business-talent-rich-world?zid=304&ah=e5690753dc78ce91909083042ad12e30

Burnett, M., Newbill, C., Lingner, Y., & Gurin. P. (Producers). (2009-2016). *Shark Tank* [Television series]. New York: American Broadcasting Company.

Buses in Rwanda used to teach IT skills. (2013, October 18). *BBC.com.* Retrieved August 8, 2016 from http://www.bbc.com/news/business-24574998

Capital Seaweed. (2016). *LinkedIn.com.* Retrieved June 5, 2016 from https://www.linkedin.com/company/capital-seaweed

Caryle Group. (n.d.). Retrieved August 4, 2016 from https://www.carlyle.com/about-carlyle

CDC group. (2013). Retrieved July 12, 2016 from http://www.cdcgroup.com/Who-we-are/Key-Facts/

Center for Disease Control. (2016, May 31). *Well-being Concepts. Health-related quality of life (HRQOL).* National Center for Chronic Disease Prevention and Health Promotion, Division of Population Health. Retrieved July 31, 2016 from http://www.cdc.gov/hrqol/wellbeing.htm

Central Intelligence Agency. (n.d.). Country comparison: Distribution of family income: GINI Index. In *World Fact Book.* Retrieved July

24, 2016 from https://www.cia.gov/library/publications/the-world-factbook/rankorder/2172rank.html

Centre for Women's Entrepreneurship at Chatham University. (2013). Barbara Span. Retrieved May 17, 2016 from https://www.chatham.edu/cwe/networking/thinkbig/2013/span.cfm

Chang, S. (2016, April 13). China's first-quarter GDP growth likely slowed to a seven-year low. *Market Watch*. Retrieved July 17, 2016 from http://www.marketwatch.com/story/chinas-first-quarter-gdp-growth-likely-slowed-to-a-seven-year-low-2016-04-12

Chimjeka, R., & Chiwaula, L. (2015, October 1). Unima invents solar fish dryer. *The Nation*. Retrieved August 5, 2016 from http://mwnation.com/unima-invents-solar-fish-dryer-equipment/

China Construction Bank Corporation Johannesburg Branch. (n.d.). About Us. China Construction Bank Corporation. Retrieved August 17, 2016 from http://za.ccb.com/johannesburg/en/gywm.html

China-Africa SME Convention. (2016, June 7-10). Reliconn. Retrieved May 5, 2016 from https://www.reliconn.com/presentation

Christensen, C. M. (2003). *The innovator's dilemma*. New York: HarperBusiness Essentials.

Clifton, J. (2011). *The coming jobs war*. New York: Gallup Press.

Clinton, W. J. (1998, March 23). Remarks to the people of Ghana [speech]. Independence Square, Accra, Ghana.

Company overview of United Nigerian Textiles Limited. (2016, June 5). Bloomberg. Retrieved from May 13, 2016 http://www.bloomberg.com/research/stocks/private/person.asp?personId=207764043&privcapId=20376911

Congo River facts. (n. d.). Retrieved July 30, 2016 from http://interesting-africa-facts.com/Africa-Landforms/Congo-River-Facts.html

Congo River. (n. d.). Research begins here. In *New World Encyclopedia.* Retrieved July 30, 2016 from http://www.newworldencyclopedia.org/entry/Congo_River

Connecting innovators with capital: Meet 40 investors from the VC4Africa Investor Network. (2013). Venture Capital for Africa (VC4Africa). Retrieved May 13, 2016 from https://vc4a.com/blog/2013/03/14/connecting-innovators-with-capital-meet-40-investors-from-the-vc4africa-investor-network/

Corporate social responsibility. (n.d.). Definition. *Financial Times.* Retrieved October 8, 2016 from http://lexicon.ft.com/Term?term=corporate-social-responsibility

Corruption Perception Index. (2015). Transparency International. Retrieved September 30, 2016 http://www.transparency.org/cpi2015?gclid=CNfvjKeQuM8CFYY7gQodxm0Ghw

Craven, M. (2015). Between law and history: The Berlin Conference 1884-1885 and the logic of free trade. *London Review of International Law 3*(1): 31-59. Retrieved April 16, from http://lril.oxfordjournals.org/content/3/1/31.full

Credit Suisse Research Institute. (2015, October). *Global wealth data book 2015.* Retrieved July 4, 2016 from http://publications.credit-suisse.com/tasks/render/file/index.cfm?fileid=C26E3824-E868-56E0-CCA04D4BB9B9ADD5

Crook, J. & Escher, A. (2015, October 15). A brief history of Snapchat. *TechCrunch.* Retrieved July 6, 2016 from https://techcrunch.com/gallery/a-brief-history-of-snapchat/slide/12/

Crowe, P. (2015, January 8). The economist who coined the term 'BRIC' thinks Brazil and Russia could get kicked out of the club. *Business Insider.* Retrieved July 9, 2016 from http://www.businessinsider.com/the-brics-could-ditch-russia-and-brazil-2015-1

Cunningham, E. (n.d.). Uganda good labour practices bloom in flower industry. Inter Press Service News Agency. Retrieved May 16,

2016 from http://www.ipsnews.net/2007/08/uganda-good-labour-practices-bloom-in-flower-industry/

Dangote, A. (2016, January). 38th pre-convocation lecture [speech]. Amadou Bello University, Nigeria, Zaira.

de Sousa dos Santos, J.F. (2015, August 4). *Why SMEs are key to growth in Africa.* WeForum. Retrieved September 4, 2016 from https://www.weforum.org/agenda/2015/08/why-smes-are-key-to-growth-in-africa/

Delevingne, L. (2015). Private investors pile into Africa. CNBC. Retrieved July 12, 2016 from http://www.cnbc.com/2015/03/17/private-equity-investors-pile-into-africa.html

Dell commitment to zero waste packaging. (2016). Dell. Retrieved August 19, 2018 from http://www.dell.com/learn/us/en/uscorp1/corp-comm/cr-earth-reduce-reuse-recycle

*Demo Africa. (*2016, August 29). *Africa Live.* [Television broadcast, 1 p.m.] China Global Television Network.

Department for Business Innovation and Skills Innovation, UK. (2014, October 14). National statistics. URN15/92. Retrieved August 6, 2016 https://www.gov.uk/government/uploads/system/uploads/attachment_data/file/467443/bpe_2015_statistical_release.pdf

Department of International Development, UK. (2014, August 27). *Africa Enterprise Challenge Fund.* Retrieved March 8, 2016 from https://www.gov.uk/international-development-funding/africa-enterprise-challenge-fund

Development Innovation Center. (n.d.). Retrieved June 19, 2016 from https://www.usaid.gov/div

Development Partners International. Retrieved August 4, 2016 from http://www.dpi-llp.com/

Development Workshop Angola. (2015). Retrieved May 8, 2016 from http://www.dw.angonet.org/

Diaspora Demo Summit. (n.d.). Diaspora Demo. Retrieved November 27, 2016 from http://diasporademo.com/

Do-it-Yourself. DIY. Retrieved June 17, 2016 from https://en.wikipedia.org/wiki/Do_it_yourself

Do-it-Yourself (DIY) Geiger Counter. Retrieved June 17, 2016 from http://ocw.mit.edu/courses/nuclear-engineering/22-s902-do-it-yourself-diy-geiger-counters-january-iap-2015/

Donna Oosthuyse, Director of Capital Markets, Johannesburg Stock Exchange: Interview. (2015, June 15). Oxford Business Group. Retrieved July 12, 2016 from http://www.oxfordbusinessgroup.com/interview/going-strong-obg-talks-donna-oosthuyse-director-capital-markets-johannesburg-stock-exchange-jse

Dudovskiy, J. (2016, August 8). SMEs in China overview. *Research Methodology.* Retrieved August 8, 2016 from http://research-methodology.net/small-and-medium-enterprises-in-china-overview/

E4Impact Foundation. (2015, September 19). A new foundation launched to support impact entrepreneurship in Africa. Lioness of Africa. Retrieved June 25 and August 18, 2016 from http://www.lionessesofafrica.com/blog/2015/9/19/a-new-foundation-launched-to-support-impact-entrepreneurship-in-africa

East African Community. (n.d.). Overview of EAC. East African Community. Retrieved November 25, 2016 from http://www.eac.int/about/overview

East African Stock Exchange: East African Stock Exchange in the works to merge buoyant. (2013, July 9). *International Business Times.* Retrieved July 12, 2016 from http://www.ibtimes.com/east-african-stock-exchange-works-merge-buoyant-profitable-markets-1338415

ECOWAS 2015 Outlook. (2015, January 16). inAfrica24.com. Retrieved November 25, 2016 from http://inafrica24.com/modernity/ecowas-outlook-2015-gdp-growth-projected-7/#sthash.9wlbadQ2.dpbs

Embassy of the United States, Brazzaville, Republic of the Congo. (n.d.). Retrieved May 19, 2016. Retrieved from http://brazzaville.usembassy.gov/grants2.html

Emekalan, K. *Africa Live.* (2016, July 11) [Television Broadcast]. China Global Television Network.

Emerging Capital Partners. Retrieved August 4, 2016 from http://www.ecpinvestments.com

Entrepreneurs-Aliko Dangote. (n.d.). In *Famous Entrepreneurs.* Retrieved June 24, 2016 from http://www.famous-entrepreneurs.com/aliko-dangote

Environmental Protection Agency, (2016, June 14). *Climate change.* Retrieved July 9, 2016 from https://www3.epa.gov/climatechange/basics/

Ernst & Young. (2015). *EY's attractiveness survey. Africa. Making choices.* Retrieved June 30, 2016 from http://www.ey.com/Publication/vwLUAssets/EY-africa-attractiveness-survey-2015-making-choices/$FILE/EY-africa-attractiveness-survey-2015-making-choices.pdf

Ernst & Young. (2014). *Women of Africa - A powerful untapped economic force for the continent.* Retrieved July 10, 2016 from http://www.ey.com/Publication/vwLUAssets/Women_of_Africa/$FILE/Women%20of%20Africa%20final.pdf

EU-Africa Infrastructure Trust Fund. (n.d.). *European Union-Africa.* Retrieved May 9, 2016 from http://www.eu-africa-infrastructure-tf.net

European Centre for Development Policy Management. (n.d.). Dossier: FAQ - Economic Partnership Agreements. Retrieved

May 28, 2016 from http://ecdpm.org/dossiers/dossier-economic-partnership-agreements/#

European Union Commission. (2016, July 8). Climate negotiations Paris. Retrieved July 9, 2016 from http://ec.europa.eu/clima/policies/international/negotiations/paris/index_en.htm

Ezeoha, A. E. & N. Cattaneo. (2011). FDI flows to Sub-Saharan Africa: The impact of finance, institution and natural resource endowment. Rhodes University, Grahamstown, South Africa. Retrieved August 15, 2016 from http://www.csae.ox.ac.uk/conferences/2011-edia/papers/294-ezeoha.pdf

Facebook. Company info. (2016). Retrieved July 6, 2016 from http://newsroom.fb.com/company-info/

Facts about water: statistics of the water crisis (2014, August, 12). The Water Project. Retrieved August 25, 2016 from https://thewaterproject.org/water-scarcity/water_stats

Fallon, A. (2014, April 26). Sweet Dreams: Rwanda women whip up popular ice cream business. *The Guardian*. Retrieved March 21, 2016 from http://www.theguardian.com/global-development/2014/apr/26/rwanda-women-ice-cream-business-sweet-dreams

fDi Intelligence, Division of Financial Times. (2015). *Foreign direct investment for Sub-Saharan Africa report*. Retrieved April 17, 2016 from http://www.ft.com/cms/s/0/79ee41b6-fd84-11e4-b824-00144feabdc0.html#axzz4HRlWalVD

FEEEDS Advocacy Initiative & FE3DS, LLC. (2016). Home Page. Retrieved June 4, 2016 from http://www.ambassadorrobinreneesanders.com

FEEEDS Advocacy Initiative's @The FEEEDS Index. (n.d.). *FEEEDS Index Backgrounder*. Retrieved May 13, 2016 from www.bit.ly/FEEEDSIndex

FEEEDS-GALLUP July 14, 2016 Event Slides. FEEEDS Cloud: www.bit.ly/FEEEDS-GALLUPSlides

FEEEDS SME Report. (2012). SME training for Bank of Industry-Western Union-FEEDS-ADM Program. FEEEDS Advocacy Initiative. Retrieved May 13, 2016 from www.bit.ly/BOI-WU-FEEEDS2012

FEEEDS. [Blog post]. (n.d.). FEEEDS Page. Retrieved May 13, 2016 from http://blogitrrs.blogspot.com/p/feeeds.html

FEEEDS-Gallup-Allafrica July 14, 2016 Event Documentation. www.bit.ly/FEEEDS-GALLUP7-14-16

FEEEDS-W.TEC. (2014, February). Nigeria Executive Summary. Africa Female SME ICT Training. W.TEC-FEEEDS Report. BOI-WU-FEEEDS-ADM. FEEEDS Cloud. Retrieved May 13, 2016 from www.bit.ly/W-TEC-FEEEDS-ICT-Female-SMEs

FEEEDS-W.TEC. (2013, November). Nigeria Final Report: Africa Female SME Special ICT Training Session. BOI-WU-FEEEDS-ADM. FEEEDS Cloud. Retrieved May 13, 2016 bit.ly/W-TEC-ICTSpecialSession

Female entrepreneurs. A driving force in African SMEs. (n.d.). Venture Capital for Africa (VC4Africa). Retrieved March 10, 2016 from https://vc4a.com/blog/2011/10/31/female-entrepreneurs-a-driving-force-in-african-smes/

Fick, M. (2016, January 28). Smart Africa: Nigerian group target 100% mobile-first market. *Financial Times*. Retrieved July 3, 2016 from http://www.ft.com/cms/s/0/0ad2bbe4-c044-11e5-846f-79b0e3d20eaf.html#axzz4DO2DXW00

Finance for all: Promoting financial inclusion in Central Africa. (2016, March 23). ECCAS Regional Conference, Congo-Brazzaville. Retrieved September 4, 2016 from https://www.imf.org/external/np/seminars/eng/2015/brazzaville/pdf/AfrilandENG.pd/f

Financing SMEs in Kenya. Key Resources. (2012, April 12). Entrepreneur's tool kit: For social and environmental entrepreneurs. Retrieved July 13, 2016 from http://www.entrepreneurstoolkit.org/index.php?title=Financing_SMEs_in_Kenya

Fingar, C. (2015, May 10). Foreign direct investment in Africa surges. *Financial Times*. Retrieved August 15, 2016 July 4, 2016 from http://www.ft.com/cms/s/0/79ee41b6-fd84-11e4-b824-00144feabdc0.html#axzz4HRlWalVD

Fjose, S., Grunfeld, L.A., Green C. (SQW). (2010, June). [SMEs and growth in Sub-Saharan Africa] identifying SME roles and obstacles to SME growth. Menon Business Economics. Menon Publications 14/2010. Retrieved September 4, 2016 fromhttp://www.norfund.no/getfile.php/132385/Documents/Homepage/Reports%20and%20presentations/Studies%20for%20Norfund/SME%20and%20growth%20MENON%20%5BFINAL%5D.pdf

Fletcher, P. (2013, May 10). Africa's emerging middle class drives growth and democracy. Reuters. Retrieved July 4, 2016 from http://www.reuters.com/article/us-africa-investment-idUSBRE9490DV20130510

Food Standards Agency, UK. (2016, August 22). GM basics: Food and safety standards. Retrieved July 4, 2016 from https://www.food.gov.uk/science/novel/gm/basics

Foundation for Advanced Studies on International Development (FASID). (n.d.). Retrieved August 4, 2016 from http://www.fasid.or.jp/e_about/

Foundation for Skills Development Nigeria. (n.d.). Retrieved June 24, 2016 from http://www.foundationforskillsdevelopment.com/about-index/

Four Global Experience to support SME development. (2016). SME Cooperation Forum. Global Alliance of SMEs/Consultative Status with UNIDO. Retrieved August 6, 2016 from http://www.globalsmes.org/news/index.php?func=detail&lan=en&detailid=945&catalog=03

Fox, J. (2012, January-February). Economics of wellbeing. *Harvard Business Review*. Retrieved July 4, 2016 from https://hbr.org/2012/01/the-economics-of-well-being

Fresh Direct. (n.d.). Retrieved December 1, 2016 from http://www.freshdirect.ng/about-us/

From colonialism to independence. (n.d.). Mapping History: Africa History. University of Oregon. Retrieved July 30, 2016 from http://mappinghistory.uoregon.edu/english/AF/AF01-04.html

Funding agencies in South Africa. (n.d.). Funding Connection. Retrieved August 1, 2016 from https://fundingconnection.co.za/funding-agencies-in-south-africa

G-77. (n.d.). Retrieved May 17, 2016 from http://www.g77.org/doc/

Gahayalinks Rwanda Handicraft Company. (n.d.). Retrieved June 19, 2016 from http://gahayalinks.com/

Gallup Analytics (2013-2015). Retrieved March, April, June, July, August 2016 from http://www.gallup.com/products/170987/gallup-analytics.aspx

Gallup Hope Index. Hope Initiatives. Retrieved July 3, 2016 from https://www.operationhope.org/Gallup-HOPE-Index

Gallup Well Being. (2016). Retrieved July 4 from http://www.gallup.com/topic/category_wellbeing.aspx

Gallup World Poll. (n.d.). Retrieved August 7, 2016 from http://www.gallup.com/services/170945/world-poll.aspx

García de Alba, M. V. (2016, January 10). A small player with a big footprint... SMEs, CSR and the SDGs. Retrieved July 17, 2016 from http://www.eoi.es/blogs/imsd/a-small-player-with-a-big-footprint-smes-csr-and-the-sdgs/

Gates Foundation. (n.d.). Retrieved May 12, 2016 from http://www.gatesfoundation.org/How-We-Work/Resources/Grantee-Profiles/Grantee-Profile-Alliance-for-a-Green-Revolution-in-Africa-AGRA

Gates Foundation. (n.d.). Retrieved April 18, 2016 from http://www.gatesfoundation.org/Who-We-Are/General-Information/History

Gavaghan, J., & Warren, L. (2012, April 9). Instagram's 13 employees share $100m as CEO set to make $400m reveals he once turned down a job at Facebook. *Daily Mail*. Retrieved July 4, 2016 from http://www.dailymail.co.uk/news/article-2127343/Facebook-buys-Instagram-13-employees-share-100m-CEO-Kevin-Systrom-set-make-400m.html#ixzz4DT28QgTV

Geertz, C. (1973). *The interpretation of culture* (2000 ed.). New York: Basic Books.

Generation 2030/Africa. (2014, August 12). Retrieved July 5, 2016 from http://data.unicef.org/gen2030/index

Ghana boosts financial support for SME development. (2014, January). Oxford Business Group. Retrieved August 1, 2016 from http://www.oxfordbusinessgroup.com/news/ghana-boosts-financial-support-sme-development

Glenn, P., & Crabtree, S. (2013, December 23). More than one in five worldwide living in extreme poverty. *Gallup*. Retrieved May 2016 from http://www.gallup.com/poll/166565/one-five-worldwide-living-extreme-poverty.aspx

Global Business: Brics Summit 2016. (2016, October 17). [Television Broadcast]. China Global Television Network.

Global Business: Taxijet Cote d'Ivoire. (2016, May 24). [Television broadcast]. China Global Television Network.

Global Entrepreneurship Summit (GES). (n.d.). Retrieved May 17, 2016 from http://www.ges2016.org/

Global homelessness statistics. (2014). *Homeless World Cup*. Retrieved May 26, 2016 from http://www.homelessworldcup.org/homelessness-statistics/#africa

Global youth unemployment: A ticking time bomb. (2013, March 27). *The Guardian.* Retrieved May 2016 from http://www.theguardian.com/global-development-professionals-network/2013/mar/26/global-youth-unemployment-ticking-time-bomb

Goffman, E. (1973). *The framing analysis: An essay on the organization of experience.* Boston: Northeastern University Press.

Goyal, M. (2013, June 9). SMEs employ close to 40% of India's workforce, but contribute only 17% to GDP. *Economic Times.* Retrieved July 3, 2016 from http://articles.economictimes.indiatimes.com/2013-06-09/news/39834857_1_smes-workforce-small-and-medium-enterprises

GSMA Intelligence. (2016, July). *Global data.* Retrieved July 3, 2016 from https://www.gsmaintelligence.com/

GSMA Intelligence. (2015). The mobile economy Sub-Saharan Africa 2015. Retrieved August 8, 2016 from https://www.gsmaintelligence.com/research/?file=721eb3d4b80a36451202d0473b3c4a63&download

GSMA Mobile Economy. (2016, July). Retrieved July 3, 2016 from http://www.gsmamobileeconomy.com/

Gulf Cooperation Council (GCC). (2015, June 9). In *Encyclopædia Britannica.* Retrieved August 7, 2016 from https://www.britannica.com/topic/Gulf-Cooperation-Council

Gulf Cooperation Council. (n.d.). Organizational Structure. Retrieved August 7, 2016 from http://www.gcc-sg.org/en-us/AboutGCC/Pages/OrganizationalStructure.aspx

Habitat. (2015). *World Habitat Day 2015 key housing facts.* Retrieved May 2016 from http://www.habitat.org/getinv/events/world-habitat-day/housing-facts

Hall, E. T. (1977). *Beyond culture.* New York: Anchor Books.

Heilbron, M. (2014, March 3). Private equity & venture capital investments in Africa growing fast - Will we see a quick shift towards SMEs? Venture Capital for Africa. Retrieved June 25, 2016 from https://vc4a.com/blog/2014/03/03/private-equity-venture-capital-investments-in-africa-growing-fast-shift-towards-smes-expected/

Helios. (n.d.). Retrieved August 4, 2016 from http://www.heliosinvestment.com/

Helliwell, J., Layard, R., & Sachs, J. (2015). *World happiness report 2015.* United Nations. Retrieved July 4, 2016 from http://worldhappiness.report/wp-content/uploads/sites/2/2015/04/WHR15.pdf

Hello Doctor. (2016). Retrieved July 2, 106 from https://www.hellodoctor.co.za/app/

Helmrich, B. (2015, January 11). Instagram for business: Everything you need to know. *Business News Daily.* Retrieved July 4, 2016 from http://www.businessnewsdaily.com/7662-instagram-business-guide.html#

Henry Ford Innovation Nation. (2016, April 2). [Television broadcast] *Columbia Broadcasting System (CBS).*

Hidden Figures. How Black Women Did the Math That Put Men on the Moon. 2016, September 25). Author Interviews. *NPR News.* Retrieved January 5, 2017 from http://www.npr.org/2016/09/25/495179824/hidden-figures-how-black-women-did-the-math-that-put-men-on-the-moon

High definition. In *Dictionary.com.* Retrieved July 12, 2016 from http://www.dictionary.com/browse/high-definition

Hilton Hotels & Resorts. (n.d.). Retrieved July 31, 2016 from http://www3.hilton.com/en/index.html?WT.srch=1 and http://www.hiltonworldwide.com/

Hippo Water Roller project. (n.d.). Retrieved May 27, 2016 from http://www.hipporoller.org/solutions/

Hirvonen, P. (2005, August). Stingy Samaritans: Why recent increases in development aid fail to help the poor. Global Policy Forum. Retrieved April 26, 2016 from https://www.globalpolicy.org/component/content/article/240/45056.html

Holodny, E. (2016, May 9). South Africa's unemployment rate just surged to a 12-year high. *Business Insider.* Retrieved May 25, 2016 from http://www.businessinsider.com/south-africa-unemployment-rate-rises-2016-5

Homestrings. Retrieved March 11, 2016 from https://www.homestrings.com/

Honde, G. J. & Abraha, F. G. (2015). *Botswana 2015.* Retrieved May 2016 from http://www.bw.undp.org/content/dam/botswana/docs/Publications/Botswana%60s%20GDP%202015.pdf

How far do EU-US sanctions on Russia go? (2014, September 15). BBC News. Retrieved July 7, 2016 from http://www.bbc.com/news/world-europe-28400218

How Rwanda's only ice cream shop challenges cultural taboos. (2014, April 10). National Public Radio (NPR). Retrieved March 21, 2016 from (http://www.npr.org/sections/parallels/2014/04/10/301414587/how-rwandas-only-ice-cream-shop-challenges-cultural-taboos

Hussain, M. N. (2000). Linkages between SMEs and large industries for increased markets for trade: The African perspective. African Development Bank, Strategic Planning and Research Department, #53. Retrieved July 1, 2016 from http://www.afdb.org/fileadmin/uploads/afdb/Documents/Publications/00157640-EN-ERP-53.PDF

ICTs delivering home-grown development solutions in Africa. (2012, December 10). World Bank.

Imbaza Mussels. (n.d.). Retrieved December 1, 2016 from http://www.companies-southafrica.com/imbaza-mussels-hgui/

Industrial Revolution [television broadcast]. A & E Network. Retrieved July 31, 2016 from http://www.history.com/topics/industrial-revolution

Innovation Prize for Africa. (n.d.) Retrieved May 6, 2016 from http://innovationprizeforafrica.org.

Instagram. (n.d.). Retrieved July 4, 2016 from https://www.instagram.com/instagram/

Inter-American Development Bank. (2016). Retrieved July 6, 2016 from http://www.iadb.org/en/inter-american-development-bank,2837.html

International Development Agency. (n.d.). Retrieved April 18, 2016 from http://ida.worldbank.org

International Finance Corporation. (2016). *Aureos Africa Fund L.L.C.* Retrieved May 4, 2016 from http://ifcext.ifc.org/ifcext/spiwebsite1.nsf/ProjectDisplay/SPI_DP26992

International Finance Corporation. (2014, February 26). Expanding women's access to financial services. Retrieved August 18, 2016 from http://www.worldbank.org/en/results/2013/04/01/banking-on-women-extending-womens-access-to-financial-services

International Finance Corporation. (2013). Closing the credit gap for formal and informal, micro, small and medium enterprises. IFC Advisory Services. Retrieved August 17, 2016 from http://www.ifc.org/wps/wcm/connect/4d6e6400416896c09494b79e78015671/Closing+the+Credit+Gap+Report-FinalLatest.pdf?MOD=AJPERES

International Finance Corporation. (2011, October). Strengthening access to finance for women-owned SMEs in developing countries. Retrieved August 17, 2016 from http://www.ifc.org/wps/wcm/connect/a4774a004a3f66539f0f9f8969adcc27/G20_Women_Report.pdf?MOD=AJPERES

International Union for the Conservation of Nature (1980). World Conservation Strategy. Retrieved May 2016 from http://www.

triplepundit.com/2010/08/origin-of-sustainability-movement-leads-to-current-challenges/#

International Institute for Education. (n.d.). Retrieved May 9, 2016 from http://www.iie.org/

International Labour Organization (2015). Global employment trends for youth 2015: Scaling up investment for decent job for youth. Geneva, Switzerland. Retrieved July 5, 2015 from http://www.ilo.org/wcmsp5/groups/public/---dgreports/---dcomm/---publ/documents/publication/wcms_412015.pdf

International Labor Organization. (2015). World employment social outlook trends. Retrieved April 16, 2016 from http://www.ilo.org/wcmsp5/groups/public/---dgreports/---dcomm/---publ/documents/publication/wcms_337069.pdf

International Labor Organization. (1996-2016). Decent work and the 2030 agenda for sustainable development. Topics. Goal #8: Decent work and economic growth. Retrieved July 17, 2016 from http://www.ilo.org/global/topics/sdg-2030/lang--en/index.htm

International Monetary Fund. (2015, December 26). Africa's middle class spearheads economic growth. Retrieved July 5, 2016 from http://www.imf.org/external/pubs/ft/survey/so/2013/INT122613A.htm

International Monetary Fund. (2015, April). Sub-Saharan Africa - Navigating headwinds. Retrieved July 24, 2016 from https://www.imf.org/external/pubs/ft/reo/2015/afr/eng/pdf/sreo0415.pdf

International Trade Administration. African Growth and Opportunity Act. (n.d.). Retrieved May 9, 2016 from http://trade.gov/agoa/

International Trade Administration. (2001-2009). Summary of AGOA I. Retrieved August 17, 2016 from http://trade.gov/agoa/legislation/index.asp

Intuit. (2016). Retrieved July 1, 2016 from http://www.intuit.com/

Investment Climate Facility for Africa. (2014, April 8). North African Women and SMEs: An opportunity hiding in plain view. Retrieved from http://www.icfafrica.org/news/north-african-women-and-smes-an-opportunity-hiding-in-plain-view

Investment Fund for Africa. (2015, December). International public and private partners invest USD 137 million healthcare in Africa. Retrieved from http://www.ifhafund.com/

iPad. (2016). Apple Inc. Retrieved July 7, 2016 from http://www.apple.com

Ilwad Elman – Leaders of Sustainable Development. (n.d.). Thomason Reuters. Retrieved January 6, 2017 from http://sustainability.thomsonreuters.com/women/authors/ilwad-elman

Jacana Partners. On *LinkedIn.* Retrieved April 21, 2016 from https://www.linkedin.com/company/jacana-partners

Japan International Cooperation Agency. (2011, March/April). JICA, the World Bank, and FASID publish a study on industrial clusters and SME growth in Africa. Retrieved May 5 and August 4, 2016 from http://www.jica.go.jp/usa/english/office/others/newsletter/2011/1103_04_08.html

Jendayi E. Frazer, Ph.D. - CIPI Director and Distinguished Public Service Professor. (n.d.) Center for International Policy and Innovation. Carnegie Mellon University. Retrieved August 17, 2016 from http://www.cmu.edu/cipi/people/frazer-jendayi.html

Johannesburg Stock Exchange. (2013). History overview. Retrieved July 12, 2016 from https://www.jse.co.za/about/history-company-overview

Jones, V. C. (2010, February 10). U.S. trade and investment relationship with Sub-Saharan Africa: The African Growth and Opportunity Act. Congressional Research Service Publication 7-5700.

Kauffman Index on Growth Entrepreneurship. (2016). Retrieved December 2, 2016 from http://www.kauffman.org/microsites/kauffman-index/reports/growth-entrepreneurship

Kalama, M. (Reporter). (2014, September 19). *Africa live newscast* [Television broadcast]. China Global Television Network.

Kalama, M. (Reporter). (2014, September 9). *Africa live newscast* [Television broadcast]. China Global Television Network.

Katura, T. N. (2014, December). The role of SMEs in employment creation and economic growth in several countries. *International Journal of Education and Research, 2*(12). Retrieved August 18, 2016 from http://www.ijern.com/journal/2014/December-2014/39.pdf

Keep up with TaxiJet Cote d'Ivoire. (2016). On *LinkedIn.* Retrieved August 6, 2016 from https://www.linkedin.com/company/taxijet-cote-d'ivoire

Kelly, D., Singer, S., Herrington, M., & the Entrepreneurship Research Association (GERA). (2015-2016). *Global Entrepreneurship Monitor 2015-2016 Global Report.* Retrieved August 4, 2016 from http://www.gemconsortium.org/report

Kelly, M. (2015, October 16). Overview of the Industrial Revolution: The United States and the Industrial Revolution of the 19th century. Retrieved July 31, 2016 from http://americanhistory.about.com/od/industrialrev/a/indrevooverview.htm

Kennedy, K. (2016, June 23). Key barriers to Kenya's SMEs growth - Study. *Capital Business.* Retrieved July 1, 2016 from http://www.capitalfm.co.ke/business/2016/06/key-barriers-to-kenyas-smes-growth-study/

Kenny, P. (2016). (2016, October 10). Africa makes progress on trade and economic integration. *Allafrica.com.* Retrieved October 14, 2016 from http://allafrica.com/stories/201610100001.html?aa_source=nwsltr-nigeria-en

Kenyan Revenue Authority. (n.d.). iTax system is now easier than ever. Retrieved June 23, 2016 from http://www.nakuru.go.ke/2015/09/02/deputy-governor-ruto-welcomes-itax-support-centre-to-nakuru-county/

Kharpal, A. (2016, September 23). Facebook's Instagram hits 400M users, beats Twitter. Retrieved July 4, 2016 from http://www.cnbc.com/2015/09/23/instagram-hits-400-million-users-beating-twitter.html

KickStart. (n.d.). Retrieved April 12, 2016 from http://kickstart.org/about-us/

Kimani D. (2015). Deputy Governor Ruto welcomes iTax support centre to Nakuru county. Retrieved June 23, 2016 from http://www.nakuru.go.ke/2015/09/02/deputy-governor-ruto-welcomes-itax-support-centre-to-nakuru-county/

KIT - Sustainable Economic Development. (n.d.). Annona Sustainable Impact Fund. Retrieved August 4, 2016 from http://www.kit.nl/sed/project/annona-sustainable-investment-fund

Klein, C. (2015, December 15). 10 Things You Didn't Know About Ada Lovelace. History in the Headlines. Retrieved November 21, 2016 from http://www.history.com/news/10-things-you-may-not-know-about-ada-lovelace

Kolster, J. (2008, February 15). Infrastructure consortium for Africa regional collaboration meeting. Regional Integration Department, Africa Region, World Bank. Retrieved May 9, 2016 from http://www.eu-africa-infrastructure-tf.net/attachments/library/ica-presentation-2008-02-15%20.pdf

Kountable. (2016). Our Mission. Retrieved September 28, 2016 from http://www.kountable.com/about/

Kuramo Capital. (2016). Retrieved June 16, 2016 from https://kuramocapital.com/

Kushnir, K., Mirmulstein, M. L., & Ramalho, R. (2010). Micro, small, and medium enterprises around the world: How many are there, and what affects the count. World Bank/IFC. Retrieved March 5, 2016 from http://www.ifc.org/wps/wcm/connect/9ae1dd80495860d6a482b519583b6d16/MSME-CI-AnalysisNote.pdf?MOD=AJPERES

Laylin, T. (2011, November). Africa's first plastic bottle house rise in Nigeria. *Inhabitat*. Retrieved June 30 and August 19, 2016 from http://inhabitat.com/africas-first-plastic-bottle-house-rises-in-nigeria/nigeria-bottle-house-1/

Lermet, C., & Branaman, A. (Eds.). (n.d.). *The Goffman Reader.* Retrieved July 22, 2016 from http://people.brandeis.edu/~teuber/goffmanbio

Les Poles de Competitivite. (n. d.). Competitiveness clusters in France. Retrieved July 1, 2016 from http://competitivite.gouv.fr/documents/commun/Documentation_poles/brochures_poles/anglais/brochure-ang-internet.pdf

LinkedIn. (2016). Retrieved July 6, 2016 from http://ourstory.linkedin.com/

Lloyd Pierson (n.d.). On *LinkedIn*. Retrieved May 19, 2016 from https://www.linkedin.com/in/lloyd-pierson-63276018

Lundin Foundation. (n.d.) Portfolio Manager. Retrieved May 30, 2016 from http://www.lundinfoundation.org/i/pdf/lundingfoundation_portfoliomanager.pdf

Made in Africa Foundation. (2015). Retrieved August 4, 2016 from http://www.madeinafricafoundation.com/

Magnier, M. (2016, January 19). China's economic growth in 2015 is slowest in 25 years. *Wall Street Journal*. Retrieved May 12, 2016 from http://www.wsj.com/articles/china-economic-growth-slows-to-6-9-on-year-in-2015-1453169398

Makhelewane Festival. (2016). Retrieved December 2, 2016 from https://twitter.com/makhelwanefest

Makoko Floating School. (n.d.). Aga Khan Award for Architecture. Retrieved December 1, 2016 from http://www.akdn.org/architecture/project/makoko-floating-school

Manufacturing in Africa: An awakening giant. (2014, February). *The Economist.* Retrieved May 12, 2016 from http://www.economist.com/news/middle-east-and-africa/21595949-if-africas-economies-are-take-africans-will-have-start-making-lo

Mara Foundation. (n.d.). Retrieved May 12, 2016 from www.mara-foundation.org

Marshall, I., & Onyekachi, O. (2014). Funding housing deficit in Nigeria: A review of the efforts and the way forward. *International Journal of Business and Social Science, 5* (13). Retrieved July 9, 2016 from http://ijbssnet.com/journals/Vol_5_No_13_December_2014/22.pdf

Martin, P. (2014, July 25). Capitalism and global poverty: Two billion poor, one billion hungry. Centre for Research in Globalization. Retrieved July 24, 2016 from http://www.globalresearch.ca/capitalism-and-global-poverty-two-billion-poor-one-billion-hungry/5393262

Martin, X. (2014, May). Rwanda: A country finding its path to financial inclusion. FinclusionLab. Retrieved July 31, 2016 from http://finclusionlab.org/blog/rwanda-country-finding-its-path-financial-inclusion

Martinetti, I. (2007). UN management reform - The role and perspective of the G77. Center for UN Reform.

Mascarenhas, H. (2014, May 22). 45 surprising facts about extreme poverty around the world you may not have realized. *WorldMic.* Retrieved May 2016 from http://mic.com/articles/89717/45-surprising-facts-about-extreme-poverty-around-the-world-you-may-not-have-realized#.ZTbscq6s

Matthee, M., & E. Finaughty. (2010, March 18-19). Trade with China: How to support African SMEs. The 7th African Finance Journal Conference. Stellenbosch, South Africa.

Mbeki, T. (1998, April 9). The African Renaissance, South Africa and the world. Speech at United Nations University, Tokyo, Japan.

McKinsey and Company. (2010). *What's driving Africa. 2010.* Johannesburg, South Africa.

McKinsey Global Institute. (2010, June). Lions on the move: The progress and potential of African economies. Retrieved from http://www.mckinsey.com/global-themes/middle-east-and-africa/lions-on-the-move

M-Cloud. M-Visions. (n.d.). Retrieved July 3, 2016 from http://maafo-visions.com/

MDG Report 2015. (2015). United National Economic Commission, African Union, African Development Bank Group, UNDP. Retrieved July 24, 2016 from http://www.afdb.org/fileadmin/uploads/afdb/Documents/Publications/MDG_Report_2015.pdf

Melber, H. (2016, May 26). The myth of Africa's growing middle class. *Independent Online.* Retrieved July 5, 2016 from http://www.iol.co.za/news/the-myth-of-africas-growing-middle-class-2026750

Mfonobong, N. (2011, November 29). The philanthropy of Africa's 40 richest. *Forbes.* Retrieved March 3, 2016 from http://www.forbes.com/sites/mfonobongnsehe/2011/11/29/the-philanthropy-of-africas-40-richest/#78c4dc8740a0

MGI lions on the move: African economies. (2010, June). Full report. Africa Pop Up Store/ McKinsey & Company. Retrieved August 9, 2016 from http://www.africapopupstore.com/documents/MGI_Lions_on_the_move_african_economies_full_report.pdf

Mijiyama, A. G. (n.d.). What drives foreign direct investment in Africa? An empirical investigation with panel data. African Center for Economic Transformation & African Development Bank. Retrieved

August 15, 2916 from http://www.afdb.org/fileadmin/uploads/afdb/Documents/Knowledge/What%20Drives%20Foreign%20Direct%20Investments%20in%20Africa%20An%20Empirical%20Investigation%20with%20Panel%20Data.pdf

Millennium Challenge Corporation. (2015). Guide to the indicators and selection process. Retrieved May 15, 2016 from https://www.mcc.gov/resources/doc/report-guide-to-the-indicators-and-the-selection-process-fy-2015

Millennium Challenge Corporation. (2014, October 9). Report guide to indicators. Retrieved May 17, 2016 from https://www.mcc.gov/resources/doc/report-guide-to-the-indicators-and-the-selection-process-fy-2015

Millennium Challenge Corporation. (n.d.) Retrieved August 17, 2016 from http://www.mcc.gov

Ministry of External Relations Brazil. (n.d.). Information about BRICS. Retrieved June 30, 2016 from http://brics.itamaraty.gov.br/about-brics/information-about-brics

Ministry of Foreign Affairs, Government of Japan. (2014). Japan's new assistance program for Africa in-line with TICAD II agenda for action. Retrieved May 2016 and July 9, 2016 from http://www.mofa.go.jp/region/africa/ticad2/agenda_n.html

Minney, T. (2016, May 5). Exchanges give SMEs a helping hand. *Africa Business Times*. Retrieved May 11 and July 12, 2016 from http://africanbusinessmagazine.com/african-banker/exchanges-give-smes-helping-hand/

Mo Ibrahim Foundation. (n.d.). Retrieved June 23, 2016 from http://mo.ibrahim.foundation/

Mo Ibrahim. (n.d.). In *Wikipedia*. Retrieved April 19, 2016 from https://en.wikipedia.org/wiki/Mo_Ibrahim_Foundation

Mo Ibrahim will participate in EU-Africa business forum. (2014). *Latest news*. Mo Ibrahim Foundation. Retrieved April 19 and

June 17, 2016 from http://mo.ibrahim.foundation/news/2014/mo-ibrahim-will-participate-in-eu-africa-business-forum/

Mobile phone users worldwide 2013-2019. (2016). Statista: The Statistical Portal. Retrieved July 2, 2016 from http://www.statista.com/statistics/274774/forecast-of-mobile-phone-users-worldwide/

Moodley, J., Holt, T., Leke, A., & Desvaux, G. (2016, August). Women matter. Africa. McKinsey & Company. Retrieved August 18, 2016 from http://www.mckinsey.com/global-themes/women-matter/women-matter-africa

Moore, C. (August 2, 2010). Origin of sustainability movement leads to current challenges - Historical perspective. Sustainable Development Land Initiative. Retrieved May 2016 from http://www.triplepundit.com/2010/08/origin-of-sustainability-movement-leads-to-current-challenges/#

MTN SA Foundation. (2009). *Entrepreneurship.* Mobile Telephone Network (MTN). Retrieved May 11, 2016 from http://services.mtn.co.za/mtnfoundation/Entrepreneurship.html

Multiple mobile device ownership. (2016). Statista: The Statistical Portal. Retrieved July 2, 2016 July 4, 2016 July 12, 2016 from http://www.statista.com/statistics/245501/multiple-mobile-device-ownership-worldwide/

Mwiti, L. (2015, October 29). Special report: 18 million, not 300 million: That's the size of Africa's 'real' middle class – and it could disappear. *Mail & Guardian Africa.* Retrieved July 4, 2016 from http://mgafrica.com/article/2015-10-27-18-million-thats-the-size-of-africas-middle-classand-with-chinas-woes-it-could-just-be-wiped-out

Nairobi Securities Exchange Limited. (2013, January 22). Nairobi Securities Exchange (NSE) launches the growth enterprise market segment (GEMS). Retrieved July 12, 2016 from https://www.nse.co.ke/media-center/press-release.html?download=6259%3Apress-release-launch-of-the-growth-enterprise-market-segment and also, found at www.nse.co.ke

Nakuru County. Retrieved June 24, 2016 from http://www.nakuru.go.ke/about/

Nasir Ahmad el-Rufai (n. d.). In *Wikipedia*. Retrieved May 3, 2016 from https://en.wikipedia.org/wiki/Nasir_Ahmad_el-Rufai

Nationals. (n.d.). Definition. In *Oxford Dictionaries*. Retrieved July 30, 2016 from http://www.oxforddictionaries.com/us/definition/american_english/national

Nelwa's Gelato. (n.d.). Nelwa's Gelato. Facebook. Retrieved November 28, 2016 from https://www.facebook.com/NelwasGelato/

New Development Bank BRICS. (n.d.). Retrieved June 30, 2016 from http://ndbbrics.org/

New Development Bank BRICS. (n.d.). Agreement on the new development bank. NDB. Retrieved June 30, 2016 from http://ndbbrics.org/agreement.html

New Faces New Voices. Retrieved April 26, 2016 from http://www.nfnv.org/

New Faces New Voices. Nomsa Daniels Biography. Retrieved June 3, 2016 from http://www.nfnv.org/home/advisory-board-founding-members/

New Faces New Voices. SME Initiatives. Retrieved June 3, 2016 from http://www.nfnv.org/initiatives/

New rival to JSE on cards as ZAR X granted license. (2016, March 31). Africa News Network. Retrieved July 12, 2016 from http://www.ann7.com/new-rival-to-jse-on-cards-as-zar-x-granted-licence/

Nigerian Stock Exchange. (2016). Alternative securities market. Retrieved July 12, 2016 from http://www.nse.com.ng/Issuers-section/listing-your-company/asem

Nike Centre for Arts and Culture. (n.d.). Nike Art.com. Retrieved August 20, 2016 from http://www.nikeart.com/

Njiraini, J. (2014, December). AGOA: The US-Africa trade dilemma. *Africa Renewal Online*. Retrieved August 11, 2016 from http://www.un.org/africarenewal/magazine/december-2014/agoa-us%E2%80%93africa-trade-dilemma

Nomsa Daniels. (n.d.). On *LinkedIn*. Retrieved April 26, 2016 from https://za.linkedin.com/in/nomsa-daniels-ba2b6439

Norfund. (n.d.). Norfund SME Funds. Retrieved May 15, 2016 from http://www.norfund.no/sme-funds/category316.html

Nsehe, M. (2011, August 2). The best African mobile apps: iCow. *Forbes*. Retrieved August 2, 2016 from http://www.forbes.com/sites/mfonobongnsehe/2011/08/02/the-best-african-mobile-apps-icow/#58d5c8161934

Octocopter. (2016) In *Oxford Dictionaries*. Retrieved August 18, 2016 from http://www.oxforddictionaries.com/us/definition/american_english/octocopter

O'Donnell, C. (2011, September 12). New study quantifies use of social media in Arab Spring. Washington University. Retrieved July 31, 2016 from http://www.washington.edu/news/2011/09/12/new-study-quantifies-use-of-social-media-in-arab-spring/

OECD. About History. Retrieved June 15, 2016 from http://www.oecd.org/about/history/

OECD. About Us. Retrieved June 15, 2016 from http://www.oecd.org/about/

OECD Better Life Index. (n.d.). Retrieved July 4, 2016 from http://www.oecdbetterlifeindex.org/

Office of Evaluation and Oversight (OVE), Inter-American Development Bank. (2014, October 11). *A comparative analysis of*

IDB approaches supporting SMEs: Assessing results in the Brazilian manufacturing sector. Retrieved August 5, 2016from https://publications.iadb.org/bitstream/handle/11319/6683/SME_BRIK_English.pdf?sequence=1

Office of National Statistics, UK. (2016, May 5). Personal wellbeing. Frequently Asked Questions (FAQ). Retrieved July 4, 2016 from http://webarchive.nationalarchives.gov.uk/20160105160709/http://www.ons.gov.uk/ons/guide-method/method-quality/specific/social-and-welfare-methodology/subjective-wellbeing-survey-user-guide/subjective-well-being-frequently-asked-questions--faq-s-.html

Office of the Special Advisor for Africa. United Nations. (n.d.) Tokyo International Conference of African Development (TICAD). Partnerships. Retrieved August 4, 2016 from http://www.un.org/en/africa/osaa/partnerships/ticad.shtml

Ogunlesi, T., & Busari, S. (2012, September 4). Seven ways mobile phones have changed lives in Africa. CNN. Retrieved July 3, 2016 from http://www.cnn.com/2012/09/13/world/africa/mobile-phones-change-africa/index.html

Olijnyk, Z. (2014, October). Jim O'Neill: The man who coined the term BRIC. BNN International. Retrieved June 30, 2016 from http://www.bnn.ca/News/2013/10/24/Jim-ONeill-The-Man-Who-Coined-The-Term-BRIC.aspx

Oliver, R., & Atmore, A (2005, February). *Africa since 1800.* (5th). Cambridge, UK: Cambridge University Press.

Open Aid Data. (n.d.). Retrieved May 17, 2016 from http://www.openaiddata.org/purpose/288/321/10/

Open Aid Data. (2014, May 28). Zambia. Retrieved May 7, 2016 from http://www.openaiddata.org/purpose/288/321/918/

Opening address by Tourism Minister Derek Hanekom. (2016, May 7). Indaba Africa's top travel show: Indaba Tourism Conference. Retrieved August 7, 2016 from http://www.indaba-southafrica.co.za/news/INDABA-2016-opening-address.aspx

Operation Hope. Home Page. (n.d.). Retrieved May 14, 2016 from https://www.operationhope.org/

Operation Hope. Banking on our future. (n.d.). Retrieved May 14, 2016 from https://www.operationhope.org/banking-on-our-future-south-africa

Organic Farms. Retrieved May 14, 2016 from http://www.organicfarmsgroup.com/

Organization for Economic Cooperation and Development (OECD). (2016). Divided we stand: Why inequality keeps rising. Retrieved July 5, 2016 from http://www.oecd.org/els/soc/dividedwestandwhyinequalitykeepsrising.htm

Organization for Economic Cooperation and Development (OECD). (2015, May 21). *In it together: Why less inequality benefits all*. Retrieved July 5, 2016 from http://www.oecd.org/els/in-it-together-why-less-inequality-benefits-all-9789264235120-en.htm, and July 21, 2016 from http://dx.doi.org/10.1787/9789264235120-en

Organization for Economic Cooperation and Development. (2014). Development aid stable in 2014 but flows to poorest countries still falling. Retrieved April 26, 2016 from http://www.oecd.org/dac/stats/development-aid-stable-in-2014-but-flows-to-poorest-countries-still-falling.htm

Organization for Economic Cooperation and Development (OECD) (2014). Global outlook on aid results of the 2014 DAC survey on donors' forward spending plans and prospects for improving aid predictability. Retrieved April 26, 2016 from http://www.oecd.org/dac/aid-architecture/GlobalOutlookAid-web.pdf

Organization for Economic Cooperation and Development (OECD). (2011, June 6). Africa should embrace new economic giants and boost social inclusion. *African Economic Outlook*. Retrieved May 2016 from http://www.oecd.org/newsroom/africashouldembracenew economicgiantsandboostsocialinclusionsaysafricaneconomicoutlook2011.htm

Organization for Economic Cooperation and Development (OECD). (n. d.). *Better life index.* Retrieved July 4, 2016 from http://www.oecdbetterlifeindex.org/#/11111111111

ORT South Africa. (n.d.). Retrieved May 8, 2016 from http://www.ortsa.org.za

Oxfam. (2016, January 18). 62 people own the same as half the world, reveals Oxfam Davos report. Retrieved from https://www.oxfam.org/en/pressroom/pressreleases/2016-01-18/62-people-own-same-half-world-reveals-oxfam-davos-report

Oxford Business Group. (2015, June 15). Oosthuyse, D. Director of Capital Markets, Johannesburg Stock Exchange: Interview. Retrieved July 12, 2016 from http://www.oxfordbusinessgroup.com/interview/going-strong-obg-talks-donna-oosthuyse-director-capital-markets-johannesburg-stock-exchange-jse

Parke, P. (2016, April 1). Why are 600 million Africans still without power? CNN.com Retrieved July 30, 2016 from http://www.cnn.com/2016/04/01/africa/africa-state-of-electricity-feat/

Pasquali, V. (2011, August 22). Income inequality and wealth distribution by country. *Global Finance.* Retrieved July 23 and July 30, 2016 from https://www.gfmag.com/global-data/economic-data/wealth-distribution-income-inequality

Pew Research Center. (2015, April 15). Cell phones in Africa: Communication lifeline. Texting most common activity, but mobile money popular in several countries. *Global Attitudes and Trends.* Retrieved July 3, 2016 from http://www.pewglobal.org/2015/04/15/cell-phones-in-africa-communication-lifeline

Piejko, P. (2016, May 18). 16 mobile market statistics you should know in 2016. Mobiforge. Retrieved July 2, 2016 from https://mobiforge.com/news-comment/16-mobile-market-statistics-you-should-know-in-2016

Plant. (n.d.). Retrieved August 20, 2016 from http://www.plantcafe.co.za/

Poll of eight African nations. (2004, June 16). Retrieved June 3, 2016 from http://www.worldpublicopinion.org/pipa/articles/brafricara/209.php?lb=braf and Retrieved April 17, 2016 from http://worldpublicopinion.org/poll-of-8-african-nations/

Population - Female (% of total) in Sub-Saharan Africa. (2014). *Trading Economic.* Retrieved August 17, 2016 from http://www.tradingeconomics.com/sub-saharan-africa/population-female-percent-of-total-wb-data.html

Population-Female (Percent of Total) in Sub-Saharan Africa. (2016). *Trading Economic.* Retrieved July 9, 2016 from http://www.tradingeconomics.com/sub-saharan-africa/population-female-percent-of-total-wb-data.html

President's Young African Leaders Initiative. (n.d.). Department of State, U.S. Retrieved August 1, 2016 from http://www.state.gov/p/af/rt/pyali/

Private Equity Africa. (2016, June 5). Jacana Partners. TAG Archives. Retrieved June 5, 2016 from http://www.privateequityafrica.com/tag/jacana/

Quadcopter. (2016). In *Oxford Dictionary.* Retrieved June 2, 2016 from http://www.oxforddictionaries.com/us/definition/american_english/quadcopter

Qureshi, R. (2016). Ericsson Mobility Report, data and forecast page. 1996-2016. Retrieved July 2, 106 from https://www.ericsson.com/mobility-report

Regional integration: Uniting to compete. (2014). Retrieved June 2016 from http://static.moibrahimfoundation.org/downloads/publications/2014/2014-facts-&-figures-regional-integration-uniting-to-compete.pdf

Republic of the Congo. (n. d.). In *Encyclopaedia Britannica Online.* Retrieved May 9, 2016 from http://www.britannica.com/place/Republic-of-the-Congo

Rheault, M., & McCarthy, J. (2016, June 13). In busy election year, African leaders enjoy high approvals. *Gallup World Poll*. Retrieved June 14, 2016 from http://www.gallup.com/poll/192584/busy-election-year-african-leaders-enjoyed-high-approval.aspx?utm_source=genericbutton&utm_medium=organic&utm_campaign=sharing

Rolex Awards for Enterprise. (2005). Ancient technology preserves food. Retrieved May 2016 from http://www.rolexawards.com/profiles/laureates/mohammed_bah_abba/project

Rosen, A. A. (2015, November 19). Credit Suisse report just debunked a huge claim about the size of Africa's middle class. *Business Insider*. Retrieved May 2016 from http://publications.credit-suisse.com/tasks/render/file/index.cfm?fileid=C26E3824-E868-56E0-CCA04D4BB9B9ADD5

Russia unemployment rate 1993-2016 [data set]. (n.d.). *Trading Economics*. Retrieved June 30, 2016 from http://www.tradingeconomics.com/russia/unemployment-rate

Rwanda Population. In *WorldOMeters Population*. Retrieved June 15, 2016 from http://www.worldometers.info/world-population/rwanda-population/xxx

Safaricom Foundation. Retrieved May 14, 2016 from http://www.safaricomfoundation.org

Safaricom. M-Pesa. (n.d.). Retrieved May 28, 2016 from http://www.safaricom.co.ke/personal/m-pesa

Salunkhe, C. (2016, February 17). Micro and macro developments will help SMEs expand. *The Times of India*. Retrieved August 6, 2016 from http://www.smechamberofindia.com/MediaCoverage/timesofindia_feb2016.pdf

Sanders, Ambassador R. R. (2013). *The legendary Uli women of Nigeria: Their life stories in sign, symbols, and motifs*. Bloomington, Indiana: Xlibris Books.

Sanders, Ambassador R. R. (2013, June 13). Sub-Saharan Africa 2013: Striving to be a more perfect continent. [Blog post] The Huffington Post. Retrieved July 27, 2016 from http://www.huffingtonpost.com/amb-robin-renee-sanders/africa-2013-the-positive-_b_3431342.html

Sanders, Ambassador R. R. (2013, June 2). The 5th BRICS Summit: Lessons for the developed world. [Blog post]. The Huffington Post. Retrieved May 2016 from http://www.huffingtonpost.com/amb-robin-renee-sanders/the-5th-brics-summit-less_b_2995658.html

Sanders, Ambassador R. R. (2012, December 12). Mobile services and E-empowerment – The developing world has the advantage. [Blog post]. The Huffington Post. Retrieved August 3, 2016 from http://www.huffingtonpost.com/amb-robin-renee-sanders/post_4203_b_2253551.html

Sanders, Ambassador R. R. (2012, December 12). Mobile services and E-empowerment – The developing world has the advantage. [Blog post]. FEEEDS. Retrieved August 3, 2016 from http://blogitrrs.blogspot.com/2012/12/mobile-services-e-empowerment.html

Sanders, Ambassador R. R. (2012, November 12). It's the economics: Refocusing & reframing Africa, part one. [Blog post]. The Huffington Post. Retrieved May 2016 from http://www.huffingtonpost.com/amb-robin-renee-sanders/its-the-economics-africa_b_2084087.html

Sanders, R. R. (2012, November 6). It's economic: Refocusing and reframing Africa. [Blog post]. FEEEDS. Retrieved May 2, 2016 from http://blogitrrs.blogspot.com/2012/11/its-economics-refocusing-reframing

Sanders, Ambassador R. R. (2011, July 1). Importance of SME development in Africa: They will produce Africa's middle class. [Blog post]. The Huffington Post. Retrieved August 3, 2016 from http://www.huffingtonpost.com/amb-robin-renee-sanders/importance-of-sme-develop_b_888407.html

Sanders, R. R. (2011, June 22). SMEs development enterprise role in national building: Recognizing the valuable role of SMEs in national development. [Blog post]. FEEEDS. Retrieved May 2016 from http://blogitrrs.blogspot.com/2011/06/smes-development-enterprise-role-in.html

Sanders, Ambassador R. R. (2011, May 26). Coining the acronym BRICA - Adding Africa's name to world regions & economies in economic boom! [Blog post]. FEEEDS. Retrieved from http://blogitrrs.blogspot.com/2011/05/coining-acronym-brica-adding-africas.html

Sani, K. S., & Gbadegesin, J. T. (2015). A study of private rental housing market in Kaduna Metropolis, Nigeria. *Journal of Resources Development and Management, 11.*

Sarah E. Moten. (2013). George Bush Presidential Center. Retrieved December 4, 2016 from http://www.bushcenter.org/people/sarah-e-moten.html

Save the Children. (2016, October 10). *Girls' Opportunity Index.* Retrieved October 15, 2016 from https://assets.savethechildren.ch/downloads/index_only_every_last_girl_print_version_inside_pages_3_10_16_3_.pdf

Schiere, R., Ndikumana, L., & Walkenhorst, P. (Eds.). (2011). *China and Africa: An emerging partnership for development?* African Development Bank Group. Retrieved March 3, 2016 from http://www.afdb.org/fileadmin/uploads/afdb/Documents/Publications/Anglaischina.pdf

Scramble for Africa. (n. d.). In *New World Encyclopedia.* Retrieved May 11, 2016 from http://www.newworldencyclopedia.org/p/index.php?title=Scramble_for_Africa&printable=yes

Second Guangzhou Africa Investment Forum. (2016, September 7-8). News Guangzhou. Retrieved September 7, 2016 from http://www.newsgd.com/news/2016-09/07/content_155386819.htm

Sedghi, A., & Anderson, M. (2015, July 31). Africa wealth report 2015: Rich get richer even as poverty and inequality deepen. *The Guardian.* Retrieved July 24, 2016 from https://www.theguardian.

com/global-development/datablog/2015/jul/31/africa-wealth-report-2015-rich-get-richer-poverty-grows-and-inequality-deepens-new-world-wealth

SEED Africa Symposium. Retrieved June 3, 2016 from https://www.seed.uno/seedas16/

SEED. (2016). Retrieved May 15, 2016 from https://www.seed.uno/about/who.html.

Seria, N. (2011, January 18). Africa's growth may not meet poverty targets, UN says. Bloomberg News. Retrieved July 22, 2016 from http://www.bloomberg.com/news/articles/2011-01-18/africa-s-growth-not-enough-to-meet-poverty-targets-united-nations-says.

Shah, A. (2016, January 7). Poverty facts and stats. [last modified May 8, 2016] *Global Issues.* Retrieved April 13 and May 30 2016 from http://www.globalissues.org/article/26/poverty-facts-and-stats

Shah, A. (2014, September 28). Foreign aid for development assistance. *Global Issues.* Retrieved April 13, 2016 from http://www.globalissues.org/article/35/foreign-aid-development-assistance

Shah, A. (2013, March 24). Global financial crisis. *Global Issues.* Retrieved July 25, 2016 from http://www.globalissues.org/article/768/global-financial-crisis

Sham, T., & Pang, I. (2014, September). China's SME development. *OCBC Wing Hang Bank Monthly Newsletter.* Retrieved July 11, 2016 from http://www.ocbcwhhk.com/webpages_cms/files/Investment%20Newsletter/English/Investment%20Newsletter_Sep_e(1).pdf

Shark Tank Television Show. American Broadcasting Company. 2009 – present. Retrieved May 2016 from http://abc.go.com/shows/shark-tank.

She.Leads.Africa. (2016). Retrieved AUGUST 5, 2016 from http://sheleadsafrica.org/

SheHive. (2016). Retrieved August 5, 2016 from http://sheleadsafrica.org/shehive-new-york/ and also from http://sheleadsafrica.org/shehive-london/

Shekhtman, L. (2012, November 2). A mobile money revolution in the developing world. Triple Pundit. Retrieved May 2016 from http://www.triplepundit.com/2012/11/mobile-money-revolution-developing-world

Small and Medium Business Development Chamber of India. (2016, February). About MSMEs in India. Empowering SMEs for Global Competitiveness. Retrieved August 6, 2016 from http://www.smechamberofindia.com/about_msmes.aspx

Small and medium-sized enterprises. (2016, July 2). In *Wikipedia*. Retrieved July 2, 2016 from https://en.wikipedia.org/wiki/Small_and_medium-sized_enterprises

Small Business Administration, U.S. (n.d.). *About SBA*. Retrieved July 1, 2016 from https://www.sba.gov/about-sba/what-we-do/history

Small Business Administration, U.S. (n.d.). *About the 8(a) business development program. Contracting.* Retrieved August 27, 2016 from https://www.sba.gov/contracting/government-contracting-programs/8a-business-development-program/about-8a-business-development-program

Small Business Administration, U.S. (n.d.). *Small business trends impact.* Retrieved March 9, 2016 from https://www.sba.gov/content/small-business-trends-impact

Small Business Administration, U.S. (n.d.). *Starting & Managing.* Retrieved July 3, 2016 from https://www.sba.gov/managing-business/running-business/energy-efficiency/sustainable-business-practices/small-business-trends

SME Ghana awards. (2016). SMEGA. Retrieved September 4, 2016 from http://www.smeghanaawards.com/introduction

SME Women South Africa. (n.d.). Women in Business. Retrieved March 10 and August 2016 from http://www.smesouthafrica.co.za/SME-Women

Smith, D. (2014, November 1). Power struggle in Burkina Faso after Blaise Compaoré resigns as president. *The Guardian*. Retrieved May 2016 from http://www.theguardian.com/world/2014/oct/31/burkina-faso-president-blaise-compaore-ousted-says-army

Smith, M. (2014, April 21). GSM vs. CDMA: What is the difference and which is better? Retrieved July 3, 2016 from www.makeuseof.com/tag/gsm-vs-cdma-difference-better/

Snapchat changes name, rolls out video-recording spectacles (2016, September 26). *CBSNews*. Retrieved September 28, 2016 from http://www.cbsnews.com/news/snapchat-snap-video-recording-spectacles/

Social Enterprise UK. (n.d.). Retrieved July 10, 2016 from http://www.socialenterprise.org.uk/about/about-social-enterprise

Sonal, S., Wagacha, N., & Nyayieka, S. (2015, March 16). A review of local content regulations in the upstream oil & gas sector in Africa. *Insights: King, Woods, & Mallesons*. Retrieved July 31, 2016 from http://www.kwm.com/en/uk/knowledge/insights/a-review-of-local-content-regulations-in-the-upstream-oil-and-gas-sector-in-africa-20150316

Songhai Centre. (n.d.). Retrieved May 27, 2016 from http://www.songhai.org/index.php/en/home-en

South Africa GDP growth rate 1993-2016. (2016). *Trading Economics*. Retrieved June 30, 2016 from http://www.tradingeconomics.com/south-africa/gdp-growth

South Africa unemployment rate. (n.d.). *Trading Economics*. Retrieved May 14, 2016 from http://www.tradingeconomics.com/south-africa/unemployment-rate

South African scientists develop the world's first digital laser. (2013, September 13). Center for Scientific and Industrial Research. Retrieved August 6, 2016 from http://ntwwl.csir.co.za/plsql/ptl0002/PTL0002_PGE157_MEDIA_REL?MEDIA_RELEASE_NO=7525990

South Africa's unemployment rate rises. (2016, May). *Business Insider.* Retrieved May 14, 2016 from http://www.businessinsider.com/south-africa-unemployment-rate-rises-2016-5

Southern African Development Community. (n.d.). SADC Facts & Figures. Retrieved November 25, 2016 from http://www.sadc.int/about-sadc/overview/sadc-facts-figures/

Southern African Venture Capital and Private Equity Association (SAVC). (2015, May). *Africa private equity confidence survey 2015.* Deloitte. Retrieved July 12, 2016 from http://www2.deloitte.com/content/dam/Deloitte/na/Documents/finance/na_za_private_equity_confidence_survey_may2015.pdf

Special Economic Zone. Investment Opportunity. Government of Tanzania. Retrieved June 24, 2016 from http://www.epza.go.tz/invest.php?p=232

Special Self-Help Fund (SSH). Diplomacy in Action. Department of State. Retrieved July 3, 2016 from http://www.state.gov/p/af/pdpa/ssh/

Startup Africa. (n.d.). Retrieved May 10, 2016 from http://startupafrica.org/conference/

Stock Exchange of Mauritius. (n.d.). Investor Education. Retrieved December 4, 2016 from http://www.stockexchangeofmauritius.com/faqs-listingon-dem

Stock exchanges for small and medium enterprises. (2016, July 13). *Africa Strictly Business.* Retrieved March 10 and July 12, 2016 from http://www.africastrictlybusiness.com/lists/stock-exchanges-small-and-medium-enterprises

Suba. (2016). Retrieved July 2, 2016 from http://www.subaapp.com/index.html

Sustainable Development Platform: Agenda 21. (1992). United Nations Conference on Environment and Development (UNCED), Rio de Janeiro, Brazil. Retrieved June 27, 2016 from https://sustainabledevelopment.un.org/outcomedocuments/agenda21

Sustainable Innovation Expo - UN Environmental Program (UNEP). (2016, May). United Nations Environmental Program. Retrieved July 2, 2016 from http://www.sustainableinnovationexpo.org

Sweet Dreams - Rwanda Women ice cream business. (2014, April 26). *The Guardian*. Retrieved March 21, 2016 from http://www.theguardian.com/global-development/2014/apr/26/rwanda-women-ice-cream-business-sweet-dreams

Tafirenyika, M. (2014, April). Intra-Africa trade: Going beyond political commitments. *Africa Renewal Online*. Retrieved July 6 and August 8, 2016 from http://www.un.org/africarenewal/magazine/august-2014/intra-africa-trade-going-beyond-political-commitments

Tafirenyika, M. (2011, April). Information technology super-charging Rwanda's economy. *Africa Renewal Online*. Retrieved July 31, 2016 from http://www.un.org/africarenewal/magazine/april-2011/information-technology-super-charging-rwandas-economy

TBL Mirror Fund. (n.d.). Private equity for high growth businesses in Africa. Retrieved April 18, 2016 from www.tblmirrorfund.com

TBY talks to Aliko Dangote, chairman of Dangote Group, on rising profits, listing on international stock markets, and plans for the year ahead. (2016). *Business Year*. Retrieved March 28, 2016 from https://www.thebusinessyear.com/nigeria-2016/solid-bet/interview

Technology: A young Kenyan invents charger shoes! (2014, December 8). *Africa Top Success*. Retrieved August 6, 2016 from http://www.

africatopsuccess.com/en/2014/12/08/technology-a-young-kenyan-invents-charger-shoes/

The Africa Fund. (2016) About Us. What is TAF. Retrieved November 12, 2012 and August 4, 2016 from http://www.aaftaf.org/en/about-us/

The African Woman's Development and Communication Network (FEMNET). (2016, February 19). *African women's decade 2010 - 2020.* Retrieved July 9, 2016 from http://femnet.co/2016/02/19/african-womens-decade-2010-2020/

The Clinton Foundation. (n.d.) The Clinton foundation history. Retrieved May 10, 2016 from https://www.clintonfoundation.org/about/clinton-foundation-history

The Heat. (2016, June 17). [Television broadcast]. China Global Television Network.

The Industrial Revolution in the United States. (n.d.). *Teacher's guide primary source set.* Library of Congress. Retrieved from http://www.loc.gov/teachers/classroommaterials/primarysourcesets/industrial-revolution/pdf/teacher_guide.pdf

The inside story of how the Clintons built a two billion global empire. (2015, June 2). *Washington Post.* Retrieved May 15, 2016 from https://www.washingtonpost.com/politics/the-inside-story-of-how-the-clintons-built-a-2-billion-global-empire/2015/06/02/b6eab638-0957-11e5-a7ad-b430fc1d3f5c_story.htm

The New Development Bank: Its Role in Achieving BRICS Renewable Energy Targets. (2016, October). Institute for Energy Economic and Finance Analysis (IEEFA). Retrieved November 26, 2016 from http://ieefa.org/wp-content/uploads/2016/10/New-Development-Bank-and-Role-in-BRICS-Renewable-Energy-Targets-October-2016.pdf

The origins of the financial crisis: Crash course. (2013, September 7). *The Economist.* Retrieved from http://www.economist.com/news/schoolsbrief/21584534-effects-financial-crisis-are-still-being-felt-five-years-article

The real history of twitter. (2016). *AboutTech.* Retrieved July 6, 2016 from http://twitter.about.com/od/Twitter-Basics/a/The-Real-History-Of-Twitter-In-Brief.htm

The Story Exchange. One Thousand Stories. (n.d.). Retrieved April 2016 from http://thestoryexchange.org/1000-stories-women-business/?gclid=COeZta2AvcsCFdcagQodftYLyw

The White House. (2007). *Africa Education Initiative.* Background. National Security Council. Retrieved August 17, 2016 from http://agsp.worlded.org/background.htm

The White House. (1998). *Promoting Peace and Democracy.* Ghana Speech. National Security Council. Retrieved April 26 & August 17, 2016 from http://clinton5.nara.gov/WH/EOP/NSC/html/nsc-01.html

The world's billionaires – 2016 ranking. (2016, March 28). *Forbes Magazine.* Retrieved May 2016 from http://www.forbes.com/profile/jan-koum/

TICAD VI Summit Nairobi. (2016). Retrieved August 4, 2016 from https://ticad6.net/

Tony Elumelu Foundation. (2016). *Elumelu Entrepreneurs Program 2016.* Startups. Retrieved June 17, 2016 from http://tonyelumelufoundation.org/teep/startups/elumelu-entrepreneurship-programme/

Tony Elumelu Foundation. (n.d.). In *Wikipedia.* Retrieved May 30, 2016 from https://en.wikipedia.org/wiki/The_Tony_Elumelu_Foundation

Top 10 healthcare apps for Africa. (2015, August 19). *IT News Africa.* Retrieved July 2, 2016 from http://www.itnewsafrica.com/2015/07/top-mobile-apps-made-in-africa/

Torota, B. (2014, May 1). Africa continues going mobile. Retrieved May 1, 2016 from http://www.gallup.com/poll/168797/africa-continues-going-mobile.aspx

TradeMark East Africa. Retrieved May 15, 2016 from https://www.trademarkea.com/

Tumwebaze, P. (2016, May 12). Rwanda: SMEs urged to embrace e-commerce. *Allafrica.com*. Retrieved May 13 and June 30, 2016 from http://allafrica.com/stories/201605120051.html

Twahirwa, A., & Makome, K. (2010, June 8). Rwanda: Women win by formalising businesses. *Women & Economy*. Retrieved August 1, 2016 from http://www.ipsnews.net/2010/06/rwanda-women-win-by-formalising-businesses/

Twenty-One African countries are pleased with the performance of its leaders. (n.d.). *Gallup*. Retrieved June 14, 2016 from http://www.gallup

Twitter. (2016). About us. Retrieved July 6, 2016 from http://twitter.about.com/od/Twitter-Basics/a/The-Real-History-Of-Twitter-In-Brief.htm

Uber. (2016). Our story. Retrieved July 2, 2016 from https://www.uber.com/our-story/

Ugandan flower exporters facing tough times. (2016, March 10). International Trade Center. Retrieved August 18, 2016 from http://www.intracen.org/blog/Ugandan-flower-exporters-facing-tough-times/

UN conference spotlights role of tourism in fighting poverty and building peace. (2016, May 21). *Johannesburg Life*. Retrieved August 1, 2016 from http://www.johannesburglife.com/index.php/sid/244260705

UN environment assembly opens in Nairobi aiming to ensure healthy planet, with healthy people. (2016). The United Nations News Center. Retrieved July 2, 2016 from http://www.un.org/apps/news/story.asp?NewsID=54014#.V3f7vod0xwE

UN Women. Africa - Where We Are. (n.d.). Retrieved April 16 and July 10, 2016 from http://www.unwomen.org/en/where-we-are/africa

UN-NGO Relations. (n.d.). *UN Non-Governmental Liaison Service*. United Nations. Retrieved April 2016 from http://www.un-ngls.org/orf/ngorelations.htm

UNCTAD 2014/2015 Annual Report. (2015). United Nations Conference on Trade and Development. Retrieved August 15, 2016 from http://unctad.org/en/PublicationsLibrary/wir2015_en.pdf.

Understanding the East African stock markets. (2016, July 3). *AFK Insider*. Retrieved July 12, 2016 from http://afkinsider.com/129044/understanding-east-african-stock-markets/

UNFCCC COP 24 [event]. (2016). IISD Reporting Services. Retrieved July 9, 2016 from http://climate-l.iisd.org/events/unfccc-cop-24/

United Nations Children's Fund. (2014, August 12). *Generation 2030 | Africa*. Retrieved May 2016 from http://data.unicef.org/gen2030/index.html

United Nations Children's Fund. (1999). *The state of the world's children*. Retrieved April 17, 2016 from http://www.unicef.org/sowc99/sowc99f.pdf

United Nations Conference on Trade and Development. (n.d.). Retrieved August 17, 2016 from http://unctad.org/en/Pages/Home.aspx

United Nations Conference on Trade and Development (2005). *Economic Development in Africa*. Report. United Nations. p. 12. Retrieved August 15, 2016 from http://unctad.org/en/docs/tdr2005_en.pdf

United Nations DESA's Population Division. (2014). World's population increasingly urban with more than half living in urban areas. Retrieved June 25, 2016 from http://www.un.org/en/development/desa/news/population/world-urbanization-prospects-2014.html

United Nations Development Program (UNDP). (2015, September 28). *Assessing progress in Africa toward the Millennium Development*

Goals. Retrieved July 24, 2016 from http://www.undp.org/content/undp/en/home/librarypage/mdg/mdg-reports/africa-collection.html

United Nations Development Program. (2015, July 1). *The Millennium Development goals report 2015.* Retrieved May 2016 from http://www.un.org/millenniumgoals/2015_MDG_Report/pdf/MDG%202015%20rev%20(July%201).pdf.

United Nations Development Program. (2015, July 6). *The Millennium Development goals report.* Retrieved April 2016 from http://www.undp.org/content/undp/en/home/librarypage/mdg/the-millennium-development-goals-report-2015.html

United Nations Development Program. (2013, September). NGOs and CSOs; A note on terminology. Annex 1. Retrieved May 2016 from http://www.cn.undp.org/content/dam/china/docs/Publications/UNDP-CH03%20Annexes.pdf

United Nations Education and Cultural Organization. (2016, February 2). UNESCO and E4IMPACT to develop cultural and education entrepreneurship in Africa. Retrieved August 18, 2016 from http://www.unesco.org/new/en/media-services/single-view/news/unesco_and_e4impact_to_develop_cultural_and_education_entrepreneurship_in_africa/#.V23b3I9OIic

United Nations High Commission for Refugees. (2015). *Global appeal 2015 update.* Retrieved April 9, 2016 from http://www.unhcr.org/ga15/index.xml

United Nations Industrial Development Organization (UNIDO). (2015). *Annual report 2014/2015.* Vienna: United Nations.

United Nations Industrial and Development Organization. (2008, August). *Foreign Direct Investment in Sub-Saharan Africa: Determinants and Location Decisions.* Research and Statistic Branch. Working Paper. p. 6. Retrieved August 16, 2016 from http://www.unido.org//fileadmin/user_media/Publications/Research_and_statistics/Branch_publications/Research_and_Policy/Files/Working_Papers/2008/WP082008%20Foreign%20

Direct%20Investment%20in%20Sub-Saharan%20Africa%20-%20 Determinants%20and%20Location%20Decisions.pdf

United Nations Industrial Development Organization (UNIDO). (2014). *Sustainable development.* Vienna: United Nations. Retrieved May 24, 2016 from https://sustainabledevelopment.un.org/content/ documents/2031UNIDO%20Annual%20Report%202014.pdf

United Nations Industrial Development Organization (UNIDO). (2009). *Annual report 2009.* p. 1. Vienna: United Nations. Retrieved May 2016 from https://www.unido.org/fileadmin/user_media/ Publications/Annual_Report/2009/10-50277_Ebookb.pdf

United Nations Industrial Development Organization (UNIDO). (2000). *Annual report 1999.* Vienna: United Nations. Retrieved August 15, 2016 from http://www.unido.org/resources/publications/ flagship-publications/annualreport/1999.html

United Nations Sustainable Development. (1992, June 3-14). *Agenda 21.* United Nations Conference on Environment & Development, Rio de Janeiro, Brazil. Retrieved June 27, 2016 from https:// sustainabledevelopment.un.org/outcomedocuments/agenda21

United Nations World Tourism Organization. (2015). *UNWTO tourism highlights.* Retrieved July 6, 2016 from http://www.e-unwto.org/ doi/pdf/10.18111/9789284416899

United Nations. (n.d.). *Tokyo International Conference of African Development (TICAD).* Partnerships. Office of the Special Advisor for Africa. Retrieved August 4, 2016 from http://www.un.org/en/ africa/osaa/partnerships/ticad.shtml

United Nations. (2016, June 13). Women and youth entrepreneurship in Africa: The impact of entrepreneurial education on development. Office of the Special Advisor on Africa. Retrieved June 15, 2016 from http://www.un.org/en/africa/osaa/events/2016/entrepreneurship. shtml

United Nations. (n.d.). *Sustainable development goal 8: promote sustained, inclusive and sustainable economic growth, full and productive employment and descent work for all.* Sustainable Knowledge Platform. Retrieved October 11, 2016 from https://sustainabledevelopment.un.org/sdg8

United Nations. (2015). *Sustainable development goals: 17 goals to transform our world.* Retrieved April 2016 from http://www.un.org/sustainabledevelopment/sustainable-development-goals

United Nations. (2015). *World population prospects: Key findings and advance tables.* Retrieved April 17, 2016 from http://esa.un.org/unpd/wpp/publications/files/key_findings_wpp_2015.pdf

United Nations. (2014, April 25). Secretary-General appoints Aurélien Agbénonci of Benin Deputy Special Representative and resident coordinator for Central African Republic [press release]. Retrieved May 2016 from http://www.un.org/press/en/2014/sga1458.doc.htm

United Nations. (2005, September 12). *Economic development in Africa report.* United Nations Conference on Trade and Development. Retrieved August 17, 2016 from http://unctad.org/en/Docs/gdsafrica20051_en.pdf

United Nations. (n.d.). *Resolutions adopted on the reports of the Second Committee. 1970-1971.* Vienna: United Nations. Retrieved April 2016 from http://documents-dds-ny.un.org/doc/RESOLUTION/GEN/NR0/348/91/IMG/NR034891.pdf

United States African Development Foundation (USADF). (2016). Retrieved August 1, 2016 from http://www.usadf.gov/apply-for-a-grant

United States Agency for International Development. (2016). *Africa diaspora marketplace.* Retrieved August 7, 2015 from http://www.diasporamarketplace.org/

United States Agency for International Development. (2015, November 2). Non-governmental organizations (NGOs). Retrieved June 2016 from http://www.usaid.gov/partnership-opportunities/ngo

United States Agency for International Development. (2014, November). *Technical brief: Use of technology in the Ebola response in West Africa.* Retrieved May 28, 2016 from https://www.msh.org/sites/msh.org/files/technology_and_ebola_response_in_west_africa_technical_brief_final.pdf

United States Agency for International Development. (2007). *Africa Education Initiative – Ambassadors Girls Scholarship Program (AEI – AGSP): Background.* Retrieved April 19 and August 17 from http://agsp.worlded.org/background.htm

United States Agency for International Development. (2016, July 26). *Development Innovation Venture (DIV).* Retrieved June 2016 from https://www.usaid.gov/div

United States Agency for International Development. (n.d.). Power Africa. Retrieved August 1, 2016 from https://www.usaid.gov/powerafrica

United States Agency for International Development/West Africa Trade Hub. (n.d.). Retrieved April 12, 2016 from https://www.watradehub.com/en/about/

United States Department of State. (n.d.). *African Women's Entrepreneurship Program.* (AWEP). Retrieved August 7, 2016 from http://www.state.gov/p/af/rt/awep/index.htm

United States Department of State. (n.d.). *President's Young African Leaders Initiative.* Retrieved July 11, 2016 from https://yali.state.gov/washington-fellowship/

United States unemployment rate 1948-2016 [data set]. (2016). *Trading Economics.* Retrieved June 30, 2016 from http://www.tradingeconomics.com/united-states/unemployment-rate

USAID trade hubs in Africa. (n.d.). U.S. Department of State. Retrieved August 7, 2016 from http://www.state.gov/p/af/rt/awep/196204.htm

U.S. Government Publishing Office (GPO). (2016, June 30). Size standards used to define small business concerns. 121.201 - Electronic Code of Federal Regulations. Retrieved July 3, 2016 from http://www.ecfr.gov/cgi-bin/retrieveECFR?gp=&SID=7780ee089107f59ef3f78b938e2282b7&r=PART&n=13y1.0.1.1.17#se13.1.121_1305

Venture Garden Group. (n.d.). Retrieved May 2, 2016 from www.venturegradengroup.com

Veras, O. *Africa's Middle Class: Anemic Growth?* (2016, July 25). Alerts. Newsletter [incoming email] *ThisIsAfrica*. Retrieved July 26, 2016 from thisisafrica@ftmail.ft.com

Veselinovic, M. (2016). Tired of catcalls? Pink taxi promises to drive women around Cairo peacefully. *CNN World*. Retrieved July 2, 2016 from http://www.cnn.com/2015/12/09/africa/pink-taxi-cairo/

Vinton, K. & Forbes Staff. (2015, May 25). The Most Powerful Women in Tech. *Forbes Tech. Forbes*. Retrieved August 5, 2016 from http://www.forbes.com/sites/katevinton/2015/05/26/the-most-powerful-women-in-tech-2015/#133a1642cab6

W.TEC Nigeria Africa SME Women's ICT Training Session. (2014). Final Report. 2014. W-TEC. Lagos, Nigeria.

W.TEC Nigeria. (2013). Final Report on Africa Female SME Special ICT Training Session. Retrieved May 13, 2016 from bit.ly/W-TEC-ICTSpecialSession

W.TEC Nigeria Women in Technology Empowerment Center. (n.d.). Retrieved May 13, 2016 from http://www.w-teconline.org/

Ward, M., & Rhodes, C. (2014, December 9). Small business and the UK economy. House of Commons Stand Note: SN/EP 6078. Retrieved August 6, 2016 from http://researchbriefings.files.parliament.uk/documents/SN06078/SN06078.pdf

Warford, L. (2016, July 14). Africa is moving toward a massive and important free trade agreement. *Washington Post*. Retrieved July 16, 2016 from https://www.washingtonpost.com/news/monkey-cage/

wp/2016/07/14/the-7-things-you-need-to-know-about-africas-continental-free-trade-area/?wpisrc=nl_cage&wpmm=1

Weisman, S. R. (1990, September 19). Atlanta selected over Athens for 1996 Olympics. *New York Times*. Retrieved June 30, 2016 from http://www.nytimes.com/1990/09/19/sports/atlanta-selected-over-athens-for-1996-olympics.html

Welcome to the AAF's technical assistance facility. (2016). Phatsia Fund Managers. Retrieved August 4, 2016 from http://www.aaftaf.org/en/

Welcome to the Youth Division of African Union Commission. (n.d.). Department of Human Resources, Science, and Technology. African Union Youth Division. Retrieved July 30, 2016 from http://www.africa-youth.org/

White, B. (2011, October 31). *Female Entrepreneurs a Driving Force in African SMEs*. VC4A. Venture Capital for Africa. Retrieved April 2016 from https://vc4a.com/blog/2011/10/31/female-entrepreneurs-a-driving-force-in-african-smes/

Will & Brothers Consulting. (n.d.). Retrieved July 12, 2016 from http://will-brothers.com/

William Elong: Africa's and Cameroon's promising entrepreneur. (2016, June 27). *TechCrunch*. Retrieved July 12, 2016 from http://techcrunch-africa.com/people/william-elong-africas

Williams, S. (2012, March 30). Africa Youth - The African Development Bank and the demographic dividend. *African Development Bank*. Retrieved March 30, 2016 from http://www.afdb.org/fileadmin/uploads/afdb/Documents/Generic-Documents/AFDB%20youth%20doc.pdf

Wilson, J. (2004). *The politics of truth: Inside the lies that led to war and betrayed my wife's CIA identity*. New York: Carroll & Graf.

WIMBIZ. (n.d.). Retrieved August 5, 2016 from http://wimbiz.org/

World Bank. (2016, April 11). Africa: Low commodity prices continue to impede growth [press release]. Retrieved July 24, 2016 from http://www.worldbank.org/en/news/press-release/2016/04/11/africa-low-commodity-prices-continue-to-impede-growth

World Bank. (2015, November). Listening to Tajikistan. Retrieved July 4, 2016 from http://pubdocs.worldbank.org/en/472971449038116674/TJK-Wellbeing-v13.pdf

World Bank. (2012). Databank. Retrieved July 24, 2016 from http://databank.worldbank.org/data/views/reports/ReportWidgetCustom.aspx?Report_Name=POV_REG_1&Id=be849c9d&tb=y&dd=n&pr=n&export=y&xlbl=y&ylbl=y&legend=y&isportal=y&inf=n&exptypes=Excel&country=SSA&series=SI.POV.NOP1,SI.POV.DDAY&zm=n

World Bank. (2012). Maximizing mobile. 2012 information and communications for development. Retrieved May 2016 from http://siteresources.worldbank.org/EXTINFORMATIONANDCOMMUNICATIONANDTECHNOLOGIES/Resources/IC4D-2012-Report.pdf

World Bank. (2009). Republic of Congo documents and reports. Retrieved September 4, 2016 from http://documents.worldbank.org/curated/en/316651468244180464/708380ESW0P1070000Final00030-06-09.docx

World Bank. (2016, January). *Sub-Saharan Africa analysis. Global economic prospects 2016.* Retrieved August 15, 2016 from https://www.worldbank.org/content/dam/Worldbank/GEP/GEP2016a/Global-Economic-Prospects-January-2016-Sub-Saharan-Africa-analysis.pdf

World Bank. (2013, January). *Sub-Saharan Africa analysis. Global economic prospects.* Retrieved August 9, 2016 from http://siteresources.worldbank.org/INTPROSPECTS/Resources/334934-1322593305595/8287139-1358278153255/GEP13aSSARegionalAnnex.pdf

World Bank. (n.d.). Tech hubs across Africa which will be legacy makers [blog post]. Retrieved April 18, 2016 from http://blogs.worldbank.org/ic4d/tech-hubs-across-africa-which-will-be-legacy-makers

World Bank Group. (2014). Women-owned SMEs: A business opportunity for financial institutions. p. 11.

World Bank Group (2011). IFC advisory service in sustainable business. Issue Brief, p. 3.

World Bank Group. (2001). What is sustainable development. Retrieved July 9, 2016 from http://www.worldbank.org/depweb/english/sd.html

World Bank Group. (n.d.). Aureos Africa Fund L.L.C./International Finance Corporation. Retrieved May 4, 2016 from http://ifcext.ifc.org/ifcext/spiwebsite1.nsf/ProjectDisplay/SPI_DP26992

World Bank Group. (n.d.). External countries Africa. Retrieved May 10, 2016 from http://web.worldbank.org/WBSITE/EXTERNAL/COUNTRIES/AFRICAEXT/0,,contentMDK:20226042~menuPK:258664~pagePK:146736~piPK:226340~theSitePK:258644,00.html

World Bank Group. (2015). Financing women entrepreneurs in Ethiopia. Retrieved May 13, 2016 from http://www.worldbank.org/en/news/feature/2015/11/16/financing-women-entrepreneurs-in-ethiopia

World Bank Group. (n.d.). Tech hubs across Africa which will be legacy makers. Retrieved from May 15, 2016 http://blogs.worldbank.org/ic4d/tech-hubs-across-africa-which-will-be-legacy-makers

World Bank IBRD-IDA. (2016). Mobile cellular subscriptions (per 100 people). Retrieved July 3, 2016 from http://data.worldbank.org/indicator/IT.CEL.SETS.P2?locations=NG

World Bank IRBD-IDA. (2016). Women Entrepreneurship Development Project. Project and operation overview. Retrieved

July 10, 2016 from http://www.worldbank.org/projects/P122764/women-entrepreneurship-development-project?lang=en

World Bank IBRD-IDA. (2015, September 1). Small and Medium Enterprises (SMEs) finance. Retrieved September 4, 2016 from http://www.worldbank.org/en/topic/financialsector/brief/smes-finance

World Bank IBRD-IDA. (2015, September). Small and medium enterprises (SMEs) finance. Finance Brief, p. 8. Retrieved July 5, 2016 from http://www.worldbank.org/en/topic/financialsector/brief/smes-finance

World Bank IBRD-IDA. (n.d.). Unemployment, youth total (% of total labor force ages 15-24). [Data set]. Retrieved July 17, 2016 from http://data.worldbank.org/indicator/SL.UEM.1524.ZS

World Bank/IBRD-IDA. (2015). *Sub-Saharan Africa population* [data set]. Retrieved August 15, 2016 from http://data.worldbank.org/region/sub-saharan-africa

World Bank/IBRD-IDA. (2012). *GINI index (World Bank estimate by country)*. Retrieved July 24, 2016 from http://data.worldbank.org/indicator/SI.POV.GINI?locations=ZA

World Bank/IBRD-IDA. (2016, March). While poverty in Africa has declined, number of poor has increased. Retrieved July 24, 2016 from http://www.worldbank.org/en/region/afr/publication/poverty-rising-africa-poverty-report

World Bank/IBRD-IDA. (2015, September 30). FAQ: Why did the World Bank decide to update the International Poverty Line, and why now? Retrieved July 30, 2016 from http://www.worldbank.org/en/topic/poverty/brief/global-poverty-line-faq

World Bank-IBRD/IDA. (2012, December). ICTs delivering home-grown development solutions in Africa. Retrieved August 7, 2016 from http://www.worldbank.org/en/news/feature/2012/12/10/ict-home-grown-development-solutions-in-africa

World Bank-IBRD/IDA. (2016). *Nigeria population* [data set]. Retrieved August 8, 2016 from http://data.worldbank.org/country/nigeria

World Bank/International Finance Corporation. (2016). Sub-Saharan Africa. SME Initiatives. Retrieved September 4, 2016 from http://www.ifc.org/wps/wcm/connect/REGION__EXT_Content/Regions/Sub-Saharan+Africa/Advisory+Services/SustainableBusiness/SME_Initiatives/

World Bank/Royal Africa Society. (2003-2004). Study 2003-2004. Retrieved May 2016 from http://www.afrobarometer.org/data and http://www.worldpublicopinion.org/pipa/articles/brafricara/209.php?lb=braf

World Commission on Environment and Development: Our common future. (1987). Report to United Nations General Assembly.

XChem Chemicals (PTY) LTD. (n.d.). Retrieved November 28, 2016 from http://www.xchem.co.za/index.html and http://www.wbs.ac.za/search-results/?q=angela+pitsi

Xilebat. (2010, June 12). 10 cases of appropriate technology. Listverse. Retrieved June 30, 2016 from http://listverse.com/2010/06/12/10-cases-of-appropriate-technology

Yewela, S. (2011). Solving Nigeria's housing problem with plastic water bottles. *Vanguard Newspaper.* Retrieved June 23, 2016 from http://www.vanguardngr.com/2011/11/solving-nigerias-housing-problem-with-plastic-water-bottles/

Young African Leaders Initiative. (n.d.). Retrieved July 11, 2016 from https://yali.state.gov/washington-fellowship/

Young, A. (2012). *The making of modern Atlanta.* Georgia State University, GA: Andrew Young Foundation and Andrew Young School of Policy Studies.

Zena Exotic Fruits. (n.d.). Retrieved May 14, 2016 from http://www.zenaexoticfruits.com/en/about

Zeng, D. (2015). Global experiences with special economic zones with a focus on China and Africa. Trade and Global Competitiveness Practice. World Bank. Retrieved June 24, 2016 from http://www.worldbank.org/content/dam/Worldbank/Event/Africa/Investing%20in%20Africa%20Forum/2015/investing-in-africa-forum-global-experiences-with-special-economic-zones-with-a-focus-on-china-and-africa.pdf

Zhang, L., & Xia, W. (2014). Integrating small and medium-sized enterprises into global trade flows: the case of China. Geneva, Switzerland: World Trade Organization. Retrieved July 11, 2016 from https://www.wto.org/english/res_e/booksp_e/cmark_chap3_e.pdf

Zipline. (n.d.). Retrieved June 23, 2016 from http://flyzipline.com/product/

Index

Acknowledgments

I would like to thank the many colleagues, friends, and public-private partners (on and off the Continent) that I have had on my incredible life journey so far. They are all in some way part of the inspiration for writing this book and are either reflected in my *slice of life* stories, or highlighted because our work together inspired me in some way to do more and to do better. In particular, I would like to thank my personal assistant Monica who helped me on both my books and all the FEEEDS-Gallup events over the last three years; my program assistants Paula and Anne (based in Nigeria); and, my policy advisor Jim Parks, who was also part of the team that helped to design and frame @ *The FEEEDS Index* and PowerHouse Nations strategy in the early days.

A big thank you goes to Danny Evans, the coordinator of *@The FEEEDS Index*, who spent countless hours on the special version of the *Index* for this book focused on issues that are important to and are affecting Africa SMEs and entrepreneurs. Special appreciation goes to Gallup World Poll – Jon, Magali, Jay, Kris, and Rachel – for supporting the FEEEDS-Gallup event each year, but more importantly for the information and data leadership role Gallup provides worldwide. One thing I have learned from working with Gallup World Poll is that no matter how well one thinks they know their subject area, data can always surprise you.

I also appreciate all the kind words and thoughtful comments from all the book reviewers, and I am immensely honored to have had two of the most forthright persons I know write the Introduction and Foreword – Ambassador Andrew Young and Mr. Aliko Dangote.

Then there is Valerie Sweeney, both an ardent fact checker and a copyeditor, who has helped me since I wrote my dissertation, assisted me on my first book, as well as for this recent work on Africa's SMEs. Thank you also to Nicole Franklin for her initial comments and fact checking as well as for her enthusiasm for this subject matter which is so near and dear to my heart.

Lastly, there is the Association for Diplomatic Studies and Training (ADST), which is such an important State Department-connected institution as it seeks to preserve the voices, life lessons, and contributions of American diplomats to U.S. policy and through its book series and program with the U.S. Library of Congress. I am privileged that ADST has reviewed, provided comments and approved this book to be part of its prestigious Memoirs and Occasional Papers (MOPS) series.

About Us

The FEEEDS Advocacy Initiative

What does FEEEDS® or the FEEEDS Advocacy Initiative mean? FEEEDS is an acronym that encompasses some of the main global issues of today – Food Security, Education, Environment-Energy, Economics, Democracy-Development, and Self-Help – that both developed and developing countries are grappling with in order to address and resolve the challenges for the world community. All of these issues are also connected to human cultural communication and how we relate to each other as people and as nations. FEEEDS represents the first letter of each word or word-phrase noted above. FEEEDS Advocacy Initiative provides lectures, contributions to think tanks, instruction, and training on the FEEEDS issues, SDGs, and other global topics and serves as a global advisor to several Africa-focused organizations. FEEEDS also publishes *@The FEEEDS Index* on key Africa polling data and partners with Gallup World Poll on an annual Africa event on topics ranging from African elections to the importance of Africa SMEs.

@The FEEEDS Index

The Index was launched April 9, 2015, at Gallup Headquarters in Washington, D.C., during a FEEEDS-Gallup-Allafrica.com partnership event on Nigeria's 2015 elections and is officially powered by Gallup Analytics polling data. The *@The FEEEDS Index* focuses on key political, election, economic, social, and development issues for Sub-Saharan Africa and also on what FEEEDS sees as PowerHouse Nations on the African Continent. The idea behind the Index is to provide actual polling data showing responses from African nationals on these overarching subject areas on aggregate and country-by-country. In addition, *@The FEEEDS Index* publishes special indices with polling data on selected issues important to and affecting the environment in which Africa SMEs and entrepreneurs operate, such as the special *@The FEEEDS Index* appearing in Chapter 11 of this book. See www.*bit.ly/FEEEDSIndex*

The Association for Diplomatic Study and Training (ADST)

In 2003 the Association for Diplomatic Studies and Training (ADST) created the Memoirs and Occasional Papers Series (MOPS) to preserve first-hand accounts and other informed observations on foreign affairs for scholars, journalists, and the general public. Sponsoring publications is one of the ways ADST, a non-profit organization founded in 1986, seeks to promote the understanding of American diplomacy and those that conduct it. See www.adst.org/publications for the current list of all titles under the MOPS series.

About the Author

Ambassador Robin Renee Sanders served as one of the U.S. Government's top diplomats on African issues over an extensive career in the United States Diplomatic Corps with senior positions ranging from Ambassador to the Republics of Nigeria and the Congo, two stints as Director for Africa at the White House, and the U.S. Permanent Representative to the West African Regional Organization ECOWAS.

Dr. Sanders received her doctorate degree from Pittsburgh's Robert Morris University in information systems and communications and is known as a thought-leader on a range of issues from national security to today's Africa development, political and economic issues. She has a particular focus on the SMEs, and the UN Sustainable Development Goals (SDGs,) the global international consensus document to combat poverty issues. She has presented at two "TEDx Talks" and has testified before the U.S. Congress on many of these topics. Ambassador Sanders is the recipient of the U.S. military's joint Chiefs of Staff Award, the highest U.S. military honor given to a civilian; serves on the U.S. Trade Representative Africa Advisory Committees; is a member of the prestigious Academy of Diplomacy of former senior U.S. Government officials; is recipient of the Presidential Medal of Honor from Congo; and has six Department of State Awards (Superior and Meritorious). Sanders also is a Distinguished Public Service Scholar at RMU, has two Master's Degrees (International Relations-African Studies and Communications) from Ohio University, and is a Visiting Scholar under the CIC Woodrow Wilson Program. Her first book, *The Legendary Uli Women of Nigeria,* can be found at: http://bit.ly/1MtEFe0. Also see www.ambassadorrobinreneesanders.com, www.blogitrrs.blogspot.com, www.huffingtonpost.com, and twitter: @rrsafrica.

About the Book

Sanders' new book credits the innovativeness and determination of Africa SMEs and entrepreneurs who stepped into the development void left by 40 years of post-independence ineffective efforts to fundamental improve the life of the average African citizen, despite $US3.5 trillion spent. Their willingness to find new paths, the convergence with technology and its mobility, and more importantly, the new responses to many age-old challenges have made the Africa entrepreneur a driver for job creation, a catalyst to grow the middle class, and a principal contributor to the region's GDP. They led; donors followed. The "Africa SME and entrepreneur" is the center piece of book given the links and ties among African nationals, African immigrants, and the greater Africa Diaspora and the small business sector. This phrasing is intentional as it is meant to include the contributions of all these communities to the region's development given the wide nature of self-definition, place of birth, history of the slave trade, and global nature of entrepreneurship. "What Africa SMEs have done is flip the old *income-generation* model to a *generating-income* model," Sanders notes in the book.